T. R. Hamzah & Yeang:
ecology of the sky

Ivor Richards

images
Publishing

First published in Australia in 2001 by
The Images Publishing Group Pty Ltd
ACN 059 734 431
6 Bastow Place, Mulgrave, Victoria, 3170
Telephone (61 3) 9561 5544 Facsimile (61 3) 9561 4860
Email: books@images.com.au
www.imagespublishing.com.au

Copyright © The Images Publishing Group Pty Ltd 2001
The Images Publishing Group Reference Number: 352

National Library of Australia Cataloguing-in-Publication data

Richards, Ivor.
T. R. Hamzah & Yeang: ecology of the sky.

Bibliography
Includes index.
ISBN 1 86470 095 5.

1. Yeang, Ken, 1948– . 2. T. R. Hamzah & Yeang.
3. Skyscrapers. 4. Architecture and climate.
5. Architecture – Environmental aspects.
6. Architecture, Modern – 20th century.
I. Title. II. Title: T. R. Hamzah and Yeang.
(Series : Millennium series (Mulgrave, Vic.)).

720.483092

Author Ivor Richards
Book design by Elaine Cheong
Coordinated by Andy Chong
Book production by The Graphic Image Studio Pty Ltd, Australia
Film by Pageset Pty Ltd, Australia
Printed by Everbest Printing, Hong Kong

T. R. Hamzah & Yeang
Website: www.trhamzah-yeang.com
Email: trhy@tm.net.my

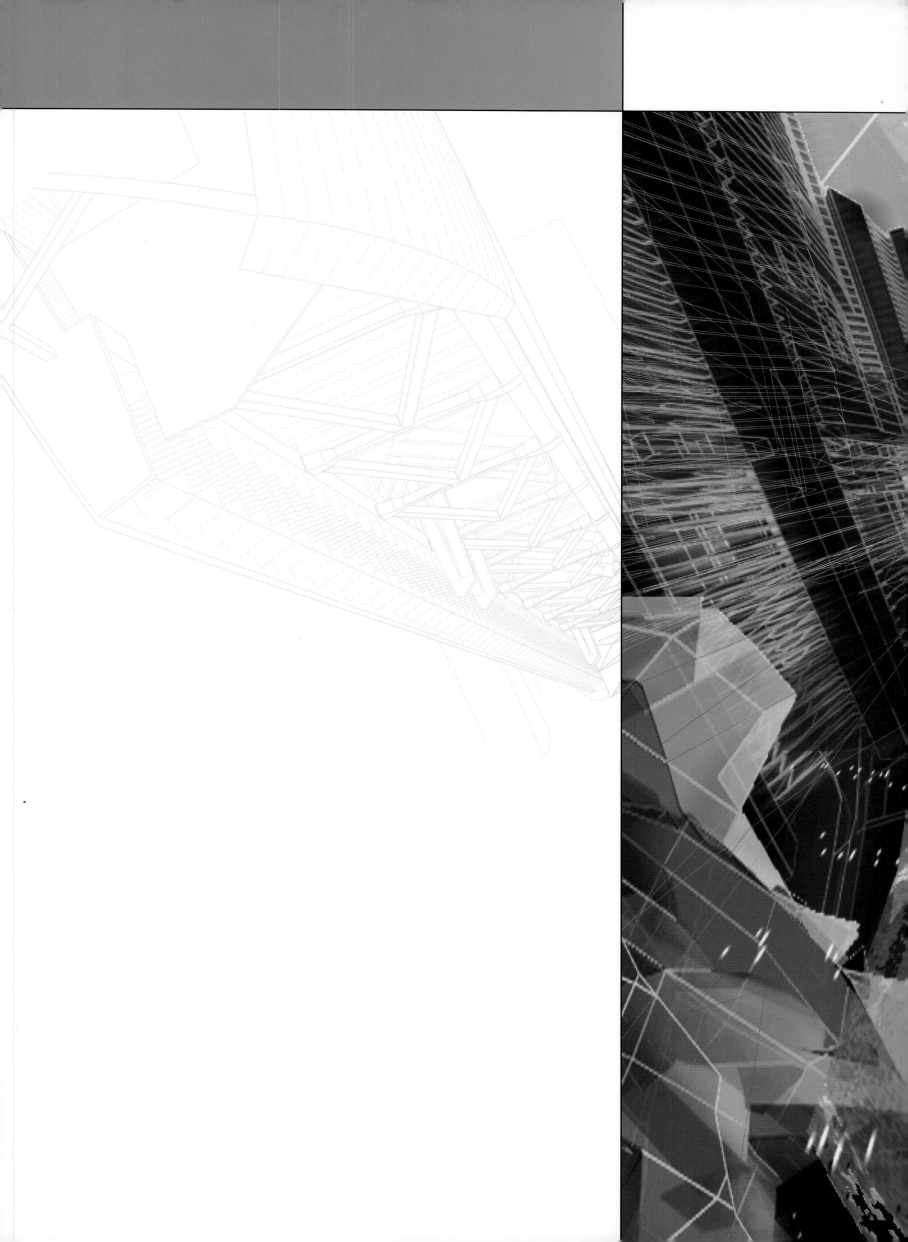

contents

illustration by Jason Yeang

Central Plaza   Menara Boustead   TA1

$$(LP) = \frac{\begin{array}{c|c} L11 & L12 \end{array}}{\begin{array}{c|c} L21 & L22 \end{array}}$$

(Ecological Design)

Yeang 1995: partitioned matrix

interconnectedness

Before any detailed discussion of Ken Yeang's architecture can take place, it is essential to understand the overall nature of his thought, philosophy and theory of systems that underlies and structures his whole output in practice – the making of 'green' buildings.

His recent treatise *The Green Skyscraper* [1] sets out his position and method very clearly, and is built upon both his Cambridge University research, which began in the 1970s, and all the subsequent development and refinement that has been enacted in the course of his extensive practice.

Yeang is therefore not an architect who is a maker of form alone, but rather a totally different designer whose understanding of ecology and sustainable systems insists that the reasons why his forms exist, develop and mutate are all an integral part of an ecologically responsive design process. At the same time his own knowledge has progressively advanced as the precision of specialist advice has increased and added to the process of his practice and research.

Two principal factors characterise Yeang's mission and research as applied to architectural production. First, is the recognition of the extensive degradation of the natural environment and the time limit on both the provision of low-cost energy and supply of irreplaceable materials that currently supports the built environment as a whole, and that cannot continue if future generations are to have appropriate access to natural resources.

Yeang concludes that

> **'It is therefore evident that designing with "green" or ecologically responsive design objectives in mind is vital. Indeed, these must certainly now be the prime objectives for the design community today.'** [2]

This statement naturally alludes to the second factor in Yeang's overall mission. This concerns the belief that all those concerned with building design can, with the application of ecological principles, make a significant contribution towards a sustainable future through the creation of a thorough 'green' architecture that is evolved from a comprehensive method, [3] and how it particularly relates to the ecological

design of both skyscrapers, and other large projects such as the National Library of Singapore, in which he is currently engaged.

While this book is entirely dedicated to Yeang's architectural output in the realm of his own developing bioclimatic series of skyscrapers and beyond, and it therefore cannot substitute as a complete theoretical treatise. It is nevertheless important to place the work in the critical context of Yeang's theory, as completely contained in his extensive writings such as *The Green Skyscraper*. [4]

The logic of tackling the scale of high-density intensive buildings in relation to ecological design gains particular relevance when their massive input and output of resources and waste is measured. Equally the increasing intensity of expansion in world cities is almost certain to continue the proliferation of major urban buildings [5] given the economics of urban land economy. Hence, Yeang's case that the skyscraper and other major urban building types require to be designed to an ecologically responsive standard as a matter of urgency for a sustainable future. However, the limitations are also defined and recognised:

> **'... the problems and technical innovations for a comprehensive holistic ecological design for intensive building types remain unresolved or have yet to be invented. But this should not lead us to assume that a technological 'fix' is the preferred solution of design problems or that it is possible for all environmental issues to be resolved overnight.'** [6]

Yeang is calling for a change in the attitude of designers universally, and for what he calls 'an intelligent start' on the application of techniques and ideas required to establish green design solutions as a basic expectation.

With regard to the progressive content of the skyscraper projects in this collection, it is important to clarify a fundamental concept. In Yeang's own terms:

> **'To avoid confusion between what is bioclimatic design and what is ecological design, we should clarify the differences. Generally, bioclimatic design is the passive low-energy design approach that makes use of the ambient energies of the climate of the locality to create conditions of comfort for the users of the building ... As an emergent bioclimatic built form, it provides a viable alternative to the existing skyscraper and constitutes a new building genre; however it must made clear that bioclimatic design is not ecological design in its entirety, but only an intermediate stage in that direction. Ecological design is a much more complex endeavour.** [7]

The crucial distinction between Yeang's theories of 'ecological design' and those of other architects is then a vital matter of definition.

---

[1] *The Green Skyscraper: The Basis for Designing Sustainable Intensive Buildings*, Ken Yeang, Prestel Verlag 2000, completely documents Yeang's ecological treatise with particular reference to the design of large buildings. This text is an essential primer and should be read as an extension and augmentation of this book.
[2] Ibid. p 7.
[3] Ibid. *The Green Skyscraper* is entirely dedicated to Yeang's definition of design principles for an ecological architecture.
[4] Ibid.
[5] Ibid. p 10, Yeang presents the case for the inevitable continuing development of intensive urban buildings.
[6] Ibid. p 11.
[7] Ibid. pp 11 & 12.

Architecture 2000 and Beyond

May 2000

by Charles Jencks

Ivor Richards

interconnectedness

In Yeang's own terms, ecological design is fundamentally about interconnectedness:

'... the emphasis here is on the interdependencies and interconnectedness in the biosphere and its ecosystems ... the crucial property of ecological design is the connectedness between all activities, whether man-made or natural; this connectedness means that no part of the biosphere is unaffected by human activity and that all actions affect each other ... Simply stated, all built systems must have a reciprocal relationship with their local environments and with the rest of the biosphere' [8] , or equally, '... the greater the adherence to the principles of applied ecology ... the greater will be the effectiveness of the ecological solution'. [9]

Related to this seminal statement are Yeang's theoretical 'interactions matrix' (see frontispiece) and his 'law of ecological design' – both deserve particular attention. As a preface to this central area of Yeang's theory, several other factors require mention.

The first is the question of the 'time-lag' that is inevitable between the design of a major building and its subsequent realisation, while in the meantime ideas and theoretical developments, and also technological solutions may all have advanced. At the same time Yeang also acknowledges that ecological design, in the complete sense, is still in its infancy:

'... current ecological design strategies should be appropriately regarded as a transition towards the ecological ideal.' [10]

Next, it is equally relevant to outline the scope of Yeang's eco-agenda:

'Ecological design ... includes not just architectural and engineering design but also other seemingly disparate disciplines such as landscape ecological land-use planning, embodied energy studies, recycling practices, pollution control ...' [11]

together with all the associated detail systems. The great importance of Yeang's comprehensive method and approach lies in the concept of 'gathering and togetherness', as he describes it:

'... the bringing together and integration of these aspects of environmental protection and control (previously regarded as separate disciplines) brought into a single approach to ecological design.' [12]

What follows from this is the summary organisation of Yeang's 'partitioned matrix', which unifies his concept of four sets of interactions into 'a single symbolic form' [13] and includes the fundamental interactions of the built and natural environments. More specifically, these are processes that occur within the system (internal interdependencies), and activities in the environment (external interdependencies). These are taken together with exchanges between system/environment and environment/system. In Yeang's summary terms:

'... internal and external relations and transactional interdependencies are all accounted for'. [14]

the skyscraper as a stack of goodies and as a series of events-in-the-sky

8 Ibid. p 12.
9 Ibid. p 9.
10 Ibid. p 14.
11 Ibid. p 15.
12 Ibid. p 15.
13 Ibid. p 65.
14 Ibid. p 65.

" Ken Yeang's architecture is beginning to synthesize elements from opposed traditions into an unlikely hybrid, the 'organitech'. With him the new skyscraper is emerging and what can be seen as five points of a new architecture. First, and derived from the past, are what he calls 'valves', the movable parts that respond to fast changing climatic conditions. It is a measure of our time that progress in the tall building may consist in windows that can actually open! Second are 'filters', again including new versions of such traditional elements as exterior louvres. Third is the design decision to locate the elevator and service cores on the sides where it is hot, thus reducing the heat gain. Fourth are the sky courts and growing plants used to cool the building, its most obviously visible feature of looking green. These courts and vegetation, if generally applied to most buildings, could also cool our overheated cities. The 'heat domes' that have recently been discovered by satellites to be raising the temperature by as much as 5 degrees, over such cities as Atlanta, could be completely cleared if such measures became widespread. And the fifth point is the contrast between sunshades and clear glass (where the view is good and the sun does not penetrate).

All of these measures lead Yeang to a new, articulate and dynamic skyscraper. They also lead to a new theory of ecological architecture that, like Corbusier's FIve Points of Modern Architecture in the 1920's, is being summarised and replicated around the world. As Ken Yeang argues, since the tall, unecological skyscraper will not go away, in the 21st century it will have to become 'bioclimatic', or more like the rest of life, related to the earth's economy. "

programme. He found that huge heat "domes" form over cities, triggering thunderstorms, increasing the production of polluting ozone, and raising local temperatures by as much as 10F (5.5C).

"Over Atlanta, the heat island is causing the city to create its own weather." he

Replacement of the trees by roads and roofs means that heat is trapped during the day, and radiated back into space at night. The extra heat makes the city less habitable, forces air-conditioning units to work at full stretch, and increases the conversion of vehicle pollution into ozone.

THE TIMES WEDNESDAY FEBRUARY 23 2000

Giant cities are creating their own weather

EXPLOSIVE urban growth is creating "heat islands" so intense that they are establishing their own local weather systems. The asphalt jungle and the lack of vegetation created by building makes cities many degrees hotter than they would otherwise be. Dr David Quattrochi, of Nasa's Marshall Space Flight Centre, said yesterday.

He has studied the phenomenon by flying Nasa aircraft over US cities and measuring temperatures using equipment developed for the space programme. He found that huge heat "domes" form over cities, triggering thunderstorms, increasing the production of polluting ozone, and raising local temperatures by as much as 10F (5.5C).

"Over Atlanta, the heat island is causing the city to create its own weather," he said. "At the end of July and the beginning of August, we have seen a series of thunderstorms generated in the early hours of the morning – when no thunderstorm would normally occur – as a result of heat rising from the city."

Nigel Hawkes reports from the American Association for the Advancement of Science in Washington

which show the growth of the city, he said. The images show that in the past 10 years Atlanta, one of the fastest growing American cities, has lost 380,000 acres of tree cover, and gained 370,000 acres of single-family housing.

Replacement of the trees by roads and roofs means that heat is trapped during the day, and radiated back into space at night. The extra heat makes the city less habitable, forces air-conditioning units to work at full stretch, and increases the conversion of vehicle pollution into ozone.

The effects of the "heat islands" has been investigated by Dr Marc Imhoff, from Nasa's Goddard Space Flight Centre. He found that it has

two countervailing effects on agricultural productivity. The extra heat lengthens the growing season but the growth of housing reduces the area available for agriculture. The net effect is a loss of output equivalent to a reduction of 20 days in the growing season.

"Human survival depends on the ability of the landscape to produce food," he said. "If the capacity of the landscape to carry out photosynthesis is substantially reduced, the ability of the planet to support human life must also be diminished." His results show that urban expansion tends to take place on the most productive land, an observation echoed by studies in Egypt and southern China.

Dr Quattrochi said that the "heat island" effect could be minimised by reflective roof

LINKS

While acknowledging that it is logistically impossible to do full justice to Yeang's extensive and prolific theory in a brief survey, it is nevertheless crucial to indicate the fundamental difference it brings to his position as an architect.

$$(LP) = \begin{array}{c|c} L11 & L12 \\ \hline L21 & L22 \end{array}$$

Yeang 1995: partitioned matrix

Key: LP = partitioned matrix   L11 = internal interdependencies
       1 = built system   L22 = external interdependencies
       2 = environment   L12 = system/environment exchanges
       L = interdependencies   L21 = environment/system exchanges

"The partitioned matrix is itself a complete theoretical framework embodying all ecological design considerations. The designer can use this tool to examine interactions between the system to be built and its environment holistically and inclusively, taking account of all the environmental interdependencies" [15]

included in the four sets of the diagram.

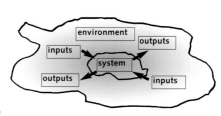

Yeang 1995:
model of a system and
its environment and the
exchanges between the two

In drawing a synoptic conclusion to Yeang's view of architecture in the domain of the earth, his 'General Systems Framework for Design' is acute and simple (see Model of System above). Of this essential drawing, he has said:

"For the purpose of developing a theory, for ecological design, we can regard our building as a system (ie. a designed system or a built system) that exists in an environment (including both the man-made and natural environments). The general systems concept is fundamental to the ecosystem concept in ecology … The crucial task in design – and similarly in any theory – is therefore to pick the right variables to be included, which are those we find essential to our resolution of the design process." [16]

Clearly, these general frameworks cannot encompass all the resultant requirements of a perfect system. Yeang has always emphasised that the process is ongoing and that various sophistications are essential:

"… one thing the (partitioned) matrix will not do is to incorporate the environmental feedback that occurs once the building is actually constructed …" [17]

as this would require a more comprehensive and complex model, yet again.

The 'partitioned matrix' for Yeang constitutes what he has described as a fundamental 'Law of Ecological Design'. [18]
"In ecological design, this 'Law' then requires the designer to look at his designed system in terms of its component

see how these interact with each other (both statically and dynamically over time, these being the four components of the partitioned matrix).** [19]

The matrix allows the designer to assess the ecological impacts and to incorporate all the necessary adjustments to produce a comprehensive, balanced design. In Yeang's terms:

"… any designed system can be conceptually broken down and analysed based on these four sets of interactions …" [20] within the matrix.

Within the extensive range of Yeang's theory, the case of application in this book is essentially about the design of sustainable intensive buildings – including skyscrapers and other building types such as malls, stadiums, etc. It is therefore a priority to relate theory to architectural practice. In this regard two further statements provide clarity:

"… holistic and ecological design takes into account local and global environmental interactions; anticipatory design is forward-looking and is also environmental in that it considers effects over the entire lifetime of the built structure … green design is also self critical … it considers its own effects on the environment and tries to eliminate negative impacts on ecosystems and terrestrial resources … the green designer takes a 'balanced budget' approach, weighing environmental costs and using global resources in the least damaging, most advantageous manner possible." [21]

This statement, in the first instance, establishes the overall context in which the essential act of design, as a process, occurs.

But, secondly the application of principles in itself, requires definition relative to actual building design:

"From the point of view of applied ecology, ecological design has essentially to do with energy and materials management concentrated in a particular locality (ie. the building site). By this (Yeang) means the earth's energy and material resources (biotic and abiotic components) are in effect managed and assembled by the designer into a temporary man-made form (for a period of intended use of 'its useful life'), then later demolished or disassembled at the end of this period, to be either reused or recycled within the built environment or assimilated elsewhere into the natural environment." [22]

Taking these two statements into account, it is important to establish that ecological design is much more than just the management of energy and materials, and that Yeang's approach in no way eliminates the 'giving of form' in the conventional sense. Moreover his insistence on analysis has much to do with the rigorous discipline of major architecture as evidenced earlier in the works of Wright, Kahn and others. It is simply that, in Yeang's case, a much wider view of the building, the use of resources, and the overall impact of its life in use, is being taken into account, together with its initial creation and the inputs that go into this process and then its outward effect on the environment – immediately and afterwards.

[15] Ibid. p 65.
[16] Ibid. pp 59–60.
[17] Ibid. p 70.
[18] Ibid. pp 65–67..

[19] Ibid. pp 65–66.
[20] Ibid. p 66.
[21] Ibid. p 67.
[22] Ibid. p 68.

Yeang's own statement summarises the inclusive nature of his method:

"... the designed system must create a balanced ecosystem of biotic and abiotic components or, what would be better, create a productive and even reparative (ie. healing) relationship with the natural environment both locally and globally ... in addition one has to consider the other conventional aspects of the design of a built system (in this case the Skyscraper): design programme, costs, aesthetics, site and so forth." [23]

The recurrent theme in Yeang's theory is that of comprehensiveness, and this is echoed again when he addresses the act of building:

"... the real test of environmental commitment and principles is on the level of human action (ie. when ground is broken), and this model (ie. Yeang's 'interactions framework'), by offering a comprehensive framework for understanding the interrelations of built systems and ecosystems allows people in various fields to act in concert and contribute to ecological design philosophy." [24]

Yeang has also crucially highlighted that the theoretical structure of the 'interactions framework' can reveal

"... holes in current design practice and research on the subject ... Green design, when pursued comprehensively, demands certain kinds of data, which will have to be developed and quantified where not available." [25]

There can be no doubt that the latter will require substantial developments to assess, assemble and disseminate the massive quantities of data involved and to ensure that is is regularly and systematically updated. However, the IT revolution and the universal availability of systems knowledge should mean that this objective is now eminently viable, as never before. A further implication of Yeang's theory and its real application must also have serious meaning for education in general, and the teaching of a responsive architectural design in particular. It should also further reinforce important areas of research, on a global basis, that can make a significant contribution to both architecture and the whole environment.

Beyond this synoptic comment there are some further observations, that relate back to the central thesis of this book and to the application of Yeang's theory:

"... while the partitioned matrix is a comprehensive frame-work, it is not programmatic. That is to say, it includes all possible issues but not ... particular situations and cases. It can act as the 'law for ecological design', but it is the individual designer who has to apply that law. All that can be predicted here is the type of design issue likely to be faced by the architect of a 'green' skyscraper and other large buildings, particularly in the area of ecosystem interactions and effects ... the interactions model and the matrix present a general, overall picture of the design problems faced by architects following green principles. In essence it is a map, which allows many paths on the way from problem recognition to resolution ... What is important is that in adapting the built system to the natural environment the designer does not neglect any of the interactions defined by the partitioned matrix; how they are addressed remains individual." [26]

23 Ibid. p 68.
24 Ibid. p 71.
25 Ibid. p 71.
26 Ibid. p 73.

the skyscraper should not be packaging

the skyscraper should not be an isolated urban fortress island

skyscraper design is not styling

skyscraper design should not be a homogenous stacking of floor plates

the skyscraper as a stack of information

The message behind Ken Yeang's The Green Skyscraper is not to say how difficult it all is but rather how much more informed and innovative we need to be in our challenge of delivering a sustainable future. I would call it a book of 'tools both theoretical and practical to aid us in applying our craft of design (architectural and engineering). Our world evolves around design, it lives and dies by its application. Take for example the simple flower. It's 'designed' to attract the insects which pollinate it, the leaves are "designed" to process sunlight to keep the plant alive whilst its roots are "designed" to draw nutrients from and to stabilise it to the earth below. The simple flower is holistic, sustainable, a well designed organism, a closed loop. When a generic accident occurs (the loop is broken) which causes a part not to function the flawed design causes catastrophic failure, the plant dies. It is of course safe to say that nature's 'designs' have evolved and are continuing to evolve in response to changes in the global environment. In man's designs however, evolution takes the form of history and perception but unlike natures evolutionary process man does not have time (resources) on his side. Which then suggests that if building design is the identification of a need then we must worry about the needs of the planet that we live on as well as our own. So quite apart from the issues of design philosophy and social relevance there are immediate urgencies, which relate to how we as designer's use the resources of the planet and how our designs interact with the world about us. Responsible (sustainable) design demands that we work with the planet in true evolutionary harmony, not against it and to do so demands knowledge. The Green Skyscraper is but a part of this.

Tony Mclaughlin
(Buro Happold Consulting Engineers)

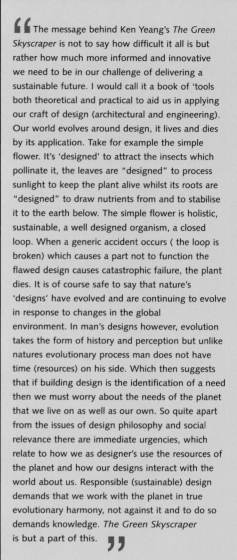

early icons
Empire State Building   Chrysler Building

Corbusier's skyscrapers with a reti-form plan

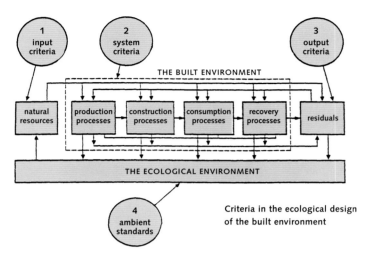

Criteria in the ecological design
of the built environment

Yeang's theoretical statements are consistently supported by his own comprehensive graphics, such as the summary diagram of 'The Built Environment' (above), which models **interactions**: in his own terms these relate to the partitioned matrix and include:

- "the management of inputs (L21)
- the management of outputs (L12)
- the management of the environmental context of the building (L22)
- the design and management of the internal operational systems of the skyscraper in relation to the other three sets of factors (L11) – to this Yeang adds a further crucial condition:
- the interactions of all the above sets acting symbiotically as a whole with the natural systems (and the other man made systems as well) in the biosphere." [27]

To this summary of interactions, Yeang has added a conclusive statement:

> "To fulfil the last (and broadest) goal, that of synchronising all the above aspects of the skyscraper (ie. its inputs, outputs, operational activities and environmental consequences) with the natural cycles in the biosphere and with other human structures, communities and activities in the biosphere, appears at first to be naively idealistic. Yet it is crucial to the realisation of green design and sustainability; however it would require economic – political decisions that lie beyond the scope of the present work and full exploitation of the opportunities of digital technologies." [28]

This universal statement epitomises the intentions, scope and promise of Yeang's philosophy, his call to order and overall understanding, and the total responsibility of his mission – that of an ecological architect. In the seminal text of *The Green Skyscraper*, the summary of his life work to date, he has expanded his address in an exhaustive survey of all the criteria and conditions that surround the process of building architecture. These areas include, in addition to his central theory:

- "Assessing what Is to Be Built
- The Environmental Context for Building
- Design Regarded as Management of Energy and Materials
- Designing the Skyscraper's Operational Systems, and
- Discussion: Ecological Design" [29]

Each of these areas of review and analysis is supported by his assembled collection of graphics, many drawn from projects and instances within his own ever expanding portfolio of architecture.

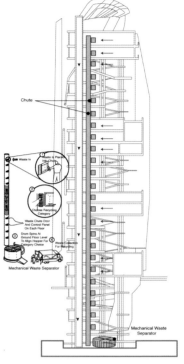

Solid-waste recycling system

EDITT Tower (see pp 110)

Rainwater Collection
and Recycling System

One further reflection on Yeang's extensive treatise, which requires study in full rather than a summary, reveals two outstanding points relative to the skyscraper. The first has to do with **modes**. In this crucial connection, Yeang – who regards each project and building as a progressive development in a series – has said:

> "At the beginning of the production of the design brief, it should be ascertained whether it is possible to meet the skyscraper's comfort requirements largely through a design incorporating passive mode measures with a direct effect. In any event, the design strategy must begin by optimising all the passive mode strategies ...

(which are exhibited in many of Yeang's early skyscraper projects included in this book).

> "Following which, the designer must endeavour to use those mixed-mode systems that are viable and acceptable. The remaining energy needs in terms of heating, cooling, electricity and ventilation should be met by those active systems powered by ecologically sustainable forms of energy." [30]

Yeang then expands on this central question of modes and systems: [31]

> "It will be useful to categorise the level of operational systems provided to our skyscraper and other intensive building types, in other words the extent of its internal environmental servicing systems ... into three levels of provision:

[27] Ibid. p 74, including diagram 'The built environment'.
[28] Ibid. p 75.
[29] pp 5, 77–89, 127, 197 & 279–287.
[30] p 84.
[31] p 85, Yeang attributes this categorisation adapted from Worthington J., 1997, p 11.

- passive mode
- mixed mode
- full mode
- productive mode

The provision of the basic level of systems at the passive-model level, if acceptable to all occupants, is ecologically ideal. It requires the optimisation of all possible passive-mode systems for the locality. The full conventional systems level of servicing is referred to here as the specialised level or the full conventional systems level of servicing is referred to here as the specialised level or the full mode. The in-between or mixed-mode level is the background level of servicing. Productive mode is the use of systems that generate energy (eg. photovoltaics). The designer must decide at the onset which of these levels of operational systems is to be provided in the building." [32]

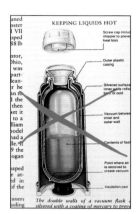

the skyscraper should not have a sealed skin as in a thermos flask

But, on the decisive question of defining the level of provision both for Skyscrapers or other large buildings, Yeang returns to the centrality of the designer's role, and to 'interconnectedness' and the partitioned matrix:

"We can conclude that in the ecological approach, the designer must start with the premise that the environmental impact increases in relation to the increase in demands by users for living conditions beyond those of a simple existence. The first question to be asked prior to design is, 'What is to be built?' and to assess its validity and consequences generically. In preparing the design brief, the designer must find out the extent of shelter and comfort that he or she must design for …

the skyscraper should not be a multi-storey refrigerator

By considering the ecological design holistically in terms of the four factors in the partitioned matrix, it is clear that ecological design must encompass not just architectural design, engineering design and the science of ecology but also other aspects of environmental control and protection such as resource conservation, recycling practices and technology, pollution control, energy embodiment research, ecological landscape planning, applied ecology, climatology, etc. The partitioned matrix here demonstrates the interconnectivity of this multitude of disciplines which must be integrated into a single approach to ecological design." [33]

the skyscraper should not be a multi-storey fortress

As far as this brief synopsis can extend, Yeang's final outstanding point has to do with **aesthetics**, together with economics and performance within the marketplace:

"… we might conclude here by declaring that in addition to meeting the systemic aspects of ecological design, the ecologically responsive or 'green' skyscraper or large building type must also be aesthetically pleasing, economically competitive and excel in performance. If it does not meet these criteria, it is likely that it will not be accepted by the public. The economics of ecological design (or ecological economics) need to be rationalised if business is to accept the benefits of green design …" [34]

the skyscraper as the multi-activity tower

[32] Ibid. pp 85 & 86.
[33] Ibid. pp 86 & 87.
[34] Ibid. p 287.

Menara TA1

"Low energy design and ecological design are applicable regardless of architectural style. Since the best opportunity for improving a building's environmental performance occurs early in the design process, it is clear then that we must at the onset make our skyscrapers and other large buildings not only ecologically responsive but aesthetically pleasing as well if green design is to be a durable proposition." [34]

In drawing together a synoptic review of Yeang's extensive overall vision of the formation of a responsive and responsible ecological architecture, the importance of his concepts of **interconnectedness** and **comprehensiveness** are absolutely central. In practice, using Yeang's theories, the importance of the architect and designer applying the principles to the design process is equally crucial in the actual realisation of truly ecological architecture. Then, in turn, what can be achieved on a global scale, is an architecture and quality of settlement that both satisfies human need and contributes to a **sustainable** environmental condition.

Yeang's summary declaration describes his theoretical work to date as **"… a set of ecological ideals or intentions, the full implementation of which may incur additional costs (over and above the conventional building costs) or societal changes (eg. standard-of-living or comfort) or the revision of current technological and design methods. While many of the ecological objectives remain currently technologically or scientifically unfulfilled, the framework … nevertheless provides a point of departure from which, hopefully, these objectives will eventually be achieved in their entirety."** [35]

With this last statement in mind, it is then possible to see Yeang's development of his own architecture as a set of projects that gradually work progressively towards the ecological objective, both within the constraints of the actual commission and those of the commercial marketplace.

In the presentation of Yeang's skyscrapers and large buildings that follows the trajectory of that development towards an ecological objective is naturally revealed in the nature of the architecture itself – inflected and new forms that are signal of a truly contemporary genre of green buildings. Beginning in the early 1980s, Yeang has already spent some two decades in that relentless development, and the active production of increasingly measured and precisely designed projects are consistently emergent from his Kuala Lumpur studio.

Collectively, and taken together with his theory, Yeang's work is steadily providing an important place of world leadership in the pursuit of architecture and sustainability.

Any overview of Ken Yeang's skyscraper architecture of the last two decades will inevitably confront his relentless pursuit of ecological design, enacted throughout his growing range of projects, typologies and developing hybrid forms.

That the urban skyscraper is central to Yeang's output is self-evident, but alongside this, two other aspects of his creative activity are both synonymous and critical. The first concerns his method, that of **research, design and development (R, D & D)** within the context of practice; the second is his inventive creation of **vertical urbanism** within the framework of the bioclimatic skyscraper.

As further background, it is fundamental to refer to his doctoral thesis, **'A Theoretical Framework for the Ecological Design and Planning of the Built Environment'**. [36] Yeang's work on ecological design and its theory emerged at Cambridge University in 1971–75, and has ever since consistently addressed the whole built environment, including architecture and urbanism. His fundamental agenda is sustainability, and in his ground-breaking thesis of 1974 he summarised his theory of ecological design:

"… it is not an architectural theory but a body of theory that is architectural. Ecological design theory, by nature of the interconnected and holistic characteristics of the earth's ecosystems, affects all aspects of human activity that have an impact on the natural environment, consequently, ecological design theory can include, besides architecture, such seemingly disparate fields as energy production, efficient utilization, waste recycling and reutilization." [37]

Yeang has consistently stressed, from the outset and his entry into architectural practice in Kuala Lumpur in the mid-1970s, that all his theory needs is to be advanced and developed through systemic application and testing via the implementation of real architectural projects. In turn this attitude is the foundation of his creative process, both in terms of technique and his form-giving in architecture.

In reviewing his theory and practice, Yeang has emphasised that:

"Crucial to our entire agenda and work is the focused methodology of research, design and development (R, D & D). This involves an approach to the craft and practice of architecture that demands research as the basis for design and, further, insists on physical implementation as the testing ground for ideas and their poetic interpretation." [38]

Yeang's R, D & D work over the last two decades, especially as applied to tall buildings, has resulted in his invention of a new building type: the bioclimatic skyscraper. In turn this typology incorporates his additional principles and spatial development of **vertical urbanism**.

This trajectory of development is evidenced in a particular set of towers selected to exemplify Yeang's architecture.

[34] Ibid. p 287.

[35] Ibid. p 287.

[36] Published as *Designing with Nature : The Ecological Basis for Architectural Design*, Ken Yeang, McGraw-Hill 1995, essentially documents Yeang's doctoral thesis from Cambridge University UK, written between 1971–75.

[37] Ibid., p. viii.

[38] 'Bioclimatic Skyscrapers' Ken Yeang, Artemis 1994, see essay 'Theory & Practice', Ken Yeang, p 16.

A review of Ken Yeang's architecture should be seen in the context of architectural history, and the earlier work of Wright, Neutra and Schindler, together with the more recent output of Foster, Rogers and Piano. Equally designers such as Victor Papanek and economist-prophet Fritz Schumacher all have established positions and principles relevant to Yeang's agenda. [39] The seminal influence of Buckminister Fuller, as inventor-architect, should also be acknowledged, as Yeang's response to region, programme, climate and context – relative to his agenda for sustainability – has encompassed the thought and principles of all these figures. But, it is the single-minded action and commitment in the area of **bioclimatic** and **ecological design** that has made Yeang's architecture significant, and his collaboration with creative engineers that has enabled much of his work to be achieved.

Just as Yeang's work should be rightly set in a global context in terms of both history and development in 20th century architecture, equally his projects for tall buildings should be seen as a constantly developing series, and not as isolated, sensational events. For in Yeang's case, it is the development of his thought and the expression that his architecture achieves, within the explosive economic climate of South-East Asia, and beyond.

What is on hand, is the emergence of an appropriate and responsive architecture for the 21st century – a sustainable architecture based on ecological principles.

In order to exemplify this architectural response, a limited set of four of his skyscrapers are taken here as a representative range of Yeang's more recent works, although these are only part of a much larger collection that this book incorporates.

The four projects include the Tokyo-Nara Hypertower 1993, the Singapore EDITT Tower 1998, the Kuala Lumpur BATC Tower 1997–99, and the recently completed Penang UMNO Tower 1995–98. However, in order to properly locate these projects in relation to Yeang's overall works and context, it is essential to first mention the benchmark tower, Menara Mesiniaga, realised between 1989–92 in Kuala Lumpur, for IBM's Malaysian agency.

Menara Mesiniaga, a 15 storey landmark office tower, is essentially configured within a circular planform and marks the culmination of Yeang's **sunpath** projects. The cylindrical form is deeply incised by a series of spiralling skycourts, which develop into three-story atria with terraces at the higher levels. These spiralling recessions are heavily planted, beginning from a splayed berm at the base, which houses entrance and computer facilities. The skycourts and atria assist the channelling of cool airflow throughout the transitional spaces of the offices and the planting provides both shade and an oxygen-rich environment. The service cores are gathered into a solar shield-tower on the east facade, while the west face is protected by louvred sun-shading. The cores, containing the lifts, stairwells and restrooms, are naturally ventilated with day-lit spaces. The office skycourts and terraces also provide release to the exterior and natural ventilation when required.

The curtain-glazed north and south walls are a response to the tropical over-head sunpath, moderating solar gain and augmenting the natural day-lit office spaces, which encircle the peripheral plan, with conference facilities forming an inner core.

The roof-level swimming pool and gymnasium are covered by an outrigger shading structure, which protects the associated terraces and pool, and provides a site for the future addition of photo-voltaic solar cells. The project also incorporates systems management to reduce energy consumption by all equipment, including air-conditioning plant.

[39] Ibid., see essay 'The Tropical High-Rise', Professor Ivor Richards, pp 9 & 10.

the Pokemon skyscraper
(Pokemon Adventures vol. 2)

the trojan horse
skyscraper

the skyscraper should
not be a series of
stacked trays in the air

the skyscraper is not
multi-storey shelving

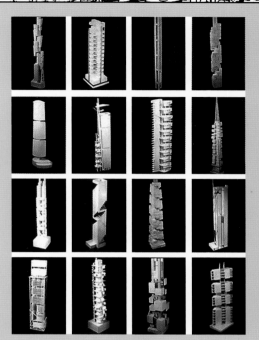

skyscraper morphology studies
(at Hong Kong University with
Professor Eric Lai OBE)

Tower of Babel

bioclimatic skyscraper in a   the skyscraper as a stack
hot humid zone by ants   of interdependent modules

vegetated skyscrapers   oreo cookiescraper

Although there is precedent in Yeang's earlier work, Menara Mesiniaga is the archetypal summary of the bioclimatic sun-path type, which exhibits the clear principles of solar-shielding and orientation, coupled with the insertion of planted skycourts and atrial recessions. Details such as sun-shading spandrels, and size and profile of protective louvres are all subjected to precise geometrical arrangement related to sun angle and path, while the materials specification throughout is related to studies of embodied energy. The external form is appropriately dominated by the spiralling planting of the courts and atrial spaces that are the signal of Yeang's bioclimatic architecture, which is significantly low-energy in operation. At the same time the building exploits the quality of the pleasant tropical climate, uniting office workers with the natural environment.

The bioclimatic skyscraper thus stands as an exemplar and in sharp contrast to the sealed, air-conditioned, centrally cored and energy-consumptive form of its essentially North American counterpart.

four towers: four types

The four towers represent progressive developments within the range of Yeang's bioclimatic series.

Tokyo-Nara Supertower is essentially a spiralling form, rotating within a controlling **circular** geometry, which extends several theoretical propositions. The Singapore EDITT Tower and the Kuala Lumpur BATC Tower are both signature forms, displaying freer **organic** plan arrangements that incorporate ideas for **vertical urbanism.** While these three are not built, the fourth project for the Pulau Pinang UMNO Tower was completed in 1998 and essentially **wind wing-walls**, applied to a constrained rectilinear plan, are the central innovation.

This series also demonstrates Yeang's designs as a progression from formal geometry to a freer organic expression. The formal progression is matched by an expanding ecological and urbanistic investigation.

TOKYO-NARA HYPERTOWER 1993

This is a project that both extends and experiments with several theoretical ideas founded in earlier works, in particular that of Menara Mesiniaga, Kuala Lumpur 1992. Both Mesiniaga and Nara tower forms are constrained within the outline of a circle and contain the principle of a vertical spiral of boundless dimensions. While the KL Mesiniaga Tower is a mere 15 storeys, the Nara Tower can be visualised and extended to 210 storeys, or 880 metres high, almost double the vertical dimensions of Pelli's Petronas Towers in Kuala Lumpur.

The Nara Tower project provided Yeang with the opportunity to realise and expressively confirm many of this theoretical ideas. The project represents a summary of his research to 1993,

"... into the nature and evolution of tall buildings ..." [40]

The central ideas in the project design and its conception are dominated by the spiral floor-plate structure festooned with **vertical landscaping**, which loops around and penetrates the form and its progression of vertical spaces. This is a direct development of the Mesiniaga principle, and in the same way the abundant foliage assists in cooling the building mass. Equally, the planted fringes of floors and atrial spaces contribute to the control of air movement within the overall structure. In this case the calculated, assembled mass of planting balances the biosystems

with the mechanical systems in a symbiotic relationship that yields a stable environment – **a bioclimatic machine a habiter**.

In response to the maintenance needs of the vertical landscaping, glazing and panel cladding systems, Yeang introduced an innovative **robot-arm** as a form of 'cherry-picker' on moveable trellises. These travelling devices move on an external track that spirals the tower in vertical, expressive circulation.

The structural system is a **tour de force** : a three-point equilateral triangle defines a tripartite primary cellular honeycomb structural frame, linked and set within the circular geometry of the robot track system. This matrix provides a support system for the **radial/spiral** arrangement of organic floor plates (described as plectrum shaped).

As the floor plates are rotated at alternative floors, the overlapping layers provide a natural shading system. This shifted pattern allows the introduction of hanging gardens, inter-floor bracing, ventilation and cooling system networks. The main structure is penetrated centrally by a pivotal cable stay mast, and this element, together with the outer triple V-form structures, define the positions for batteries of vertical transportation. The floor plate spiral shift also creates variations of atrial space that are further infused with terraces, internal courts, private gardens and skycourts.

Throughout, Yeang envisaged his first principles of **vertical urbanism**. These included principally: **mixed occupancy** such as offices, apartments, hotels and communal facilities; **skycourt oases**, the equivalent of green parks; and the **atrial spaces** as a public areas of movement, vistas, air and light. The skycourt oases, located at regular vertical intervals, provide major breaks in the built volume – a form of suspended natural park, introducing fresh air and acting as the Tower's lungs, distributing via the atrial voids and essential airflow, while insulated from the city beneath. The atrial network of spaces, winding within the tower, provides a sheltered interaction of walkways, bridges and stairwells – a pedestrian system of routes, open to the environment but particular to the tower itself. Taken together with the central core, these elements provide an overall system of **wind-flues**, which bring wind to inner parts of the building, with adjustable dampers. This principle has been further developed in the wind wing-wall system used in the Penang UMNO Tower.

As with the Mesiniaga Tower, the **lift and service** cores are laid defensively on the east-west axis of the sunpath to absorb the maximum quantity of solar gain. The cooler facades on the north-south axis are, conversely, more open with clear glazing and atrial voids, echoing the earlier precedent. In the same bioclimatic tradition the **shielding and glazing** systems are orientated to resist solar gain. The east-west facing sides are more solidly glazed, with cast and perforated metal cladding – selected for qualities of reflection, weight and structural capacity. And again, the north-south faces of the form are equally legible by the open louvres, tiered sunshades and clear glazing in response to the lower exposure to the sun.

The vast spiral form of this bioclimatic supertower is intended to rise independent of the polluted lower city beneath, reaching into the inhabitable upper atmosphere, in Yeang's words **"...at the edge of the sky"**. Armoured against solar gain and strategically opened to introduce natural ventilation, the overall spatial composition and functional mix offers the possibility of a new form of urban life.

40 'Tokyo-Nara Tower', Ken Yeang, project profile and notes, 1993

Were it to be realised, Yeang would doubtless add to the design many further principles developed in later projects such as rain irrigation, ecosystem hierarchy, recycling and embodied energy assessment.

In its present form as an earlier project (1993) it remains both as an iconic statement, and as the key link between the diminutive Mesiniaga Tower and the current series of supertowers in which Yeang has been subsequently engaged. As the scale of the projects increases, the **ecological design agenda** expands.

SINGAPORE EDITT TOWER 1998

The design for the EDITT Tower, on a site owned by the Urban Redevelopment Authority (URA) for an urban corner site in Singapore, is a hybrid form. In its initial current state it fulfils the client's programme requirements for an **Exposition Tower**, but the nature of its design formation allows future **transformation** to offices or apartments.

The 26-storey tower project, situated at the junction of Middle Road and Waterloo Street, is remarkable in two principal respects. First, the design advances Yeang's ideas for a civilised **vertical urbanism** – the continuous extension of street life into the elevated levels of the skyscraper. Second, Yeang uses the project to explore and demonstrate his consolidated **ecological** approach to tower design. This involves an even wider agenda than that he has applied in earlier projects. Finally, the design and its inherent plan **geometry** displays a freer, organic composition – related both to public space and circulation – and therefore marks a departure from the KL Mesiniaga and Tokyo-Nara Towers, whose forms are controlled within a circular plan particulary towards a new ecological aesthetic.

The overall programme of uses is defined by the nature of an Expo event project and includes retail areas, exhibition spaces and auditorium uses as well as more conventional open office spaces on the upper levels, which are adaptable.

The controlling V-form structural geometry is evident in the plan form level 1 above ground, but the three-dimensional form does not express this clearly until level 12. This is largely due to the inclusion of groups of **pedestrian ramps**, which alternate, within the vertical progression from the north to the south faces of the tower. At levels 20 to 23, the ramp systems are so extended that they occupy the whole western sector of the plan, between the north and south faces, extending an expressive principle of public circulation that is similarly first signalled at the introductory levels between ground, and level 1 through to 3.

Otherwise, the plan organisation reveals the signature hallmarks of Yeang's designs. These include vertical landscaping, here further developed; skycourts, atrial spaces and plazas; and very heavy solar-shielding of the eastern face, with a cranked, unified 'wall' of stairtowers, lifts and restroom accommodation.

The two central propositions of **place making** and public circulation, coupled with an extended **ecological agenda** both take their place as major forces and expressive elements within the design. They are the root and content of the whole architectural form, whose elegant inflection has resulted in a design of great freedom and substance.
In addition, Yeang's approach here substantiates his earlier statement, that

> **"... the design of energy-efficient enclosures has the potential to transform architectural design from being an uncertain, seemingly whimsical craft, into a confident science".** [41]

It is also delivering a new, environmentally responsible version of the modernist canon, where sociable openness and climate informs its essential spatiality.

[41] Yeang 'Bioclimatic Skyscrapers' (essay 'Theory and Practice'), op. cit. p. 17.

Tokyo-Nara Tower
(see p 068)

woodcut of a ventilated costume that is cool in summer and warm in winter (1877)
(in Dupre J., 1996, p 54)

EDITT Tower

interconnectedness

Yeang has made a crucial point in the design of the EDITT Tower in that the major issue in the urban design of skyscrapers

> **"... is poor spatial continuity between street-level activities with those spaces at the upper-floors of the city's high-rise towers ..."**[42],

in the conventional case, which is based on repetitious, physical compartmentalisation of floors within an inherently sealed envelope.

Yeang's central manifesto is that urban design involves 'place making'. In the EDITT Tower he has applied this principle with conviction:

> **"... in creating 'vertical places', our design brings 'street-life' to the building's upper-parts through wide landscaped-ramps upwards from street-level. Ramps are lined with street activities: stalls, shops, cafes, performance spaces and viewing decks, up to the first six floors. Ramps create a continuous spatial flow from public to less public, as a 'vertical extension of the street', thereby eliminating the problematic stratification of floors inherent in all tall buildings typology. High-level bridge-linkages are added to connect to neighbouring buildings for greater urban connectivity."**[43]

In addition to the consideration of public space and circulation, Yeang added an **analysis of views** to enable upper-floor design to have greater visual connectivity with the surroundings. In Singapore, with its superb seaboard location, this is a significant factor, and rightly exploited.

But, it is the manipulation and integration of the **ramp**, within the form and function of the project, that emerges as the fundamental precept of the architecture and its manifestation of public space and use. In common with the early projects of le Corbusier, and more recently Richard Meier, the ramp is once again celebrated here as a symbolic notation, and the visible expression of the **promenade architecturale**.

Aside from the abundant, spiralling landscape of indigenous vegetation which assists ambient cooling of the facades, two further elements appear foremost in the form-giving process. These include the curvilinear rooftop **rainwater collector**, and the attendant **rainwater facade collector scallops**, which form the rainwater collection and recycling system. Equally the extensive incorporation of photovoltaic panels, as a major formation on the east facade, adds a further level of formal detail residual in the overall bioclimatic discipline, towards reduced energy consumption.

In this case, Yeang's ecological response begins with an extensive analysis of the **site's ecology**. This exhaustive analysis of ecosystem hierarchy, determines that this site is an urban **'zero culture'**. Consequently, this is a crucial determinant, which focuses the design approach towards the restoration of organic mass, which will enable **ecological succession** to replace the inorganic nature of the site, in its current urban state of devastation.

This policy is manifest in the planted facades and terraces of the project, which are continuously ramped upwards from the ground plane to the roof-summit level and constituting a significant proportion of planted to useable floor area. Yeang included a survey of indigenous planting within a 1 mile radius of the site in order to select species that will not compete with those already present in the locality. **Sustainability** underscores every move.

Otherwise, Yeang's ecological design process includes a further series of significant analyses. Perhaps most important is to submit the project to a **'loose-fit'** philosophy, which will enable the building to absorb change and refitting over a life-span of 100/150 years. Overall, this allows conversion from the expo-condition to possible office use, with a high level of floor occupation efficiency. This involves removable partitions and floors, reuse of skycourts, mechanical jointing, which enables future recovery of materials, all within a matrix that is based upon **flexibility** as a paramount condition.

In addition, Yeang introduced a series of systems and assessment procedures that further underscore the ecological design of the tower. As well as **water recycling and purification** associated with rainwater and grey-water reuse, the project includes **sewage recycling, solar energy use, building materials' recycling and reuse, together with natural ventilation and 'mixed-mode' servicing.** The latter optimises the use of mechanical and electrical servicing so that both mechanical air-conditioning and artificial lighting systems are reduced, relative to the locality's bioclimatic responses. Ceiling fans with demisters are used for low-energy comfort cooling. **Wind** is also used to create internal comfort conditions by the introduction of 'wind-walls', that are placed parallel to the prevailing wind to direct airflow to internal spaces and skcourts, to assist breeze cooling.

Finally, the whole material fabric and structure of the tower were subjected to an **embodied energy and CO_2** emission assessment, in order to understand the environmental impact of the project, and to define a balance between embodied and operational energy content.

While these methods are neither unique nor overly new in themselves, it is the co-ordinated collective effect of their application in Yeang's architecture that signals his ecological attitude to design, and provides the basis for development in following projects.

KUALA LUMPUR BATC SIGNATURE TOWER 1997

In order to describe the Signature Tower adequately it is essential to place it in the context of the overall development to which it belongs, as a key component.

The Business Advancement Technology Centre forms a massive mixed-urban development, incorporating some university faculties on the Semarak Campus of the Universiti Teknologi Malaysia. The site is also related to the Central Business District of Kuala Lumpur. As both the Multimedia Super Corridor (MSC) and the Kuala Lumpur City Centre (KLCC) are located less than 2 kilometres from the campus site it became strategically obvious to further expand its potential and develop the overall site into a Satellite MSC, in a synergistic relationship with the MSC itself. In principle, the project incorporates major educational, research and development and electronic commerce related activities.

The project is organised as a collaboration between the university, as landowner, and a property developer.

As an integrated urban masterplan, the project represents one of the largest proposals Yeang has designed, and opens the opportunity to demonstrate the principles of his bioclimatic approach as applied to the design of tall buildings, and a larger high technology urban village with transportation infrastructure.

[42] 'EDITT Tower', Ken Yeang, project profile and notes, 1998.   [43] Ibid. 'Place Making'.

The 47 acre site is envisaged as a landscaped park within which the buildings are placed and serviced by a central series of public plazas, boulevard walk-ways and controlled car access routes. The rapid transit system (LRT) forms a central spine with a station at the mid-point junction between retail, commercial and university facilities.

The site is divided, therefore, into three zones. A central north-south zone of the major public spaces and activities, edged on the east and west by two further fluid parkland areas into which the array of facilities are inserted and attached to the central V-form spine. The 60-storey Signature Office Tower and the five, 30-storey office towers are sited within the parkland areas, as part of this ensemble.

As landscaping is applied to the entire development, the whole immense project viewed from the peripheral roads is seen as a grand park with the buildings located and immersed within this natural setting. The towers are accessed via the mounted landscaped ground plane of the site, while water gardens and soft landscaping are introduced to enhance the pedestrian routes throughout the site in general. Many of the routes provide weather-protected, semi-covered pedestrian circulation, free of vehicular intrusion. This is a principle, related to the tropical climate that has it origins in Yeang's earlier work, such as his conceptual proposals for the Tropical Verandah City of 1987. [44]

Related to the overall principles of a landscape concept, landscaped and terraced skycourts have been incorporated at intervals in the office tower floors as they ascend, providing both an amenity for relaxation, and a continuous visual and physical linkage, threading together all storeys. The **vertical urbanism**, in this case, accords with a vertical ascension of public **gardens and parks**. This concept is further supported with Yeang's incorporation of **public places in the sky** – the amenities of a traditional city, but vertically located in the tower forms. Thus, in the instance of all six towers for the BATC masterplan, the principles Yeang employed for the Singapore EDITT Tower are first enacted into a major exposition of the bioclimatic skyscraper. In turn these tall buildings all incorporate integrated Building Management Systems to control internal conditions by monitoring the immediate, external surroundings through a series of environmental sensors located on the roof – effectively Yeang's version of a **bioclimatic weather station**.

The significance of the BATC Towers lies in the fact that they exist as a part of a much larger idea, centred on a harmony of bioclimatic principles, and framed within the urban master plan, as a whole. The BATC Centre and Branch Campus of UTM contains a School of Advanced Education Programmes in high technologies catering for 5000 students. This is coupled with industry, research and development centres for 20 institutions, in order to advance business opportunities arising from the research. The associated High-Technology Office Park houses companies involved in the advanced technology industry, including IT and multimedia, and provides these occupants with the shared use of super-capability computer facilities as a basis for a significant centre of innovation. The masterplan also incorporates major convention and exposition centres, information and resource centres and a Multimedia and IT College. Each of these facilities occupies either a linked edge site or a part of the spinal arrangement. Further public facilities include a major theme mall for retail entertainment and recreation via multimedia applications; residential blocks to house students, researchers and office workers; a four-star hotel for visitors and tourists, with fully equipped business centres.

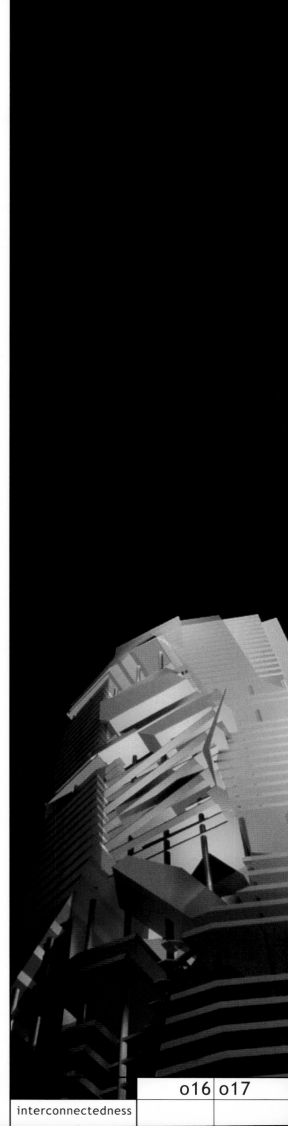

BATC Tower

[44] 'The Tropical Verandah City', Ken Yeang, Longman (Kuala Lumpur), 1987.
These proposals discuss the concept of semi-covered, shaded pedestrian circulation areas for the tropical city.

All this diverse provision is underscored by the system of public park land within the site, whose lush greenery and landscaped contributes towards an environment that enables high business activity and related research endeavours. A main boulevard system structures the site in vehicle-free conditions that encourage public use with covered pedestrian walkways, or the alternative of an air-conditioned Internal Rapid Transit System, which provides movement within the site, with links to the outer LRT system of Kuala Lumpur.

The 60-storey Signature Office Tower is the singular landmark, vertical event of the BATC Masterplan, counterbalanced by the horizontal mass and spaces of the central plaza and spinal facilities.

The Signature Tower occupies a central site on the western parkland of the project, with longer sides of its cranked rectilinear plan facing north and south, and the eastern face typically solar shielded with service cores, elevators and restroom clusters. The sunken lower levels incorporate escalator banks serving the centre of the form up to level 4. Above level 32, two systems of **pedestrian ramps** alternate on the outer north and south faces up to level 40, reducing to the south face only from level 48 through to 60. As with the Singapore EDITT Tower, these ramp formations are an important part of the building's expression of public circulation and the notion of **vertical urbanism**, seen as a hierarchy within the tower-form. Otherwise, the dominant composition elements are the two massive vertical landscape parks occupying a large area of the atrial voids and skycourts at the higher levels. These are augmented by a ramping park at the base, and ten other smaller parks distributed over the height of the building's section.

As the central and most prestigious flexible office facility for the whole development, the innovative bioclimatic design offers a first-class daily environment for its occupants. The intermissions of restaurants, sky-plazas and special gallery spaces, with the overall development of the vertical gardens, park and extensive skycourt voids, taken together, mark Yeang's most flamboyant tower project of his current series. On another level, much of the technical innovation of the Singapore EDITT Tower could be expected to appear, when the project is ultimately realised.

The Signature Tower summarises Yeang's vision of the **Skyscraper as the Vertical City-in-Sky**. This is primarily achieved through the vertical coupling of multiple programmes of space use, within the overall programme of the tower as a spatial construct. This idea is then further emphasised by a three-tier hierarchy of circulation systems, and the system of vertical landscaping, parks and squares both ascending and cross-cutting the overall form. The singular force of the concept is perhaps best conveyed in Yeang's coloured elevational notations of his tripartite vision.

Beyond the tower itself, however, the most significant impact of the total masterplan is the application of bioclimatic principles to the overall urban design of the BATC complex, regardless of type.

PENANG UMNO TOWER 1995-98

The UMNO Tower is one of a series of projects that Yeang developed and built between 1992–98, using slim rectilinear plan forms on dense urban site locations. These projects include Central Plaza, and the Budaya Tower, both in Kuala Lumpur and realised between 1992–96. While all these towers were designed within the framework of Yeang's bioclimatic agenda, the UMNO project for downtown Penang is singularly distinguished by its concentration on **natural ventilation** and the development of **wind wing-walls** in this connection.

The thin-elongated urban site-plan of the tower is situated at the junctions of Jalan Zainal Abidin and Jalan Macalister, resulting in the extended longitudinal facades being exposed to a south-east or north-west orientation. This is often a function of such valuable urban-land locations.

The 21-storey tower design responds with a virtually solid solar shield-wall of elevators, staircases and restrooms with service cores, as in Yeang's other bioclimatic projects. In this case the shield-wall not only protects the critical south-eastern face from solar gain, but its projecting planar terminals, at the north and south extremities, form two of the wind wing-walls that are particular to the natural ventilation strategy of the project and its office spaces.

The base of the UMNO Tower contains a deeply recessed, double-height banking hall, together with the glass-canopied main entrance raised on a shallow podium and accessed from Jalan Macalister, the main thoroughfare. The base also contains the main plant spaces and car-ramps that give access to parking areas on levels 2 through 5. Level 6, the principal occupied floor, houses an auditorium for meetings and assemblies. Above this rise, 14 floors of office floor space for let. Several floors, such as level 9 and 12, have extensive break-out roof terraces, and the roof levels are shielded by a steel-structured, elevated shade canopy.

The solar shield-wall accommodation of elevator lobbies and restrooms are naturally sun-lit and ventilated, and typically accord with Yeang's low-energy agenda. Similarly, all office floors, although designed to be air-conditioned, can be **naturally ventilated**. The thin plan-form, of each floor-plate, means that no desk location is more than 6.5 metres distant from an openable window, enabling all office users to receive natural sunlight and ventilation. Although the project was originally designed for tenants to install their own split unit air-conditioning, due to expected low rental rates in Penang, ultimately a central air-conditioning system was installed. The design for **natural ventilation**, in its realised form, thus provides a back-up system for the building, in the event of power-failure.

Major sun-shaded installations on the curvilinear north-west office wall are solar orientated, and outrigged shield-shades are provided to the carpark floors, also on this facade.

But, it is the **wind wing-wall** system, which in this case dominates the streamlined form of the UMNO Tower architecture, and it is perhaps significant that Yeang has persistently compared the vertical-scale of the building, to the aerofoil form of one to a one and a half times the length of a typical jumbo-jet aircraft. The symbolic inference of building-airstream-aircraft, and the cross-referencing of the sophisticated serviced shell, has long existed in Yeang's essays and in certain projects, such as this, comes closer to a transferable vision.

The architect's own notes on the development of the wind wing-wall design are of significance, as they describe his system of research and application:

> **"The building has wind wing-walls to direct wind to special balcony zones that serve as pockets with air-locks, having adjustable doors and panels to control the percentage of openable windows, for natural**

ventilation. **This building is probably the first high-rise office (tower) that uses wind as natural ventilation for creating comfort conditions inside the building ... For internal comfort as in this building, a higher level of air-change per hour is required. Here, we tried to introduce natural ventilation at point of entry, rather than create suction at the leeward side. To create pressure at the inlet, a system of 'wing-walls' to 'catch' the wind from a range of likely directions (are introduced). The wing-walls are attached to a balcony-device with full-height sliding doors. The placements of the wing-walls and air-locks within the floor-plate are based on the architect's assessment from the locality's wind-data. The wing-wall cum air-lock device is of course, experimental, and site verification with CFD analysis indicates that this device worked reasonably well. Experience from the project, will enable the architect to further develop the device for other projects."** [45]

And this has indeed been the case, for the design of the EDITT Tower for Singapore uses the same principles to create internal comfort conditions, by the incorporation of 'wind-walls' as an integral device, in the natural ventilation strategy. These examples not only demonstrate Yeang's R, D & D strategy in a sequence, but they also point up the process which informs his architectural expression – a process that allows functional low-energy design to bring sophisticated form to what would otherwise be just an office tower, in the conventional sense. In creating the **bioclimatic skyscraper**, Yeang has not just evolved a new type, but has developed both low-energy architecture and the **spatiality of vertical urbanism.**

Further, it has been said of Yeang's work, that

"... his towers as they ascend in Kuala Lumpur or Penang or Ho Chi Minh City seem, in their paradoxical mix of orders and desires, to achieve a synthesis exactly appropriate to the cultural promise of South-East Asia, their warrior-like stance ready for the economic revolutions of the new century". [46]

The fact that Ken Yeang has brought about his sustainable architecture, and its range of achievements, within a harsh commercial environment, in itself is memorable, but even more important is the fact that his work and the improved environments his buildings offer, has affected the quality of life for countless occupants for the better.

Ivor Richards
School of Architecture
Planning & Landscape,
University of Newcastle
UK
May 2001

UMNO Tower

[45] 'MENARA UMNO', Ken Yeang, project profile and notes, 1998.
[46] Yeang, 'Bioclimatic Skyscrapers' (essay 'Architecture for a New Nation', Alan Balfour) op. cit. p. 8.

solar

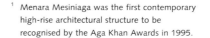

Within the rigorous development of any new **typeform**, certain projects emerge which embody and summarise all the significant principles that are applied, and configure these into an elegant and mature formal order – Menara Mesiniaga exemplifies the characteristics and significance of such a project.

Although only 15 storeys in height, this tower – while being clearly grounded in the basics of Menara Boustead – can be extended as a type, to create great leaps of development, such as Yeang's 80-storey Tokyo-Nara Tower project.

Central to this iconic summary of the low-energy, passive-mode sunpath type are the principles of solar-shielding and orientation, combined with the implementation of multi-height planted skycourts and atrial recessions coupled into a beautiful spiral-form, gathered into a pure circular plan. Details of attached sun-shading spandrels and protective sun-louvres all reach a stage of precise and sophisticated design related to sun angle and path, in the overall conception and its constructed reality.

That this project, which stands on the outer threshold of Kuala Lumpur city, has been the subject of multiple publications that demonstrate its significance also measures its importance, but it is equally noteworthy that the building has received international acclaim in the form of awards for architecture. [1]

The Mesiniaga Tower is essentially a regional headquarters building, in this case for IBM's Malaysia agency. With its commanding position, the building both exploits the qualities of the local, ambient tropical climate and the magnificent vistas to the surrounding hillside landscape.

Yeang's modest description, first cast in 1994, belies the archetypal nature of the project as a first-rate exemplar of bioclimatic architecture:

And, leaving aside the later UMNO Tower of 1995–98, and its subsequent development of the **'wind wing-wall'** principle with its expressive consequences, Mesiniaga remains as a supreme architectural statement:

"... the most striking design feature is the planting which is introduced into the facade and the skycourts, starting from a three-storey-high planted mound (a berm) and spiralling up the face of the building. Triple-height recessed terraces towards the upper part of the building are also planted. These atriums enable the

[1] Menara Mesiniaga was the first contemporary high-rise architectural structure to be recognised by the Aga Khan Awards in 1995.

menara mesiniaga

channelling of a cool flow of air throughout the buildings transitional spaces while the planting provides shade and an oxygen-rich atmosphere. Curtain wall glazing is used only on the north and south facades to moderate solar gain. All the windows areas facing the hot east and west faces have external aluminium fins and louvres to provide sun shading. Glazing details allow the light-green glass to act as a ventilation filter, protecting the interior without totally insulating it. Terraces are provided for all the office floors, and have sliding full-height glass doors to control the extent of natural ventilation (when required). Lift lobbies, stairwells and toilets have natural ventilation and sunlight. The lift lobbies do not need pressurisation for fire protection. [2]

What Yeang is describing constitutes the major low-energy elements of the design, which, in turn, greatly enhance the quality of life of the office occupants. These ideas are coupled with the internal occupation concept of enclosed rooms such as conference spaces being located at the core of the plan, while the work stations encircle the periphery ensuring good natural light and views to the distant landscape. The terraces provide excellent break-out spaces into the external environment – an extra facility that relieves and enlivens the working day.

The pure, circular plan is surrounded by four pairs of major circular structural columns, which emerge at high level as roof masts. The major cluster of elevators and service spaces are situated outboard on the eastern face and the skycourt terraces rotate clockwise and upwards, providing a different plan form at each level. The resultant form is a loosely defined cylinder encircled with a sheath of detached spandrels and louvre elements. At the same time, the cylinder is grounded in the berm and crowned with rooftop facilities. The summary result is both simple in conception and outstandingly clear in its resolution – all of Yeang's elements of the **bioclimatic skyscraper** typology are brought together into his first iconic maste piece.

[2] Yeang, 'Bioclimatic Skyscrapers', op. cit. p 59.

owner Mesiniaga Sdn Bhd
(IBM Sole Agent in Malaysia)
'Mesiniaga' = business machine
location Subang Jaya, Selangor, Malaysia
latitude 3.7°N
nos of storeys 15 storeys
(including one basement)
date start 1989 (June)
completion date 1992 (August)
areas
Total nett (office) area 6,741 sq m
Total net non-office (ie. gym, cafe, etc.) 476 sq m
Balconies, skycourts & pool-deck 981 sq m
Circulation & toilets 2,318 sq m
Mechanical rooms 1,424 sq m
Carpark (basement) (145 bays) 404 sq m
site area 6,503 sq m
plot ratio 1:1.6

design features • The building brings together the principles of the bioclimatic approach to the design of tall buildings developed over the previous decade by Yeang. In particular, the building has the following features:
• 'Vertical landscaping' (planting) introduced into the building facade and at the 'skycourts'. The planting starts by mounding up from ground level to as far up as possible at one side of the building. The planting then 'spirals' upwards across the face of the building with the use of recessed terraces (as skycourts).
• A number of passive low-energy features are also incorporated: All the window areas facing the hot sides of the building (ie. east and west sides) have external louvres as solar-shading to reduce solar heat gain into the internal spaces. Those sides without direct solar insolation (ie. the north and south sides) have unshielded curtain-walled glazing for good views and to maximise natural lighting.
• Lift lobbies are naturally ventilated and are sun-lit with views to the outside. These lobbies do not require fire-protection pressurisation (ie. low-energy lobby). All stairways and toilet areas are also naturally ventilated and have natural lighting.
• The sunroof is the skeletal provision for panel space for the possible future placing of solar-cells to provide back-up energy source. BAS (Building Automation System) is an active Intelligent Building feature used in the building for energy saving.

1995 AGA KHAN AWARD FOR ARCHITECTURE

jury citation

❝ For having boldly designed a meaningful tall building in a tropical climate. Eschewing the box like curtain-wall structures so common in corporate office buildings, this project promotes a new language that punches out parts of the structure and wraps a spiralling series of interactive open gardens around the main core buildings. It raises the kind of architectural debate in which the corporate world generally, and the Muslim world more specifically, can fruitfully engage. ❞

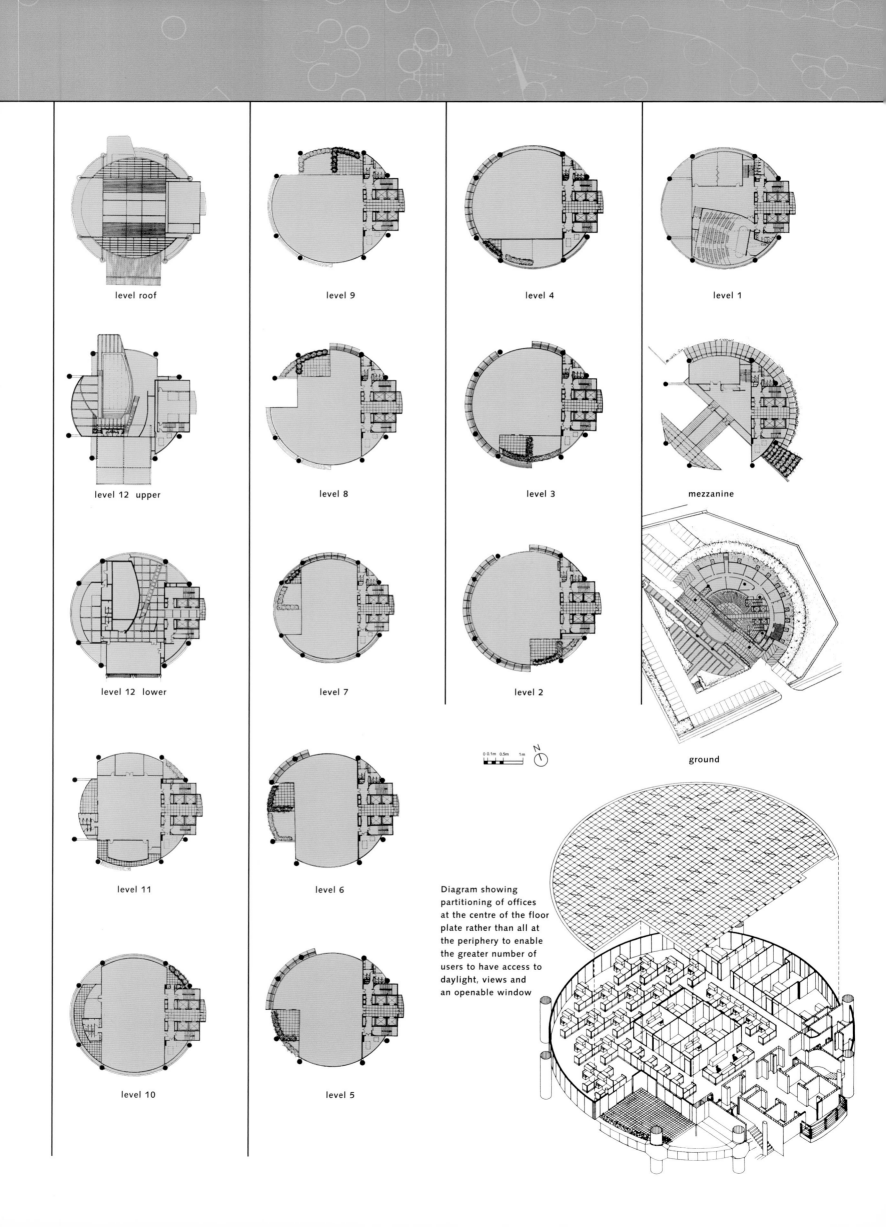

level roof

level 12 upper

level 12 lower

level 11

level 10

level 9

level 8

level 7

level 6

level 5

level 4

level 3

level 2

0 0.1m 0.5m 1m

N

level 1

mezzanine

ground

Diagram showing partitioning of offices at the centre of the floor plate rather than all at the periphery to enable the greater number of users to have access to daylight, views and an openable window

The three-storey planted berm base, a major formal element, houses entrance lobbies, computer suites, and below underground car parking in sheltered basements. At the top end, a roof-level sun terrace is covered with a sunroof of trussed steel and aluminium. Locally known as the 'flycatcher' this shading structure filters daylight over the swimming pool and the curved roof form of the high-level gymnasium. This filigree structure also provides a site for the future installation of photovoltaic cells – as an active contributor to the building's energy requirements. In addition, the project is fitted with a range of automated systems to reduce energy consumption by both equipment and the air-conditioning installation.

This project also provokes questions of aesthetics and architectural expression. In its effortless formation, the resultant architecture is the pure product of principles and geometry – there is not a trace of applied formal imagery nor any reference to Malay tradition, only to climate and global position:

"... the architectural zeitgeist is expressed through technology and materials, state-of-the-art thought and attitude and the incorporation of climate and lifestyle principles as a contemporary translation of context ... Emotive references to traditional materials and forms are avoided, an attitude validated from a realistic position that proposes a Malaysian architecture for the 21st century, very different from its historical origins. This is an open attitude that can absorb change. It is also an intelligent reflection of a polyculture establishing a positive identity as a collective, through abstract contemporary form." [4]

4 Professor Ivor Richards, 'The Tropical High-Rise', op. cit. p 14

swimming pool at level 12 upper

evaluation of service core position options and OTTV Values

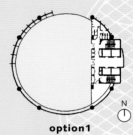

option 1

north = 37.0
east = 55.7
south = 38.8
west = 52.0
total OTTV = **43.3 W/m²**
(less 90%)

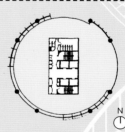

option 2

north = 37.0
east = 61.7
south = 38.8
west = 52.0
total OTTV = **47.5 W/m²**
(less 99%)

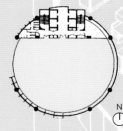

option 3

north = 39.0
east = 53.0
south = 38.8
west = 52.0
total OTTV = **47.6 W/m²**
(100%)

OTTV = **Overall Thermal Transmission Value**

The diagrams inform how building configuration (eg. location of service cores) can optimise the passive-mode strategy to result in a low-energy design

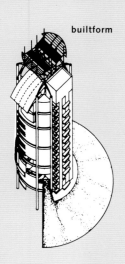

builtform

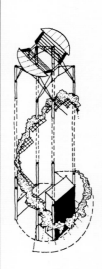

orientation

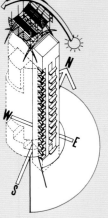

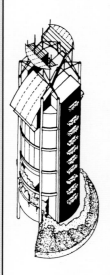

interstitial spaces

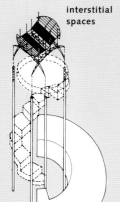

glazing & shading

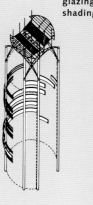

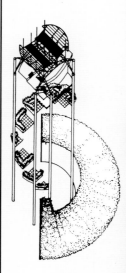

roof assembly

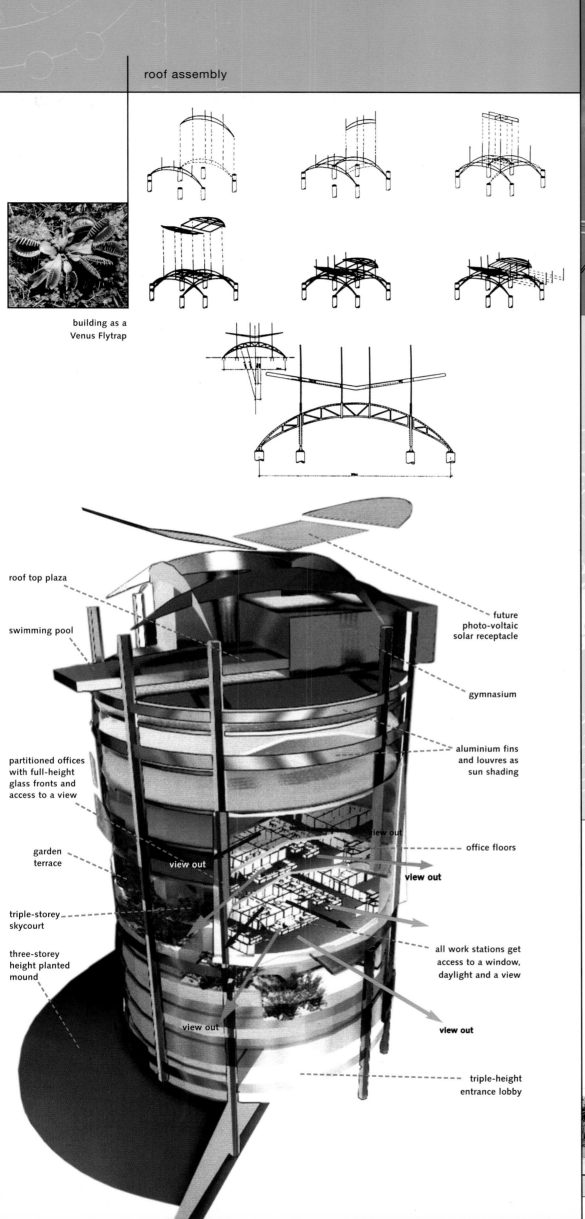

building as a
Venus Flytrap

roof top plaza

swimming pool

partitioned offices
with full-height
glass fronts and
access to a view

garden
terrace

triple-storey
skycourt

three-storey
height planted
mound

future
photo-voltaic
solar receptacle

gymnasium

aluminium fins
and louvres as
sun shading

view out

view out

view out

office floors

view out

all work stations get
access to a window,
daylight and a view

view out

triple-height
entrance lobby

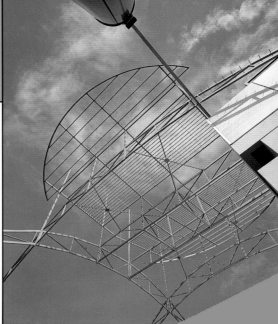

Jumping Out of the Glass Box

in THE ASIAN WALL STREET JOURNAL (JULY 1994)
Susan Berfield

" … Of all the ways to divine the spirit
of a city, perhaps the most telling is to get a fix
on its coordinates, Yeang believes. A city's
latitude determines its climate, and 'climate' says
Yeang 'is the most durable aspect of a place and has
to be the first factor in design.' When it is,
then 'the design is always indigenous and reflects
the place' … The firm's most recently completed
project, Menara Mesiniaga, the HQ for IBM's
Malaysian distributor, is its best known. The 15-
story building, by far the firm's most adventurous,
is nonetheless eminently logical. The untrained
observer needs only a minute to see how this
cylindrical mass of steel and glass resting on eight
columns makes sense. Most striking is that Menara
Mesiniaga's exterior is neither sealed nor uniform.
Yeang carved a series of planted terraces, or
skcourts as he calls them, into the building. They
spiral around the tower's perimeter, providing
shaded outdoor sanctuaries and absorbing some of
the sun's heat. He also reshaped the building's
'skin'; aluminium screens and strips are designed to
minimize the impact of the sun at some points and
to allow more light to penetrate at others. Yeang
experimented with the building's interior as well,
he placed workstations along the edges of each
floor and private, glass-partitioned offices in the
centre to allow everyone to work in a naturally lit
space with a view. "

gymnasium at level 12

Architecture Beyond Architecture

ACADEMY EDITIONS, LONDON (1995)

Cynthia Davidson

" This striking interpretation of the corporate 'landmark' skyscraper explores a new direction for an often pompous building type. Instead of a typically authoritarian and introverted statement of a multi-national corporation, the IBM tower is a robust, informal and open expression of an emerging technology. The architects calls this new type the 'bioclimatic tall building' and provides it with sensible, energy-saving climatic controls. Most notable are the two spirals of green 'sky gardens' that twist up the building and provide shade and visual contrast with the steel and aluminium surfaces. The reinforced concrete frame is further punctuated by two types of sun-screen and a glass and steel curtain wall, which, along with the sloping base and metal crown, make the essentially High Tech image much more organic; one of the jurors termed the building 'organitech'. Further ecological sensitivity includes the placement of the core functions on the hottest (east) side of the tower and the extensive use of natural light, ventilation and greenery.

Kenneth Yeang's 'bioclimatic architecture' recalls the climatic architecture of the 1950s and Frank Llyod Wright's skyscraper projects, in a move towards a new architecture for the 1990s. The result is an alternative to the reigning mode of corporate towers and a new synthesis for contemporary architecture that is responsive to the climate of a particular place and finds inspiration for a new architectural language from forces that are ultimately cosmic.

Menara Mesiniaga brings to fruition the architect's decade-long research into bioclimatic principles for the design of tall buildings in tropical climates.

It features strong spatial organisation with a specific hierarchy. The building has a tripartite structure that consists of a raised 'green' base, a spiralling body with horizontal, terraced garden balconies and external louvres that shade the offices, and an uppermost floor that houses recreational facilities, a swimming pool and sunroof. The reinforced concrete and steel-frame structure of the building is completely exposed; the tower is cooled by both natural ventilation and air conditioning. The distinctive tubular composition that crowns the tower will provide for the future installation of solar panels to further reduce energy consumption.

Yeang's interest in experimenting with ecologically and environmentally sound tall towers – the bioclimatic skyscraper - is to reduce the costs of a building by lowering its energy consumption and to develop benefits for the users by emphasizing ecological values, that is designing with the climate in mind. Yeang believes that a climatically responsive building is a successful building, and both client and users of Menara Mesiniaga attest to the success of his approach.

The design features of the tower are bold, and are not intended to blend with the immediate physical environment, even though its climatic adaptation is a priority. The tower has also become a landmark, and has increased the value of the land around it. "

Menara Mesiniaga energy study

Norman Disney & Young Sdn Bhd

Consulting Engineers

An energy analysis of the same building constructed of conventional unshaded curtain wall construction is prepared here to show its implications. The arrangement of the building is reviewed and we have recalculated the building cooling loads based on the following arrangement:

1 All sun-screen removed.

2 The low-height brickwall behind sun-screen replaced with glazed curtain wall

3 All shading effect from the balconies removed.

We have not taken into consideration the impact on lighting systems as we anticipate that this would be minimal.

The total increase in cooling load on the building is calculated to be approximately 125KW with a corresponding increase in supply fan motor power of approximately 15KW. From our analysis the estimated increase in installation and operating cost are as follows:

1 Installation/first cost $160,000.00

2 Operating cost per annum $42,000.00

and the basis of the assumptions are set out in the attached calculations.

Indirect cost associated with increased plant maintenance costs due to the increased operation have not been included in the latter figure. A simple 'pay back' calculation can be performed to establish the time required to recoup the cost of the sunshading to the building by dividing the annual energy savings into the cost of the sunshading. This calculation does not include for inflationary trends in energy and material costs, however for the purpose of an initial study a simple payback formula should suffice.

In preparation of our research paper, the following energy saving factors should also be considered in the design of the Menara Mesiniaga:

1 Use of the Building Automation System to save energy by performing the following functions:
- Lighting switching/control after hours.
- Optimum air-conditioning plant start up based on historical plant performance.
- Night "purge" to relieve excess thermal inertia in the building.
- Chiller control to optimise the operating characteristics of the chillers and reduce operating costs.
- Time switching of plant to prevent excessive operation.

2 Use of perimeter light switching system to either dim or turn perimeter lighting off when outdoor solar light levels are sufficient to meet perimeter lighting needs.

3 Use of Variable Air Volume systems which have been proven to reduce the total fan horsepower required over a normal day.

Items 1 and 3 are standard element of NDY's design. Item 2 can be incorporated but usually at an additional cost to be building owner. It is our opinion that trends or clearly identified energy saving devices installed and commissioned correctly in office, industrial and hotel projects should be rewarded by an incentive scheme sponsored by the Government.

Calculation of increase cooling load and air flow requirements (include removal of shading from balconies)

Floor	with shading		without shading		without sun-screen shading		cooling load increase	air quantity increase
	TC (W)	Q (L/S)	TC (W)	Q (L/S)	TC (W)	Q (L/S)	TC (W)	Q (L/S)
2F	74,572	4,404	93,386	6,444	98,072	6,391	23,500	2,040
3F	63,985	3,779	84,121	5,516	83,035	5,364	20,136	1,737
4F	60,606	3,505	81,634	5,312	80,010	5,061	21,026	1,807
5F	76,948	4,778	91,124	5,867	90,493	5,814	14,176	1,089
6F	70,107	4,929	81,109	5,831	71,731	5,093	10,002	902
7F	72,758	5,180	87,724	6,381	73,144	5,240	14,966	1,201
8F	73,293	5,255	86,080	6,281	-	-	12,787	1,026
9F	72,245	5,091	79,257	5,852	-	-	7,012	761
10F	77,561	5,486	-	-	-	-	-	-
11F	67,070	4,837			-	-	-	-
						total increase:	124,000	10,563

Calculation of increase in operating costs for a building with complete curtain wall – no shading

Formula

The formula used is as follows:

Annual Operating Cost Increase (Chiller Plant) $= (A \times F \times H \times D_w \times W_y \times E_t \times C_e)$

Where

A = Increase in cooling load

F = Diversity factor to allow for changes in sun azimuth and altitude during a normal year.

H = Hours of operation per day (12)

D_w = Days operation per week (5.5)

W_y = Weeks per year (52)

E_t = Electricity ($0.24/Kwh)

C_e = Chiller Plant Efficiency (0.21 Kw/KwR)

Annual Operating Cost Increase (Fans/Pumps) Amps $= (PF_p \times H \times D_w \times W_y \times E_t)$

Where

PF_p = Fan/Pump Power Increase

H = as above

D_w = as above

W_y = as above

E_t = as above

Hence we calculate as follows;

Savings Chiller Plant = $125 \times 0.8 \times 12 \times 5.5 \times 52 \times 0.24 \times 0.21$ = $17,297.28

Savings Fan Power = $15 \times 12 \times 5.5 \times 52 \times 0.24$ = $12,355.20

Savings Pump Power = $15 \times 12 \times 5.5 \times 52 \times 0.24$ = $12,355.20

= $42,007.68

" ... The architects' approach is best exemplified by the Menara Mesiniaga Tower (1992), an office tower situated near Kuala Lumpur International Airport, and the MBF Tower (1994), a residential and mixed-use building in Georgetown, Penang. Both towers are distinguished by exposed 'megastructure' frames, recessed 'skycourts', free-standing, naturally ventilated service cores, and a variety of sunscreen devices, combining international and regional influences in a free and creative manner ... "

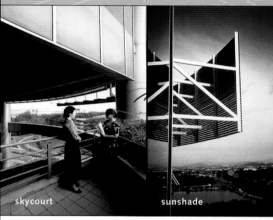

skycourt sunshade

Encyclopedia Britannica, Yearbook of Science and the Future

ENCYCLOPEDIA BRITANNICA INC., USA (1995)

" ... example of an environmentally sensitive building, deriving its quiet beauty from expressing the inherent truths of its being. The tower's form evolved from a rational response to the effects of the tropical sun, along with respect and regard for the needs of the building's occupants. The richness of its circular form come from the skillfully blended articulation of recessed windows, louvers, indented garden terraces, and balconies that form an exterior climbing helix and from a vertical exterior service core. Humanely, the architect Ken Yeang provided natural light and ventilation in the elevator lobbies, stair shafts, rest rooms ... "

sunpath

sunshades

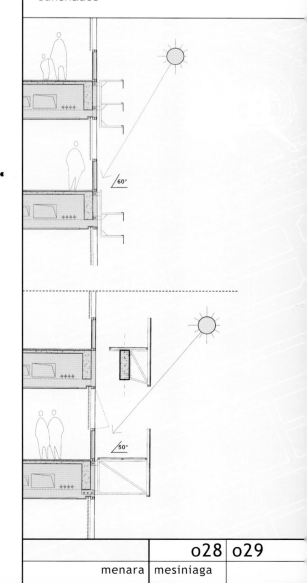

/60°

/50°

main reception
at level1

Following the completion of Menara Mesiniaga in 1992, Yeang embarked on a series of bioclimatic city-centre towers in Kuala Lumpur and Penang: these include both Menara TA1 and Central Plaza both sited in Kuala Lumpur's 'Golden Triangle', and UMNO Tower in central Penang. While the UMNO project in Penang is distinguished by the development of particular natural ventilation innovations – 'wind wing-walls' – and is dealt with separately, all three share certain constraints and formal similarities, and in this sense they form a set.

Each tower has almost identical programmatic characteristics, but with varying site conditions and orientation. But, in each case, the resultant forms are similar in essence, and present the problem of a slim slab-tower with the inherent difficulties of two exposed elongated facades with thin ends. In his feasibility sketches, Yeang has described this condition as a **"... cigarette pack ... slim form"**.

The towers each incorporate a plinth of car-parking floors with generous naturally ventilated entrance courts, together with retail facilities such as banking halls and restaurants at the ground levels. Above the parking floors, the separated office spaces all incorporate perimeter columns to yield the maximum free floor plate area. Each tower has some communal uses at roof level, such as the fabric-covered terrace atop Menara TA1 or the swimming pool at Central Plaza.

In both cases, it is the plan form that is of particular note and the impact of the design decisions on the overall formal order. In both cases one long edge zone is occupied by all services, elevators and primary circulation, which is functionally expressed as a north-east shield in Menara TA1 and south facing in Central Plaza. The Menara TA1 plan is capsule shaped with rounded end-forms – a resultant of the non-coincidence of site and sun-path geometry. This shaping geometrically reduces the length of the north-south and east-west external walls, and thus the direct insulation. The Central Plaza plan has expressed V-form cross-bracing at the east and west ends of the ultra-slim tower, and on the west face the glazing is withdrawn behind this framework to provide shading and incidental sky-courts with planting on the east face. Central Plaza incorporates stepped planting – a complete plan zone – on the north face, with the north-east corner glazed into a curved form, with solar-reflective glass, that gives views to the distant Ampang hills. Menara TA1 incorporates an extended semi-enclosed atrium on the southern facade, which is expressed by paired exposed columns and intermediate steel skycourt balconies.

mezzanine level

Selangor, Malaysia

owner ERF Properties Sdn Bhd
location 1, Jalan Lau Yew Swee,
Kuala Lumpur, Malaysia
latitude 3.7°N
nos of storeys 37 storeys
date start 1992
completion date 1996
areas
Total nett area 36,719 sq m
Service area 14, 699 sq m
Gross area 51,418 sq m
Carpark (458 bays) 15,024 sq m
Total built-up area 66,442 sq m
site area 4,868.5 sq m
plot ratio 1:10.6

design features • This rectangular site is orientated diagonally north-south, which is not an ideal orientation along latitudes near the Equator. The site conditions here are such that the geometry of the site and the geometry of the sun-path do not coincide.
• The external skin is glazed with a louvred sunshade system on the west but remains unshielded on the north and south corners (since there is minimum solar insolation on these surfaces).
• The core (which consists of the lift lobby, toilets, fire stairs and M&E rooms) is located on the east side of the slab, thus keeping the morning sun out of the offices while allowing natural lighting and natural ventilation into the core areas.
• The typical internal office floors are column-free and on alternate floors, they open out to a transitional space on the south-west face as an atrium.
• Off the atrium are 'steel skycourts' as transitional spaces that happen at various alternate levels up the building.
• A clear maximum span of 18 metres was made possible by the use of prestressed beams.
• The communal space at the top of the building is part of the Planning Authority requirements. It provides a space for corporate entertainment on the roof terrace. The tensile membrane roof canopy offers protection from the sun and gives the building its landmark status.
• The ground entrance lobby is recessed and remains open, ie. naturally ventilated.

structural system • Reinforced concrete structural frame with prestressed concrete beams, brick-in-fill.

external skin • Tempered float glass.

roofing • R.C. slab on roof terrace, tedlar-coated pvc membrane on painted m.s. structure.

finishes • Solid aluminium cladding to front columns and entrance lobby, white marble to lift lobby walls, green granite to ground and mezzanine lobbies, slate to office lobbies floors, plaster and paint on office walls, ceramic tiles to toilets, mineral fibreboard ceiling to offices, painted gypsum board ceiling to lobbies.

energy consumption • Basing on 2,288 hours of operation per annum and GFA of 51,418 sq m, the total cooling load (equipment capacity) is 0.155 kw/sq m. The estimated energy required for the air-conditioning for the building is 97.5 kwh/sq m/annum; and the total energy consumption is 157.1 kwh/sq m/annum.

The Central Plaza and TA1 plans, as outlined, are amongst the most stringently minimal arrangements Yeang has produced. Essentially the central linear plan area is empty and flexible, with the long and short faces of the plan envelope each carefully crafted to incorporate an integrated installation of both functional and bioclimatic features.

While the orientation, the variety of forms and structural innovations are generated largely by climatic concerns in response to context, as the plans readily demonstrate each of the design elements, is related to the economical provision of floor plates. At the same time, the principles of Yeang's bioclimatic agenda are inter-related with his concepts of vertical urbanism – the act of bringing life and incident to the experience of rising and changing levels.

As a set, these towers not only establish a new and fundamental **type**, but they also incorporate an increasingly sophisticated range of materials and detailing, including marble and laminated float glass. In addition Yeang has experimented with a range of whole-building colour types, from pink at Central Plaza to white at TA1. Within the ruthless constraints of the commercial property market Yeang has delivered both a developing typology of strict controlled form and a marketable product.

Since the completion of these buildings, there has been accumulating evidence that the market place is aware that Yeang's architecture offers much more than just commercially acceptable development. TA1 and Central Plaza epitomise an enhanced minimum, and form a threshold to the more sophisticated and articulated projects that follow, opening up the possibilities of vertical urbanism and ecological architecture.

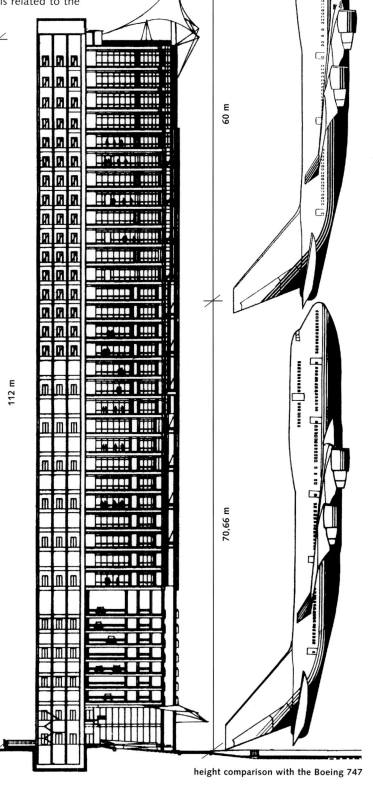

112 m

60 m

70,66 m

height comparison with the Boeing 747

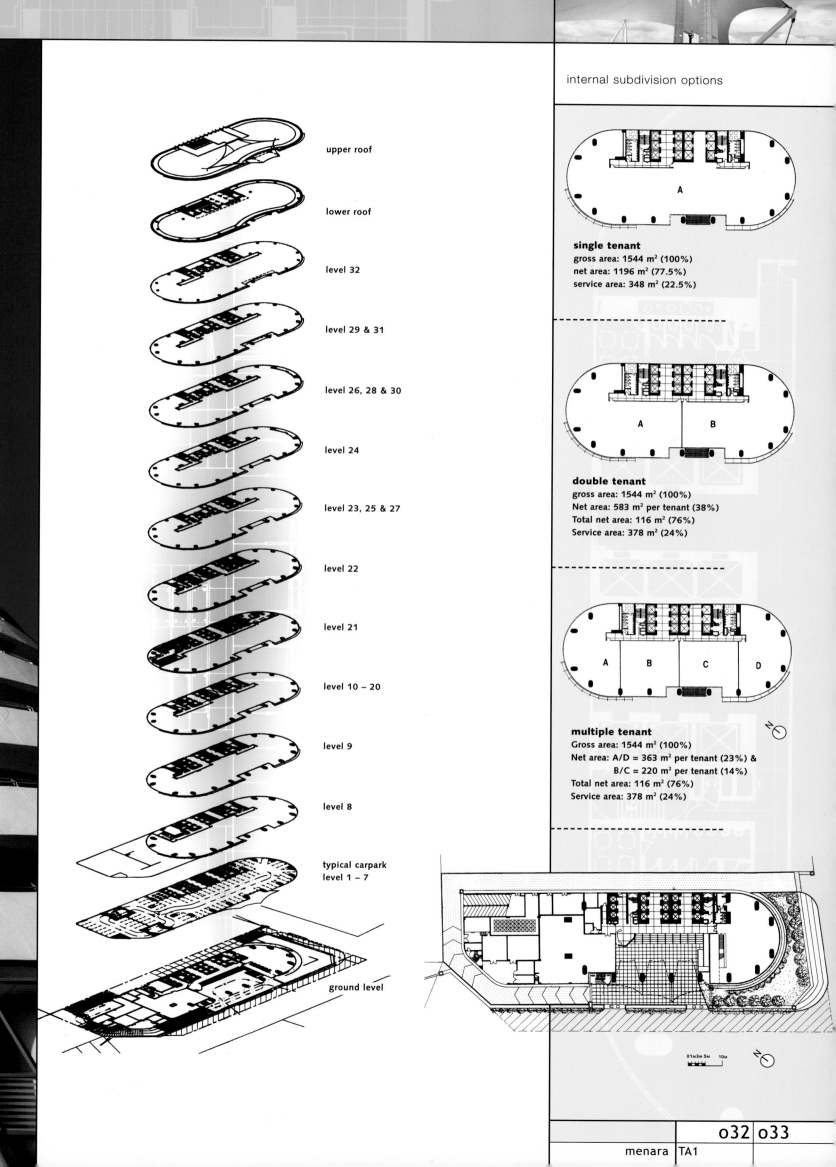

upper roof

lower roof

level 32

level 29 & 31

level 26, 28 & 30

level 24

level 23, 25 & 27

level 22

level 21

level 10 – 20

level 9

level 8

typical carpark
level 1 – 7

ground level

internal subdivision options

A

single tenant
gross area: 1544 m² (100%)
net area: 1196 m² (77.5%)
service area: 348 m² (22.5%)

A   B

double tenant
gross area: 1544 m² (100%)
Net area: 583 m² per tenant (38%)
Total net area: 116 m² (76%)
Service area: 378 m² (24%)

A B C D

multiple tenant
Gross area: 1544 m² (100%)
Net area: A/D = 363 m² per tenant (23%) &
      B/C = 220 m² per tenant (14%)
Total net area: 116 m² (76%)
Service area: 378 m² (24%)

01м 3м 5м   10м

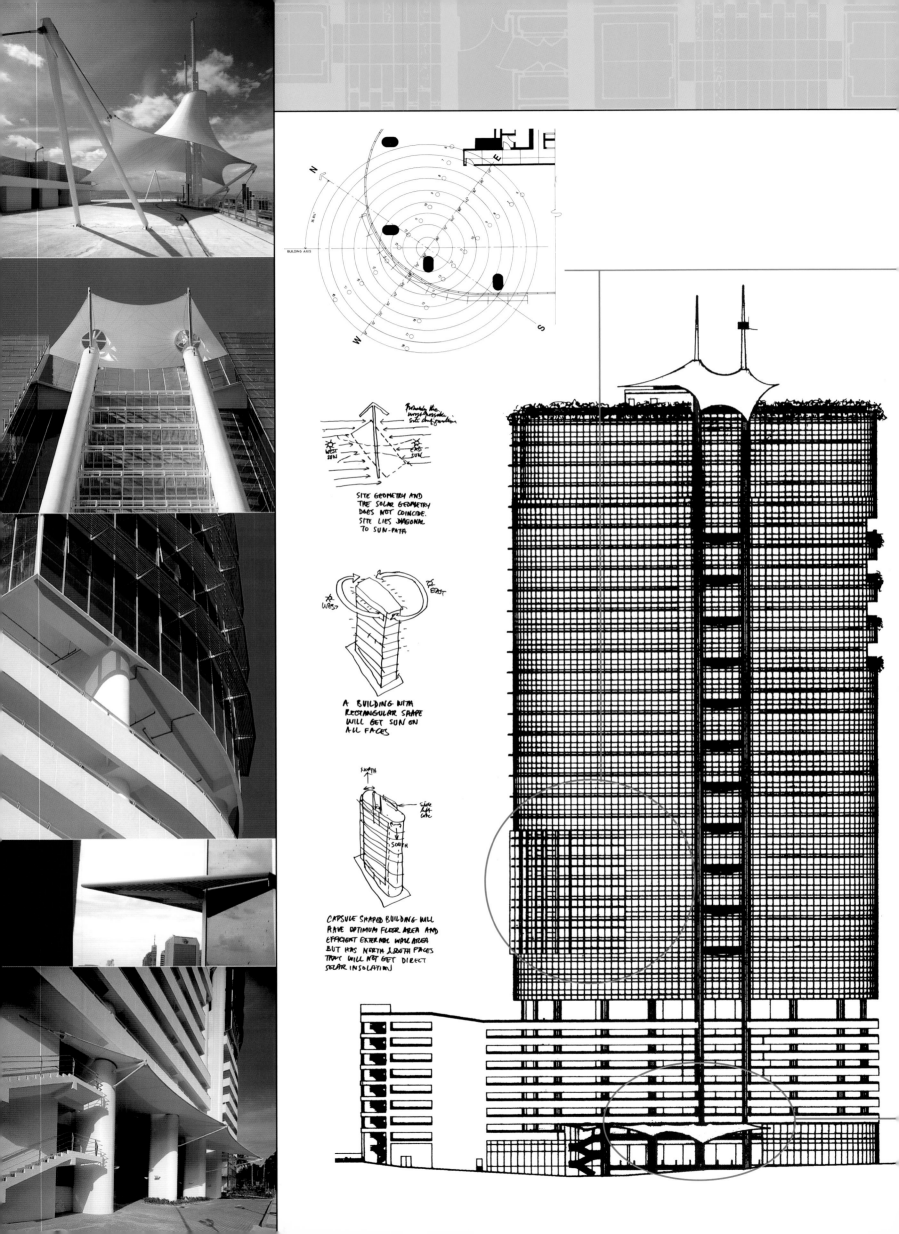

SITE GEOMETRY AND
THE SOLAR GEOMETRY
DOES NOT COINCIDE.
SITE LIES DIAGONAL
TO SUN-PATH

A BUILDING WITH
RECTANGULAR SHAPE
WILL GET SUN ON
ALL FACES

CAPSULE SHAPED BUILDING WILL
HAVE OPTIMUM FLOOR AREA AND
EFFICIENT EXTERNAL WALL AREA
BUT HAS NORTH & SOUTH FACES
THAT WILL NOT GET DIRECT
SOLAR INSOLATION

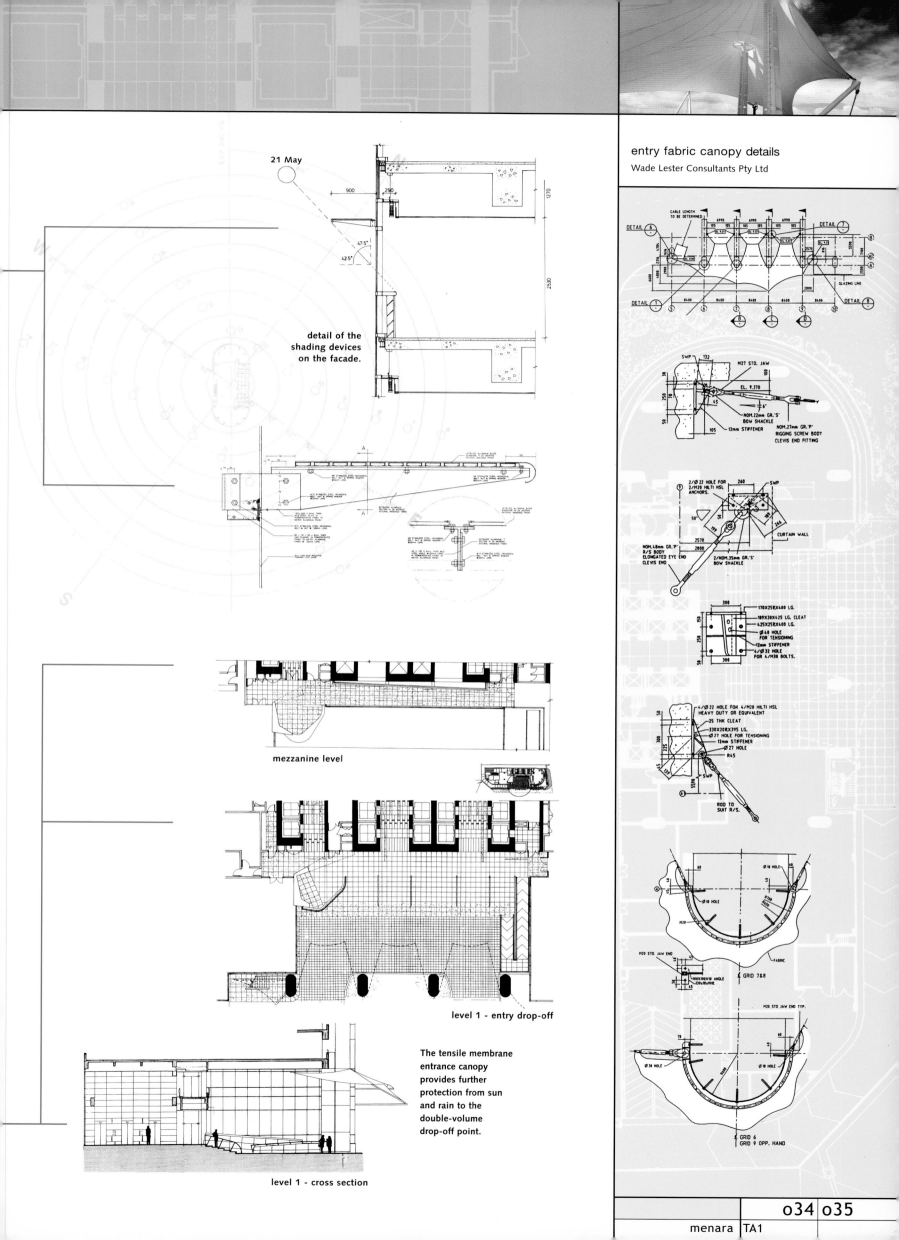

21 May

900 250

1270

47.5°

42.5°

2530

detail of the
shading devices
on the facade.

A

A

mezzanine level

level 1 - entry drop-off

The tensile membrane
entrance canopy
provides further
protection from sun
and rain to the
double-volume
drop-off point.

level 1 - cross section

entry fabric canopy details
Wade Lester Consultants Pty Ltd

DETAIL 6

DETAIL 7

DETAIL 1

DETAIL 8

Vertical Visions

in *ARCHITECTURAL REVIEW* (September 1996)
Ivor Richards

" ... Menara TA1 and Central Plaza (37 and 27 storeys respectively) in Kuala Lumpur's 'Golden Triangle', and UMNO Tower (25 storeys) in central Pulau Pinang, form a set: each tower has almost identical programmatic characteristics but with varying site conditions and orientation.

The towers all incorporate a plinth of seven car-parking floors with generous covered and naturally ventilated entrance courts, together with retail facilities such as banking halls and restaurants at ground level. Above the parking floors, the lettable office spaces all in corporate perimeter columns to yield the maximum free floor plate area. Each tower also has some communal uses at roof level, such as a terrace garden or swimming pool, and all incorporate some form of vertical atrium or skycourt.

... the towers of TA1, Central Plaza and UMNO are all for multilettable occupancy, and are realised on slim, restricted urban sites in high land-cost locations with exacting construction budgets. Essentially these towers represent the acid test both of Yeang's philosophy and his ability to deliver added value in a highly competitive marketplace.

The crucial factors that make of these office building a user-friendly experience are all functions of Yeang's bioclimatic agenda. Astute design decisions on orientation result in elements such as lift cores (usually naturally ventilated and daylit) acting as solar shields; plan shaping to reduce insolation; natural ventilation options for the office spaces related to 'thin' plan forms (also a function of the site plan) and the incorporation of painted balconies and recesses together with eggcrate and louvre solar shading. Northern facades are fully glazed to permit strategic views, often to distant hills.

While the orientation, the variety of forms and structural innovations are generated largely by climactic concerns, each of these design elements is also related to the economical provision of floor plates. The principles of Yeang's bioclimatic agenda are laced with his concepts of vertical urbanism. As a set, these towers incorporate an increasingly sophisticated range of materials and detailing, including marble and laminated float glass, and display a range of whole-building colour types, from pink (Central Plaza) to white (TA1).

Taken together, the three towers provide proof of Yeang's ability to develop a strict topology and deliver a marketable product. Perhaps equally significantly, the marketplace is gradually coming to recognise that his architecture offers much more than commercially acceptable development. Ken Yeang's studio has a slogan posted conspicuously on a wall: 'Everything depends on execution, having a vision is no solution'. However, his bioclimatic agenda is also a vision, and it continues to supply a real solution to the problems of contemporary architecture. "

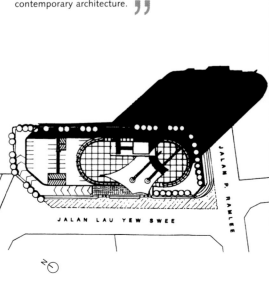

JALAN LAU YEW SWEE

JALAN P. RAMLEE

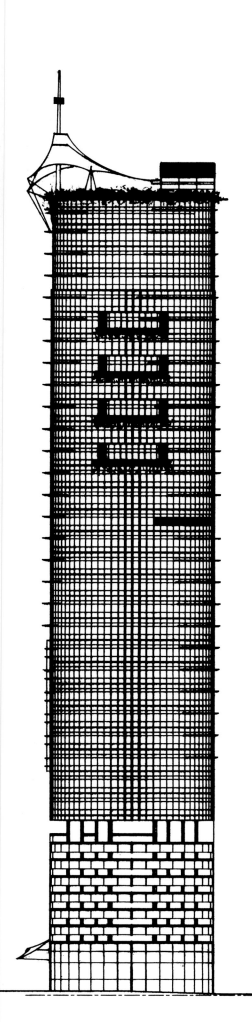

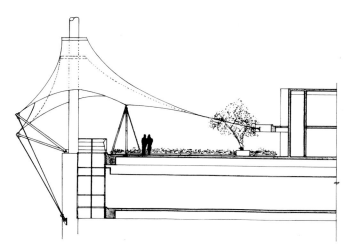

roof top canopy

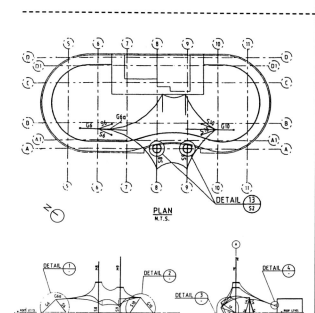

PLAN
N.T.S.

DETAIL 13
S2

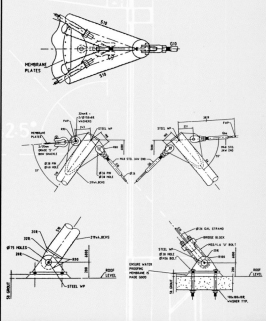

DETAIL 1

DETAIL 2

DETAIL 4

DETAIL 3

ELEVATION
N.T.S.

SOUTH-EAST ELEVATION
N.T.S.

notes

1 The contractor shall provide and leave in place until bracing elements are constructed. Such temporary bracing as is necessary to stabilise the structure during erection.

2 All workmanship and materials shall be in accordance with A.S.4100.

3 Welding shall be performed by an accredited operation in accordance with A.S.1554; electrode E48XX or WS8X to be used.

4 The ends of all tubular members are to be sealed with normal thickness plates and continuous fillet weld UNO.

5 All RHS and CHS members are to be grade 350 MPa UNO. All other steel to be grade 250 MPa.

6 Except where otherwise shown welds to be 6 mm continuous fillet.

7 All bolts, nuts and washers to be galvanised.

8 Bolt type 4.6/5 – commercial bolts of strength grade 4.6 to AS 1111.

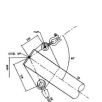

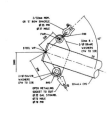

Centre of it all

in *WORLD ARCHITECTURE* (ISSUE 51, NOVEMBER 1996)
Nicola Turner

" The client, the Chuang's Group, a Hong Kong public listed company (the Malaysian branch of which is called Malview Sdn Bhd), inherited Yeang from the previous client. The site in fact had three different owners before the current design was formalised. The Chuang's Group wanted a prestigious building that would give them value for money with maximum rentable space – and a strong corporate image, which they believed would most successfully be achieved with a 'hi-tech' look. Yeang relates the tale of seeing the client in Hong Kong, and being told, as they gazed out of the window at Norman Foster's landmark Hong Kong and Shanghai Bank, "I want something like that". Yeang is not used to being dictated to by his clients. His philosophy is to ask the client for "the budget and the total area, and leave the architecture to me". But the image of Foster's bank appealed to him, and the strong visual line of the cross-bracing on the east and west facades, and the high quality of detailing both inside and out, reflect the Hong Kong example.

However, the bracing is more than a nod to 'Western' precedents, and is fundamental to the structure of the tower. In order to increase the size of the floor plates and provide a column-free interior, a hypothetical middle row of structural columns of reinforced concrete were omitted. The brace therefore compensates for this and prevents the tower from swaying. Most high-rise buildings throughout Malaysia are still concrete – as opposed to steel – frame, due to the availability and therefore expense of steel, although this is slowly changing. Central Plaza is no exception, and is clad in solid aluminum panels, tinted a distinctive rose colour using fluorocarbon paint. The glazing is tinted to match. The structural frame continues beyond the roofline of the tower, with the theoretical provision for expansion – although this would be highly unlikely, given the expense required to create and service what would probably only amount to one more floor. Two characteristic Yeang spikes complete the frame – strictly decoration only. The roof is occupied by a swimming pool, which sits on the concrete slabs like a giant ice-bucket, clad in slate tiles, and reached via a curved steel staircase. The cleaning track around the circumference of the pool, doubles as a bench. Palm trees contribute to the feeling of escapism … "

Selangor, Malaysia

owner Malview Sdn Bhd, subsidiary of Chuang's Group, public listed company (Hong Kong)

location 34 Jalan Sultan Ismail, Kuala Lumpur, Malaysia (Kuala Lumpur's "Golden Triangle Area")

latitude 3.7° N

nos of storeys 27 storeys (including 1/2-level basement)

date start 1992 (June)

completion date 1996 (June)

areas

Total net area 17,099 sq m

Service area 5,272 sq m

Gross area 22,371 sq m

Carpark (334 bays) 13,121 sq m

Total built-up area 57,863 sq m

site area 2,982 sq m

plot ratio 1:7.5

design features • The typical office floor in this 'wafer-thin' tall building is to be column-free (as a marketing requirement of the client). To enable this, structural cross-bracing is provided at the end columns of the east and west facades.
• Vertical planting steps up diagonally along the north face of the building up to the pool-side at the top of building.
• A system of louvres and balconies are located on the hot west facade.
• The core, which consists of the lift lobby, stairways and toilets, has natural ventilation and natural lighting.
• A curved fully glazed curtain-wall on the north face gives an uninterrupted view of the distant hills (ie. Ampang). As this face does not receive direct solar insolation, its sunshade-free elevation becomes a form of geographical indication of the northerly direction.
• The east and west glazing of the building are recessed from the structure for sun-shading.
• The escape staircase is an 'open-to-the-sky' staircase.
• The main staircase is naturally ventilated.
• The toilets are naturally ventilated.
• The east wall has balconies as sun-shading.
• The lift lobbies are partially naturally ventilated.
• The ground floor lobby is naturally ventilated.

structural system • Reinforced concrete structural frame with prestressed beams, brick-in-fill.

external skin • Laminated float glass
• solid aluminium cladding.

roofing • RC slab on roof terrace.

finishes • Granite on lobby floor and walls.
• Glass to entrance canopy.
• Plaster and paint to internal walls.
• Ceramic tiles to wet areas.
• Mineral fibre board to office ceilings.
• Fibrous plaster to lobby ceilings.

100 m

120 m

50 m

70.66 m

height comparison with the Boeing 747

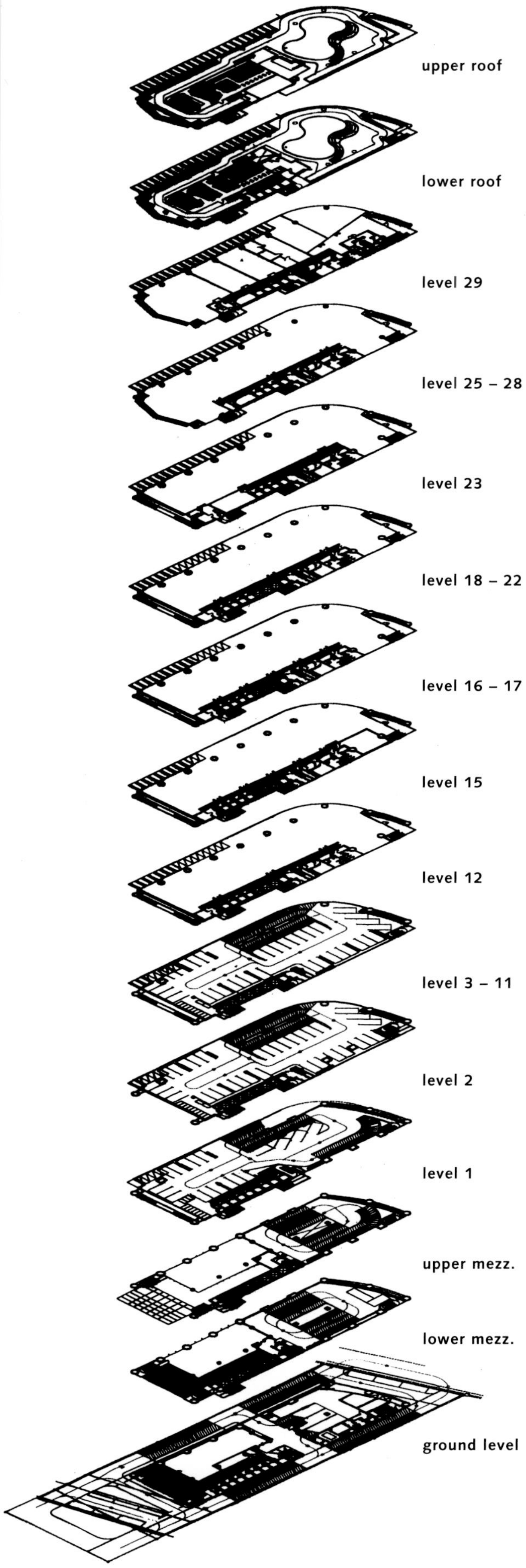

upper roof

lower roof

level 29

level 25 – 28

level 23

level 18 – 22

level 16 – 17

level 15

level 12

level 3 – 11

level 2

level 1

upper mezz.

lower mezz.

ground level

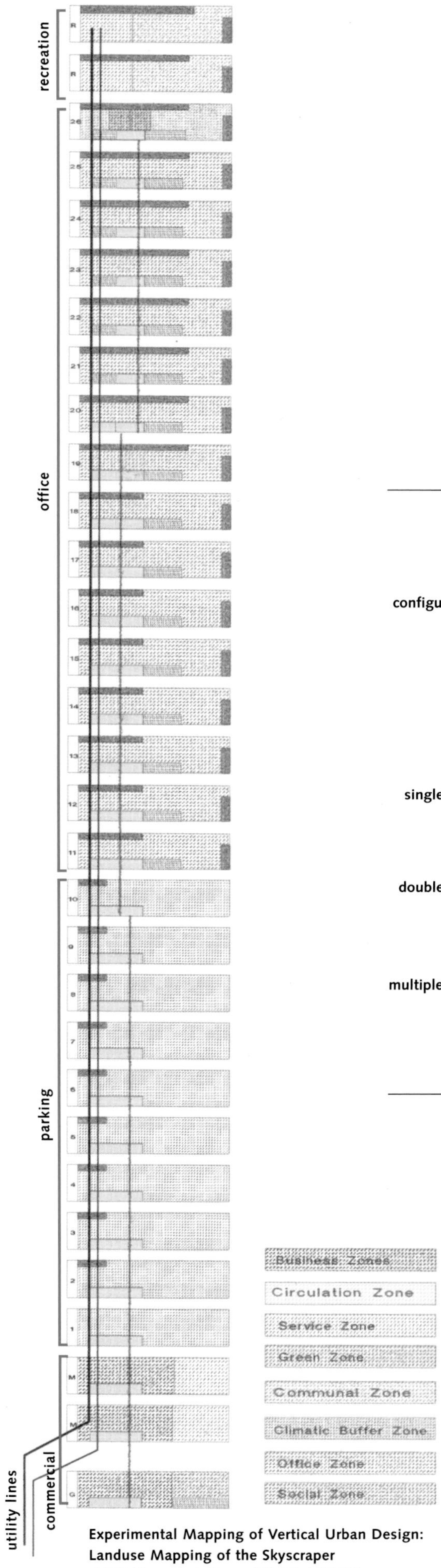

recreation

office

parking

utility lines

commercial

Business Zone
Circulation Zone
Service Zone
Green Zone
Communal Zone
Climatic Buffer Zone
Office Zone
Social Zone

**Experimental Mapping of Vertical Urban Design:
Landuse Mapping of the Skyscraper**
© T.R.Hamzah & Yeang Sdn Bhd (2001)

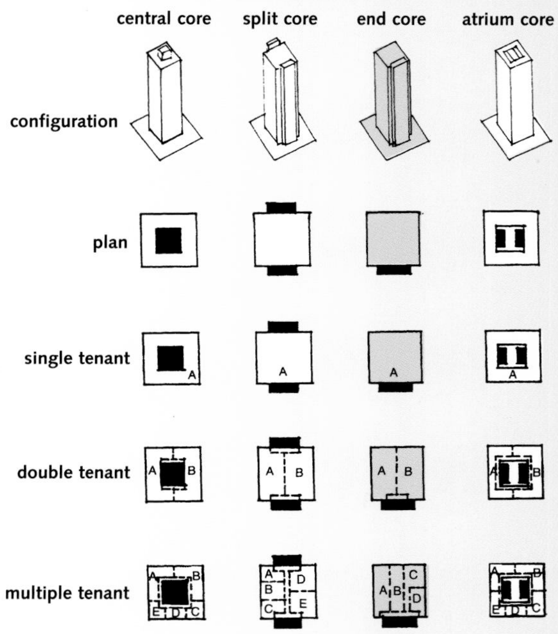

	central core	split core	end core	atrium core
configuration				
plan				
single tenant				
double tenant				
multiple tenant				

core position
configuration of
Central Plaza

Centre of it all

in *WORLD ARCHITECTURE* (ISSUE 51, NOVEMBER 1996)
Nicola Turner

" Attention to detail

Detailing is often overlooked in high-rise building throughout the major cities of South-East Asia. Yeang's attention to quality materials and construction is therefore what distinguishes most of his buildings from their neighbours. The naturally ventilated lobby immediately gives visitors the impression of a "quality" building. A structural glazed wall on the north side reveals the security room, traditionally hidden from view. A bank of television screens and flashing lights contribute to the hi-tech image. Opposite the security room, sand-blasted glass "fish-scales", secured by steel bolts, "float" above the elevator doors. Looking out of the lobby the glass theme is continued with a transparent glass entrance canopy, through which natural lights is filtered, and reflected on the granite-clad floor and walls.

Inside the elevators, more frosted glass – illuminated from the floor up – and curved perforated metal screens lighten an otherwise oppressive space. On the ceilings of the corridors running the length of the fifteen office floors, elliptical recesses house light fittings with suspended frosted glass discs. Each major office door is fitted with a sophisticated Phillippe Stark-designed door handle. "

… the glass-dominated lobby, with structural glass wall screening the security room, and glass "fish scales" floating above the elevator doors …

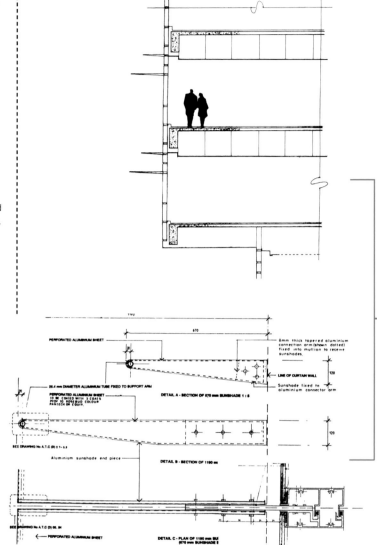

sun shade
detail

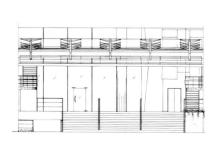

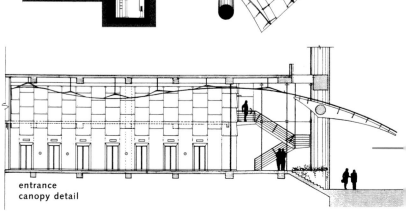

entrance
canopy detail

R=4007

canopy cast arm detail
by MERO Raumstruktur GMBH & Co.Wuerzburg

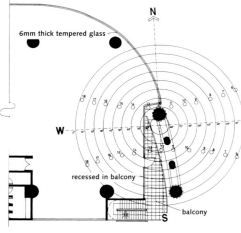

6mm thick tempered glass

N

W — — — E

recessed in balcony

balcony

S

Centre of it all

in *WORLD ARCHITECTURE* (ISSUE 51, NOVEMBER 1996)
Nicola Turner

" ... So how far has this design progressed since Yeang's first rumination on bioclimaticism in his 1972 PhD thesis 'Design with Nature: the Ecological Basis for Design'? He explains that his built work, more or less, divides into four series. The first (up to 1988) was largely experimental and dealt with one big idea in a single building, such as exterior planting or natural ventilation. the second (from 1989–1992) is the aggregate of these ideas, including Menara Mesiniaga, the Aga Khan award-winning tropical "venus flytrap" skyscraper on the outskirts of Kuala Lumpur. The third series (1992–1995) focuses more on the architectural aesthetics, for example the Shanghai Tower and UMNO Tower and the fourth – and current series – focuses on the mapping of the skyscraper; the creation of the "city in the sky".

Due to the time it takes to construct a tower from planning stage to completion, Central Plaza, perhaps surprisingly, falls within the second series, although Yeang describes it as "transitional", along with Menara TA1. It incorporates a "green" element in the vertical planting steps climbing diagonally up the north facade to the pool-side. Natural ventilation is facilitated in the lobby and washrooms, and the escape staircase on the south side is left "open to the sky". The west facade is shaded with system of louvers and balconies, and the glazing on both the west and east faces are recessed from the structure for sun-shading. The core of the building, incorporating the lift lobby, stairs and washroom is located to the south. The curved fully-glazed curtain- wall on the north facade gives an uninterrupted view of the distant hills, its sunshade-free elevation forming a geographical indication of the northerly direction.

If the client had agreed with Yeang, and decided on a development with two thirds offices and one third hotel, the design would have been quite different. The two zones would have been split by a swimming pool cut out two thirds of the way up the tower. This would have reflected Yeang's current investigative research into the "mapping" of these vertical cities. Central Plaza as it is, is hardly revolutionary in this aspect – partly due to the client's final brief, but also because it was designed in the less refined "second series". Most Asian buildings these days are oriented east-west, and have the service core to one side, maximising floor space. But despite these reservations Central Plaza is still quite obviously a Hamzah & Yeang building. It stands head and shoulders above its neighbours, even if not in height, then in quality and design. "

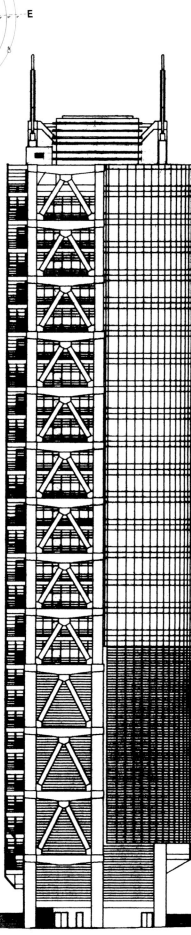

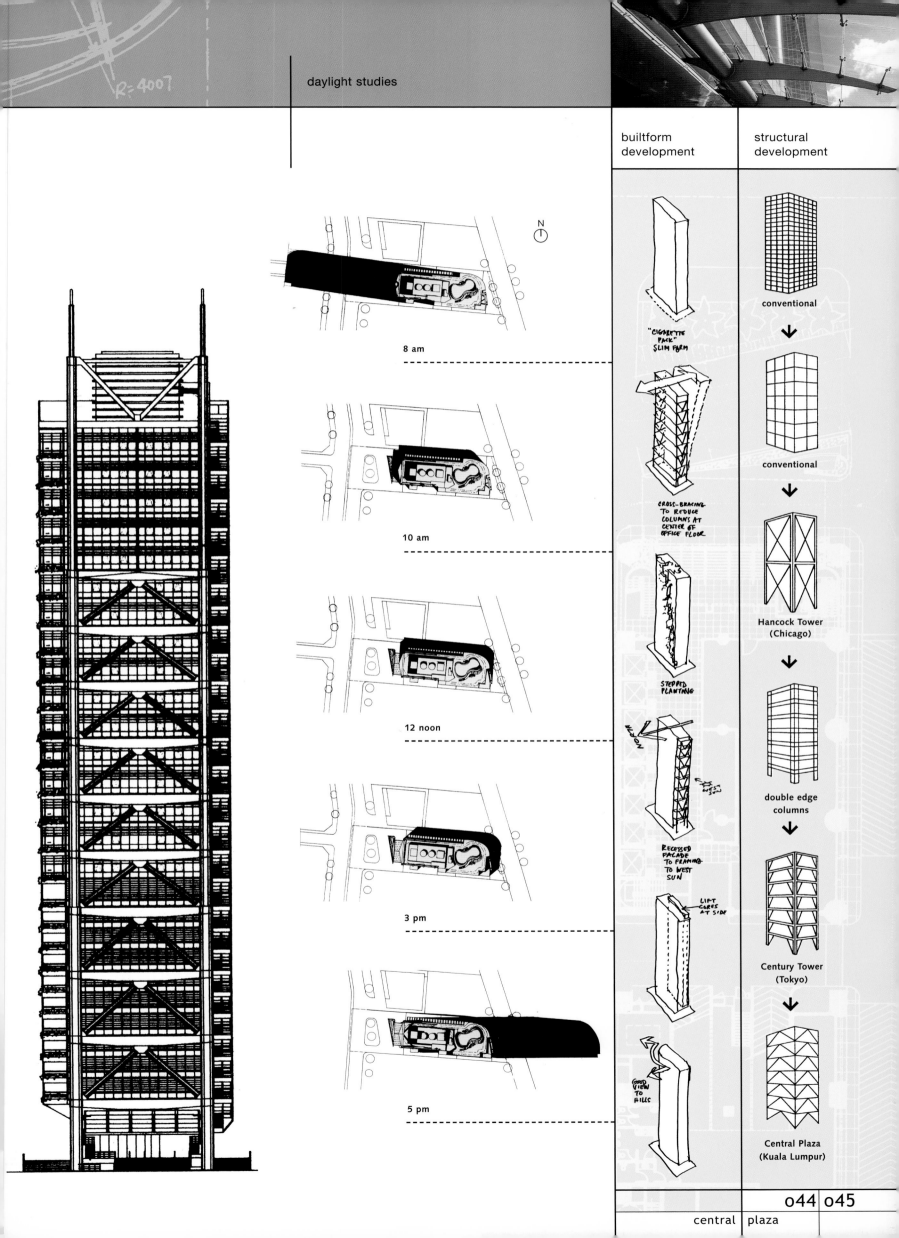

builtform development

"CIGARETTE PACK" SLIM FORM

CROSS-BRACING TO REDUCE COLUMNS AT CENTER OF OFFICE FLOOR

STEPPED PLANTING

RECESSED FACADE TO FRAMING TO WEST SUN

LIFT CORES AT SIDE

GOOD VIEW TO HILLS

structural development

conventional

conventional

Hancock Tower (Chicago)

double edge columns

Century Tower (Tokyo)

Central Plaza (Kuala Lumpur)

8 am

10 am

12 noon

3 pm

5 pm

N

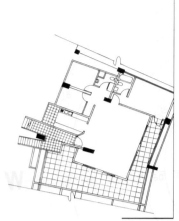

Casa Del Sol stands relatively alone amongst Yeang's **bioclimatic** projects, in that it is essentially a tall slab, and not a point-block skyscraper in the generic sense. Conceived as a **semi-circular form**, the building is a pure product of the **sun-path**. The project includes 160 residential units of accommodation together with a communal clubhouse and swimming pool.

The overall design is dominated by two key issues – the protection of the residential accommodation by a western band of circulation galleries that are separated by an **air-gap** from the main structure, and the provision of eastern facing **views** from the apartments to the valley setting.

Hence, the **naturally ventilated**, single-loaded circulation acts as a massive buffer to the hot west afternoon sun, and assists the **cross-ventilation** of the apartments themselves. The building includes planted and terraced skycourts that are spatially interconnected, stepping outwards from the centre of the building in a diagonal formation. Where they occur, these external spaces not only provide natural light and ventilation opportunities for specific apartments, but also contribute to the comfort conditions of adjoining residential spaces.

In addition, the major lift-lobby and staircase is located centrally in the semi-circular form, and again is a **naturally lit** and **ventilated**, open assembly.

casa del sol apartments

owner Metrolux Sendirian Berhad

location Bukit Antarabangsa, Selangor, Malaysia

latitude 3.7°N

nos of storeys 11 storeys

date start 1992

completion date 1996

areas Total net area 22,115 sq m
Gross area 26,903 m

site area 18,288 sq m

plot ratio total: 160 units of apartments
density: 1:3.5

As in the work of the Le Corbusier before him, it is inevitable that Yeang's work, seen as a whole, should incorporate the **universal slab-form**.

Taken as a **typeform**, Casa Del Sol represents Yeang's almost singular enquiry into the organisational and formalistic possibilities of the linear-slab arrangement, which emerges in this project as an overt exercise in **natural ventilation** and the conditions of **prospect**.

Casa Del Sol, at first sight, is a direct application of sun-path principles to the arrangement of a linear residential condominium. However, if this **typology**, and its inherent considerations, were taken further in Yeang's work it would almost certainly reveal a **different urbanism** from his skyscraper series. For in this instance and with regard to public space, it is the encircled garden courtyard of Casa Del Sol, with its clubhouse and pool, that is the equivalent to the vertical atria, of the tower projects.

In this sense, the **linear** nature of Casa Del Sol is a point of departure, and one which has great potential in the context of Yeang's work, seen overall, and in relation to a form of garden-city.

design features • The built form is a semi-circular slab with the following features:
• A series of skycourts (with planting and terraces) provide terraced areas, natural lighting and natural ventilation for abutting residential units.
• All the apartment units are accessible by means of a single-loaded corridor that faces the hot west side of the site. The corridor is separated from the tower-slab by an air gap to give some privacy to the apartment units. This access corridor also acts as buffer and sunshade from afternoon sun on the west.
• The access corridor has natural ventilation and natural lighting.
• The main lift lobby and staircase are located in the centre of the tower-slab with natural lighting and natural ventilation.
• All the apartment units are designed with cross-ventilation.
• The entire curved tower-slab is separated into two sections where the middle consists of the lift-shaft and a staircase that begins at the lowest floor as a small plaza-terrace that leads to the clubhouse, poolside and communal space.

programme • The client's programme was to build 160 units on the green-field site for sale. The site faces a valley, hence the semi-circular shape to give views from each apartment towards the valley. The central open space holds a swimming pool and a communal clubhouse.

structural system • Reinforced concrete structural frame. Cement-sand and clay brick-in-fill with plastering over.

external skin • Masonry and glass windows.

roofing • Metal deck roof with insulation.

finishes • Plaster and paint to walls, broken marble to main floor areas, skimcoat to ceiling.

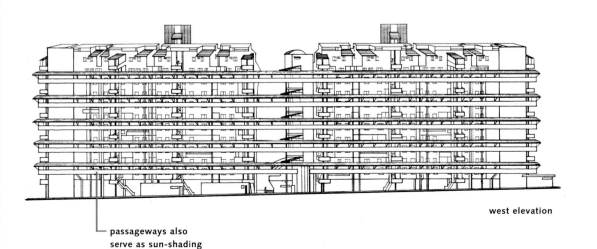

planted terraces east elevation

passageways also serve as sun-shading

west elevation

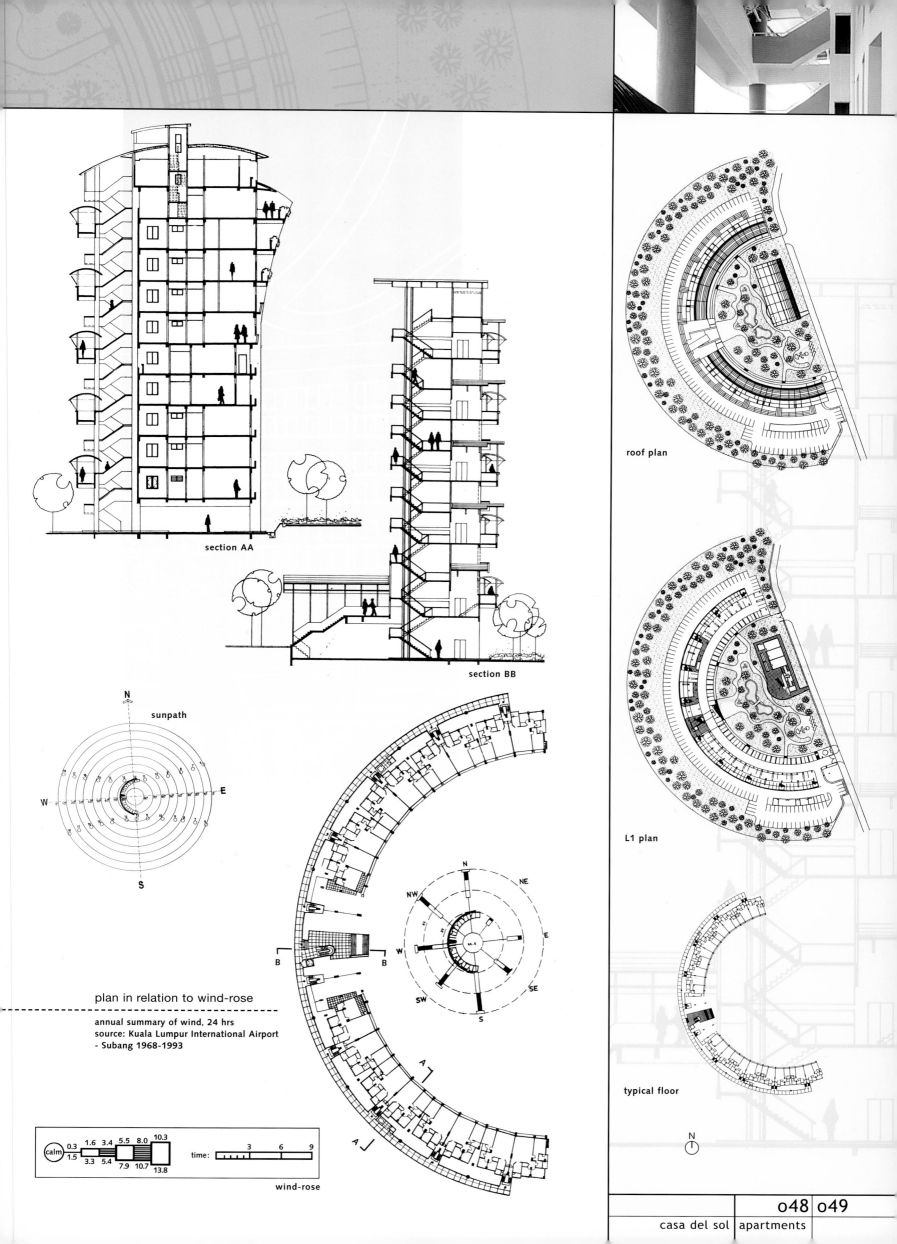

section AA

section BB

N

sunpath

W — E

S

plan in relation to wind-rose

annual summary of wind, 24 hrs
source: Kuala Lumpur International Airport
- Subang 1968-1993

B — B

N

NW — NE

W — E

SW — SE

S

A

A

| calm | 0.3 | 1.6 | 3.4 | 5.5 | 8.0 | 10.3 |
| | 1.5 | 3.3 | 5.4 | 7.9 | 10.7 | 13.8 |

time: 3 6 9

wind-rose

roof plan

L1 plan

typical floor

N

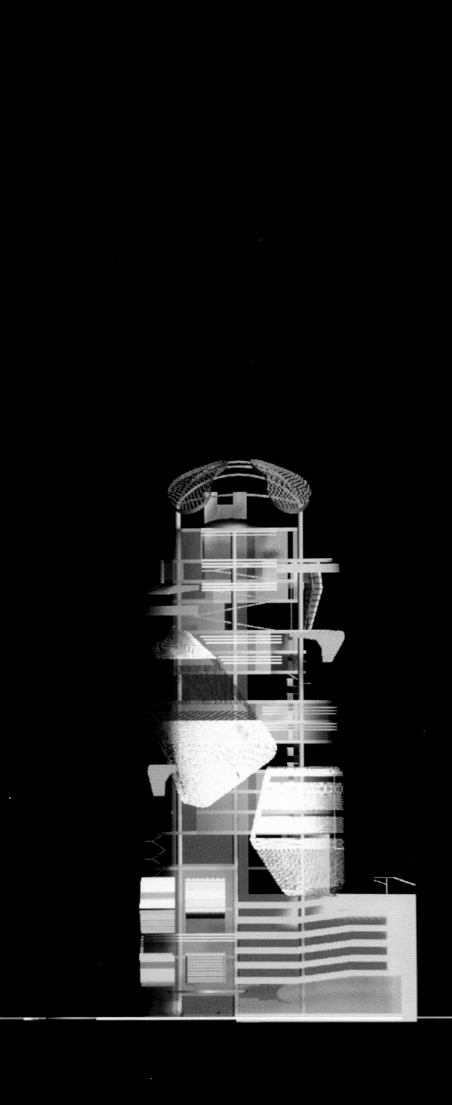

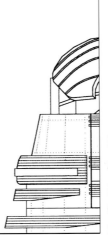

Plaza Atrium (1986) and Menara Mesiniaga (1992) are both signal projects that mark key points of development and change in Yeang's bioclimatic series. Similarly, the Hitechniaga Tower signals a further development which includes both the Shanghai Armoury Tower (1997) and the EDITT Exposition Tower (1998) – a new generation of highly expressive and innovative forms, which both further the evolution of an **ecological aesthetic and architecture** and exemplify Yeang's proposition for a **vertical urbanism**.

Essentially, the Hitechniaga project reflects Yeang's progression beyond a strict interpretation of the volumetric brief, to a point where he begins to expand the narrative of the form into an expressive dimension. This tendency is to continue with greater elaboration, into his subsequent works.

At first sight, the vertical clustering of the tower form, set against a rising backbone of vertical circulation and service space, recalls in passing the Japanese metabolist works of architects such as Kurokawa from the 1960s. But, this formal analogy is superficial and belies the more serious intention of Yeang's fluid manipulation of vertical spatiality. The overall form is composed in two distinct parts: a seven-storey base of car-parking floor-planes and a sub-tower of training rooms and auditorium. Above this rises a series of occupied levels for the activities of the computer and software company that the tower houses. These upper levels are dramatically sliced open by major **skycourts** at levels 10 and 13, with extensive landscaping. Above this, the presentation and convention floor at level 16 is joined to the Hitechniaga Management at levels 17, 18 and 19 by an eastern flank of **circulatory ramps**, that are additional to elevators and stairs on the vertical western face. This is one of the first instances of Yeang's incorporation of high-level pedestrian ramps, into the spatial movement pattern of the tower itself.

Both the eastward flank of ramps and the service core towers on the westward face provide part of the natural bioclimatic shielding on the hot solar sides – signal features of Yeang's low-energy architecture. At the same time, the skycourts and linked terraces provide **'ventilating-zones'** and external release for occupants throughout the higher levels.

In addition, a series of perforated-metal **'shields'** are included, as outriggers to the main form, to sun-shade the building. But, in this case, both the scale and curvilinear scallop-shaping of these elements extends far beyond mere function and mark a point in Yeang's formal articulation of the bioclimatic tower aesthetic. At one and the same time, these mechanisms are both solar-defensive and demonstrative. Taken together with the highly articulated form, the architecture assumes a 'warrior-like stance',[1] crowned at the tower's summit by

[1] See footnote 46 of introductory essay ('Interconnectedness, Sustainability and Skyscrapers')

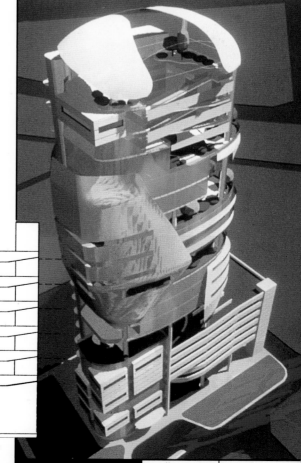

Kuala Lumpur, Malaysia

hitechniaga tower

owner Hitechniaga Sendirian Berhad
location Sri Hartamas, Kuala Lumpur, Malaysia
latitude 3°N
nos of storeys 19 storeys
date start pending
areas Nett area 6,374 sq m
Gross area 8,623 sq m
site area 1,308 sq m
plot ratio 1:6.6

design features • The site is located 20 minutes from the city centre of Kuala Lumpur.
The client wanted a distinctive corporate HQ building in line with his company's products (computers and innovative software).
The site is at a prominent corner lot adjoining a series of clusters of four-storey shop-offices (to be built).
The proposed tower on this site is 19 storeys and will contain spaces for reception and computer data centre at the ground floor at Level 1. At Levels 2 to 6 are meeting rooms and an auditorium. These are also accessible by a separate stair (away from the main tower lifts).
Above this are 14 floors of office space.
The features of the building are:
• Bioclimatic low-energy features such as: all the lift lobbies, staircases and toilets have natural sunlight and ventilation making the building low-energy and safe to use (ie. naturally lit stairs and lobbies in the event of power failure or other emergencies) and also to operate.
• Skycourts and 'ventilating zones' are located throughout the upper floors of the building. These are linked by additional staircases and ramps to increase accessibility.
• Perforated-metal 'shields' are used to sun-shade the building to shape and add form to the building.

by further shielding devices, developed from the earlier principles of Menara Mesiniaga.

Although Hitechniaga, as yet, remains as a project it decisively fulfils two central purposes. First, the form itself provides exactly the forward-looking imagery demanded by the client, for a distinctive corporate HQ reflecting the nature of an innovative computer and software company, based in Kuala Lumpur, within an emergent nation. Next and finally, it remains as a signal point of development in Yeang's pursuit of the ideal combination of elements, within the composition of the **bioclimatic skyscraper.**

In this latter respect, Hitechniaga stands on the entry threshold to a whole range of further projects that Yeang has undertaken in the following years beyond 1995–97.

0   5   10M

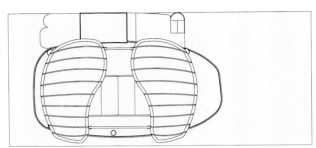

roof level

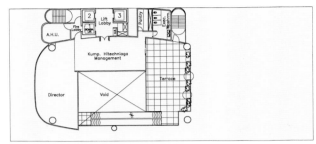

level 19

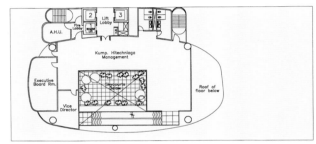

level 18

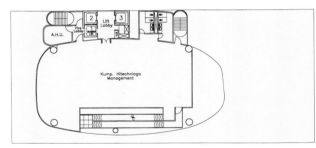

level 17

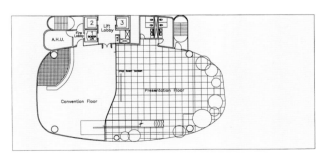

level 16

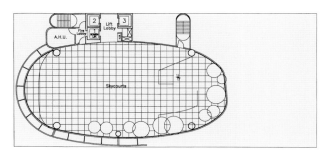

level 13

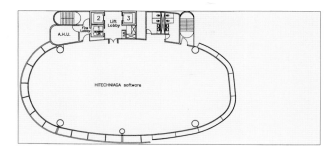

level 11 + 12

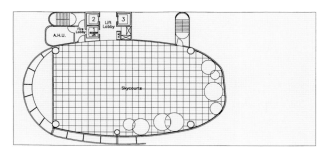

level 10

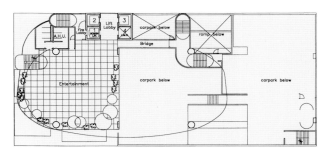

level 6

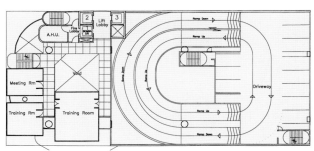

level 2

Penang, Malaysia

MBf Tower

owner MBf Holdings Berhad
location Jalan Sultan Ahmad Shah, Penang, Malaysia
latitude 5.24°N
no of storeys 31 storeys (68 units apartments)
date start 1990
completion date 1993
areas Total built-up area 17,538 sq m
nos of carpark bays 94 bays
site area 7482 sq m

design features • The tower is a development of the tropical high-rise ideas where the upper parts of the tower have large two-storey-high 'skycourts' as the building's key feature that provide better ventilation and deck space for planting and terraces.
• The lift lobbies are naturally ventilated with bridged walways leading to the apartment units.
• Stepped landscaping planter-boxes are located on the main facade of the building.

site • Consists of a regular-shaped site along the Jalan Sultan Ahmad Shah, Penang. The site is close to Pesiaran Gurney and faces the north beach head of Penang. The land is about 2 miles from the town centre and is along the road that links the beach hotels further down in the Tanjung Bungah Area to Georgetown.
• The adjoining sites on the east and west sides are lots zoned for commercial development. The site is generally oriented north-south with the access road from the north boundary. At the south-east boundary is a cul-de-sac from Salween Road.

programme • The site previously had a multi-storey apartment block by another architect but was demolished by City Hall while still under construction when the foundations were found to be faulty. Subsequently, T.R.Hamzah & Yeang were appointed as the new architects when the previous architect was discharged.
• The project consists of a podium for office and banking hall with a tower block containing luxury apartments (68 units).

structural system • The structural frame is constructed out of reinforced concrete with slip-form for the side service cores for the lift shafts. The typical floors are designed to be column free. The lower block for the apartment is RC frame construction with brick-in-fill.
• The tower columns are the periphery of the apartment units and are transferred to the columns at the podium.

major materials • Materials used include granite, marble, ceramic tiles and spray tile on the other wall area.

mechanical system • The office floors are intended to be cooled with central water-cooled package air-conditioning units with variable-air-volume control. The apartment units are to be naturally ventilated.

The predominantly residential apartment content of the MBf Tower, and the potential for separation and **openness** that this affords, has resulted in a singular statement that evokes Yeang's thematic idea of **'places in the sky'**, and at the same time is so directly expressive of the principles of **natural ventilation** and vertical landscaping.

The site is seaward-facing on the western edge, and is located in the north-east area of Penang island. This dramatic prospect and the lush tropical climate has given rise to the building's distinct form – a partial 'step-section' and the sliced, open plan-form – the former embracing the views with large residential terraces, and the latter providing cross-ventilation. The whole tower form is structured in an exposed concrete mega-frame and the finish throughout is **white** – placing the project within Yeang's 'white-cubic' series.

A six-storey podium, housing commercial facilities, is topped by a luxuriant swimming pool terrace, and alongside rises the apartment tower of 68 units, of various sizes. The step-section affords larger luxury apartments at the first half of the tower section, and also creates an internalised open atrium adjacent to the pool.

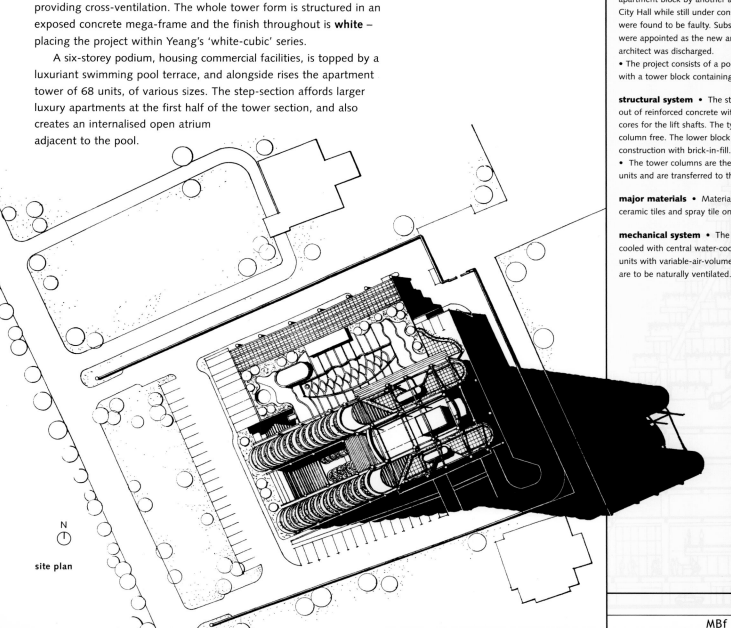

N

site plan

What merits most attention in this project is the articulation of the plan and section of the residential apartment floors as a demonstration of the basic principles of ventilation, prospect and planting, as depicted in Yeang's earliest sketches.

The residential floor is oriented approximately north-south, with the residential layers located on the line closest to the east-west axis, possible within site arrangement. The western seaward facing apartments have deep overhanging terraces, with planting, to create natural shading.

The triple-banded plan has four apartments at each floor level, on the north and south edges. These are separated by a central area of access galleries, elevator cores and staircases. In turn, all these elements are further separated with floor slots and gaps, both horizontal and vertical. In addition, the upper levels of the tower have generous, two-storey **skycourt-'cut-out'** openings which penetrate the entire section. Taken together, this intensification of the articulation of elements in both plan and section creates a flowing three-dimensional inner volume, which is laced with cool, cross-ventilation channels, lowering the thermal load of both circulation and apartments alike. This is supported by a vertical landscape which festoons skycourts, terraces and planters with a profusion of nature and natural shading.

To experience the openness and outward prospect of the residential galleries is a memorable and rare event – one that is further enhanced by the views west to the ocean.

In all of Yeang's work to date, this residential tower stands amongst his most successful projects. While its image is heroic-futurist, in use and for the occupant it offers a utopian ordinariness and a sublime sense of elevated sanctuary.

Reaching For the Skies

in *ARCHITECTURAL DESIGN PROFILE*, (NO 116, LONDON, 1993)
Maggie Toy

" This multi-storey block, located close to Pesiaran Gurney – facing the north shore of Penang – was built on the site of a similar building that had to be demolished when the foundations were found to be faulty. Again two elements are used to differentiate the different functional divisions within the building; offices in the podium and luxury apartments in the tower.
This tower further develops the architect's ideas on tropical high-rise buildings and his attempts to integrate these structures seamlessly with the natural environment. To achieve this large two storey 'skycourts' or terraces are utilised to provide natural ventilation for the apartments and deck space for planting and terraces. Even the lift lobbies are naturally ventilated with bridged walkways leading to the apartment units, and stepped planter-boxes are located on the main facade of the building. "

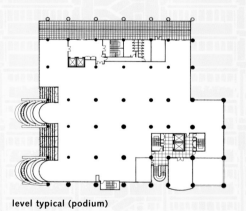

level typical (podium)

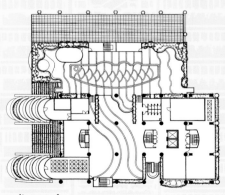

podium roof

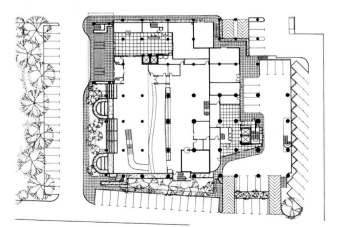

level ground

level typical (tower)

0   10M

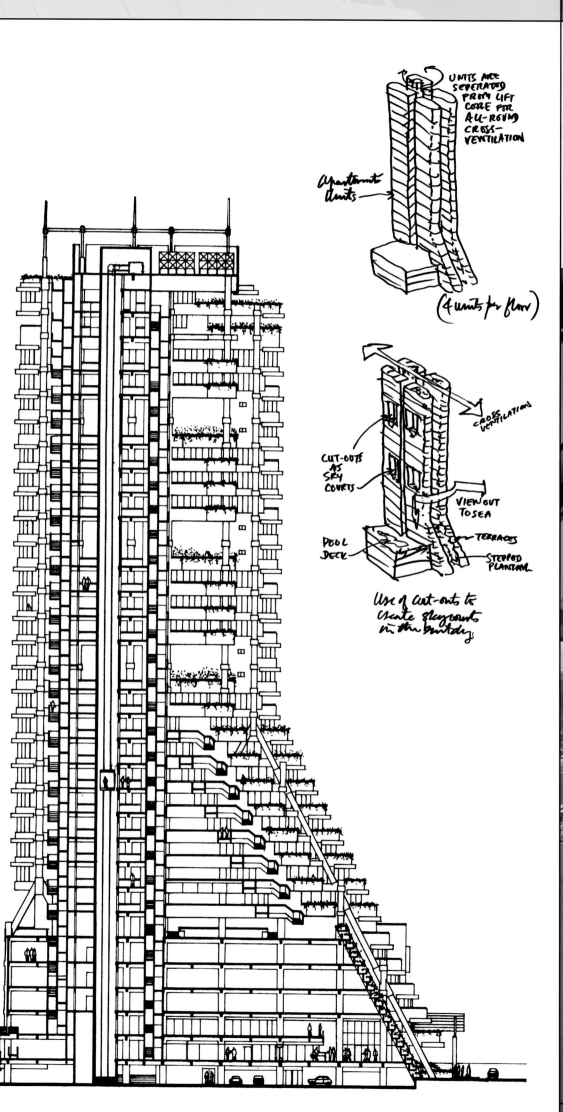

UNITS ARE SEPERATED FROM LIFT CORE FOR ALL-ROUND CROSS-VENTILATION

Apartment Units

(4 units per floor)

CROSS VENTILATION

CUT-OUTS AS SKY COURTS

VIEW OUT TO SEA

POOL DECK

TERRACES

STEPPED PLANTER

Use of cut-outs to create skycourts in the building

Sir Bannister Fletcher's
A History of Architecture,
and the Future
ARCHITECTURAL PRESS (12 EDITION 1995)
Cruikshank, D.

" ... The architects' highly original approach is best
exemplified by ... and the MBF Tower (1994),
a residential and mixed-use building in Georgetown,
Penang ... are distinguished by exposed 'megastructure'
frames, recessed 'skycourts', free-standing, naturally
ventilated service cores, and a variety of sunscreen
devices, combining international and regional influences
in a free and creative manner. "

the skyscraper as gardens-in-the-sky

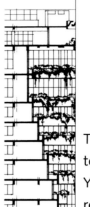

The Plaza Atrium
tower is amongst
Yeang's earliest
realised projects for
a landmark commercial building,
designed for sale and rental.
Standing on the threshold of Yeang's
bioclimatic skyscrapers, the incised heavy
white masonry form is not typical of
Yeang's mature architectural projects,
which generally incorporate lightweight
demountable cladding.

The lower floors incorporate space for
retail and bank use, with integrated car
parking. Office space occurs from the
second floor upwards.

The forshortened triangular plan-form
is a direct function of the restricted site,
with the major shielding clusters of stairs,
lifts and restrooms located on the
predominant north and south faces,
again not typical of Yeang's later, classic
bioclimatic projects. The resultant exposed
west, and particularly the south-eastern
facades, are therefore heavily clad masonry
profiles, with deeply incised horizontal
glazing bands.

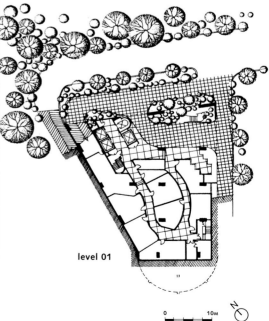

level 01

0   10M

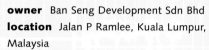

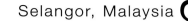

But, the project is precisely inflected by a single passive-mode environmental device – a soaring naturally ventilated atrium, serving the office floors and rising on the north-eastern sector of the overall plan. The cascading, planted balconies of the office spaces all relate to this crucial interstitial volume, which unlike conventional office towers of this period, is open to the air and acts as a giant wind-scoop. Although, in this project, the wind-scoop idea appears incidental, in fact it foreshadows Yeang's later use of wind wing-walls, such as UMNOTower in Penang, and other later projects, which are more sophisticated in their use of natural ventilated spaces.

Of Plaza Atrium, Yeang has made this statement:

"… Unlike most atriums, this space is not located within the building envelope but in the transitional space between the interior and exterior. The atrium is capped by a louvered roof using Z-profile louvres. This filters out rain while allowing hot air from within the atrium to flow out and diffused sunlight to enter. The entire atrium acts as a giant wind-scoop, capturing airflow high up on the building and enabling wind to enter the typical upper floors, controlled by the sliding doors of the terraces facing the atrium void …. The office floors facing the atrium are setback and lined with land-scaped terraces with views down into the atrium space."[1]

Thus, in this earliest of Yeang's commercial bioclimatic skyscrapers, the incidence of passive-mode intervention is evidenced, which marks the overall form of the architecture.

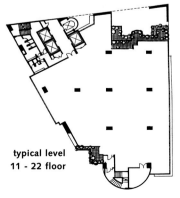

**typical level
11 - 22 floor**

[1] Yeang, 'Bioclimatic Skyscrapers', op. cit. p 55.

owner Ban Seng Development Sdn Bhd
location Jalan P Ramlee, Kuala Lumpur, Malaysia
latitude 3.7°N
nos of storeys 24 storeys
date start 1981
completion date 1986
areas Built-up area 10,700 sq m
site area 2,024 sq m
plot ratio 1:6.5

design features • The building consists of a office tower on a restricted site.
• The dominant feature of the building is the large semi-enclosed atrium to which all the office floors face with cascading terraces. This space is located not within the building envelope (as would be in common instances of atriums) but is located in a transitional space that lies between the inside of the building and the outside, ie. in the 'in-between' space with the outside.
• The atrium is topped by a louvred-roof of a Z-shaped profile louvre that acts as a filter in that it filters out the rain, permits accumulated hot-air within the atrium to flow through and enables diffused sun into the spaces below.
• The entire atrium space acts as a giant wind-scoop to capture the ai-flow at the upper regions of the tall building directed into the facade. The floors facing the atrium are set-backed and are lined with landscaped terraces; looking down into the atrium.

programme • The client's programme is to provide a landmark commercial building for sale and for rental, utilis-ing permitted plot ratio to the maximum. The permitted maximum plot ratio of 1:6.5 is to be utilised. Ground floor and first floor for shoplots or bank use with car-parking integrated into the built form and offices above.

structural system • Reinforced concrete-frame construction with piled foundations, 'slip-form' concrete construction is used for the elevator shaft. The louvred-roof over the atrium is cast-in-situ concrete.

major materials • Exterior finish – spray-on resin finish over plastered masonry walls. Tinted glazing to all windows with curtain-wall glazing to windows facing atrium. Other windows facing the outside are recessed for solar protection. Ceramic tile covering to floors with granite to lift lobby at ground floor. Interior areas – vinyl-tile surface, suspended acoustical ceiling, concrete-screeded floors with carpets, ceramic tiles to toilet areas.

mechanical system • For carpark floors: forced tempered air-ventilation system.
• For office areas: air-conditioning system.
• Wlevators: three normal high-speed elevators with one external glass elevator.

Sir Bannister Fletcher's A History of Architecture, and the Future

ARCHITECTURAL PRESS (12THE EDITION 1995)
Cruikshank, D.

" The Plaza Atrium (1983), in the capital's Golden Triangle district, by Hamzah and Yeang, is one of a series of experiments by its architects to develop a high-rise 'bioclimatic' architecture appropriate to the tropics, based on rational principles of climatic control. Partly inspired by shophouse arcades, the upper floors on one corner of the Plaza Atrium are stepped back under a canopy roof, leaving the corner exposed like a portion of a giant arcade. The architects' highly original approach is best exemplified by the Menara Mesiniaga Tower (1992), an office tower situated near Kuala Lumpur International Airport, and the MBF Tower (1994), a residential and mixed-use building in Georgetown, Penang … "

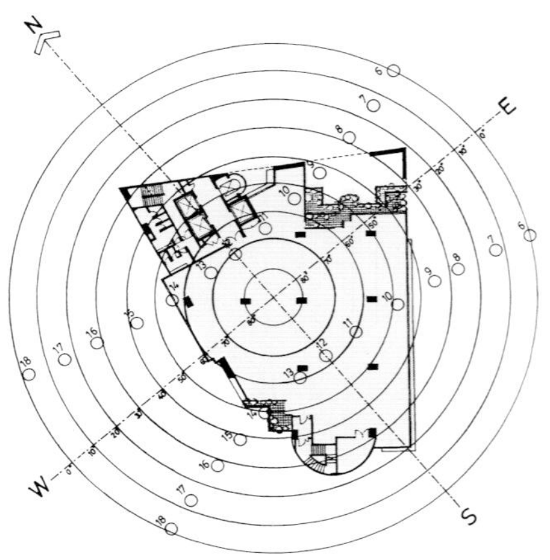

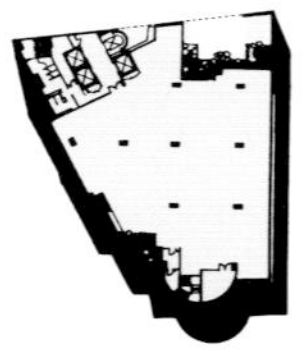

11am

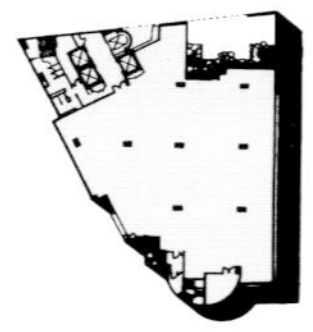

12 pm

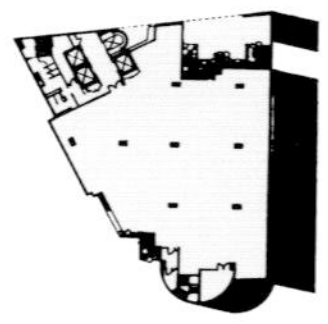

1 pm

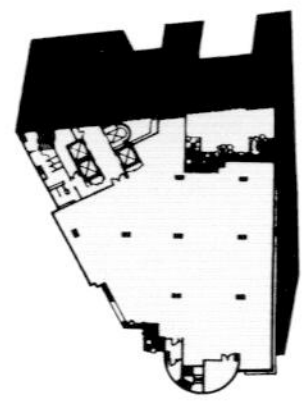

2 pm

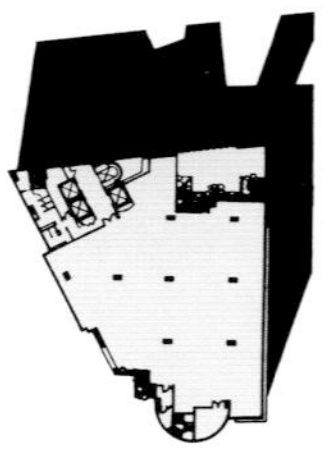

3 pm

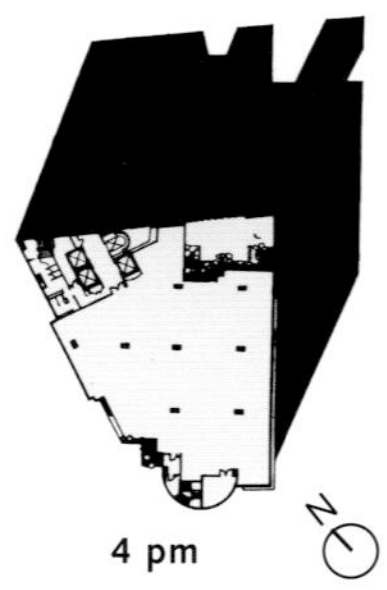

4 pm

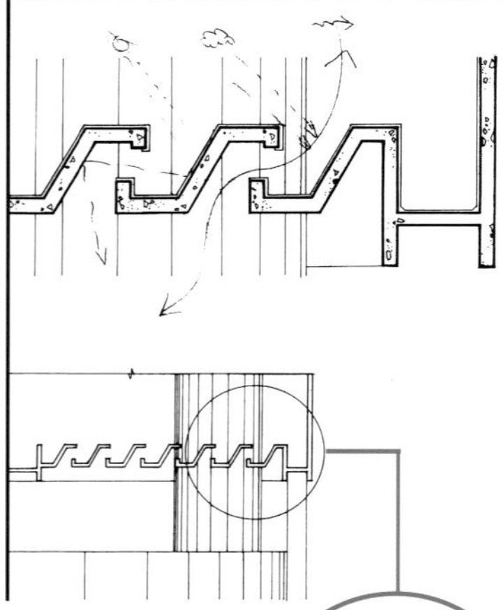

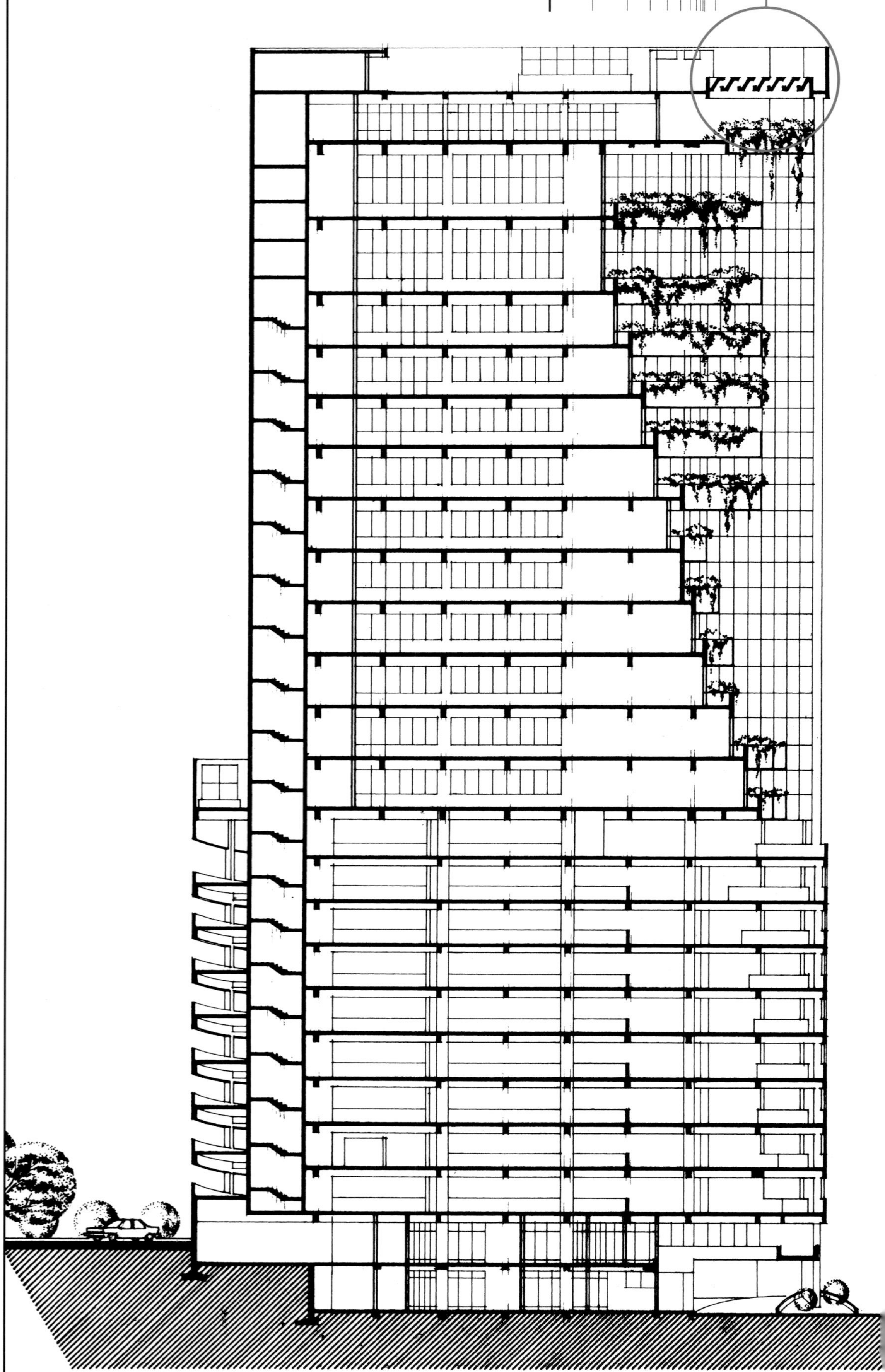

the atrium in the multi-storey building should not be inside the building as this makes it high-energy to maintain

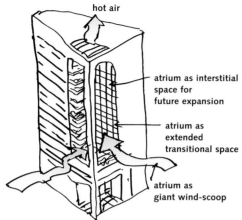

hot air

atrium as interstitial space for future expansion

atrium as extended transitional space

atrium as giant wind-scoop

THE MULTI-STOREY VERANDAH

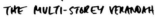

protection from sun and rain

the ubiquitous shophouse

courtyard as interstitial space

verandah way permits movement by pedestrians between buildings under protection from sun and rain

verandah as traditional transitional space

THE TRADITIONAL SHOPHOUSE

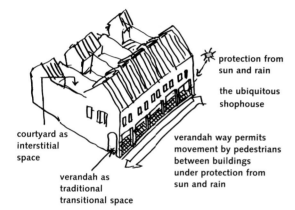

plot ratio 1:6 building without cut-outs

same GFA

atrium as 'in-between' space

recessed terraces

cut-outs as interstitial space

plot ratio 1:6 building with cut-outs as interstitial space; cut-outs allow for future extension

stage 1

stage 2 (later date when increased F.A.R. permits)

same building with cut-outs fully filled. new plot ratio 1:9

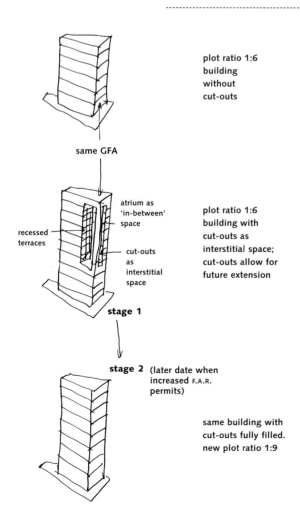

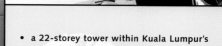

- a 22-storey tower within Kuala Lumpur's Golden Triangle Area
- the design sets out to provide an urban design prototype for an extremely built-up area in Kuala Lumpur
- design effort to redefine the huge porches from our architecture heritage

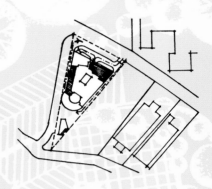

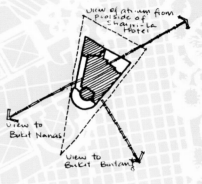

View of atrium from poolside of Shangri-La Hotel

View to Bukit Nanas

View to Bukit Bintang

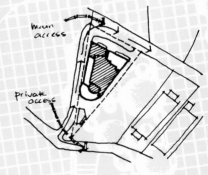

main access

private access

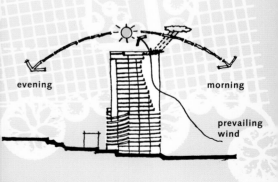

evening

morning

prevailing wind

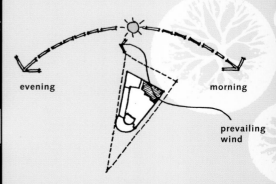

evening

morning

prevailing wind

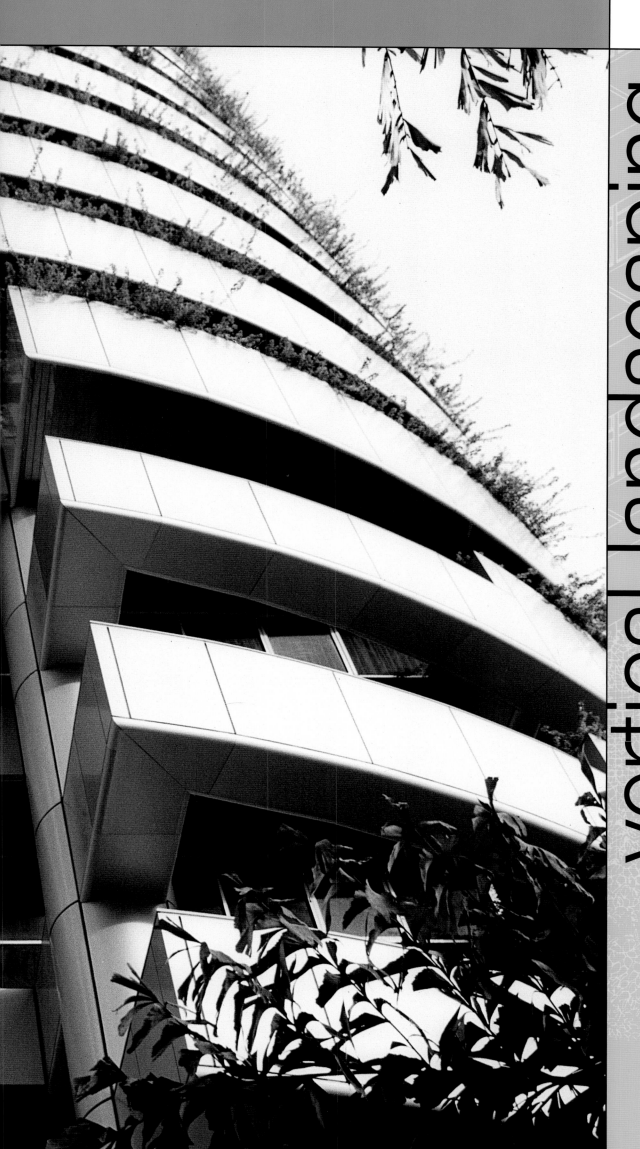

vertical landscaping

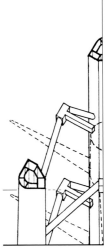

Singularly Yeang's most significant theoretical project of the mid 1990s, the Tokyo-Nara Tower is an experimental design that allowed the architect to investigate and realise ideas and research that had been accruing within his ongoing practice of tall buildings.

Essentially, the design can be summarised as the architecture of the **hollow, rotating spiral**. Although this concept may bear some basic resemblance to the diagram of Menara Mesiniaga, it is otherwise a completely free, organic invention and foreshadows many of the developed versions of Yeang's future projects.

The idealised plan-form is orientated with the shielding vertical circulation cores on the outer east and west faces. These serve the rotating floor plates, which shift position on alternate floor levels. Yeang has described these planes of occupation as **'plectrum-shaped'** – an abstracted rounded triangular element, loosely assembled onto a free grid of columns. In looking at it now this first concept of structure appears as a residual of earlier work, and is superseded in the design development by a triangular three-masted circulation-core system with a further central mast that carries circulation, and cantilever arms supporting the floor planes – the whole form being encircled by tension-rods and linear service tracks.

Were the initial concept to be redesigned and engineered today, in the 21st century, there can be little doubt that contemporary engineering principles that incorporate fractal geometries would give rise to a more sophisticated and integrated structure, that in turn would support the overall spatial construct.

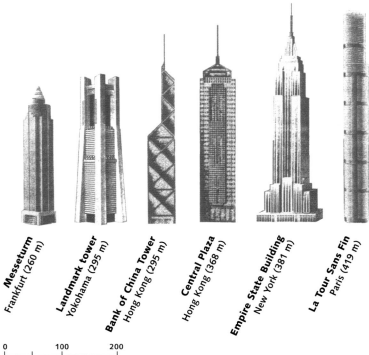

Messeturm
Frankfurt (260 m)

Landmark tower
Yokohama (295 m)

Bank of China Tower
Hong Kong (295 m)

Central Plaza
Hong Kong (368 m)

Empire State Building
New York (381 m)

La Tour Sans Fin
Paris (419 m)

0   100   200

tokyo-nara tower

owner Nara Triennale, Nara Municipal Office
location Urban site between Tokyo and Nara
latitude 35.42°N
nos of storeys 180 storeys (approx. 880 m)
areas Gross area 4,828,160 sq m
Total nett area 4,603,603 sq m
Total built up area 4,828,160 sq m
site area site footprint 122,500 sq m
plot ratio 1:40

However, and as with all great ideas, all these supporting systems ultimately serve a new architectural conception. Overriding everything else, in this case, is the central principle of **spiralling vertical landscape**.

Yeang's compulsive and compelling sketches describe the attributes of the project much more succinctly than words, but these include:

- **Stepped terraces and planters – with intermediate and roof-to-gardens, serving a mixed-use occupancy including commercial, office and residential accommodation.**
- **Extensions of the garden and sky court principles.**
- **Wind flues to bring wind ventilation to the inner parts of the building with adjustable dampers.**
- **Rotating, moveable sun shades and wind shields.**
- **Service tracks that spiral up the building to carry mobile 'cherry-picker' devices that care for the prolific planting spiral.**

Gathered together, all these ideas and the benefits they bestow to the occupant – such as the natural shading and cooling resultant from the planting to the atrial and occupied inner spaces – are also the emergent signals of Yeang's pursuit of an **ecological architecture** that is both balanced and all encompassing. All that is missing from this project is his later incorporation of informal circulatory pedestrian ramps and linkages between the host of levels.

But, this aside, in every other respect the Tokyo-Nara Tower is Ken Yeang's first major exposition of his concept of **Vertical Urbanism**. In this singular respect, it remains significant.

design features • This is a conceptual project, prepared for the World Architecture Exposition in Nara, Japan to exemplify the ideas for the climatically responsive skyscraper. The tower physically realises many of the theoretical ideas expounded by Yeang, and represents a significant stage in their ongoing research into the nature and evolution of tall buildings. The ideas behind its conception can be summarised as follows:
• Most visually apparent is the vertical landscaping – spiralling around, through and within the built form. This element performs many important functions:
- the verdant foliage acts to cool the building, both by way of shading and by chemical photo-cooling
- the fringing of floors and atrial spaces allows careful planting to control air movements within the built structure
- the mass of planting relative to the built structure is favourable comparable; thereby ensuring that biosystems are acting symbiotically with mechanical systems to provide a balanced built environment.
• The maintenance of the vertical landscaping, as well as the upkeep of external fixtures, glazing and cladding panels is ensured by specialised mechanical devices. These devices, constructed in the form of multipurpose 'robot-arms' as 'cherry-pickers' on moveable trellises that travel along an external track that spiral and circulates the tower.
• The radial/spiral movement of floor planes creates a particular built form which allows:
- the floors to shade themselves as they spiral upward
- the displaced pattern to more efficiently exploit the benefits of hanging gardens, inter-floor bracing and ventilation / cooling systems
- a constantly changing atrial space, articulated by terraces, internal courts and private gardens.
• Located at regular intervals, the skycourt oases provide inhabitants with environmentally sound 'breaks' in the built structure. These green parks, suspended high above the city, would benefit from fresh air, and be constantly maintained as part of the buildings own system. They would act as Tokyo-Nara Tower's lungs, breathing life into the floors above and below, via the atrial voids.
• The communications sub-tower, set in the upper floors of Tokyo-Nara provide satellite links and other facilities appropriate to advancing 'global village' communications.
• The atrial spaces, winding within Tokyo-Nara Tower, are the arterial routes by which floors interact. Terraces and courts, looking down on each other, fed by channels of through-flowing air, are semi-communal areas. The atrial network, bridged by walkways and flanked by stairwells, constitute a microcosm of activity, within the tower and (while open to the environment) insulated from the city.
• The service cores of the building are orientated according to solar conditions.
- Laid along the East-West axis, these lift and service cores absorb a significant percentage of heat gain
- The cooler facades on the north-south axis are left open by clear glazing and atrial voids.
• The shielding and glazing systems are orientated to solar gain.
- Those sides of the building along the east-west axis are more solidly glazed, with cast and perforated metal cladding (a preferred material for reflective, weight and structural qualities)
- The north-south axis can be identified by open louvres, tiered sunshades and clear glazing. This is as a consequence of lower exposure to the sun.
• Note: The World Architecture Exposition, Nara, Japan. This event stretches over a period of nine years, and constitutes number of activities. The first involved a competition for the proposal of a convention centre for the City of Nara, the second an exhibition of work by several internationally notable architects, culminating in the foundation of a permanent museum of Architecture in the City of Nara. The separate events are scheduled at three year intervals – the entire programme completed in 1998.

Jin Mao Building
Shanghai (421 m)

Asia Plaza
Kaohsiung Taiwan (427 m)

Sears Tower
Chicago (442 m)

Petronas Towers
Kuala Lumpur (450 m)

Chongqing Tower
Kuala Lumpur (457 m)

Millennium Tower
Japan (800 m)

Tokyo-Nara Tower
Tokyo-Nara (880 m)

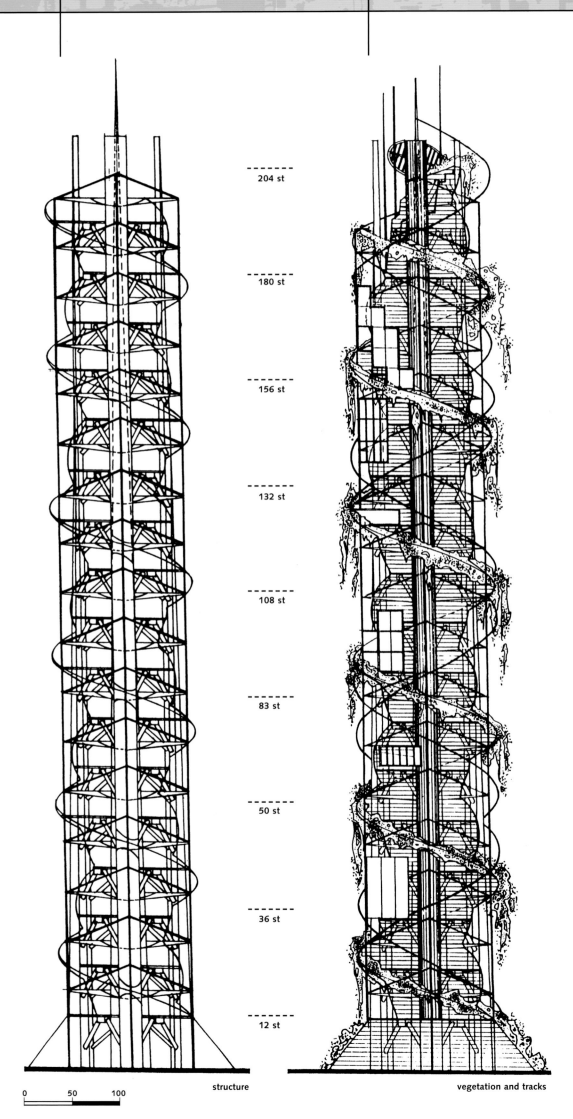

structure

elevation

- - - - - - 204 st

- - - - - - 180 st

- - - - - - 156 st

- - - - - - 132 st

- - - - - - 108 st

- - - - - - 83 st

- - - - - - 50 st

- - - - - - 36 st

- - - - - - 12 st

0   50   100

structure

vegetation and tracks

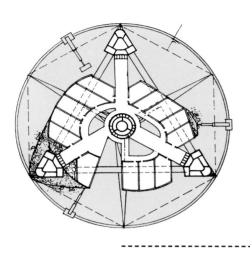

apartment floor

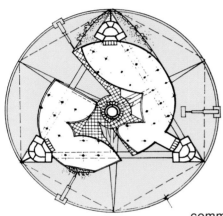

communal facilities floor

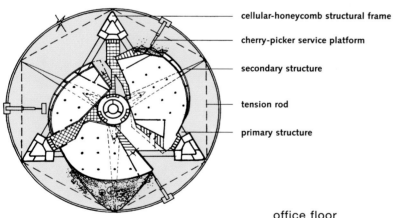

cellular-honeycomb structural frame

cherry-picker service platform

secondary structure

tension rod

primary structure

office floor

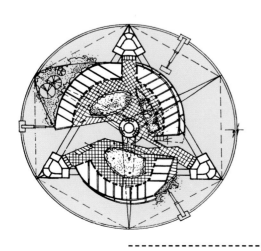

hotel floor

----

0   50   100

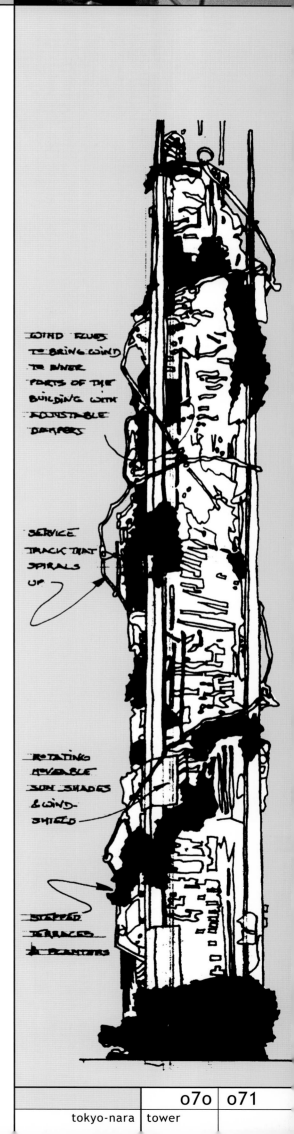

WIND FLUES
TO BRING WIND
TO INNER
PARTS OF THE
BUILDING WITH
ADJUSTABLE
DAMPERS

SERVICE
TRACK THAT
SPIRALS
UP

ROTATING
MOVEABLE
SUN SHADES
& WIND
SHIELD

STEPPED
TERRACES
& PLANTERS

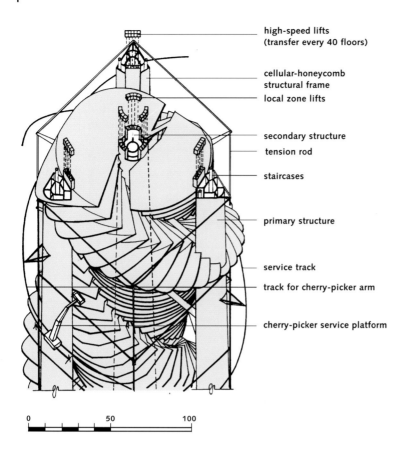

high-speed lifts
(transfer every 40 floors)

cellular-honeycomb
structural frame
local zone lifts

secondary structure

tension rod

staircases

primary structure

service track

track for cherry-picker arm

cherry-picker service platform

0   50   100

primary structure

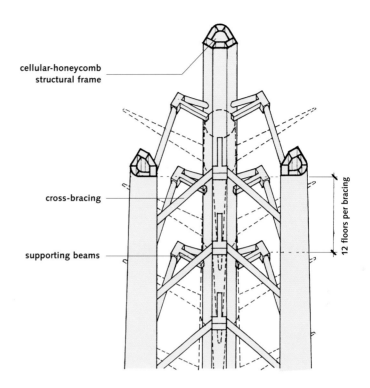

cellular-honeycomb
structural frame

cross-bracing

supporting beams

12 floors per bracing

floor plates and structure

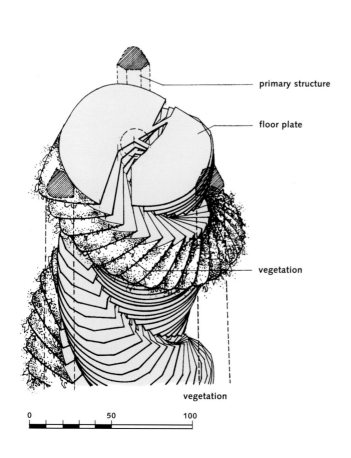

primary structure

floor plate

vegetation

vegetation

0   50   100

secondary structure

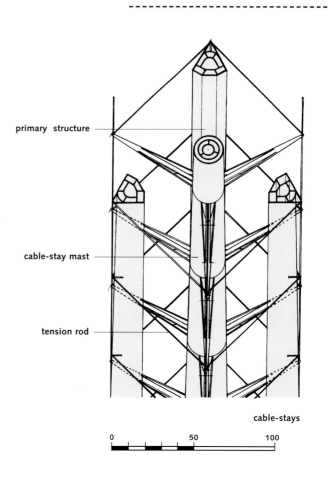

primary structure

cable-stay mast

tension rod

cable-stays

0   50   100

seasonal changes

humidity

Humidity varies throughout the year, however it is the greatest at ground level and within cloud cover.

wind velocity

The friction of the earth's surface and building landscape reduce airflow.

wind velocity

The friction of the earth's surface and building landscape reduce airflow.

climate predictability

Climate is a complex interaction of the atmospheric forces of radiation, air movement and atmospheric pressure. Near the sun's face, micro climatic forces become more influential and the global understanding become less predictable.

air temperature

Air temperature drops with height.

air pressure

As the density decreases with height, so does its air pressure.

views

Surrounding buildings at low level obstruct views. At higher level cloud cover will also reduce visibility.

solar radiation

As the sun's rays pass through the atmosphere its energy is reduced. However, as it hits the cloud level it is reflected, intensifying radiation towards the tower at lower levels.

air density

The density of the atmosphere reduces with height.

torsion and wind forces

Wind forces twist the tower. The torsion is greatest at the base where the tower is restrained, reducing with height.

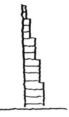

vertical movement

The movement of people increases towards the entrance at the base of the building.

rainfall

Clouds precipitate water which falls to the ground. As it falls some is lifted by rising air currents and some is evaporated so that its intensity is reduced.

ground noise

Street noise, for example, is less noticeable beyond five storeys.

bending stresses due to horizontal wind loads

Wind bend twist the tower. The bending stresses are the greatest at the base where the tower is restrained, reducing with height.

horizontal sway

As the wind passes around the tower the pressure disbalance causes the tower to sway.

speed of climatic change

The ground provides a source of thermal inertia, moderating sudden climatic variations.

concentration of pollution

The main sources of pollutants are from vehicles and industry. Vehicles deposit more pollutants at ground level, whereas industry deposits it at high level.

horizontal shear force due to wind load

Wind forces generate shear stresses, which the tower accommodates towards its base where the shear forces are the greatest.

horizontal deflection

As the wind hits the tower it deflects. The greatest deflection is the furthest point from the supports at the ground.

engineering strategy
by Chris McCarthy
Battle McCarthy Consulting Engineers

As a general comment, the floor plates are very deep, to break them up so that no floor plate is deeper than 12–15 m deep otherwise the buildings will not be day-lit and can not be naturally ventilated during mid season period.

Propose that the tower is considered as 8, 25-storey blocks stacked on each other supporting the one above but each experiencing different climatic condition in terms of temperature, solar radiation, daylight, noise, wind velocity and frequency, air quality and density, and humidity.

Have developed the highest block as it is less usual and should be compared to living on the peak in Penang or Surrey.

structural design

The tower has been subdivided into eight sustainable blocks stacked upon each other, the axial load is carried by an arrangement of diagonal struts and ties, the ties are provided with dampers to minimise the peak impact forces. The structure is founded on a combination of a basement raft and piles. The primary structural elements reduce in sectional thickness with height. Composite material is proposed for stiffness and high strength–weight ratio.

environmental design

All working areas are day-lit and naturally ventilated during mid season. In the summer periods the structure will be cooled down by the cooler night air. In the winter the building will be mechanically ventilated via a heat pump, fresh air is pre-heated via a solar collector.

energy, water and waste

Each of the eight building blocks are to be sustainable in energy, water and waste management. Each block will have its own energy centre which will incorporate a water treatment works. The nominal energy demand of the low energy building will be provided by wind power, water power, solar power and waste power (including waste from planting).

construction

As the building is constructed, people will occupy each block as is complete. The building will be a continuos building site as the top floor will be complete the lower floors will be being refurbished.

In general the higher the building unit the less it will experience seasonal change and it will exist in a wider and cooler climate with greater direct solar radiation. However the climatic change even though it occurs within a smaller margin will happen more rapidly than we are used to at ground level.

The higher blocks will need to maximise solar gain for heating, open area will need shelter from the wind and the facades will need to be alert and responsive to climatic changes within minutes rather than within a year.

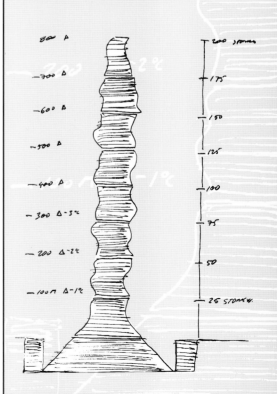

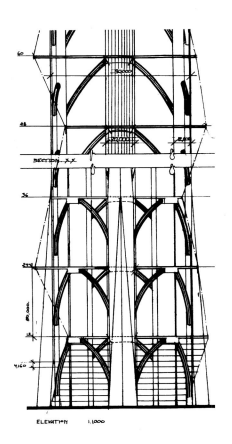

ELEVATION 1:1,000

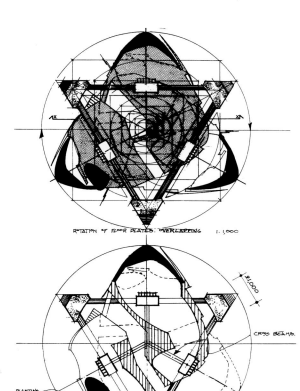

ROTATION OF FLOOR PLATES: OVERLAPPING 1:1,000

TYPICAL FLOOR PLAN 1:1,000

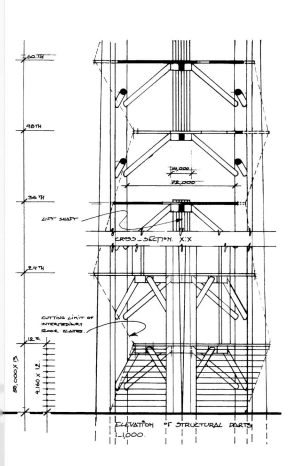

CROSS SECTION X:X

ELEVATION OF STRUCTURAL PARTS 1:1,000

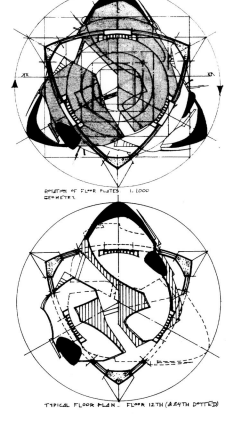

ROTATION OF FLOOR PLATES 1:1,000 GEOMETRY

TYPICAL FLOOR PLAN. FLOOR 12TH (& 24TH DOTTED)

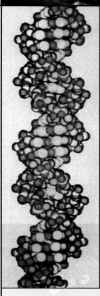

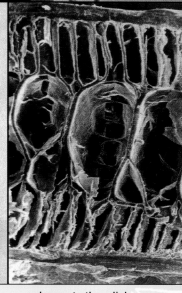

DNA tower   analogous to the cellular structure of the needle of the porcupine

the skyscraper should not be a stack of homogenous concrete plates

the anthill as a bioclimatic skyscraper

rotated magazine stack analogy

Taken together with Plaza Atrium, the IBM Plaza is another version of Yeang's early **white-cubic** towers and untypical of his later, mature designs. It is however infused with some basic characteristics of the bioclimatic series, notably orientation, solar shielding, shading and facade planting. The complex also has an urbanistic interface and incorporates an early glimpse of Yeang's ideas for a **vertical urbanism** – in this case a fragment – in the form of a mid-level breezeway floor, and the high-level shaded roof terraces.

The design was intended to reflect the progressive nature of the company for whom it was commissioned, and is composed of two forms – the tower itself, which includes both car-parking and office space, and a two storey restaurant/food court, which is linked by a curvilinear bridge. This complex is contained in a ground level plaza, surrounded by paved, pedestrian roads related to the grid of the adjoining shophouses.

The overall plan form of the tower responds to two geometries – that of the skewed sun path and the regular site grid of site context and roads. The tower plan is essentially a nine-bay square, orientated north-south relative to sunpath, with the outboard service cores on the hot east and west sides, providing solar shielding and aligning with the site geometry. Two additional features relate to the tropical climate: at ground level the lift lobby is open and naturally ventilated, revealing the pilotis and signalling the external plaza. Equally, the top levels of the tower are celebrated by a crowning open-louvred sun-filter, whose pitched sectional form is intended to evoke the memory of the traditional Malay house.

ibm plaza

owner TTDI Development Sdn Bhd
location Taman Tun Dr Ismail, Kuala Lumpur, Malaysia
latitude 3.3°N
nos of storeys 24 storeys
date start 1983
completion date 1985
areas
Total built-up area (excl. carpark) 26,057 sq m
Total built-up area (incl. carpark) 41,885 sq m
Carpark area 15,828 sq m
Hawker's centre 52 sq m
site area 8,096 sq m
plot ratio 1:4.1

These two elements of **openness**, at the base and the crown of the tower, are linked by vertical facade planting:

"… the local landscaping and planting are introduced in an innovative vertical escalating system of planter-boxes and trellises which start from a mound at the ground floor and rise diagonally up the face of the building. At mid-level, these planters traverse horizontally across the breeze-way floor – a Hawkers' Centre – and escalate again diagonally up the other face of the building to the roof terraces." [1]

This extensive geometrical feature of diagonally inflected vertical landscaping, which suggests a spiral of natural envelopment, is further developed in Yeang's more sophisticated projects such as the Nara Tower and others.

In this case, the diagonal vertical landscaping is counterbalanced by the overhung floor spandrels, producing deep recesses and sunshading. At the upper levels the floors and spandrels are skewed and extended outwards in a reversed stepped form, which provides additional wedge-shaped projections and further shading.

As well as having a climatic reference and purpose, these shifts in the form of the overall design are intended to announce a move away from the conventional modernist office slab-tower, and suggest a freer more responsive alternative.

While IBM Plaza is not a central project in Yeang's overall bioclimatic series, it is nevertheless part of the general evolution of the type, incorporating the principles of orientation, shielding, shading and elements of natural ventilation.

design features • The building consists of a office tower linked by a curvilinear bridge to a two-storey restaurant /food-court lower-block. The two forms are juxtaposed in a plaza in which the surrounding roads are pedestrianized and paved to meet the adjoining shophouses.
Two geometries are recognised: one of the sun (ie. the sun's path) and the other of the site in relation to the road (ie. contextual geometry). The typical floor is orientated aligning north and south in relation to the sun's path and geometry. The services-core (lifts, stairs and toilets) are on the hot sides of the tower (ie. the east side and the west side) and follows the geometry of the site. By this configuration the layout of the built-forms respond to the local hot–humid tropical climate in its planning and disposition.
The top of the tower is pitched to be reminiscent of the traditional vernacular house form. The local landscaping and planting are introduced uniquely into this tall building in an innovative vertical escalating-system of planter boxes. These rise diagonally up the face of the building. Then at mid-level, the planters traverse across the floor and escalate diagonally again up the other face of the building to the roof terraces. The ground-floor entrance lift lobby that leads to the plaza is opened to the outside and is naturally ventilated. The upper floors are extended in an asymmetrical pattern resulting in the wedge-shaped projection in the upper floors. This generated an overall form which is non-regular and thereby deviates from the purist modernist slab-form for the tower.

programme • To provide a landmark and headquarter building for the developers of Taman Tun Dr Ismail that reflects the contemporary progressive nature of the development company and at the same time, to retain a regional character in the architecture. Maximum plot ratio of 1:3 to be utilised. The major part of the building is to be leased to IBM Corporation.

structural system • Reinforced concrete-frame construction, piled foundations, slip-form concrete elevator shaft construction, basement retaining walls.

external skin • Precast tiled sunshading.
• Tinted glazing with half solid panel.
• Ceramic tile covering to external wall.
• Precast glass-reinforced concrete louvres roof over last floor.

interior • Tiled surface, gypsum plaster ceilings, suspended acoustical ceiling, concrete floor with carpets and vinyl asbestos tile.

mechanical system • For basement carpark: forced tempered air-ventilation system.
• For office: air-conditioning system.

detail of planter box with gravity-fed watering and nutrients feed system

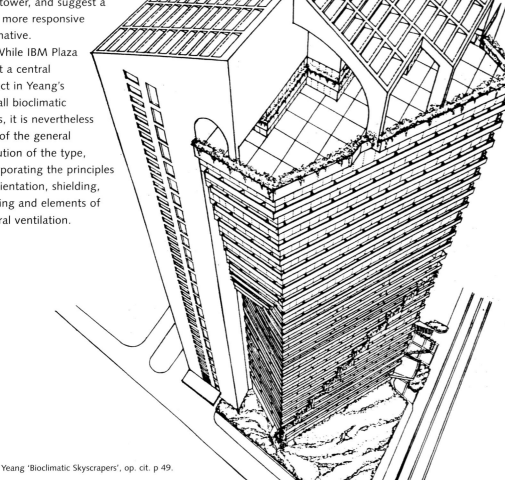

[1] Yeang 'Bioclimatic Skyscrapers', op. cit. p 49.

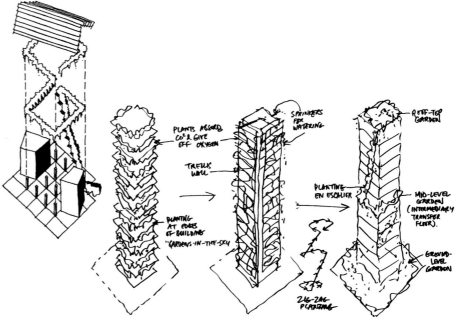

shadow studies

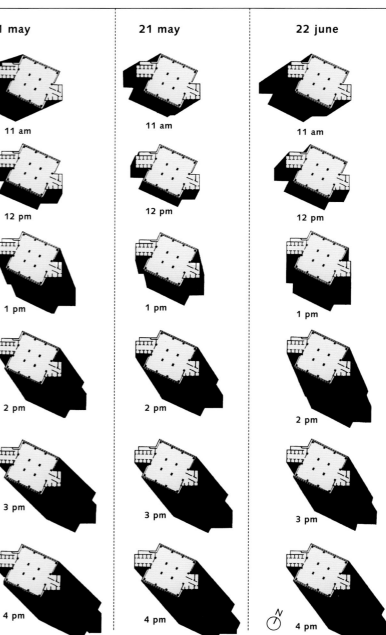

1 may	21 may	22 june
11 am	11 am	11 am
12 pm	12 pm	12 pm
1 pm	1 pm	1 pm
2 pm	2 pm	2 pm
3 pm	3 pm	3 pm
4 pm	4 pm	4 pm

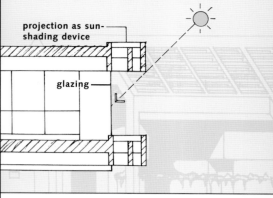

sun shading

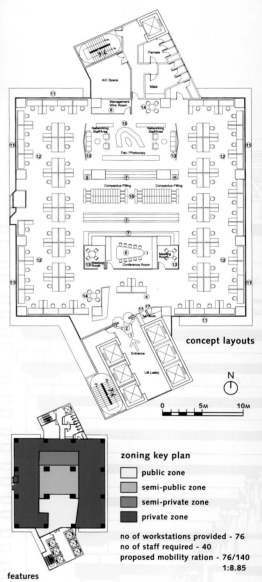

projection as sun-shading device

glazing

hot-desking layout

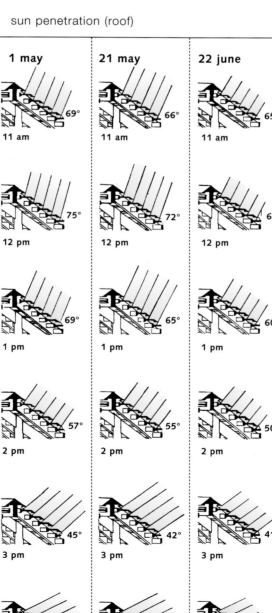

concept layouts

zoning key plan

- public zone
- semi-public zone
- semi-private zone
- private zone

no of workstations provided - 76
no of staff required - 40
proposed mobility ration - 76/140
1:8.85

features

- workstation to be arranged in groups
- accommodation discussion table within workstation groups
- promotes interaction by introducing open concept in staff networking area
- compacters to be locked next to mobile pedestals and filing cabinets
- workstations receive natural daylight

zoning

- public zone: meeting rooms and conference room to be located near reception
- semi-public zone: compactors, mobile pedestals and filing cabinets
- semi-private zone: staff networking and fax/photocopy
- private zone: workstation

sun penetration (typical floor)

1 may	21 may	22 june
69° 11 am	66° 11 am	65° 11 am
75° 12 pm	72° 12 pm	68° 12 pm
69° 1 pm	65° 1 pm	60° 1 pm
57° 2 pm	55° 2 pm	50° 2 pm
45° 3 pm	42° 3 pm	41° 3 pm
29° 4 pm	28° 4 pm	27° 4 pm

sun penetration (roof)

1 may	21 may	22 june
69° 11 am	66° 11 am	65° 11 am
75° 12 pm	72° 12 pm	68° 12 pm
69° 1 pm	65° 1 pm	60° 1 pm
57° 2 pm	55° 2 pm	50° 2 pm
45° 3 pm	42° 3 pm	41° 3 pm
29° 4 pm	28° 4 pm	27° 4 pm

N

0 5m 10m

Menara Boustead is essentially a transitional work within Yeang's early series of **bioclimatic skyscrapers,** standing between the initial white-cubic towers such as Plaza Atrium (1981) and the definitive silver-cylindrical Menara Mesiniaga (1989).

Although the tower, as a basic commission, is a corporate headquarters building incorporating just office space and car-parking, the intention of the design was to go beyond the conventions of stacked office-floor types. The project therefore includes several important innovations that reoccur in Yeang's future works – principally these are the introduction of skycourts, solar shielding with service cores, and rain and heat-check aluminium skin.

The plan-form is based on a square, with protrusions, and encircled in part by an outer layer. This formation allows the introduction of both **skycourts and terraces** in the outer corners of the plan, and characteristically marks the overall form of the tower throughout its height. These external transitional spaces perform several environmental functions: the balconies incorporate irrigated planting and landscaping and the sun-shading they provide allows full-height openable glazing, which contributes both natural-light and ventilation to the inner office spaces, enhancing user quality and comfort conditions. The skycourt terraces also provide a flexible zone for additional services, such as supplementary air-conditioning units.

The dominant effect of the planted terraces, which incise the partial-cylindrical form, is to striate the whole precise mass and festoon its surface with rich, colourful planting layers. Given its height and the intensified urban location, this comes as a relief. The skycourt, as a device, is an element that is developed significantly in Yeang's future designs, but the basic combined principles of deep facade recesses, balcony terraces, planters and heat-sink cladding and overall solar configuration, are all grounded in the Boustead design.

Kuala Lumpur, Malaysia

owner Boustead Holdings Berhad

location Jalan Raja Chulan, Kuala Lumpur, Malaysia

latitude 3.2°N

nos of storeys 31 storeys

date start Phase I (first 16 floors of office building and first 8 floors of carpark building): 1986 (May) Phase II (17th to roof of office building, basement levels, 9th to roof of carpark annexe): 1986 (October).

completion date 1986

areas Total built-up area 29,840 sq m
Carpark area 15,630 sq m

nos of carpark bays 400 bays

site area 1,920 sq m

plot ratio 1:6.97

Finally, as the overall plan orientation of Boustead is configured to respond to the tropical sun-path, this has several consequences that are significantly expressed in the overall form: in particular the massive lift cores, toilet restroom clusters and stairs are located on the hot west and east faces providing solar-shielding. In addition, as the lift lobby cores are located at the edge of the plan, this facilitates natural light and ventilation to these spaces. This shift, in contrast to the normal in-board core, not only makes circulation more pleasant to use, but also safer in the event of power-failure.

As well as the application of sun-shading to all west and east facing fenestration, and the cooling effect of the planting, the whole cladding system of this fast-tracked structure is noteworthy. This consists of a suspended double outer-layer, faced in a rain-screen aluminium skin that both checks and dissipates heat, by separation, before it can be transmitted to the main inner structure.

The tower itself is topped with a roof terrace – a feature that is also greatly developed in Yeang's subsequent projects.

The Boustead project is tightly controlled and yet innovative, while remaining commercially viable. Its low-energy, passive-mode characteristics both enhance its use and aesthetic appeal. It remains a summary statement for Yeang, at that point in 1986.

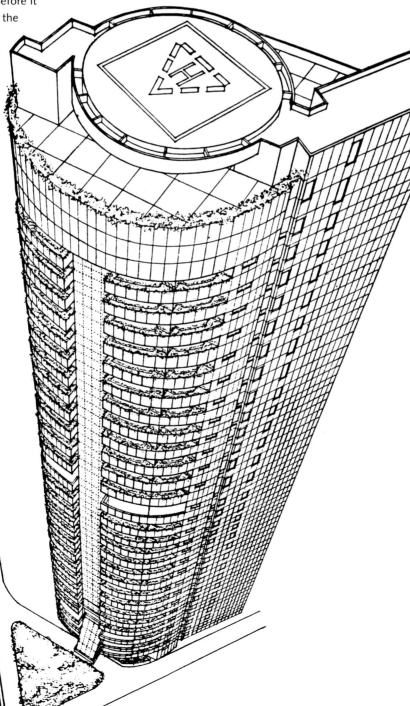

design features • The objective was to design the office building to be more than series of multiple enclosed concrete trays stacked in the air. Here in this building are **'corner terraces'** on each floor. These terraces are located at all corners all the way up the building. These terraces or skycourts permit:
- the introduction of planting and landscaping in the upper floors
- a flexible zone for potential of future addition of executive washrooms
- adequate sun-shading to allow for full-height glazing to enhance the quality of light in the office work space
- the potential for the location of supplementary air-conditioning units. This is currently not possible in most existing buildings.

• The overall conception of the building responds to the tropical sun. Cladding the building with ventilated aluminium skin enables the heat to be trapped and dissipated before it can be transmitted to the main structure.

• The typical floor plan best exemplifies the ideas for a typical high-rise type. The features are:
- lift cores and toilets are located on the hot-sides of the building. ie. on the West and on the east
- lift lobbies have natural sunlight and ventilation
- all windows are sun-shaded
- deep balconies at corners as skycourts.

site • Consists of two contiguous sites located in the commercial area of Kuala Lumpur called the 'Golden Triangle Area'. The location is a prime site for upmarket office and commercial development.
The adjoining west side of the site is a vacant lot for another proposed office tower. On the east side is an eight-storey existing office building belonging to the same owner. Surrounding buildings are high-rise offices and hotel buildings.

programme • The owner required a building for its corporate headquarters being a large public-listed company with interests in plantation (rubber and palm oil), engineering, shipping and insurance. The client wanted a building with exceptional design features of a high-level quality in finishes and have it constructed in the shortest time possible to achieve a foothold in a competitive real-estate market. It was decided to fast-track the project from design to occupancy. Construction period is 18 months.

structural system • The structural frame is constructed out of reinforced concrete, designed to withstand earthquakes to a force of 6.5 on Richter Scale. Prestressed reinforced concrete beams are used to carry the large span (column free) office floors (111 ft. maximum clear span). All the lift cores are cast using a continuous slipform. The exterior of the building is clad in an aluminium frame and *Alucobond* (aluminium) panels with Fluorocarbon paint (Kynar 500) finish (14,563 sq m). The main lift lobby is finished in dark rose coloured granite and dark brown marble with Alucobond (aluminium) ceiling. Shopfronts and window-frames are natural anodized aluminium.

major materials • Materials used include granite, marble, ceramic tiles and spray tile on other wall area.

mechanical system • The office floors are cooled with central watercooled package air-System:conditioning units with variable-air-volume control. A 'clean' electrical power supply-line installed for sensitive electronic equipment (computers) and a master antennae system for television signal reception.

dispersed planting

intermixing

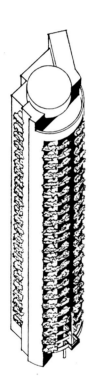

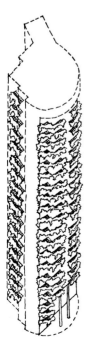

Scotiabank

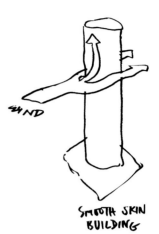

SMOOTH SKIN BUILDING

BUILDING WITH COOLING-FINS (ENGINE-CYLINDER COOLING FINS ANALOGY)

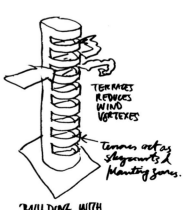

TERRACES REDUCES WIND VORTEXES

Terraces act as skycourts & planting zones.

BUILDING WITH RECESSED TERRACES

1 unprotected curtain wall

unprotected glazing

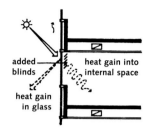

added blinds

heat gain in glass

heat gain into internal space

2 deep recesses and balconies

recessed glazing and balconies

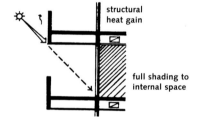

structural heat gain

full shading to internal space

3 recessed windows

recessed windows

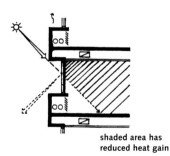

shaded area has reduced heat gain

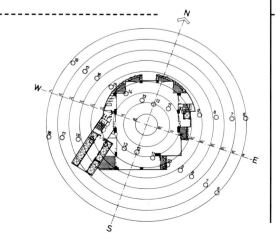

4 horizontal fins

horizontal fins

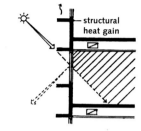

structural heat gain

4 vertical fins

vertical fins

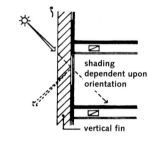

shading dependent upon orientation

vertical fin

6 deep recesses combined with balcony terraces, planters, heat-sink cladding

double skin with recessed balconies

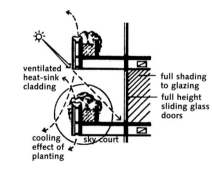

ventilated heat-sink cladding

cooling effect of planting

sky court

full shading to glazing

full height sliding glass doors

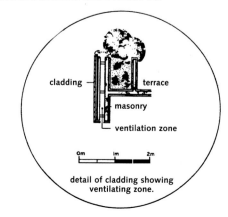

cladding

terrace

masonry

ventilation zone

detail of cladding showing ventilating zone.

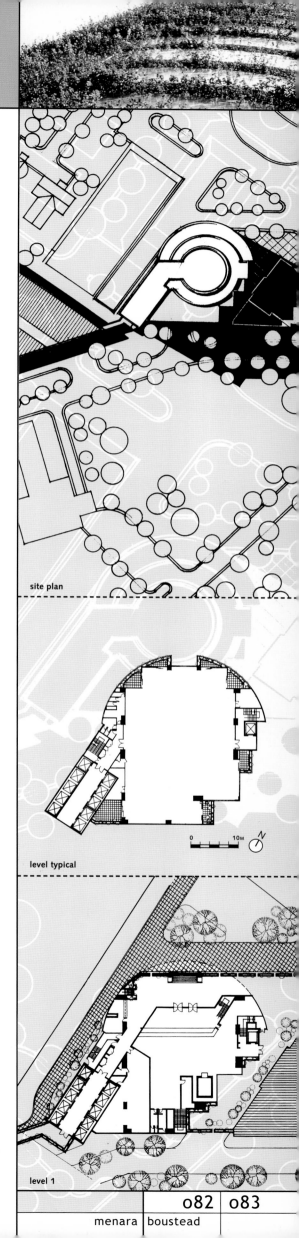

site plan

level typical

0   10M   N

level 1

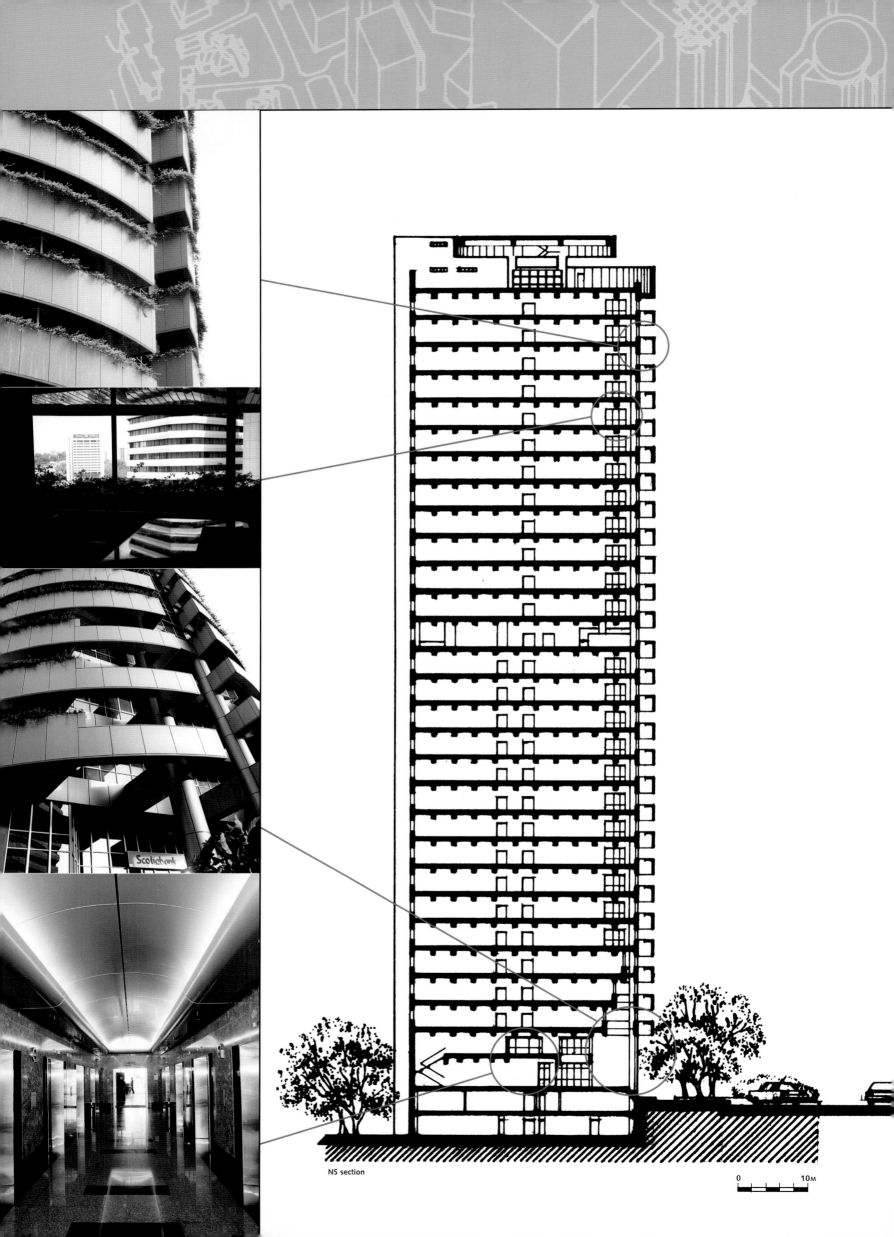

NS section

0   10м

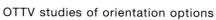

design features

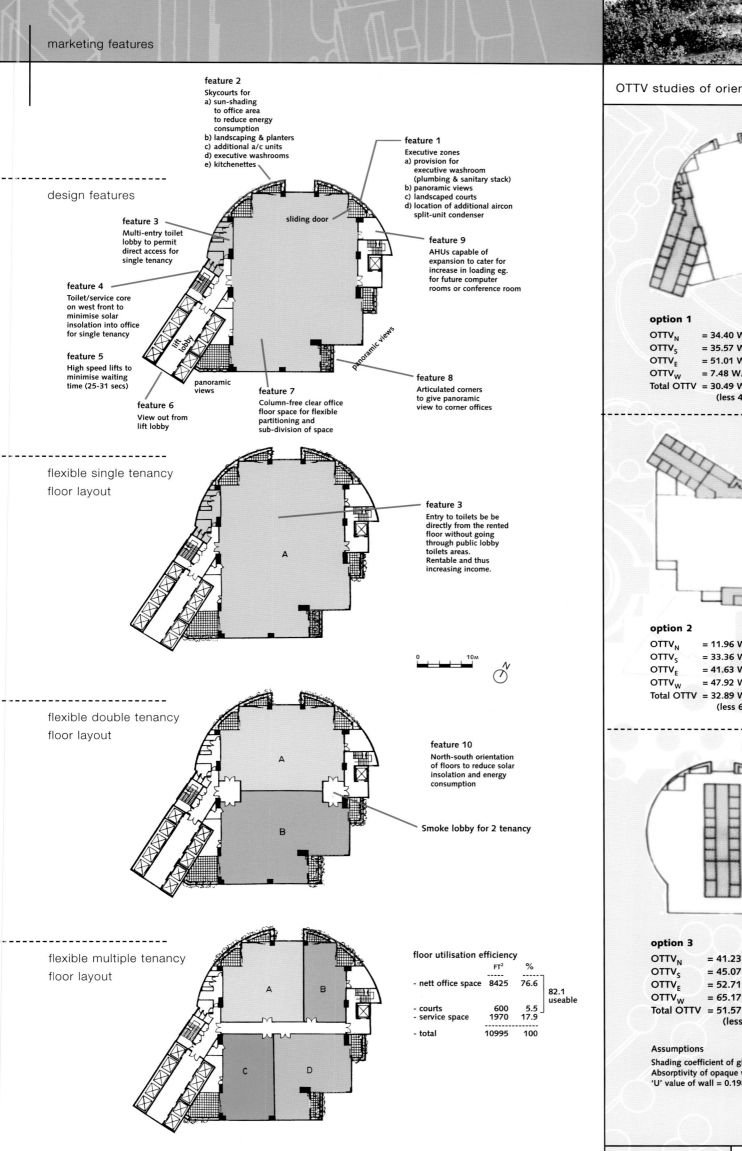

feature 2
Skycourts for
a) sun-shading
   to office area
   to reduce energy
   consumption
b) landscaping & planters
c) additional a/c units
d) executive washrooms
e) kitchenettes

feature 1
Executive zones
a) provision for
   executive washroom
   (plumbing & sanitary stack)
b) panoramic views
c) landscaped courts
d) location of additional aircon
   split-unit condenser

sliding door

feature 3
Multi-entry toilet
lobby to permit
direct access for
single tenancy

feature 9
AHUs capable of
expansion to cater for
increase in loading eg.
for future computer
rooms or conference room

feature 4
Toilet/service core
on west front to
minimise solar
insolation into office
for single tenancy

lift lobby

feature 5
High speed lifts to
minimise waiting
time (25-31 secs)

panoramic views

feature 7
Column-free clear office
floor space for flexible
partitioning and
sub-division of space

feature 8
Articulated corners
to give panoramic
view to corner offices

feature 6
View out from
lift lobby

panoramic views

flexible single tenancy floor layout

A

feature 3
Entry to toilets be be
directly from the rented
floor without going
through public lobby
toilets areas.
Rentable and thus
increasing income.

0   10M

N

flexible double tenancy floor layout

A

B

feature 10
North-south orientation
of floors to reduce solar
insolation and energy
consumption

Smoke lobby for 2 tenancy

flexible multiple tenancy floor layout

A   B

C   D

floor utilisation efficiency

	FT²	%
- nett office space	8425	76.6
- courts	600	5.5
- service space	1970	17.9
- total	10995	100

82.1 useable

OTTV studies of orientation options

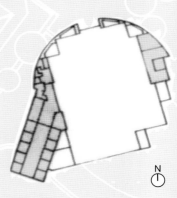

option 1
$OTTV_N$ = 34.40 W/m²
$OTTV_S$ = 35.57 W/m²
$OTTV_E$ = 51.01 W/m²
$OTTV_W$ = 7.48 W/m²
Total OTTV = 30.49 W/m²
              (less 40%)

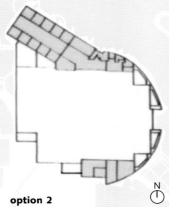

option 2
$OTTV_N$ = 11.96 W/m²
$OTTV_S$ = 33.36 W/m²
$OTTV_E$ = 41.63 W/m²
$OTTV_W$ = 47.92 W/m²
Total OTTV = 32.89 W/m²
              (less 64%)

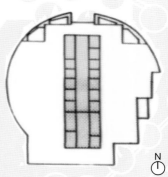

option 3
$OTTV_N$ = 41.23 W/m²
$OTTV_S$ = 45.07 W/m²
$OTTV_E$ = 52.71 W/m²
$OTTV_W$ = 65.17 W/m²
Total OTTV = 51.57 W/m²
              (less 100%)

Assumptions
Shading coefficient of glass = 0.80
Absorptivity of opaque wall = 0.50
'U' value of wall = 0.1989

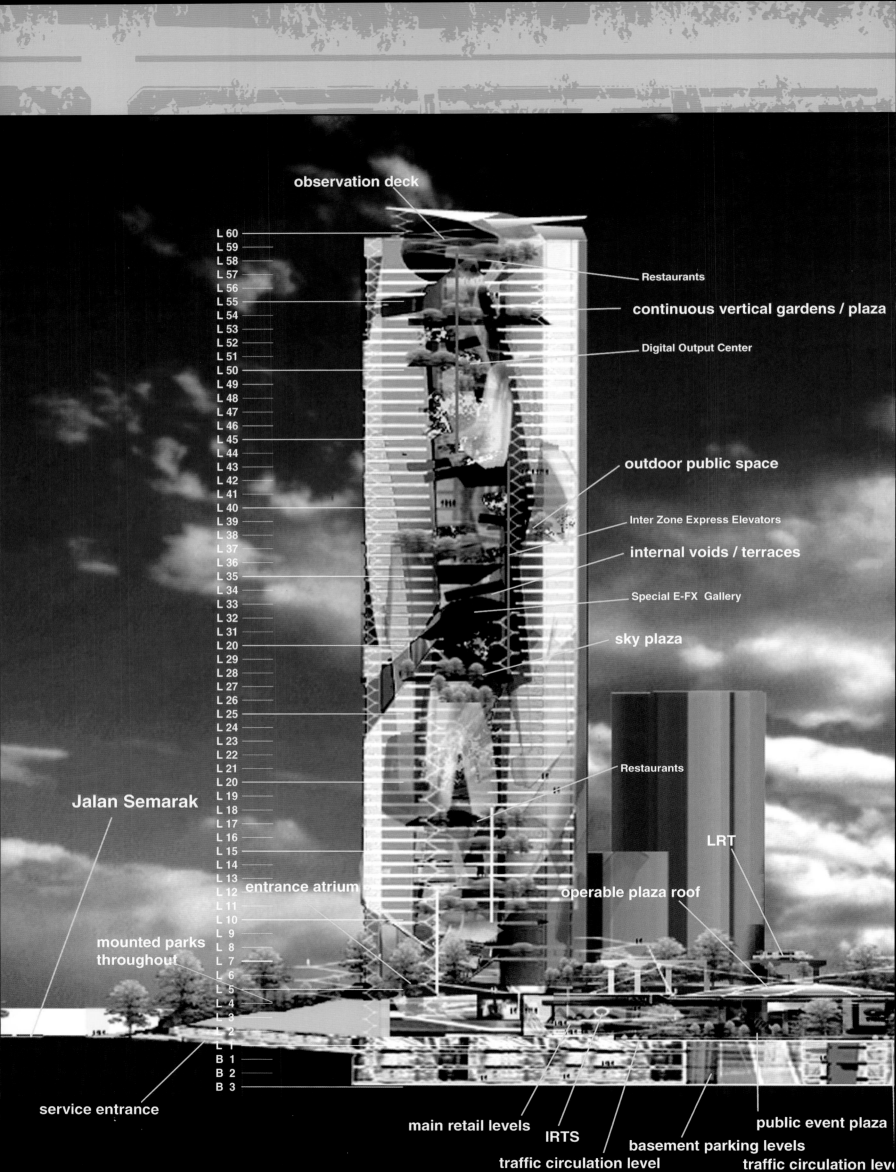

observation deck

Restaurants

continuous vertical gardens / plaza

Digital Output Center

outdoor public space

Inter Zone Express Elevators

internal voids / terraces

Special E-FX Gallery

sky plaza

L 60
L 59
L 58
L 57
L 56
L 55
L 54
L 53
L 52
L 51
L 50
L 49
L 48
L 47
L 46
L 45
L 44
L 43
L 42
L 41
L 40
L 39
L 38
L 37
L 36
L 35
L 34
L 33
L 32
L 31
L 20
L 29
L 28
L 27
L 26
L 25
L 24
L 23
L 22
L 21
L 20
L 19
L 18
L 17
L 16
L 15
L 14
L 13
L 12
L 11
L 10
L 9
L 8
L 7
L 6
L 5
L 4
L 3
L 2
L 1
B 1
B 2
B 3

Jalan Semarak

Restaurants

LRT

entrance atrium

operable plaza roof

**mounted parks
throughout**

service entrance

main retail levels

IRTS

basement parking levels

traffic circulation level

public event plaza

traffic circulation lev

owner TRC Development Sdn Bhd
location Lot 4582, Mukim of Setapak,
Kuala Lumpur, Malaysia
latitude 3.2°N
nos of storeys 60-storey signature office tower
five 30-storey office towers
date start Pending
areas Total gross area 708,178 sq m
Total net area 530,669 sq m
site area 167,286 sq m
plot ratio 1:4

design features
• The scheme consists of a 47 acre landscape park
within which the buildings are set and is serviced by a
central series of public plazas, boulevard walkways and
a car access routes. the LRT System is integrated into
the site with a centralised station at the junction between
the retail, commercial and university facilities.

• The building brings together the principles of the
bioclimatic approach to the design of tall buildings and urban
design developed over the previous decade by the firm
In particular, the scheme has the following features:
• Landscaping is applied to the entire development.
The building is accessed via the landscaped ground plane
of the site. Water gardens and soft landscaping enhance
the pedestrian routes throughout the site.
• All areas within the site are linked by an integrated
pedestrian transport system. Providing shaded car-free
access to all facilities within the site.
• Landscaped and terraced skycourts have been
incorporated at the floors of the office towers providing
building occupants the opportunity to relax in pleasant
surroundings. to maintain connectivity between floors,
these skycourts form a continuos vertical link, both visually
and physically threading together all storeys.
• Integrated Building Management Systems control building
internal conditions by monitoring the immediate (external)
surroundings through a series of environment sensors located
on the roof.

apartment tower

office tower

main entrance to
the exhibition gallery

IRTS

main retail block

service entrance

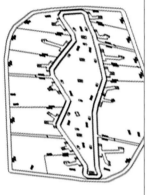

The BATC Tower is a **signature high-rise office development**, which stands at the centre of a massive proposal for Kuala Lumpur.

At the level of urban design, the overall project is one of the largest assemblies that Yeang has ever proposed. The scheme, for 47 acres of landscaped park space, is serviced by a central range of public plazas, boulevard walkways and public car access routes, together with a centralised station for the LRT System, which is situated at the junction between the retail, commercial and university facilities.

In addition to the BATC Tower, the development includes five 30-storey office towers all designed within the principles of the **bioclimatic agenda** and incorporating Yeang's ideas for **vertical urbanism**.

In overall content, this project for the Business and Advanced Technology Centre (BATC) and a Branch of UTM (University Teknologi Malaysia) will incorporate facilities for a School of Advanced Education programmes and an integrated research and development complex for some 20 institutes and centres. The proposal has resonances with similar developments in major universities, such as Cambridge (UK), and other locations on a global basis. Together with this, Yeang has proposed a high-tech office park; convention and exposition centres; a multimedia and IT college; mega-theme mall for retail and entertainment; major outdoor public spaces with cultural uses; residential accommodation for students, post-graduates and academic researchers; a four-star hotel for visitors, tourists and local residents with business centres and facilities; and a public park and boulevard that runs throughout the development project. The central theme is that of a **landscaped setting** and a sheltered traffic-free environment.

The central spine of the project running north to south, is essentially surrounded by the major higher forms, that include the BATC Tower on the western side.

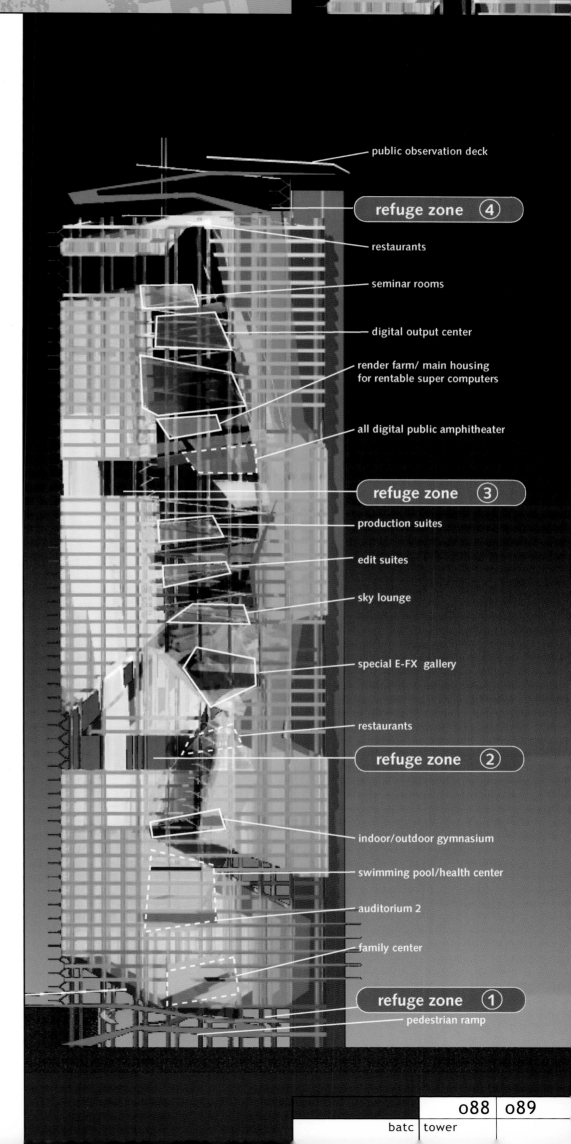

- public observation deck
- **refuge zone** ④
- restaurants
- seminar rooms
- digital output center
- render farm/ main housing for rentable super computers
- all digital public amphitheater
- **refuge zone** ③
- production suites
- edit suites
- sky lounge
- special E-FX gallery
- restaurants
- **refuge zone** ②
- indoor/outdoor gymnasium
- swimming pool/health center
- auditorium 2
- family center
- **refuge zone** ①
- pedestrian ramp

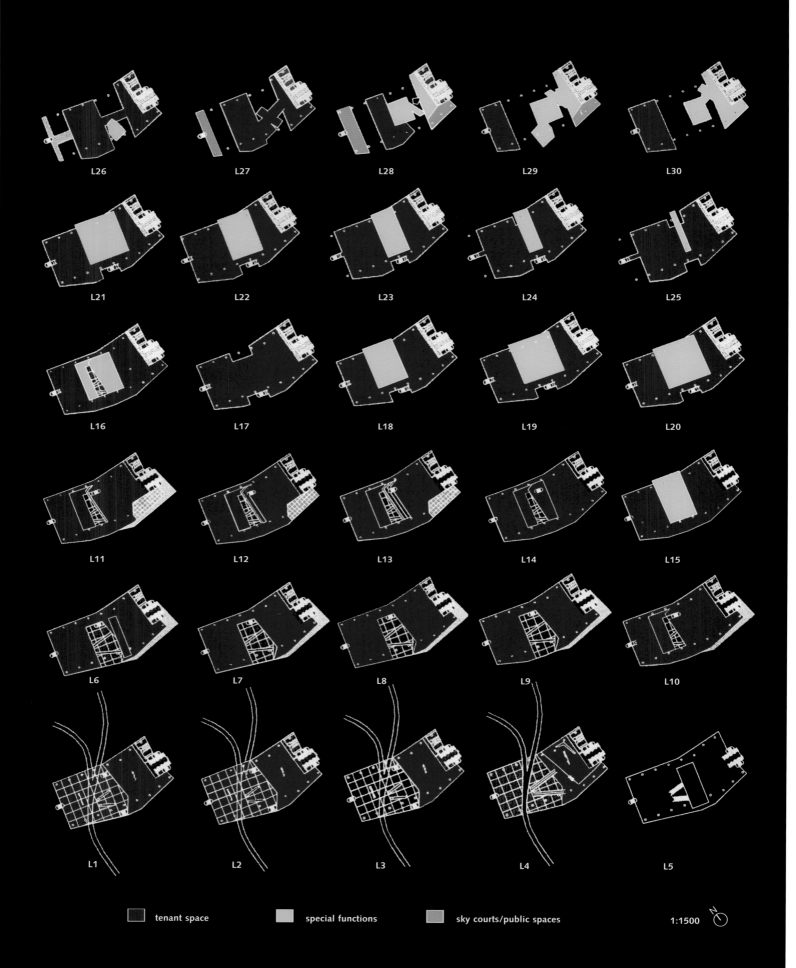

tenant space   special functions   sky courts/public spaces

1:1500

In itself, the BATC signature Tower stands amongst the most significant of Yeang's **bioclimatic skyscrape**r proposals. United within this major form are two major principles: first the inclusion of vertically linked, continuous landscaping applied to **terraced skycourts**, and second the application of **vertical urbanism**, which Yeang describes as **'places-in the sky'** – the amenities of a city, vertically distributed throughout the tower-form. While this has become a recurrent, objective proposition in Yeang's work, the BATC Tower is one of the richest designs that he has composed in this respect. The design is further strengthened by the extensive facilities of the related plaza and Exposition Centre, which share a similar **climatic openness.**

In reviewing the BATC Tower floor plans, over some 60 or more levels, several features are immediately clear. The lower levels are marked by the entrances and transportation links, and the higher levels by extensive linked tenant areas, interspersed with special functions, skycourts and public spaces. Throughout the vertical arrangement, linkages in the form of pedestrian ramps are included at intervals, augmenting the elevator systems and facilitating a flowing spatiality of movement.

The special functions include restaurants at various upward locations, an E-FX Gallery, and a Digital Output Center. These are supported by sky plazas, outdoor public space, internal atria and continuous vertical gardens. The whole assembly is capped by a planar wing-form roof, which shelters high-level observation decks.

The skyscraper has four refuge zones distributed vertically, which define the sets of tenant floors and public uses that are incorporated. At the lower levels gymnasia, swimming pool and health center are accompanied by an auditorium and family center. Similarly at the higher levels, seminar rooms, computer and production suites are mixed together with tenant spaces, sky lounges and an all-digital public amphitheatre. These groupings serve merely as examples of the extensive range of provision and occupancy that Yeang has induced within the rising vertical framework – a continuously upward flowing **urbanistic spatiality**.

Characteristically, the hot eastern tower facade is solar protected by a rising range of services and elevators, with the longest elevations facing south and north. The canted semi-rectilinear plan is sliced open at intervals to allow air-flow ventilation to both offices and public spaces. Together with the skycourts, fabric engineering and Integrated Building Management Systems (which control internal conditions by monitoring the immediate external surroundings through environmental sensors located on the roof), the entire building is part of a **bioclimatic entity**, which applies to the whole project and site.

Although it remains as a project to date, the BATC Tower and its associated master-plan summarise an important stage in Yeang's work, seen overall, and many of the innovations contribute to its future development.

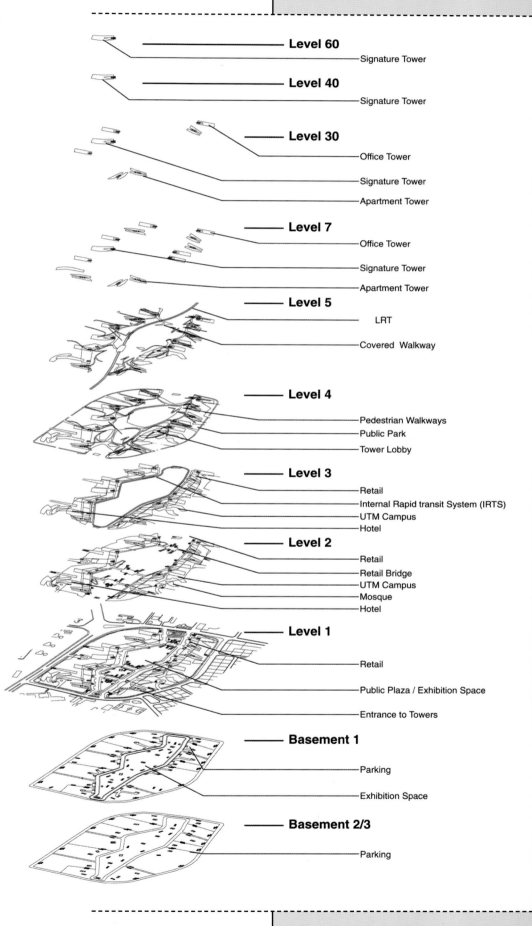

Level 60
- Signature Tower

Level 40
- Signature Tower

Level 30
- Office Tower
- Signature Tower
- Apartment Tower

Level 7
- Office Tower
- Signature Tower
- Apartment Tower

Level 5
- LRT
- Covered Walkway

Level 4
- Pedestrian Walkways
- Public Park
- Tower Lobby

Level 3
- Retail
- Internal Rapid transit System (IRTS)
- UTM Campus
- Hotel

Level 2
- Retail
- Retail Bridge
- UTM Campus
- Mosque
- Hotel

Level 1
- Retail
- Public Plaza / Exhibition Space
- Entrance to Towers

Basement 1
- Parking
- Exhibition Space

Basement 2/3
- Parking

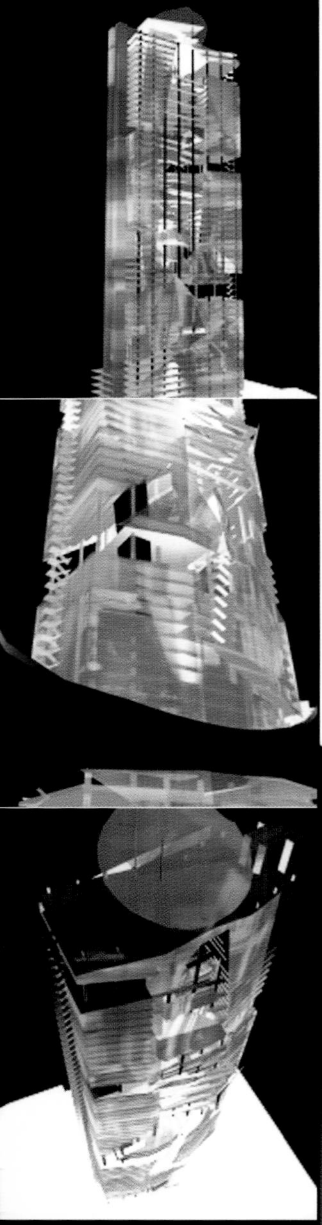

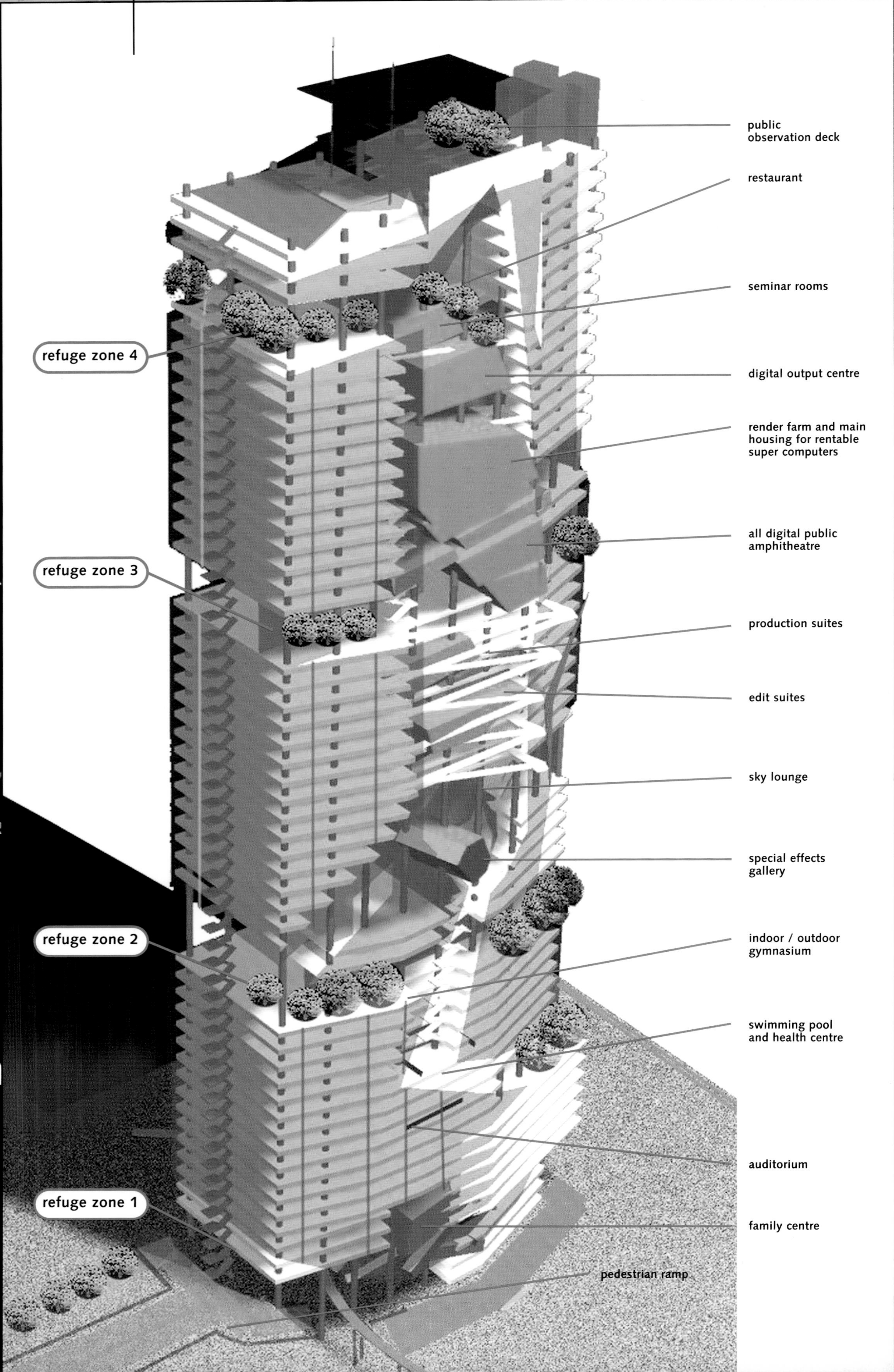

public observation deck

restaurant

seminar rooms

digital output centre

render farm and main housing for rentable super computers

all digital public amphitheatre

production suites

edit suites

sky lounge

special effects gallery

indoor / outdoor gymnasium

swimming pool and health centre

auditorium

family centre

pedestrian ramp

refuge zone 4

refuge zone 3

refuge zone 2

refuge zone 1

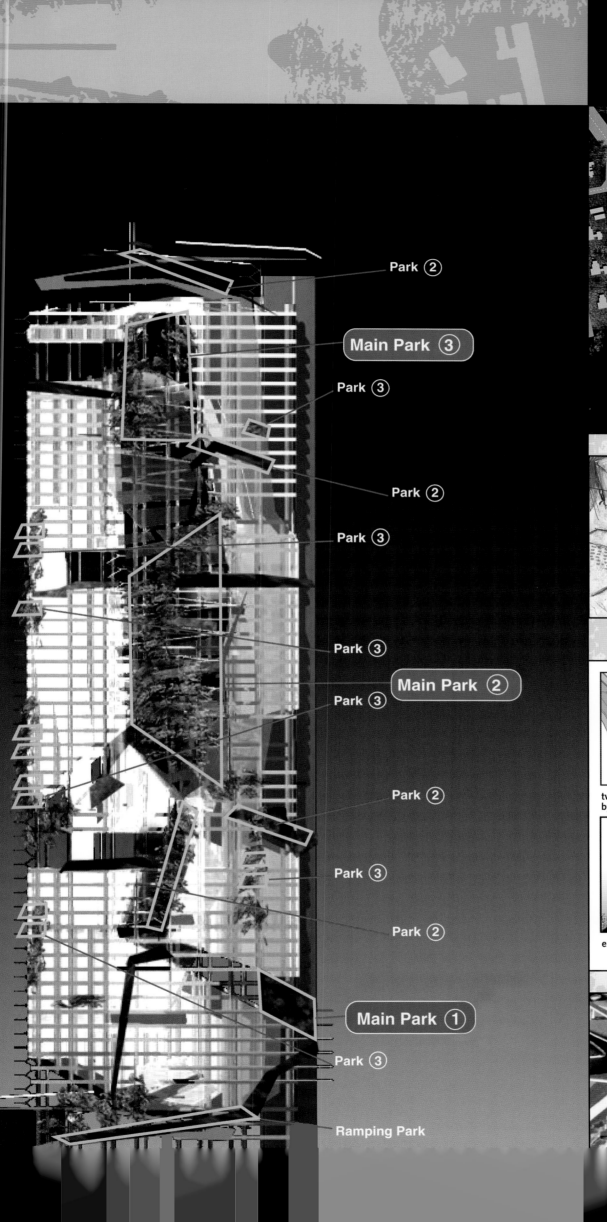

Park ②

Main Park ③

Park ③

Park ②

Park ③

Park ③

Main Park ②

Park ③

Park ②

Park ③

Park ②

Main Park ①

Park ③

Ramping Park

improving connectivity by
enabling increase in biodiversity

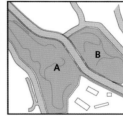

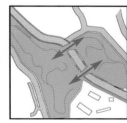

two sites separated
by road

landscaped bridge
over road

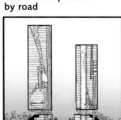

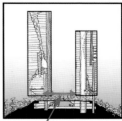

existing

landscaped bridge improves
ecosystem connectivity

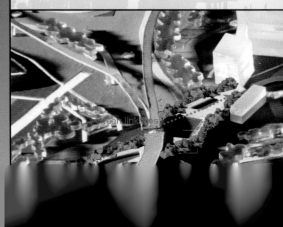

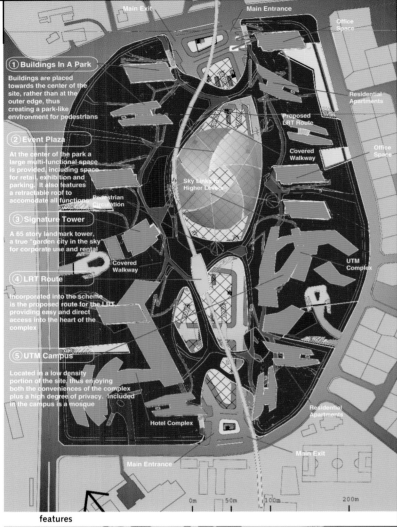

① Buildings In A Park

Buildings are placed towards the center of the site, rather than at the outer edge, thus creating a park-like environment for pedestrians

② Event Plaza

At the center of the park a large multi-functional space is provided, including space for retail, exhibition and parking. It also features a retractable roof to accomodate all functions.

③ Signature Tower

A 65 story landmark tower, a true "garden city in the sky" for corporate use and rental

④ LRT Route

Incorporated into the scheme is the proposed route for the LRT, providing easy and direct access into the heart of the complex

⑤ UTM Campus

Located in a low density portion of the site, thus enjoying both the conveniences of the complex plus a high degree of privacy. Included in the campus is a mosque.

features

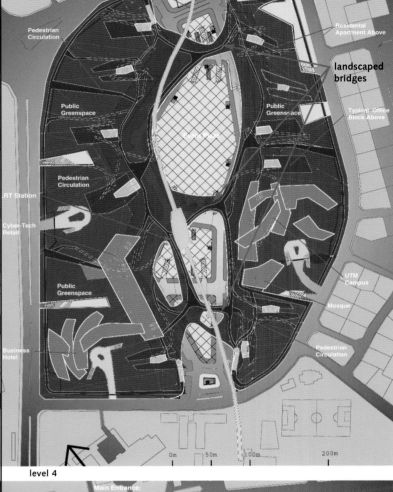

landscaped bridges

level 4

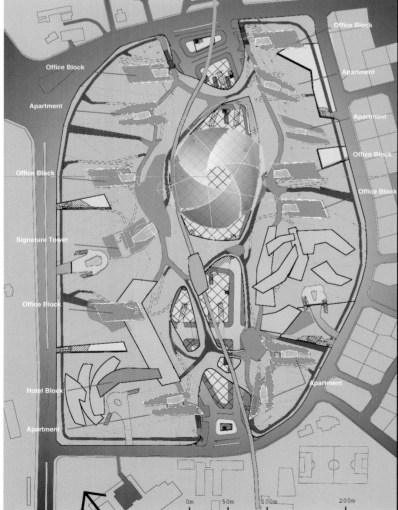

level 7

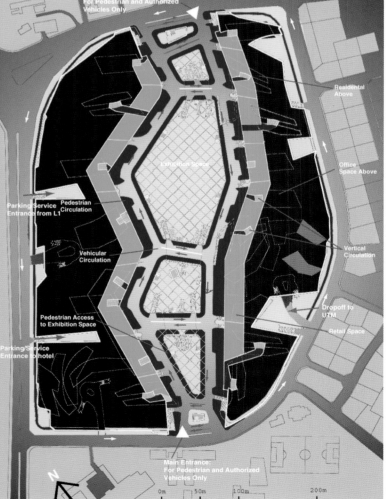

level 1

signature tower

plaza

multi-use events plaza
with retractable "camera-shutter" canopy

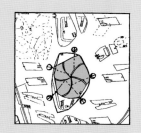

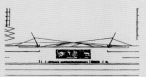

cultural use

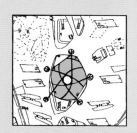

exhibition use

recreation use

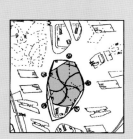

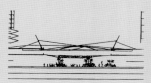

general use

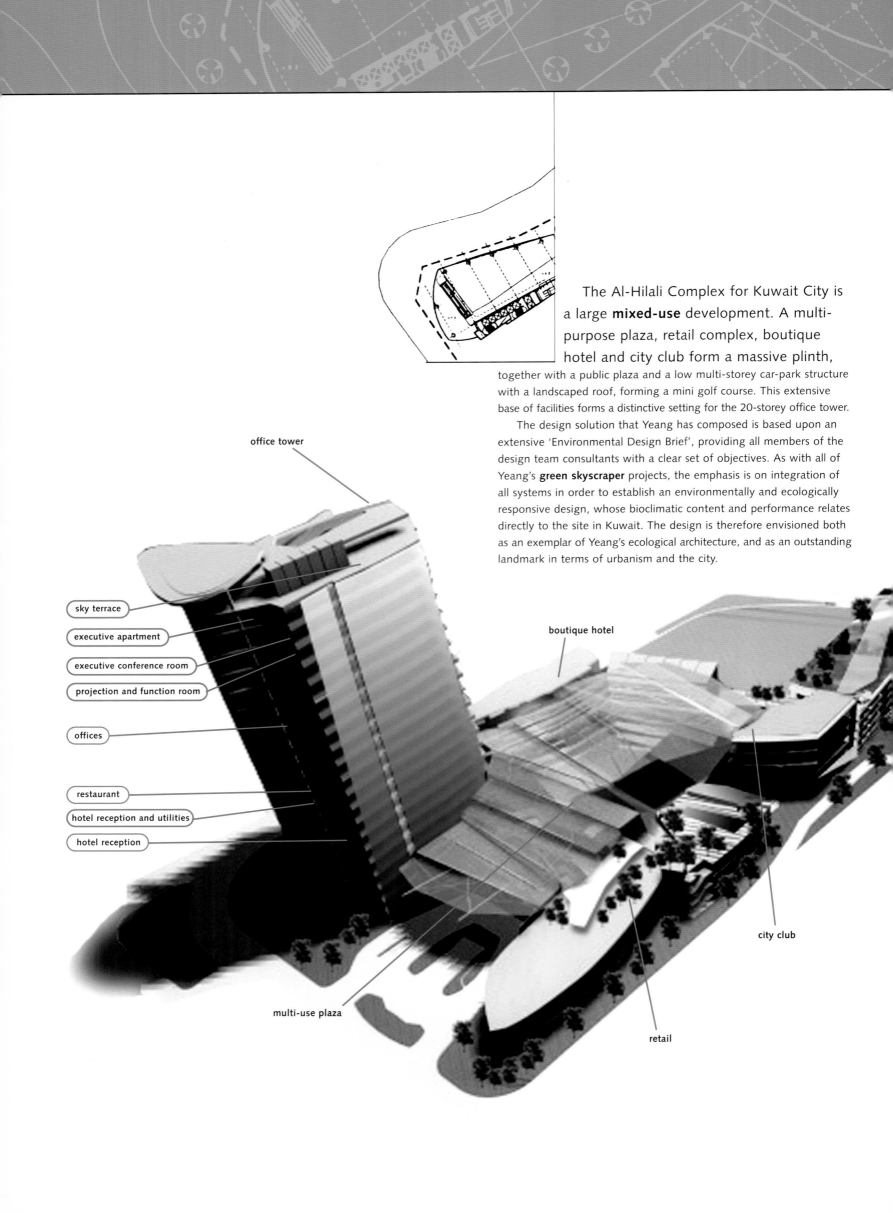

The Al-Hilali Complex for Kuwait City is a large **mixed-use** development. A multi-purpose plaza, retail complex, boutique hotel and city club form a massive plinth, together with a public plaza and a low multi-storey car-park structure with a landscaped roof, forming a mini golf course. This extensive base of facilities forms a distinctive setting for the 20-storey office tower.

The design solution that Yeang has composed is based upon an extensive 'Environmental Design Brief', providing all members of the design team consultants with a clear set of objectives. As with all of Yeang's **green skyscraper** projects, the emphasis is on integration of all systems in order to establish an environmentally and ecologically responsive design, whose bioclimatic content and performance relates directly to the site in Kuwait. The design is therefore envisioned both as an exemplar of Yeang's ecological architecture, and as an outstanding landmark in terms of urbanism and the city.

office tower

sky terrace

executive apartment

executive conference room

projection and function room

offices

restaurant

hotel reception and utilities

hotel reception

boutique hotel

city club

multi-use plaza

retail

al-hilali tower

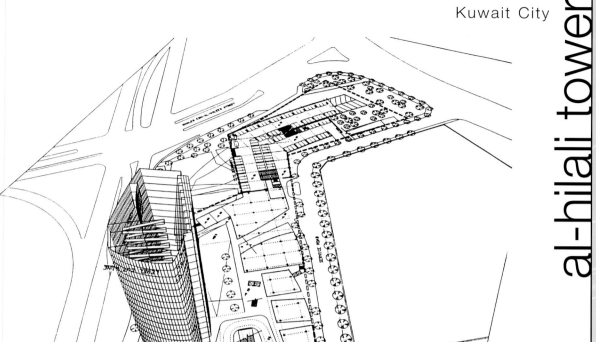

owner Kuwait Real Estate Company
location Kuwait City
latitude 29.3°N
nos of storeys 20 storeys + 1 mezannine floor
date start –
completion date –
areas Gross area 32,044 sq m
Nett area 24,755 sq m
site area 13,000 sq m overall
4,000 sq m for commercial complex
plot ratio 1:2.46

design features • The client's brief was to develop the site to accommodate:
- a commercial complex with three levels retail mall and an office tower above
- a multi-storey carpark block
- surface car-park and a public garden.

The strategy is to respond to the brief with a solution which will be bioclimatically and ecologically responsive to the site. The design is also to be recognisable landmark for the area and serve as an example of a site-specific design solution. A unique design feature is the wedged-shape landscaped roof over the car-park that mounds up to the roof of the retail podium. Air wells are cut into this wedge to bring light and ventilation into the submerged car-parking block.

The design strategy and solutions adopted are as follows:

• Separation of enclosed spaces and transitional spaces (being non-enclosed or semi-enclosed spaces which vary in enclosure depending on the seasons of the year).
The scheme has the following areas as transitional spaces:
- the central plaza, which has an openable glass roof over that opens or shuts depending on the climatic conditions
- skycourts within the office towers
- semi-enclosed access passageway to the boutique hotel rooms.
• Skycourts serve as buffer zones between interior and exterior spaces. Besides providing shading, they enable users to step out from the enclosed floor areas to directly experience and view the external environment.
• In adapting the solar-path, the tower complex is located on a west-east axis in order to reduce solar insulation on the longer sides of the tower. Service cores are positioned to serve as ;solar buffers;. Windows areas are positioned to face the direction requiring the least solar insulation.
• In the plaza and foodcourt areas are water features and planting which contribute to creating a cooler environment.
• The west facade and east facades will have a double-skin flue wall as a ventilating space, with its volume increasing with height. These flue walls exhaust air as ventilation through the facade construction and at the same time minimize solar heat gain.
• Optimising of diurnal wind-rose by shaping of the tower floor plate and external walls for natural ventilation and cooling, thus reducing need for mechanical, ventilation and air-conditioning. Service core areas (ie. lift lobbies, staircases, toilets) are located on the periphery to receive natural ventilation and natural sunlight.
• Solar shading is provided by sun-shading devices of perforated panels.
• Narrow width of floor plates and use of clear window glass is adopted to reduce need for artificial lighting thus reducing lighting costs.
• Vegetation on the facade and rooftops (over the car-park) balances the site's inorganic and organic composition and stabilizes the micro-climate.

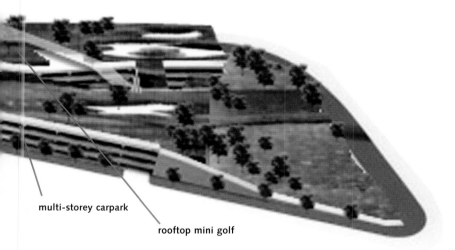

multi-storey carpark

rooftop mini golf

Yeang's environmental design brief incorporates much of his **green design theory**, and provides a thorough, comprehensive basis for the achievement of a complex of sustainable intensive buildings, across the whole spectrum of design issues involved. This ranges from the general considerations of **transitional spaces** through semi-enclosed to **enclosed spaces**, related to the whole project, and the detailed analysis of **building configuration** and its relationship with the ambient environment and the resolution of this in, for example, the design of the office tower.

A major instance of **transitional** space underpins the design of the Central Plaza within the shopping complex. This space, intended for multi-seasonal activities and foodcourt includes major ramps for peripheral pedestrian circulation. The key element is an **operable glass roof**, a layered transparent covering, which opens or shuts depending on climatic conditions and the seasons of the year. For example, the roof is fully closed in hot summer months acting as a shading device, and open during other seasons. It can also be opened at night, for heat flushing of the space.

penthouse with indoor / outdoor garden at level 17–20

helicopter landing platform

north tower facade

flue wall with sun-shading for maximum solar protection at hot west facade

south west tower facade

east face is to have a double-layered flue wall as a ventilating space

solar shading throughout the east facade will provide sufficient protection against morning sun

north tower facade

photovoltaic cells are located at south facade to maximize collection of passive solar energy

south tower facade

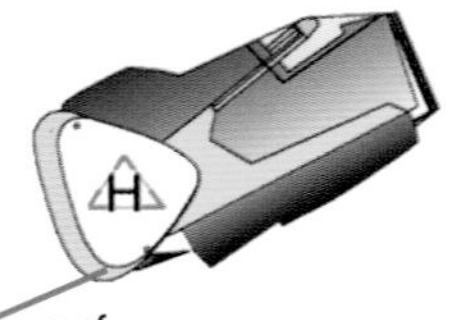

roof

public circulation/space

office

elevators/stairs

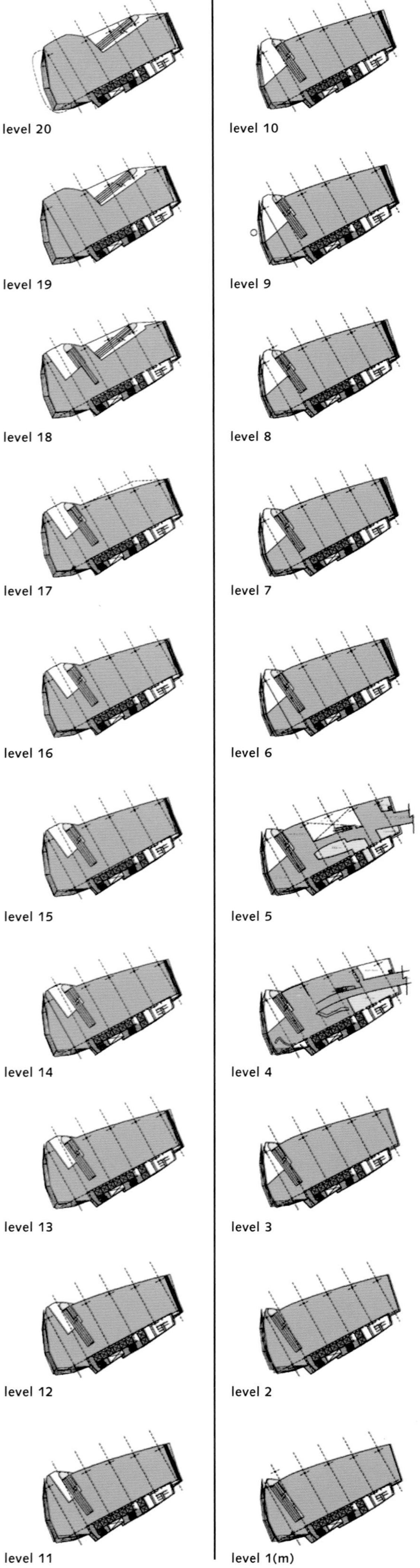

level 20

level 19

level 18

level 17

level 16

level 15

level 14

level 13

level 12

level 11

level 10

level 9

level 8

level 7

level 6

level 5

level 4

level 3

level 2

level 1(m)

Similarly, the office tower incorporates a series of **skycourts** as transitional spaces and in accord with Yeang's design principles for buffer zones between interior and exterior spaces, which also provide shading and locations for planted and landscaped terraces.

The low-rise retail buildings incorporate a series of vertical shafts, or **chimneys**, which permit air from the lower spaces to exhaust above the roof level – a system similar to the 'wind-towers' of the Dubai Towers project.

What emerges overall is that Yeang is defining very clearly the range of space types within a massive construct, identifying those which benefit from passive principles and then using a range of means to reduce energy consumption and provide sustainability to enclosed serviced spaces.

A prime example of this integrated, concentrated design methodology is evidenced in the **enclosure options** of the **office tower** and its shell, and the adaptation of the **building configuration** to its local environment, the Al-Hilali site being 29.30° north of the equator.

The office tower is related to the solar-path, with the shaped plan-form located on a west-east axis in order to reduce solar impact on the longer sides of the tower. The key element of the plan is the linear grouping of **service cores** – lifts, stairs and service spaces, on the southern side of the form, in order to act as a **solar-buffer**, or shield-wall on the hot face. Each facade is considered in detail, in order to reduce **solar-heat** gain to the interiors and to provide opportunities for **fresh-air ventilation** – both as an acoustic barrier and to augment the **expression** of Yeang's green skyscraper aesthetic.

In this connection, both east and west facades incorporate a double layered **flue-wall** as a ventilating space, with a canted section whose volume increases with height. This arrangement exhausts air as ventilation through the facade construction, and at the same time minimises solar heat gain, together with external sun-shading devices. Yeang has then explored the detailed ventilation facilities these facades offer, including the Coanda effect, which produces a stable and draught-free air movement within the interior space, together with natural and night ventilation, which exploits temperature extremes. In addition, the **flue-wall** protects the building in summer by ventilation and in winter, in a closed condition, as insulation.

In contrast, the north facade of the tower is a full-height glazed curtain-wall, and the protective south facade shield incorporates photo-voltaic cells to maximise the collection of passive solar energy.

The overall **organic form** of the tower is shaped to induce natural ventilation and cooling – a basic of sustainable design. Within, the tower floor-plans are marked by the inclusion of ramps connecting the floor levels, in addition to the elevators, and without a four-floor-high penthouse and roof gardens cap the summit of the north façade, with an oversailing helipad.

In the overall performance agenda, Yeang has again applied the criteria of embodied energy assessment, low-energy operation – for example by the use of 'thin'-plan floor plates – which reduce artificial lighting and optimise natural lighting, and the consideration of recycling of materials.

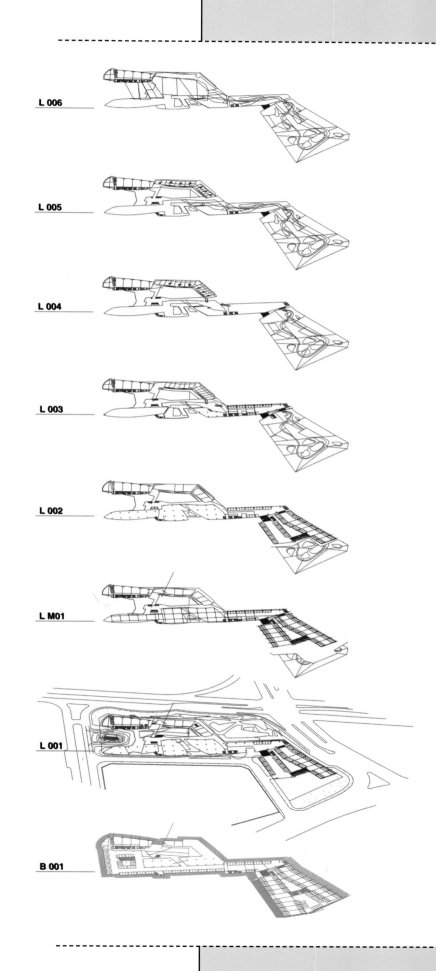

L 006

L 005

L 004

L 003

L 002

L M01

L 001

B 001

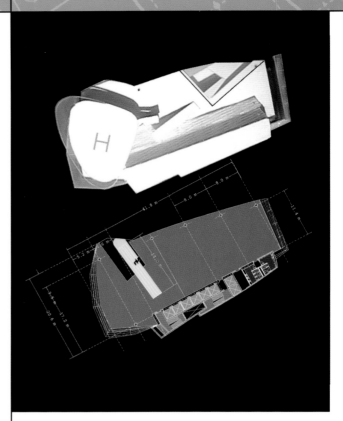

tenant occupancy options

tower occupancy with ramp option | tower occupancy without ramp

level 11 — A | level 11 — A

single tenant

level 11 — A / B | level 11 — A / B

double tenant

level 11 — A / B / C | level 11 — A / B / C

triple tenant

level 11 — A / B / C / D | level 11 — A / B / C / D / E

multiple tenant

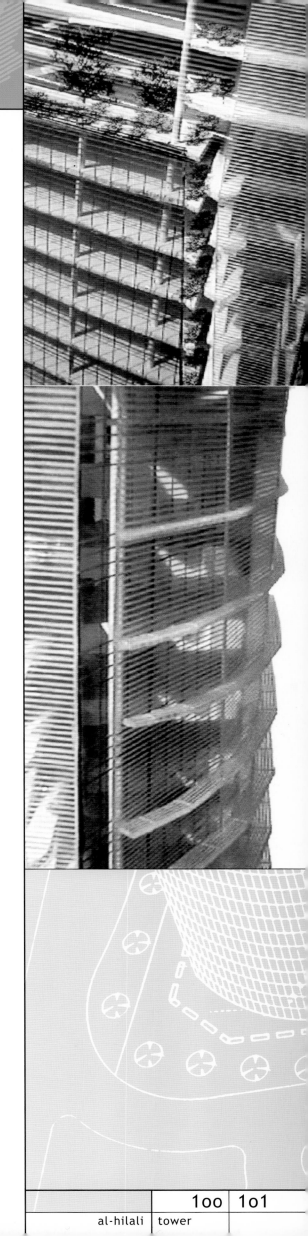

As with all of Yeang's projects, the crucial factor of the ecological design of the skyscraper is the act of **balance** between **inorganic** and **organic** content of the form – achieved by the incorporation of rich, extensive vertical landscaping. In this case, the vertical is augmented by the horizontal landscaping of the base.

This is yet another case, where the design, its objectives and criteria and their application, are **documented** in such a way that enables the **client** to understand and participate in the process and realisation of the total project.

Related to the context of Kuwait, Yeang has made specific the **nature and qualities** of his architecture that reach towards a **sustainable** future.

site plan

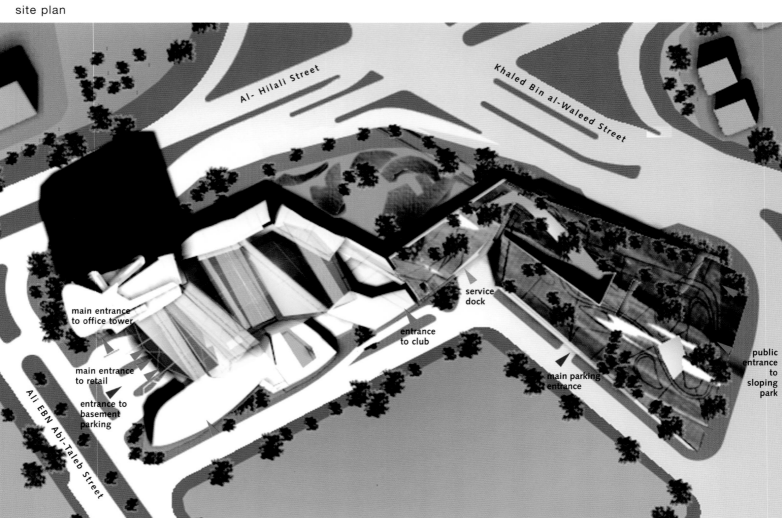

main entrance
to office tower

main entrance
to retail

entrance to
basement
parking

Ali EBN Abi-Taleb Street

Al- Hilali Street

Khaled Bin al-Waleed Street

service
dock

entrance
to club

main parking
entrance

public
entrance
to
sloping
park

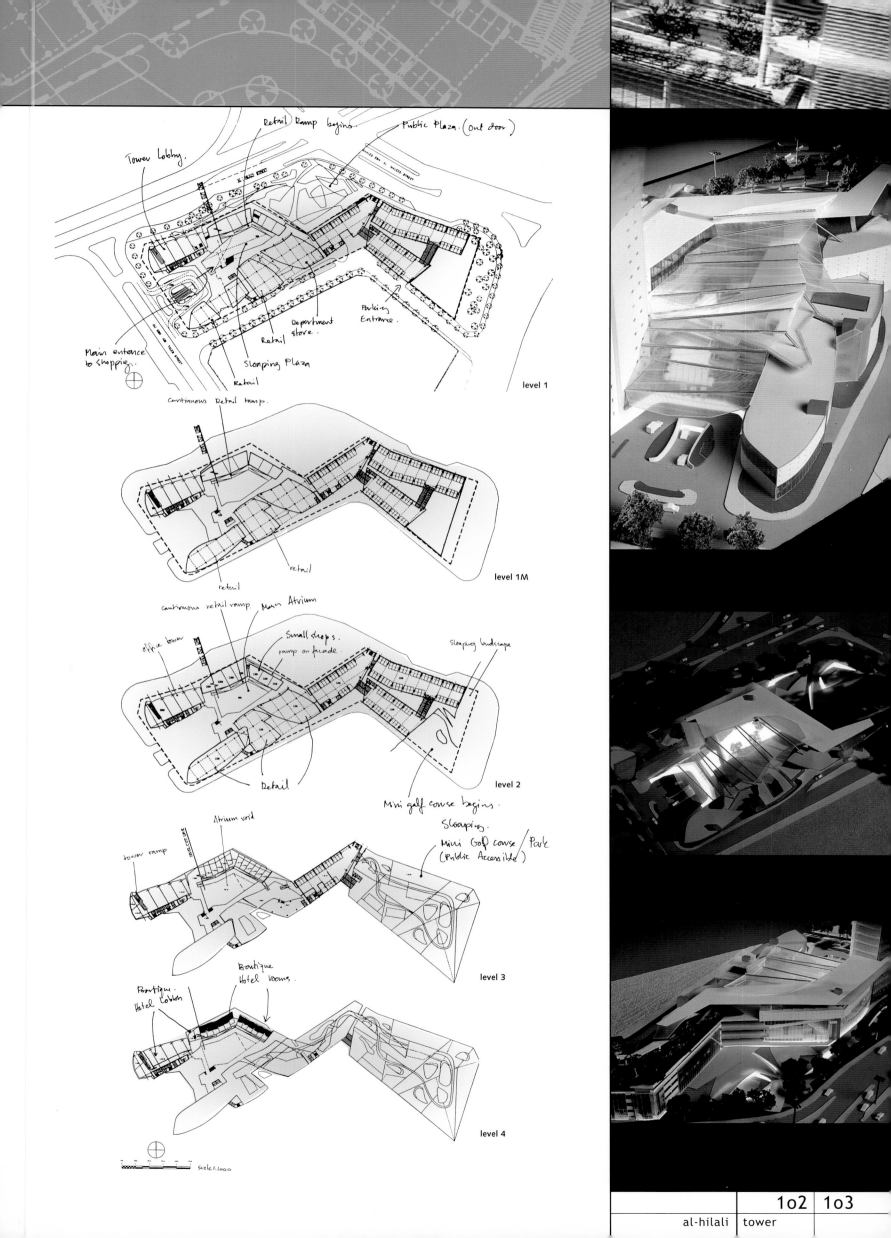

Tower Lobby.

Retail Ramp begins.

Public Plaza. (Out door)

Main entrance to shopping.

Department store.

Parking Entrance.

Retail

Sloaping Plaza

Retail

level 1

Continuous Retail ramp.

retail

retail

level 1M

Continuous retail ramp. Main Atrium

office tower

Small shops. ramp on facade.

Sloaping landscape

Detail

level 2

Mini golf course begins.

Sloaping.

Mini Golf course / Park (Public Accessible)

Atrium void

tower ramp

level 3

Boutique Hotel rooms.

Boutique. Hotel Lobby

level 4

Scale 1:1000

louvred roof system keeps plaza area bright and cool

operable sliding roof gives a different experience when open

retail at L1

pathway of boutique hotel
overlooks main plaza

office tower

ramping shopping arcade

retail at LM 1

sloping plaza leading down
to basement retail area

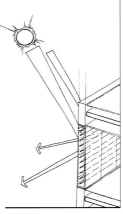

The building project is essentially that of an office tower with a **linear central atrium**, and an associated parking structure for cars.

The lower levels include a major **banking hall** for the Hong Kong Bank, associated with main entrance and atrium space. Above the banking hall levels, rise a series of floors all dedicated to banking business activities, distributed on the east and west flanks of the atrium space. Below the main plaza level entrance at level 2, a lower recessed floor at level 1 contains communal facilities, including crèche, gymnasium and canteen with a sunken garden terrace. This lower level also provides for general deliveries, a separate cash delivery bay, and the entrance to the car-parking structure.

Aside from the major double-height volume of the banking hall, which dominates the main entrance area, the **central atrium**, with its series of high-level interconnecting bridges, glazed elevator cars and escalator systems, is the principal spatial focus of the project. The major ground level vista through the atrium space is contained by a stepped range of **garden terraces** that recede beyond, and serve to visually shield the car-parking structure.

Yeang's site analysis and design responses lead to a very direct and integrated solution. This process of assessment includes a geomancy analysis, which positions the preferred entry point and its angle, and results in the main entrance and the atrium itself. Next, the traffic and pedestrian routes of Petaling Jaya are summarised by a pedestrian zone related to the building, its vehicular drop-off and the continuation of the public promenade through the atrium. Finally, there are the studies of **sun-path** and **wind-path**, both of which have a major impact on the building design. In overall terms, the sun-shading devices screen both east and west surfaces of the double-glazed facades, shielding both morning and afternoon sun and resulting in a sophisticated striated form. The wind-path study is determined by the inclusion of major louvre banks, on the vertical ends of the naturally lit and ventilated atrium, capturing and channeling the cross-flow of both north-west and south winds. The atrium conditions provide both light and internal views for the surrounding offices, and skycourts are introduced on the outer faces of the upper floor levels.

The **atrium** is announced at the entrance by a major hovering canopy, and is partnered at high-level by a planar rooftop pavilion.

Throughout the project, and particularly in the public plaza and rising levels of the public space, **vegetation** is used to create a pleasant environment and to soften the transition between the tower and associated parking – the **hanging gardens** descending from the car-park roof.

What is evidenced here is the elegant **simplicity** that results from the direct application of Yeang's design principles – aspects of his green skyscraper agenda and the pursuit of a low-energy, bioclimatic response in the most commercial of circumstances.

Regional Training (RGT)
Atrium
Regional Training (RGT)

level 13

Telephone Banking (PTB)
Roof Garden
Atrium
Personal Recovery (PRU)

level 12

Network Services (NSC)
Atrium
Atrium
Network Services (NSC)

level 9-11

Information Technology (IT)
Atrium
Information Technology (IT)

level 08

Information Technology (IT)
Atrium
Information Technology (IT)

level 07

Card Product (CPD)
Atrium
Card Product (CPD)

level 06

0 2m 10m 20m   z

Card Product (CPD)
Atrium
Roof
Void Over Garden Terraces
Roof Garden Option
Card Product (CPD)

level 5

Hongkong Bank (P.J.Branch)
Atrium
Void Over Garden Terraces
Carparking (79 cps)
Hongkong Bank (P.J.Branch)

level 3

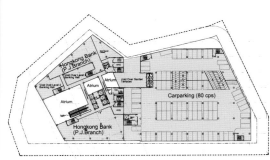

Hongkong Bank (P.J.Branch)
Atrium
Void Over Garden Terraces
Carparking (80 cps)
Hongkong Bank (P.J.Branch)

level mezzanine

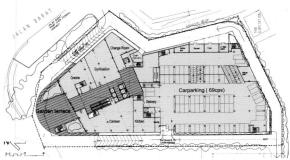

JALAN BARAT
Change Room
Gymnasium
Creche
Carparking (69cps)
Garden terrace
Canteen
Kitchen
Delivery

level 1, b1, b2   0 2m 10m 20m   z

(drawing by Huat Lim)

Selangor, Malaysia

hongkong bank tower

client Hong Kong Bank Malaysia Berhad
location Petaling Jaya, Malaysia
latitude 3.07°N
nos of Storeys 13 storeys + 1 mezzanine floor
date Start Design
completion date Pending
areas
Total gross area 79,248 sq m
Total net area 59,436 sq m
Car-parking 54,559 sq m
site area 23,099 sq m
plot ratio 1:5.2

design features • The building is configured as a tower block with two wings separated by a central atrium space, with interconnecting bridges, and an attached car-park block.
• The atrium is naturally lit and ventilated and provides additional internal views for the offices.
• The tower is wrapped in sun-shading louvres as a passive solar device.
• Vegetation is used to create a pleasant internal environment, and to soften the transition zones between the car-parking block and the tower. A stepped planter extends from the ground floor of the atrium up to the roof of the car-parking block, as a key design feature.

design responses

geomancy analysis

Preferred Entry Point and Angle
→ Preferred Entry Point and Angle to Proposed Hongkong Bank Building

response

main entrance orientation into bank building
N22.5°W

pedestrian traffic

■→ Traffic Direction
■■ Pedestrian Routes
⚑ Bus Stop

response

Atrium
Jalan Barat
Federal Highway
pedestrian zone to the Hongkong Bank building
■ Promenade Zone

sun path

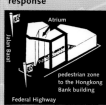

morning sun
South
North

response

sun-shades screening the east and west facades from the sun
afternoon sun
☐ Sun
■ Sun Shades

wind path

South
North

response

south wind
north-west wind
louvres filtering wind into atrium
■ Wind Louvers
☐ Wind

triple-glazed ventilated wall with plane blinds (east and west elevation)

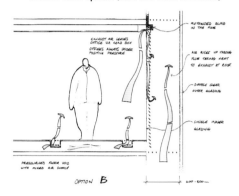

OPTION A

double-wall option (east and west elevation)

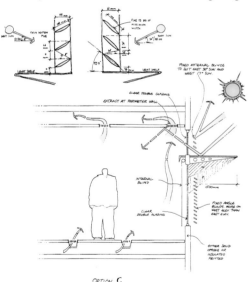

OPTION B

light shelf and blinds with clear double glazing

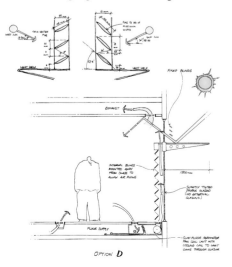

OPTION C

full-height glazed wall with light shelf

OPTION D

full-height glazing with external adjustable blinds and perimeter coil units (east and west elevation)

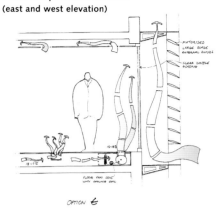

OPTION E

potential water conservation strategy

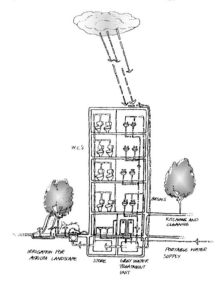

water conservation strategy

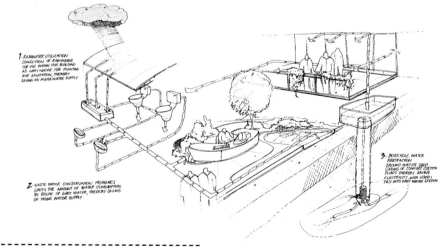

solar thermal panel system schematic

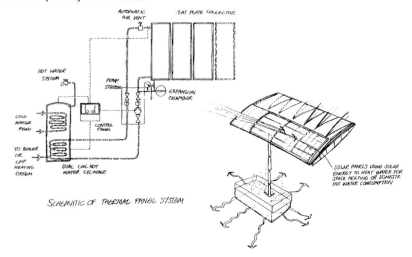

SCHEMATIC OF THERMAL PANEL SYSTEM

wind turbine system schematic

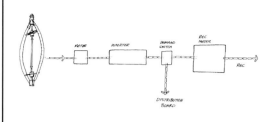

wind turbine

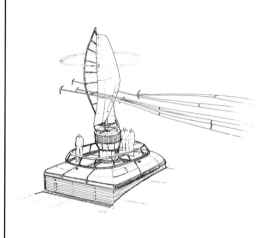

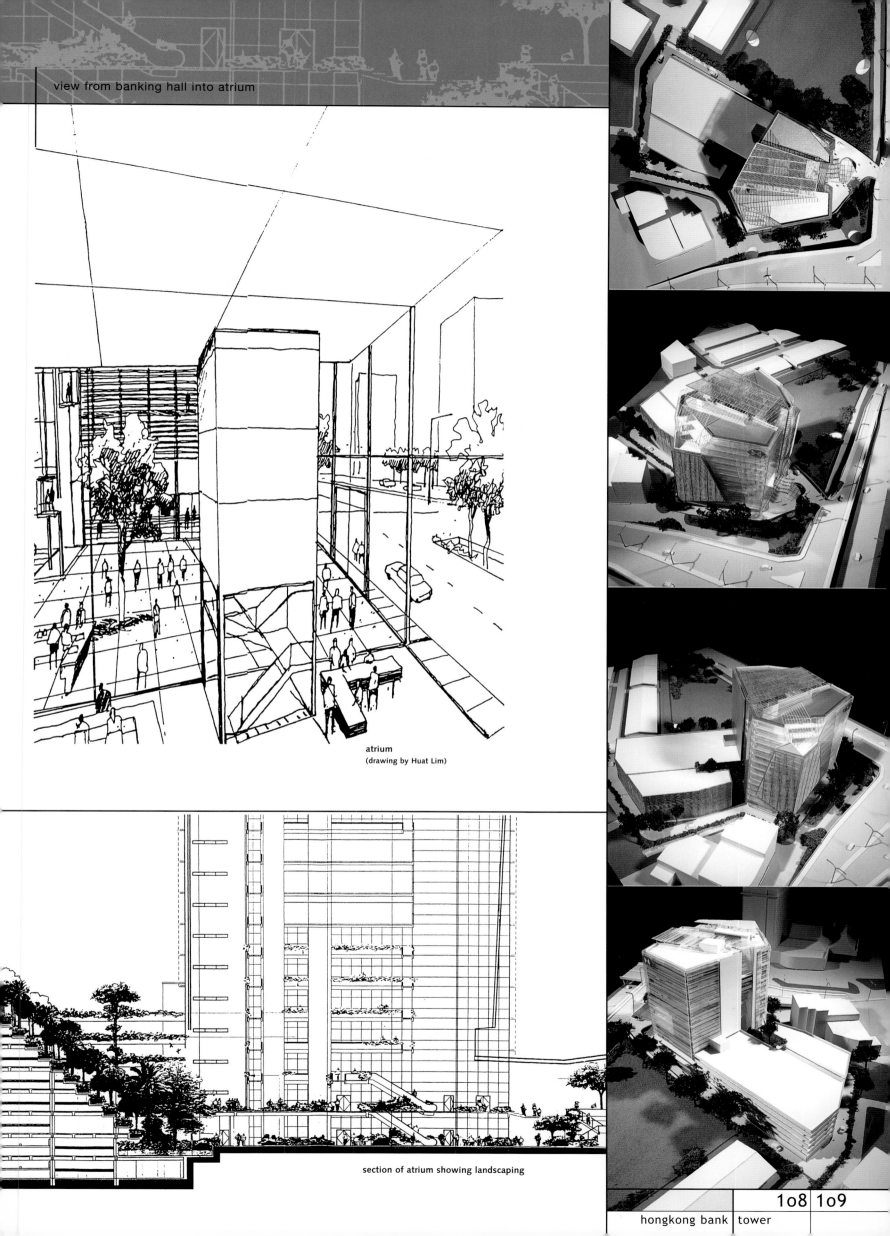

view from banking hall into atrium

atrium
(drawing by Huat Lim)

section of atrium showing landscaping

In certain key respects, the EDITT Tower is closely related to both the BATC Tower and particularly the Nagoya 2005 Tower, with the common themes being in the realm of **vertical urbanism** and **exposition** uses.

The Urban Redevelopment Authority of Singapore Competition for an Exposition Tower provided Yeang with a similar opportunity to the Nagoya project, but on a smaller scale and on a restricted corner site in the Singapore urban downtown of major commercial tower forms.

While meeting the client's programme requirements for an exposition tower, including retail, exhibition spaces, auditoria and related facilities, Yeang used this as an integrated basis to demonstrate much of his agenda for an **ecological architecture**. The pursuit of this ideal, through his many projects, leads to the establishment of his comprehensive vision of the **'green skyscraper'**. The EDITT Tower is therefore significant as an exemplar of the 'green skyscraper' agenda, which has a major impact on the design and the method of its assembly, operation and future life as a reusable framework.

The nature of Yeang's **ecological design** and its foundation of **interconnectedness**[1] is explored in the introductory essay, and the direct application of those principles is evidenced in the EDITT Tower more completely than in any previous project. It is therefore very much a part of Yeang's evolution and the direct application of his thought, just as Menara Mesiniaga forms a benchmark project in the earlier **bioclimatic skyscraper** series.

[1] The introductory essay 'Interconnectedness' is a brief survey of ecological design as the basis of the 'green skyscraper', incorporating Yeang's methodology.

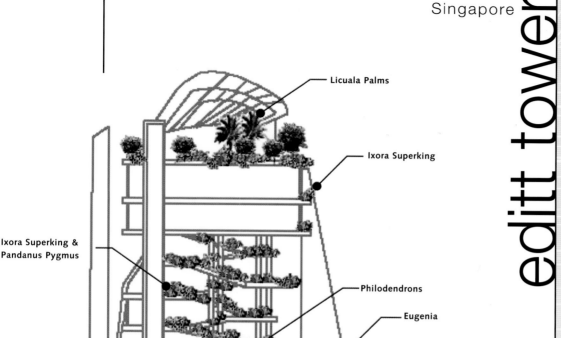

Singapore

editt tower

Licuala Palms

Ixora Superking

Ixora Superking & Pandanus Pygmus

Philodendrons

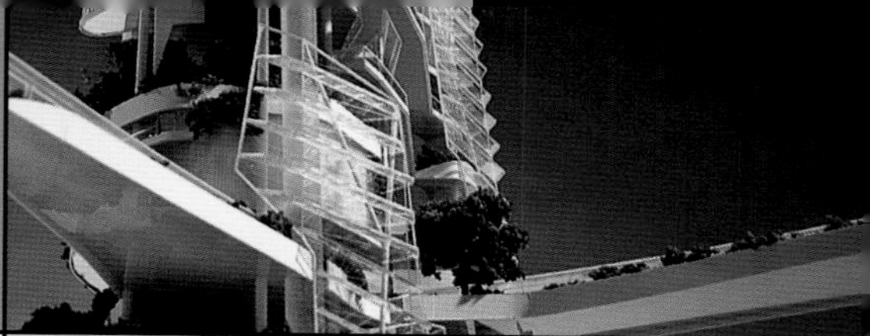

Eugenia

Livistonia Palms

Bougainvillaea

Bougainvillaea

Pandanus Pymeus & Hymenocallis

Eugenia Grandis

Philodendrons

Hymenocallis (Tropical Shrub)

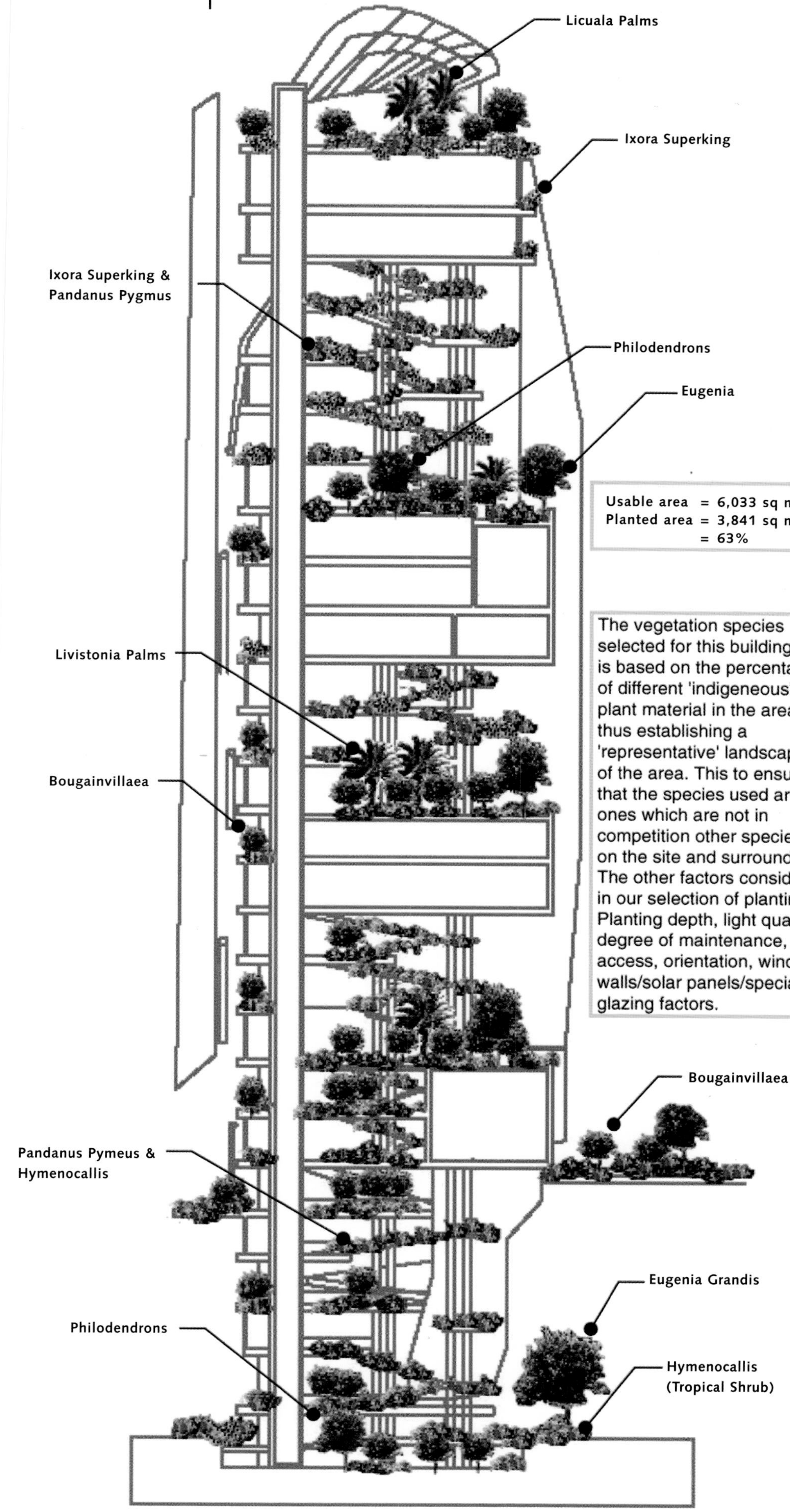

Usable area = 6,033 sq m
Planted area = 3,841 sq m
= 63%

The vegetation species selected for this building is based on the percentage of different 'indigeneous' plant material in the area thus establishing a 'representative' landscape of the area. This to ensure that the species used are ones which are not in competition other species on the site and surroundings. The other factors considered in our selection of planting are: Planting depth, light quality, degree of maintenance, access, orientation, wind walls/solar panels/special glazing factors.

client URA (Urban Redevelopment Authority) Singapore (Sponsor)
EDITT (Ecological Design in The Tropics) (Sponsor)
NUS (National University of Singapore) (Sponsor)
location Junction of Waterloo Road and Victoria Street, Singapore
latitude 1.2°N
nos of storeys 26 storeys
date start 1998 (competition: design)
completion date Pending
areas
Total gross area 6,033 sq m
Total net area 3,567 sq m
Total area of plantation 3,841 sq m
site area 838 sq m
plot ratio 1:7

design features • Our design sets out to demonstrate an ecological approach to tower design. Besides meeting the client's program requirements for an exposition tower (ie. for retail, exhibition spaces, auditorium uses, etc.), the design has the following ecological responses:

• response to the site's ecology
Ecological design starts with looking at the site's ecosystem and its properties. Any design that does not take these aspects into consideration is essentially not an ecological approach. A useful start is to look at the site in relation to an 'hierarchy of ecosystems' (see below):

Ecosystem Hierarchy	Site Data Requirements	Design Strategy
• Ecologically-Mature	Complete Ecosystem Analysis and Mapping	• Preserve • Conserve • Develop only on no-impact areas
• Ecologically-Immature	Complete Ecosystem Analysis and Mapping	• Preserve • Conserve • Develop only on east-impact areas
• Ecologically Simplified	Complete Ecosystem Analysis and Mapping	• Preserve • Conserve • Increase biodiversity • Develop only on low-impact areas
• Mixed-Artificial	Partial Ecosystem Analysis and Mapping	• Increase biodiversity • Develop on low-impact areas
• Monoculture	Partial Ecosystem Analysis and Mapping	• Increase biodiversity • Develop in areas of non-productive potential • Rehabilitate ecosystem
• Zeroculture	Mapping of remaining ecosystem components (eg. hydrology, remaining trees, etc.	• Increase biodiversity and organic mass • Rehabilitate ecosystem

From this hierarchy (above), it is evident that this site is an urban 'zero culture' site and is essentially a devastated ecosystem with little of its original top soil, flora and fauna remaining. The design approach is to rehabilitate this with organic mass to enable ecological succession to take place and to balance the existent inorganicness of this urban site.
The unique design feature of this scheme is in the well-planted facades and vegetated-terraces which have green areas that approximate the gross useable-areas (ie. GFA @ 6,033 sq m) of the rest of the building.
The vegetation areas are designed to be continuous and to ramp upwards from the ground plane to the uppermost floor in a linked landscaped ramp. The design's planted areas constitute 3,841 sq m which is @ ratio 1:0.5 of gross useable area to gross vegetated area.

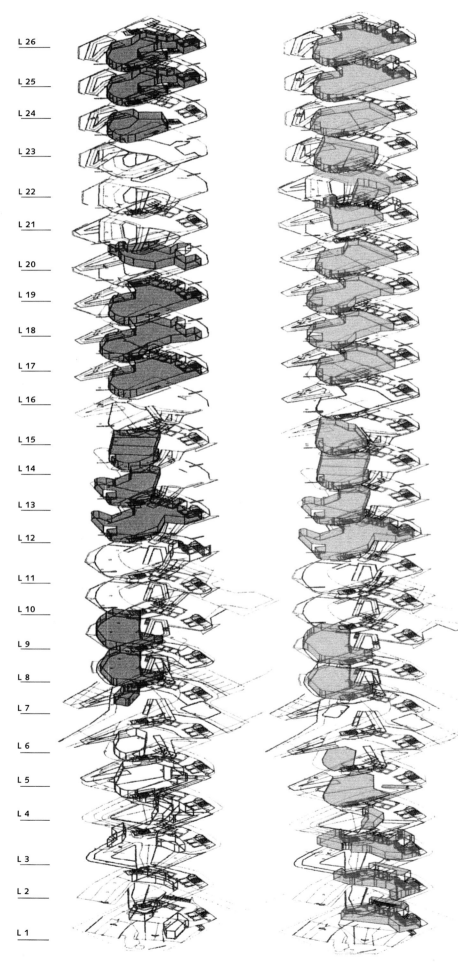

L 26
L 25
L 24
L 23
L 22
L 21
L 20
L 19
L 18
L 17
L 16
L 15
L 14
L 13
L 12
L 11
L 10
L 9
L 8
L 7
L 6
L 5
L 4
L 3
L 2
L 1

Yeang's first analysis is concerned with what he describes as a **'response to the site's ecology'**, carried out in relation to a **'hierarchy of ecosystems'**. From this he concludes that the site is an urban 'zero culture' condition – **'a devastated ecosystem with little of its top soil, flora and fauna remaining.'** [2] His response lies not only in the rehabilitation of the site's organic mass, but in the introduction of planted facades and terraces which ramp upwards from the ground level to the summit of the tower, in a continuous spiral – a **'landscaped ramp'**. Detail recommendations are then given for the selection of appropriate planting species, based on a survey of the locality.

The concept of the continuous planted facades and terraces, in itself, is integral to most of Yeang's projects, but in this case the **vertical landscaping** occupies an area equal to approximately half the usable area – an extraordinarily high proportion. Therefore the **scale** of landscaping provision, which is based on species that do not compete with those existing in the vicinity engendering diversity, and most importantly ensuring ambient cooling of the facades, coupled with the continuously shifting organic plan form results in a tower that is literally a **landscape-form**.

Further studies that are applied to the design, and result in special elements of the architecture, include water-recycling and purification, sewage recycling, solar energy use, building materials recycling and reuse, natural ventilation and mixed-mode servicing, and an embodied energy and CO_2 analysis. All of these studies form part of Yeang's ecological design agenda and are integral to the form-giving process, in the main.

For instance, the summit of the tower takes the form of a massive **rainwater collector** – a 'roof catchment pan', and is accompanied by **facade-scallops** to catch rainwater run-off – all part of a recycled grey-water system. Similarly batteries of photovoltaic panels contribute both to the façade architecture, and crucially to the reduction of electricity demand and cooling load. In analysing each system, a contribution is made to a **sustainable architecture** which has its own unique identity.

In addition to the vertical landscaping, two further aspects of the design content are noteworthy – these include **'Place Making' and 'Loose Fit'**. [3] In addition, the overall plan-form is configured with a solar-shielding-wall curvature of elevators, stairs and services on the hot east face, and the design incorporates **'wind-walls'** to assist both internal comfort conditions and that of the skycourts – developing the principles applied in the UMNO Tower. The plan arrangement is also deeply inflected by the extensive use of **pedestrian ramps**, which provide additional vertical linkage and form part of the expressive language of the architecture.

The **ramp-systems** are also an important element of Yeang's **vertical urbanism** strategy, in what he describes as a **'vertical extension of the street'**, these movement spaces are intended to be lined with street activities such as **'... stalls, shops, cafes, performance spaces, viewing decks ...'** [4] through the first six major floor levels. The design also incorporates a **'views analysis'**, to ensure that upper-level occupants have the best of the surrounding vistas of the city.

[2] Ken Yeang: 'EDITT Tower', Project Notes, 1998
[3] Ibid.
[4] Ibid.

In this instance, Yeang has also applied a **'loose-fit'** policy and has studied the possible change of use of the tower to offices or apartments, over the building's life-span of 100/150 years. The implications of this are, for example, the occupation of **'skycourts'** for office use, removable partitions and floors, and the use of **'mechanical jointing'** of materials to enable future recovery and recycling.

What the building exemplifies is an early application of the more complex principles of Yeang's ecological design approach, and the increasing involvement of multi-disciplinary design teams contributing to a comprehensive, interconnected assessment of all aspects of the site, the architecture and its formation. At the same time, Yeang is raising the expectation and the standards of the immediate future and the requirements of a genuine **green architecture**.

Tower of Babel

energy requirement for materials (GJ/Tonne)

very high energy		medium energy		
aluminium	200 - 250	lime		3 - 5
stainless steel	50 - 100	clay bricks & tiles		2 - 7
copper	100+	gypsum plaster		1 - 4
plastics	100+	concrete	precast	0.8 - 1.5
high energy			blocks	0.8 - 3.5
steel	30 - 60		in situ	1.5 - 8
lead, zinc	25+	**low energy**		
glass	12 - 25	sand lime bricks		0.8 - 1.2
plasterboard	8 - 10	sand, aggregate		<0.5
		flyash, RHA, volcanic ash		<0.5
		soil		<0.5

structural design
Battle McCarthy Consulting Engineers

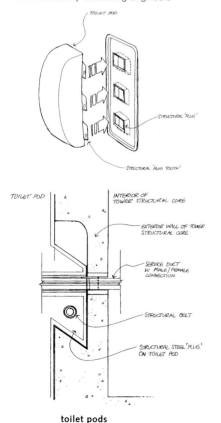

toilet pods

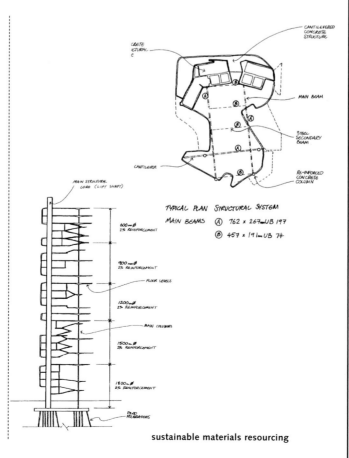

sustainable materials resourcing

• response to the site's ecology
Design began with the mapping in detail of the indigenous planting within a 1 mile radius vicinity of the site to identify species to be incorporated in the design that will not compete with the indigenous species of the locality.

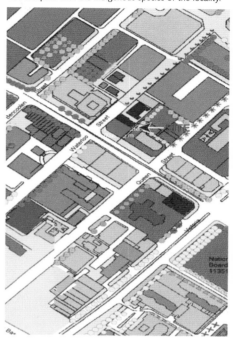

This plan shows our survey of the existing vegetation species located within the surrounding areas to the site (surveyed by our Landscape Architect).

• place making
A crucial urban design issue in skyscraper design is poor spatial continuity between street-level activities with those spaces at the upper-floors of the city's high-rise towers. This is due to the physical compartmentation of floors (inherent in the skyscraper typology). Urban design involves 'place making'. In creating 'vertical places', our design brings 'street-life' to the building's upper-parts through wide landscaped-ramps upwards from street level. Ramps are lined with street-activities: (stalls, shops, cafes, performance spaces, viewing-decks, etc.), up to first six floors. Ramps create a continuous spatial flow from public to less public, as a 'vertical extension of the street' thereby eliminating the problematic stratification of floors inherent in all tall buildings typology. High-level bridge-linkages are added to connect to neighbouring buildings for greater urban connectivity.

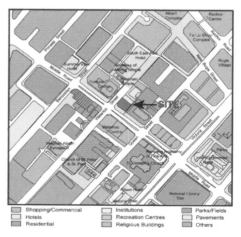

rainwater purification system

A prototype for a new generation of high buildings in the tropics, this Singapore tower explores Yeang's principles of bioclimatic design more extensively than ever before. it adds many new ideas and contextual touches.

Yeang has long been associated with tall eco-friendly projects, what he calls bioclimatic skyscrapers (see for instance AR February 1993 and AR September 1994). But up to now, though his buildings have shown steady evolution, they have been constrained by clients with understandably quite restricted programmes. The chance to try out ideas on a more speculative, yet possibly achievable level has come from a proposal by the Singapore Urban Redevelopment Authority who asked him to make proposals for an exhibition tower: one that could contain exhibition spaces of all kinds, retail uses, and auditoria. This is projected to be what he calls "a prototype ecological building design" in which his green ideas can be pursued with more freedom than usual, and with greater rigour, over a wider range of issues of ecological concern.

At the junction of Waterloo and Victoria Streets, the site is not far from the fabled cluster of slender (and by no means inelegant) towers that heraldically symbolize Singapore's CBD. But when this 26-storey structure is built, it will be completely different from them: it will be covered with vegetation, eroded to allow for internal terraces and sky courts, brimmed with shades, helm-masked with shining solar panels and wrapped in ramps. The latter are intended to make 'vertical places', gently and easy transitions between levels of what Yeang calls the "inevitable physical compartmentation of floors inherent in the skyscraper typology". The most important ones run up the lowest six or seven floors to make what Yeang hopes will be a "vertical extension of the street". Wide landscaped ramps conduct you upwards from road level, and are lined with street activities like stalls, cafes, shops, bars and so on; they lead onto the lower levels of the great exhibition building. The aim is to recreate the wonderful mix of uses, people and spaces which made streets of the richer cities of South-East Asia (Singapore, Hong Kong, and to some extent Kuala Lumpur) magically alive in the middle of this century. The buildings were modern concrete structures, but the wild mix of functions (from department stores to housing, restaurants to workshops) was far more varied, lively and picturesque than anywhere else (sadly, modern development has replaced many of these wonderful but shabby tenements with uni-functional object buildings).

Yeang's towers have always been intended to be shaggy, intimately related to vegetation, which he uses not only as an amenity bit as a means of providing shade and improving interior microclimate and oxygenation. In the Singapore project, he proposes to go further. He regards the site as ecologically "devastated", and has carried out a survey of local species to find which plants will be most suitable for the new building, and re-evoking the original eco-system. They are to make a continuous garment from street to crown of the building, winding through the ramps and vertical places. They will be nourished by rain which will be collected on the roof and in a series of "scallops" on lower floors. Rain will be augmented by grey waste water and the two will be filtered and kept in a tank on the roof to feed the irrigation system and lavatory cisterns.

The plants will be the only climate modifiers. Of course, there will be air conditioning, but its use will be minimized by built-in shading, fixed and movable, and by wind walls placed parallel to the prevailing wind to direct breezes to sky courts and internal spaces. Ceiling fans with de-misters will be used for cooling before the full air-conditioning system comes into play. The photovoltaic arrays are intended to reduce demands on the national electricity grid to power refrigeration and lighting. Solar thermal collectors will head most of the domestic hot water.

One of the key concepts behind the building is loose fit, an idea that has been around for three or four decades, but which is rarely a conscious determinant of design. Yeang suggests that the tower could be converted wholly or in part to office or residential use, and has prepared a scheme for converting the entire building to offices at 75 per cent net to gross efficiency. Partitions and even floors will be removable, but solid enough to provide sound insulation where necessary.

Yeang also believes that the whole thing should be capable of being demolished with minimum waste of energy and materials. Hence, he proposes making all structural joints by mechanical rather than fusion methods (that is, in the case of the frame, bolting the steel rather than welding it). So the structure will be demountable and re-usable, and so will elements like the floors, which he suggests will be made of innovative structural timber cassettes.

There are numerous other ingenious ideas in the concept: for instance methods of handling the building's waster (such as packaging and unused food), and composting solid sewage. It will be marvelous if the whole proposal can be realized, but even if only three quarters of the ideas are implemented, the shaggy tower should be an example for development in all tropical regions.

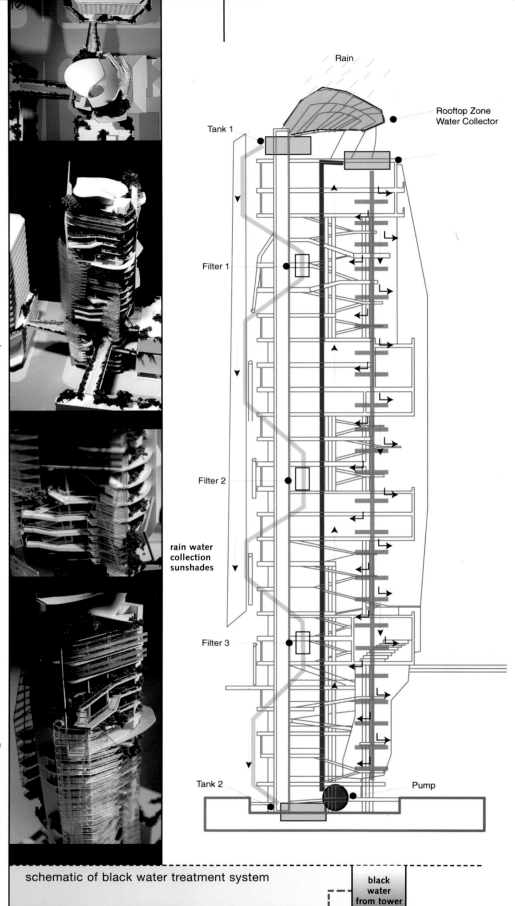

Rain

Rooftop Zone Water Collector

Tank 1

Filter 1

rain water collection sunshades

Filter 2

Filter 3

Tank 2

Pump

schematic of black water treatment system

black water from tower

treatment plant buried in ground
• sealed – no odour
• low running cost

vacuum

soil conditioner

incineration

sludge

irrigation to fuel

drying by solar or biogas

electricity

biogas

incineration

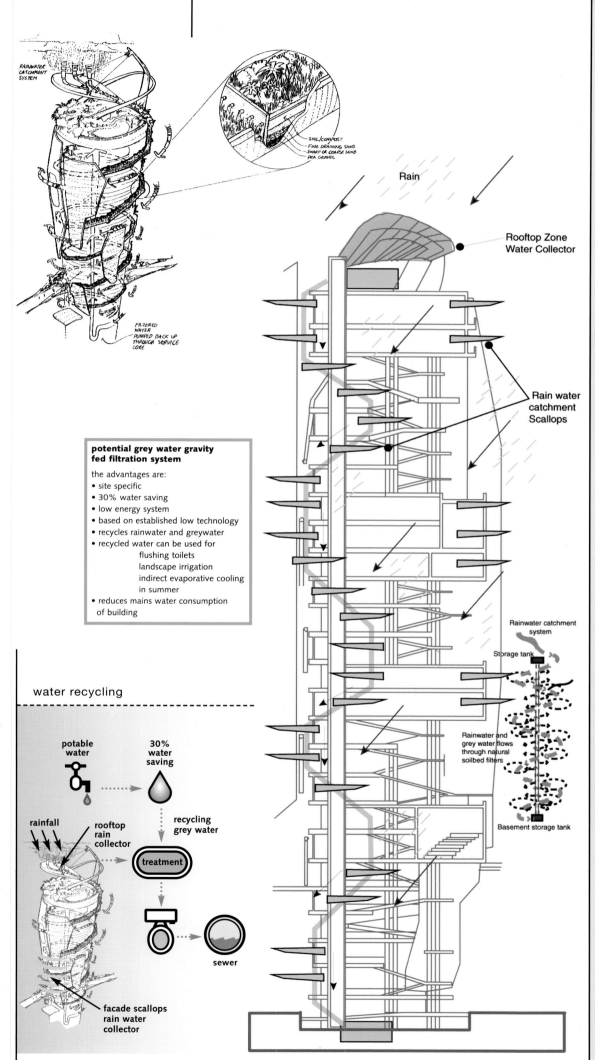

RAINWATER
CATCHMENT
SYSTEM

SOIL/COMPOST
FINE DRAINING SAND
SHARP OR COARSE SAND
PEA GRAVEL

FILTERED
WATER
PUMPED BACK UP
THROUGH SERVICE
CORE

Rain

Rooftop Zone
Water Collector

Rain water
catchment
Scallops

**potential grey water gravity
fed filtration system**

the advantages are:
• site specific
• 30% water saving
• low energy system
• based on established low technology
• recycles rainwater and greywater
• recycled water can be used for
   flushing toilets
   landscape irrigation
   indirect evaporative cooling
   in summer
• reduces mains water consumption
  of building

Rainwater catchment
system

Storage tank

Rainwater and
grey water flows
through natural
soilbed filters

Basement storage tank

water recycling

potable
water

30%
water
saving

rainfall

recycling
grey water

rooftop
rain
collector

treatment

sewer

rainfall

facade scallops
rain water
collector

• **vertical landscaping**

Vegetation from street level spirals upwards as a continuous ecosystem facilitating species migration, engendering
a more diverse ecosystem and greater ecosystem stability
and to facilitate ambient cooling of the facades.

As mentioned earlier, species are selected not to compete
with others within surroundings. 'Vegetation percentages'
represent of area's landscape character.

Factors influencing planting selection are:
• planting depths   • light quality
• maintenance level • access
• orientation   • wind-walls/solar-panels/
                       special glazing

Vegetation placements within the tower at different
heights respond to the microclimates of each individual
sub-zone at the tower.

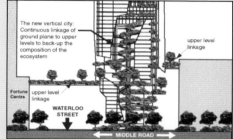

ground plane relationship

Vegetation from the street level is spiralled up the building
as a continuous ecosystem. This facilitates species
migration and engenders a more stable urban ecosystem.

• **views to the surrounding**

A 'views analysis' was carried out to enable upper-floor
design to have views of surroundings.

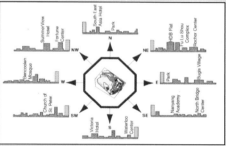

• **'loose-fit'**

Generally, buildings have life-spans of 100–150 years and
change usages over-time. The design here is 'loose-fit'
to facilitate future reuse. Features include:
• 'Skycourts' (ie. convertable for future office use)
• Removable partitions
• Removable floors
• 'Mechanical-jointing' of materials (as against to
  chemical bonding) to facilitate future recovery.
• Flexible design (eg. initially a multi-use expo building,
  its future use may be offices [net lettable area of
  9,288 sq m @ 75% efficiency] or apartments).

A set of plans to show conversion to office use has also
been prepared @ 75% net to gross floor efficiency.

• **water-recycling**

Water self-sufficiency (by rainwater-collection) in the
tower is at 31%.
• Total nett area = 3,567 sq m
• Building population = 1 person/10 sq m
                     = 3,567/10 = 356 persons
• Water consumption = 30 litres/day/person
• Total requirements = 30 x 356 persons
                     = 10,680 litres/day
                     = 10.68 m³ per day x 365 day
                     = 3,898 m³ per annum
• Total rain-fall catchment area = 518 sq m
• Singapore average rainfall/annum = 2.344 m
• Total rain-water collection = 1,214 m³ per annum
• Water self sufficiency = 1,214 ÷ 3,898 x 100 = 31%

• **water-purification**

Rainwater-collection system comprises of 'roof-catchment-pan'
and layers of 'scallops' located at the building's facade to
catch rain-water running off its sides. Water flows through
gravity-fed water-purification system, using soil-bed filters.
The filtered-water accumulates in a basement storage-tank,
and is pumped to the upper-level storage-tank for reuse (eg.
for plant-irrigation and toilet-flushing). Mains water is only
here for potable needs.

concrete recycling

by Battle McCarthy Consulting Engineers

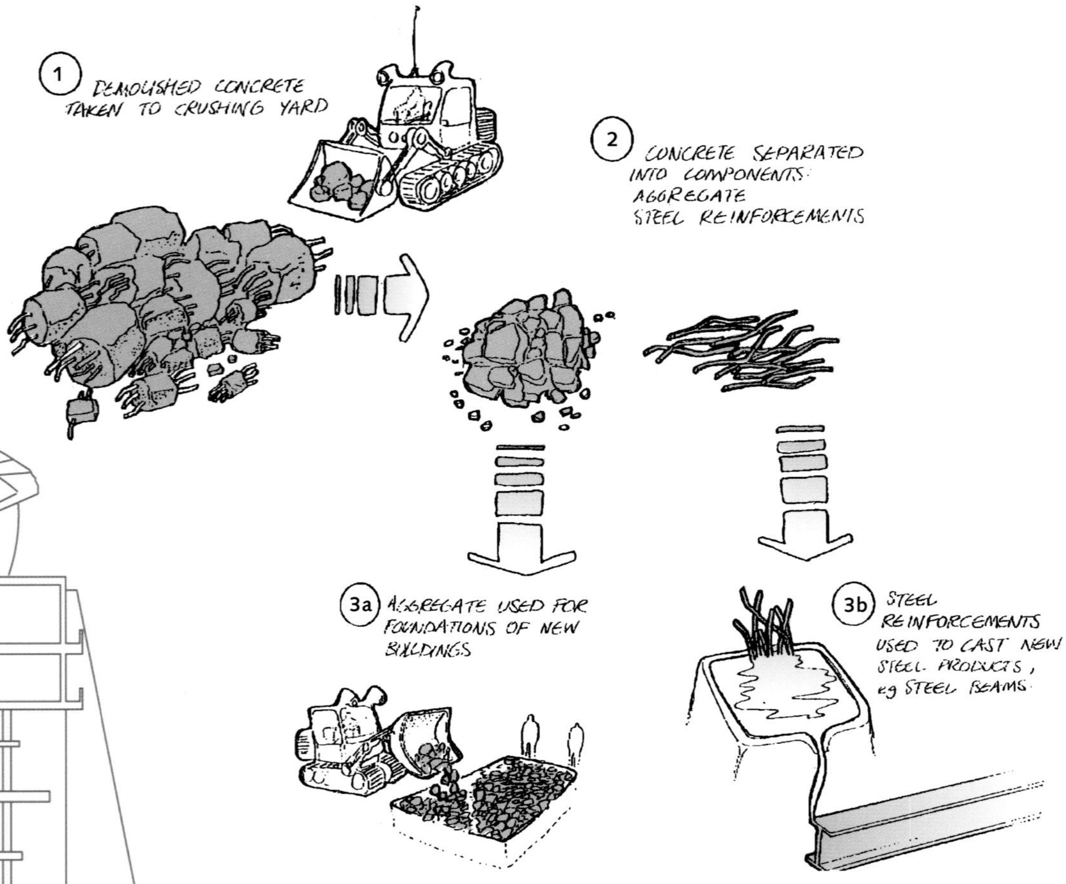
1 DEMOLISHED CONCRETE TAKEN TO CRUSHING YARD
2 CONCRETE SEPARATED INTO COMPONENTS: AGGREGATE STEEL REINFORCEMENTS
3a AGGREGATE USED FOR FOUNDATIONS OF NEW BUILDINGS
3b STEEL REINFORCEMENTS USED TO CAST NEW STEEL PRODUCTS, eg STEEL BEAMS

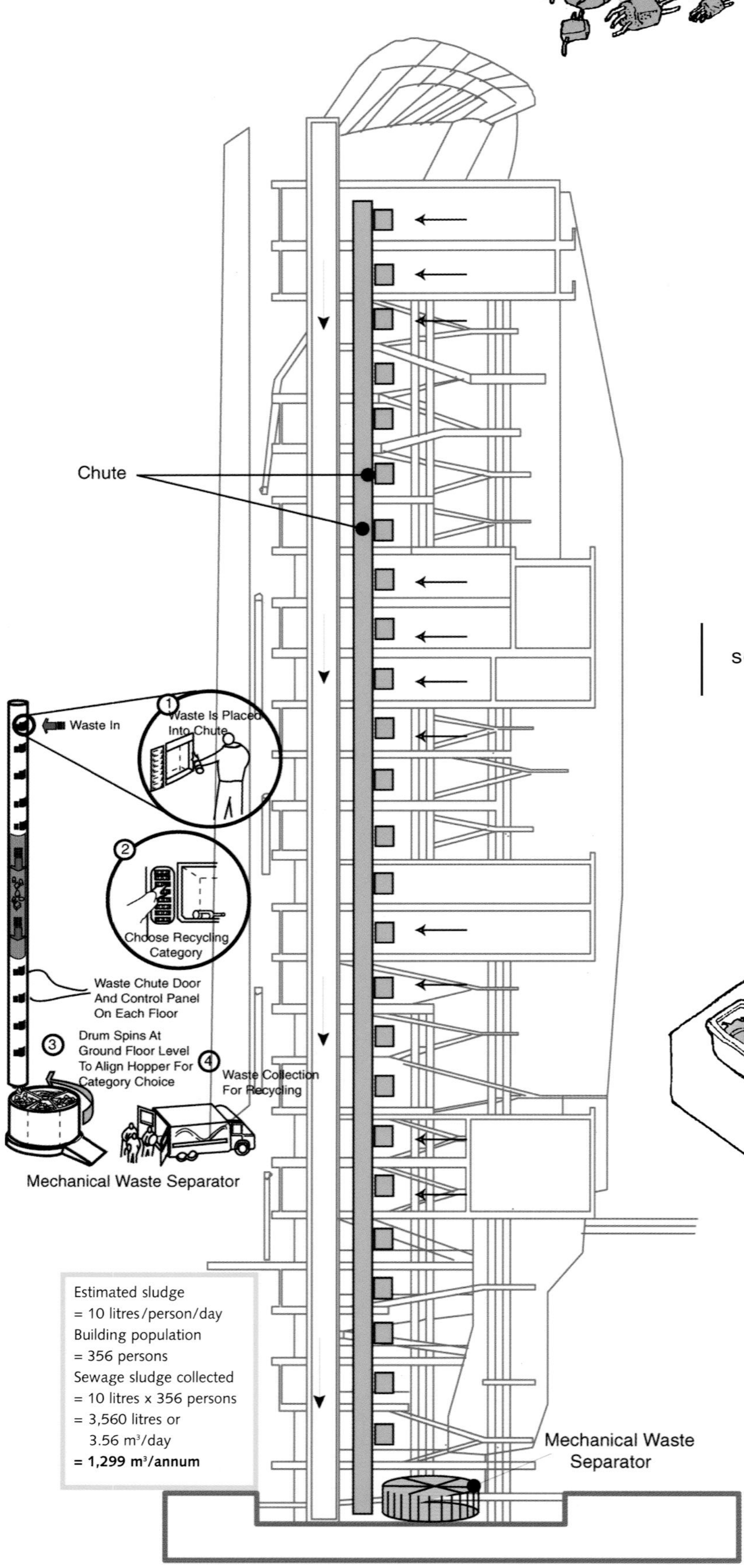
Chute
Waste In
1 Waste Is Placed Into Chute
2 Choose Recycling Category
Waste Chute Door And Control Panel On Each Floor
3 Drum Spins At Ground Floor Level To Align Hopper For Category Choice
4 Waste Collection For Recycling
Mechanical Waste Separator
Mechanical Waste Separator

Estimated sludge
= 10 litres/person/day
Building population
= 356 persons
Sewage sludge collected
= 10 litres x 356 persons
= 3,560 litres or
3.56 m^3/day
= 1,299 m^3/annum

solid waste recycling

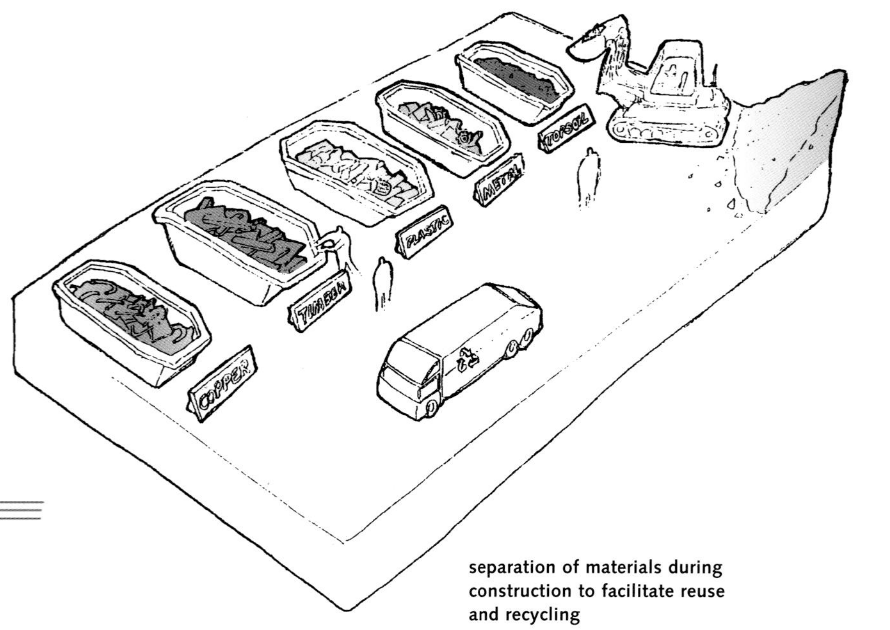
COPPER
TIMBER
PLASTIC
METAL

separation of materials during construction to facilitate reuse and recycling

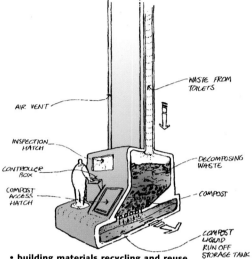

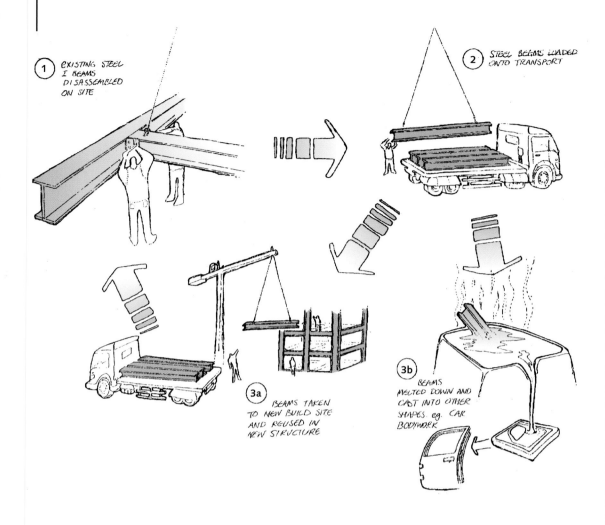

① EXISTING STEEL I BEAMS DISASSEMBLED ON SITE

② STEEL BEAMS LOADED ONTO TRANSPORT

③a BEAMS TAKEN TO NEW BUILD SITE AND REUSED IN NEW STRUCTURE

③b BEAMS MELTED DOWN AND CAST INTO OTHER SHAPES eg. CAR BODYWORK

timber cassettes recycling

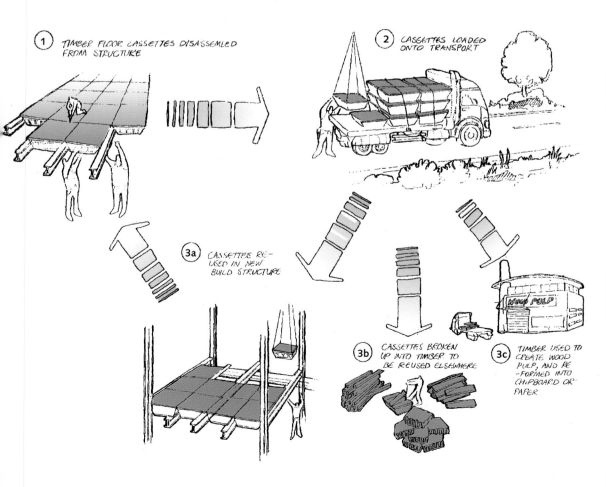

① TIMBER FLOOR CASSETTES DISASSEMBLED FROM STRUCTURE

② CASSETTES LOADED ONTO TRANSPORT

③a CASSETTES RE-USED IN NEW BUILD STRUCTURE

③b CASSETTES BROKEN UP INTO TIMBER TO BE REUSED ELSEWHERE

③c TIMBER USED TO CREATE WOOD PULP, AND RE-FORMED INTO CHIPBOARD OR PAPER

• sewage recycling

The design optimises recovery and recycling of sewage waste:

- Estimated sludge = 10 litres/person/day
- Building population = 356 persons
- Sewage sludge collected = 10 litres x 356 persons

$$= 3,560 \text{ litres or } 3.56 \text{ m}^3/\text{day}$$

$$= \textbf{1,299 m}^3/\textbf{ annum}$$

Sewage is treated to create compost (fertilizer for use elsewhere) or bio-gas fuel.

• sewage waste treatment

AIR VENT

WASTE FROM TOILETS

INSPECTION HATCH

CONTROLLER BOX

COMPOST ACCESS HATCH

DECOMPOSING WASTE

COMPOST

COMPOST LIQUID RUN OFF STORAGE TANK

• building materials recycling and reuse

Design has an in-built waste-management system. Recyclable materials are separated at source by hoppers at every floor. These drop-down to the basement waste separators, then taken elsewhere by recycling garbage collection for recycling. Expected recyclable waste collected /annum:

~ paper / cardboard = 41.5 metric-tonnes
~ glass / ceramic = 7.0 metric-tonnes
~ meta = 10.4 metric-tonnes

The building is designed to have mechanically joined connections of materials and its structural connections to facilitate future reuse and recycling at the end of building's useful life.

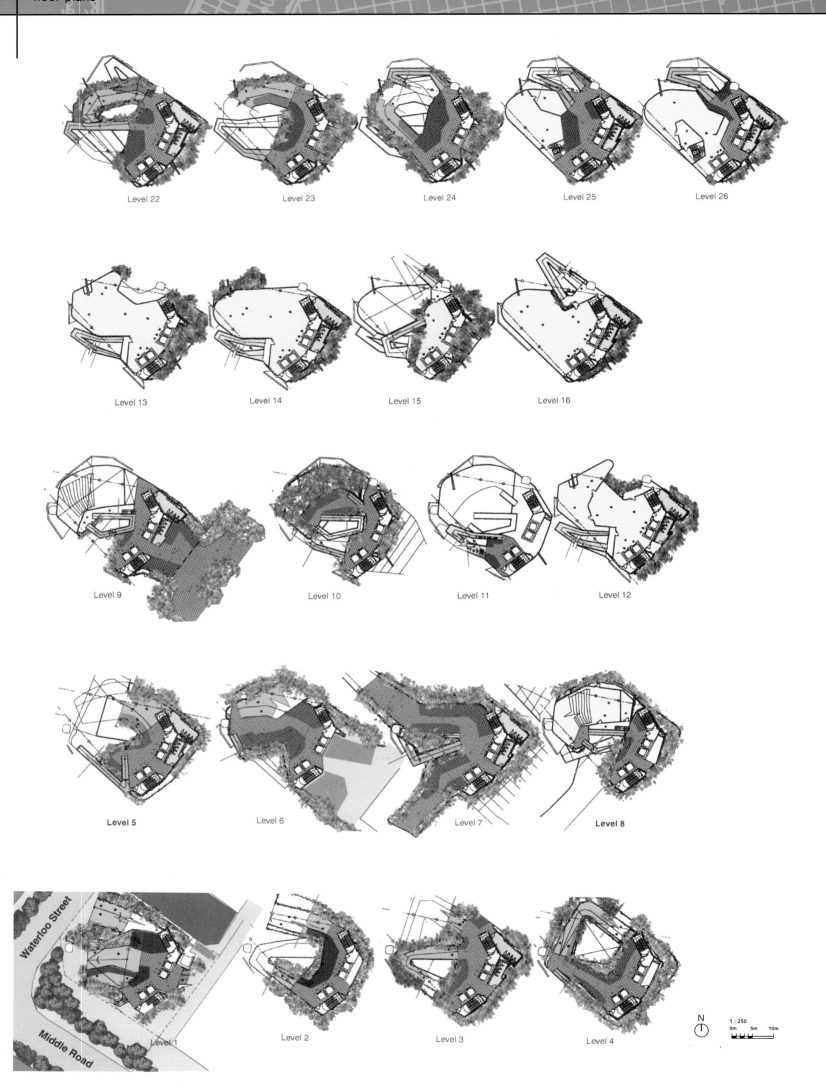

Level 22   Level 23   Level 24   Level 25   Level 26

Level 13   Level 14   Level 15   Level 16

Level 9   Level 10   Level 11   Level 12

Level 5   Level 6   Level 7   **Level 8**

Waterloo Street

Middle Road

Level 1   Level 2   Level 3   Level 4

N

1 : 250
0m   5m   10m

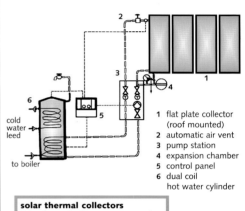

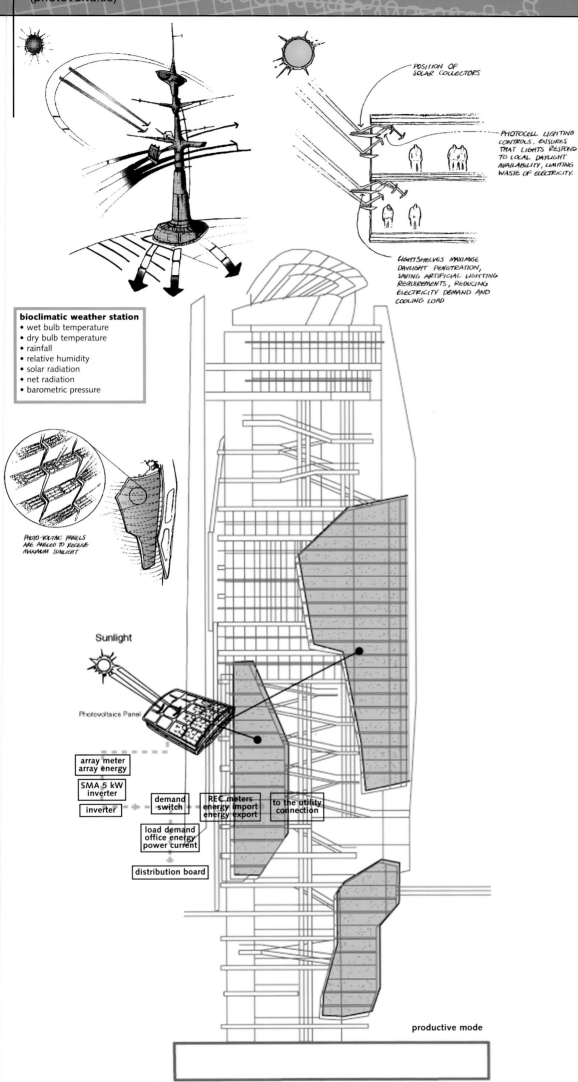

POSITION OF
SOLAR COLLECTORS

PHOTOCELL LIGHTING
CONTROLS. ENSURES
THAT LIGHTS RESPOND
TO LOCAL DAYLIGHT
AVAILABILITY, LIMITING
WASTE OF ELECTRICITY.

LIGHTSHELVES MAXIMISE
DAYLIGHT PENETRATION,
SAVING ARTIFICIAL LIGHTING
REQUIREMENTS, REDUCING
ELECTRICITY DEMAND AND
COOLING LOAD

bioclimatic weather station
• wet bulb temperature
• dry bulb temperature
• rainfall
• relative humidity
• solar radiation
• net radiation
• barometric pressure

PHOTO-VOLTAIC PANELS
ARE ANGLED TO RECEIVE
MAXIMUM SUNLIGHT

Sunlight

Photovoltaics Panel

array meter
array energy

SMA 5 kW
inverter

inverter

demand
switch

REC meters
energy import
energy export

to the utility
connection

load demand
office energy
power current

distribution board

productive mode

• **solar energy use**
Photovoltaics are used for greater energy self-sufficiency.
• Average photovoltaic-cell energy output = c 0.15 kWh sq m
• Total sunlight hours per day = 7 hours
• Daily energy output = 0.15 x 7 = 1.05 kWh sq m
• Area of photovoltaic = 855 sq m
  Total daily energy output = **898 kWh**
• Estimated energy consumption @ 0.097 kWh /sq m
  enclosed & 0.038 kWh/sq m unenclosed =
  (0.097 x 3,567 sq m) + (0.038 x 2,465 sq m) = 439.7 kWh
• Estimated daily energy consumption = 10 hrs x 439.7
  = **4,397 kWh**
• % self sufficiency is 898 ÷ 4,397 = **20.4%**

cold
water
leed

to boiler

1 flat plate collector
  (roof mounted)
2 automatic air vent
3 pump station
4 expansion chamber
5 control panel
6 dual coil
  hot water cylinder

solar thermal collectors
Solar thermal collectors convert solar
energy into hot water and they may
be used to supplement the hot water
provision in the building. They should
be mounted at roof level as a stand-
alone panel system

• **embodied energy and CO₂**
Embodied-energy studies of the building are useful to
indicate the building's environmental impacts. Subsequently,
estimates of CO_2 emissions arising from building materials
production may be made. Design's embodied energy
(prepared by our expert) is:

	Element	GJ/sq m GFA
Structural System	• Excavation	764.0
	• Steel and concrete	43,850.2
	• Formwork	3,113.10
Floor	• Steel	13,013.10
	• Timber & other material	22,648.00
	• Staircases & railings	1,752.50
	• Floor finishes	7,793.00
External wall	• Curtain wall and bricks	5,550.30
	• Aluminium cladding	2,864.50
	• Solar panels	12,435.70
External wall and partitions	• Bricks	5,482.20
	• Other materials	6,078.30
Roof and ceilings	• Concrete & membrane	5,439.00
	• Water catchment and drainage	8,439.80
	• Ceiling	1,390.70
Fittings	• Doors	1,736.60
	• Sanitary fittings	490.20
	Total	**142,841.20**

Energy sources affect CO₂ emissions associated with
embodied energy. If the majority of energy sources is
petroleum-related (with some gas and electricity), 80 kg
CO₂ per GJ of energy averages. The building here is
associated with emissions of c. 11.5 thousand tonnes CO₂.
Embodied-energy ratio to gross floor area (GJ/m² GFA) is
generally between 6 and 8, but may be more depending on
methodology used. The design's ratio is at the high end
(@ 14.2 GJ/m² GFA) but differs from others since using
solar-panels having high embodied-energy will significantly
offset operational energy saved over building life. High
embodied energy materials used (eg. aluminium and steel)
are however easily recyclable and therefore halving their
embodied-energy when reused. Replacing concrete floors
with composite timber-floors cassettes will reduce embodied-
energy by c. 10,000 GJ.

by Professor Bill Lawson (Sydney)

natural ventilation of toilet pods

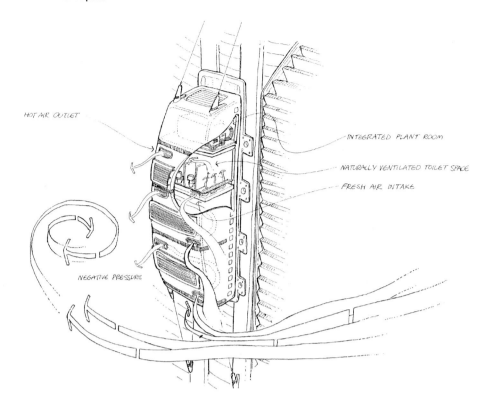

HOT AIR OUTLET

INTEGRATED PLANT ROOM

NATURALLY VENTILATED TOILET SPACE

FRESH AIR INTAKE

NEGATIVE PRESSURE

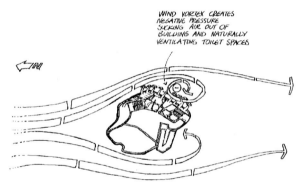

WIND VORTEX CREATES
NEGATIVE PRESSURE
SUCKING AIR OUT OF
BUILDING AND NATURALLY
VENTILATING TOILET SPACES

IN

local wind effects
by Battle McCarthy Consulting Engineers

active wind manipulation

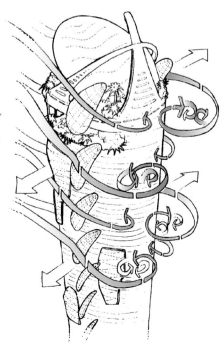

Idea for inflatable wind 'fins' positioned strategically on elevations of tower creating vortices on alternate sides behind the tower

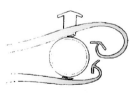

Negative and positive pressures create lateral force on tower at right angles to direction of wind

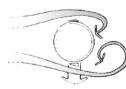

Adjacent fin (below) creates lateral force in opposite direction therefore stabilising tower and allowing more lightweight construction methods

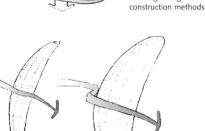

deflated   inflated

• natural ventilation and 'mixed-mode' servicing
The options for the M&E servicing modes for any ecological building are:
- passive mode
- background (mixed) mode
- full (specialised) mode.

The design here optimises on the locality's bioclimatic responses using 'mixed mode' M&E servicing. Mechanical air-conditioning and artificial-lighting systems are reduced. Ceiling-fans with de-misters are used for low-energy comfort cooling.

Wind is used to create internal conditions of comfort by 'wind-walls' that a placed parallel to the prevailing wind to direct wind to internal spaces and skycourts for comfort cooling.

local wind effects
computational fluid dynamics simulations

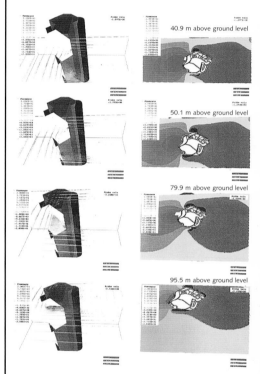

40.9 m above ground level

50.1 m above ground level

79.9 m above ground level

95.5 m above ground level

cities in the sky

 The Shanghai Armoury Tower, a project that follows from Hitechniaga, is distinct in two principal respects. First, it is deliberately designed as an iconic symbol – in Yeang's words

"… the design is intended to create a modern urban (icon) form, for the clients' progressive and valiant march into the 21st century". [1]

Second, the programmatic content is mixed-use including hotel and office spaces.

On an environmental level, as a design for a real building, the project extends beyond Yeang's former work with the incorporation of a vertical **internal atrium**, and **double-skin façade** – both functions of a **natural ventilation strategy.**

Up to that date in 1997, the Shanghai project is the most potent combination of symbolic imagery and technical innovation, within Yeang's overall portfolio of designs.

On a physical level, the design is intensively developed to produce a thoroughly responsive bioclimatic organism and an operationally energy-efficient building, that above all exploits the coastal climatic conditions of Shanghai and enables the occupants to be aware of both seasonal change and the outward prospect of the urban landscape through panoramic vistas.

As with Yeang's other related projects, such as Hitechniaga, landscaped skycourt-gardens occur at vertical intervals providing internal-external buffer zones and acting as 'green lungs', which regenerate the microclimate of the building's periphery. In addition to these, the major features of the inflected cylindrical form include the expressive vertical circulation systems, the introduction of zones of public space and the major formal element of external weather shields.

[1] Ken Yeang: 'Shanghai Armoury Tower', Project Notes

Shanghai, People's Republic of China

owner Northern Pudong Open Economy Company

location Shanghai Pudong Golden Bridge Area, Pudong, Shanghai, People's Republic of China

latitude 31.14°N

nos of storeys 36 storeys

completion date 1997 (Design)

areas Built-up area 46,750 sq m
Site area 9,100 sq m

plot ratio 1:5.13

building plinth 25%

building height 125 m

motor vehicle parking 137 carparking spaces

bicycle parking 578 sq m nett

These are beautifully summarised in Yeang's characteristic and simple diagrams, which seen together, speak of his persistent development of **vertical urbanism**.

Otherwise, what is of particular note in this project is the manner in which the shift in geographical location brings about a form that, particularly in cross-section, responds to seasonal climatic variation and change. Both the double-skin facade and the important central atrium play significant roles in the modification and control of natural ventilation and air-insulation relative to the studies of summer, mid-season and winter conditions. Equally, the incorporation of huge **wind-breaker shields,** which are adjustable to seasonable wind conditions, and the application of sun-shading devices, both bring solutions to functional needs and add layers of great expressive force to the architecture – literally and symbolically.

The rich innovations of these combined elements – especially the variable functions of the central atrium, sky-courts and double-skin facade, stand together as an important moment in the development of Yeang's architecture and the move towards a full ecological resolution of its basis.

In giving the Shanghai Armoury Tower its proper place in this evolution, the major attributes that are carried forward are those of a **seasonal-responsive form**, and the potential for that form to carry with it a **cultural-symbolic** message. While in overall technical terms, the analysis of the fabric, systems and operational modes, flexibility and future adaptability are increasingly acute, and presented as integral to the project's conception.

design features • The China Armoury Tower is located in the Pudong District of Shanghai. The design is intended to create a modern urban icon for the client's progressive and valiant march into the 21st century.
• The 36-storey skyscraper is a symbolic interpretation of components found in military armaments. The sweeping panels of metallic screens on the exterior facade alludes to the armour of the Chinese warrior. The curved solar panel atop the building depicts the helmet, while the soaring tower piece is the 'victorious torch'. The stair plan suggests the trigger of a gun.
• The China Armoury Tower is a low-energy high-quality building. The external and internal design features use a bioclimatic approach to produce an operationally energy-efficient building that makes most of the coastal climatic conditions of Shanghai and allows for the occupants to experience and be aware of the changing seasons of the year.
• Landscaped sky terraces placed at strategic points in the tower represent buffer zones between the inside and outside. In addition the act as oxygen generating 'green lungs', which refresh the microclimate of the periphery of the building. The external weather-screen performs as a multi-functional filter against extreme climatic conditions while allowing generous panoramic views of the surrounding urban-space.
• The blending of bioclimatic devices into the architecture of the Shanghai Armoury Tower will produce a building outstandingly unique in design and style and a proud and distinguished symbol of the owners.

engineering design objectives • In order to achieve an efficient and low-energy performance building of high environmental quality, through the creative use of materials and skills, these building engineering objectives have been set.

1 Maximise human comfort in terms of:
   • good daylight and views
   • good air quality
   • appropriate room acoustics and insulation
   • good thermal control
   • adequate humidity control
   • good security and safety provisions
   • good personal control
   • high degree of adaptability.

2 Minimise running costs and energy consumption by:
   • maximising the use of free energies, such as daylight, sun, wind, precipitation and temperature changes
   • high levels of thermal insulation
   • reliable and appropriate control systems
   • efficient building systems and plant
   • use of low cost fuels at off peak rates
   • maximum use of low energy and renewable materials.

3 Minimise capital cost by:
   • reducing size of mechanical services
   • efficient design of services
   • reducing complexity of services
   • co-ordination of structure and services.

4 Minimise maintenance costs by:
   • utilising durable materials
   • long-life equipment
   • reliable and simple environmental control systems
   • good access for maintenance

5 Maximise useable space by:
   • efficient planning
   • minimising plant area
   • removing the necessity for false ceilings
   • maximising structural/service integration.

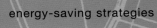

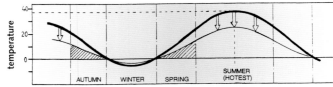

strategy of moderating the internal temperature by passive means
and extending the 'mid-season' in Latitude 31.14°N (Shanghai)

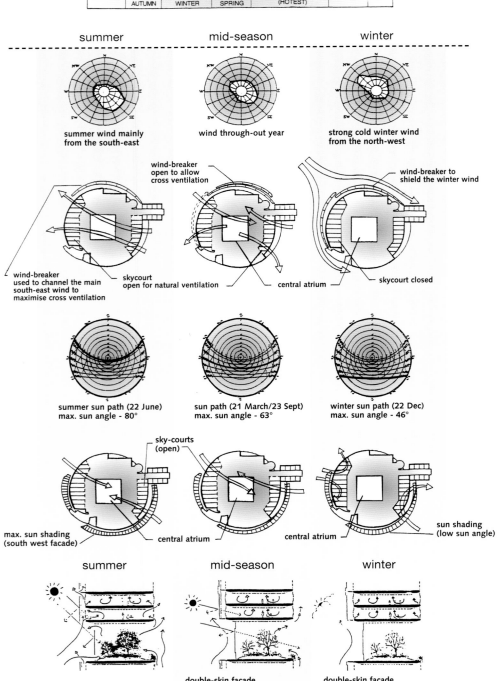

| summer | mid-season | winter |

summer wind mainly
from the south-east

wind through-out year

strong cold winter wind
from the north-west

wind-breaker
open to allow
cross ventilation

wind-breaker to
shield the winter wind

wind-breaker
used to channel the main
south-east wind to
maximise cross ventilation

skycourt
open for natural ventilation

central atrium

skycourt closed

summer sun path (22 June)
max. sun angle - 80°

sun path (21 March/23 Sept)
max. sun angle - 63°

winter sun path (22 Dec)
max. sun angle - 46°

sky-courts
(open)

max. sun shading
(south west facade)

central atrium

central atrium

sun shading
(low sun angle)

| summer | mid-season | winter |

double-skin facade
-in summer it allows for
natural ventilation by opening
windows in the inner skin

double-skin facade
-in mid-seasons the
natural ventilation is
controlled by adjustable
louvres in between the skins

double-skin facade
-in winter the louvre
shutters can be closed so
that the cavity becomes an
insulating cushion of air

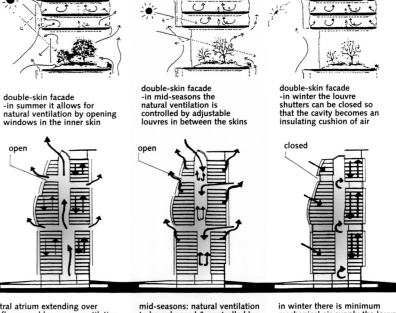

open

open

closed

the central atrium extending over
several floors enables cross-ventilation
of the building & therefore the natural
ventilation of the office spaces & hotel
corridor next to the atria

mid-seasons: natural ventilation
to be enhanced & controlled by:
- thermal stack effects by
  thermal flue (atrium)
- wind suction

in winter there is minimum
mechanical air supply the louvres
inside the double-skin facade are
closed in order to insulate the
building with air cavity

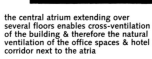

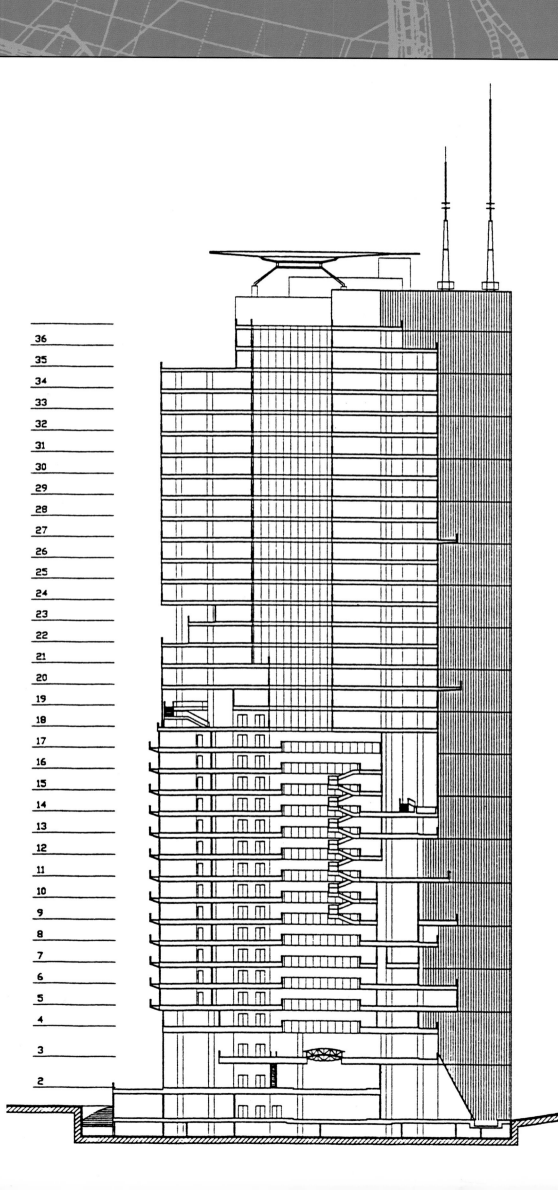

36	
35	
34	
33	
32	
31	
30	
29	
28	
27	
26	
25	
24	
23	
22	
21	
20	
19	
18	
17	
16	
15	
14	
13	
12	
11	
10	
9	
8	
7	
6	
5	
4	
3	
2	

6 Efficient planning in terms of:
- good orientation and views
- manageable security
- ease of adaptability and flexibility
- efficient circulation systems.

7 Design for change:
- simple and modular design to cope with future change
- ease of re-routing services to changing functions
- interchangeable modular design for partitions.

8 Maximise creative space by:
- utilising the interaction of structure and materials, with the climate to provide a space conducive to working and increasing an awareness of occupants environment.
- maximising the qualities inherent in construction materials.
- demonstrating the skills of local workmanship.

9 Protect and enhance ecological values by:
- integrating local fauna and wildlife
- generating green and blue conditions
- scientific landscaping
- collection of rainwater and recycling
- effective waste management and recycling.

energy-saving strategies
Battle McCarthy (consulting engineers)

- Towers may be considered as vertical infrastructure from which humans may perform on plates in the sky.
- Shanghai Armoury Tower was conceived as an armature of structural grid and power and communication wire ways which are enclosed by elemental building enclosures sliced by floor plates.
- For the majority of the year the offices are naturally ventilated. Natural ventilation is enhanced by the air being drawn from the building floor plates by wind and solar-induced effects.
- During the winter and extreme summer periods the offices are mechanically ventilated with preheated or pre-cooled air respectively. The energy demand is supplemented by renewable energies such as sun, wind and ground water cooling.
- The structure consists of a rigid space frame supporting floors and perimeter cladding. The cladding consists of lightweight panels which moderate energy flow between outside and inside.
- The floors are serviced from a primary service core which runs for the full height of the building.

energy management
global warming
- Increased CO_2 emissions into the atmosphere will result in further global warming. At the Earth Summit in 1992 in Rio, and 1995 in Berlin world governments set out a directive to reduce CO_2 emissions.
- Yet the world energy consumption is expected to rise by 40% over the next 15 years to satisfy the needs of growing population and increased housing standards.
- 90% of the energy will be generated from housing fossil fuels (gas, oil and coal). This will result not in a reduction of CO_2 emissions but an increase of 30% with possible catastrophic impact on our ecology as we know it.
- 50% of the world energy is consumed by servicing buildings. The Armoury Tower will demonstrate that high internal comfort conditions may be achieved economically without huge dependence upon fossil fuel consumption.

running cost saving and reduced CO_2 emissions
- The tower is a low -tower which uses renewable energies to supplement the use of fossil fuel consumption.

- Typical office blocks of this scale would consume at least **600 Kwhr/m² per year prime energy** which would contribute to at least 400kg/m² of CO_2 emissions per year, equivalent to a total of 20,000 tons per year.
- The proposed tower design will consume less than a third of the energy of a traditional air-conditioned building. CO_2 emissions may be further reduced by the successful insulation of wind generators and solar collectors, ie. the resultant CO_2 emissions may be quarter of those from a conventional building.

facade options
Battle McCarthy (1997)

ventilation strategy
Battle McCarthy (1997)

ventilation strategy
initial proposal by
Battle McCarthy (1995)

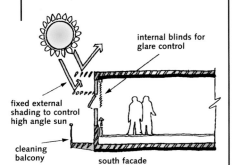

- internal blinds for glare control
- fixed external shading to control high angle sun
- cleaning balcony

south facade

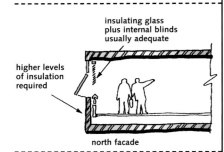

- insulating glass plus internal blinds usually adequate
- higher levels of insulation required

north facade

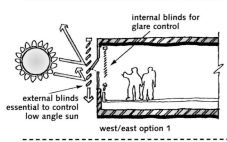

- internal blinds for glare control
- external blinds essential to control low angle sun

west/east option 1

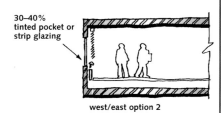

- 30–40% tinted pocket or strip glazing

west/east option 2

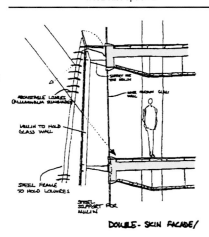

DOUBLE-SKIN FACADE/

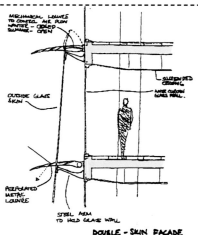

DOUBLE-SKIN FACADE

For most of the year between the extreme cold of winter and the heat of summer the building may be naturally ventilated. To moderate the winter and summer climatic extremes, solar gain is optimised in the winter whilst night time cooling is optimised in the summer.

The exposed soffit of the concrete slab provides a degree of thermal inertia and heat store. The more surface exposed to the air movement the greater the effect.

The building makes use of solar gains and a wind tower, to move air through the offices. When used in combination with night time ventilation, these help to flatten out peak temperature within the office areas.

winter

offices – winter day
- During winter, mechanical air is supplied to each floor. Air is extracted at high level from the offices.
- A heat recuperator and/or mixing section within the air handling unit will ensure that only a minimum of additional fresh air heating is required.
- The air handling units will operate on full fresh air, if necessary, to maintain a high level of air freshness and a temperature of 20–21°C.

winter
- The building is sealed and mechanical air is supplied to the offices to provide the minimum fresh air requirement to the occupants.
- Heat recovery within the air handling unit makes use of the heat produced by the occupants' office equipment and also utilises solar gains.

mid-season

offices – mid-season day
- During periods of mild weather (over 50% of the year) the building utilises combination of mechanical displacement ventilation and passive night time cooling of the structure to maintain acceptable comfort conditions. The heating system will be switched off and opening windows on the facade will permit cross ventilation.
- The exposed concrete soffit, which is pre-cooled overnight, will absorb the peak heat of the day and ensure that comfort is maintained.
- During sunny periods shading will control solar penetration into the offices.

offices – mid-season night
- By night the air temperature falls and high level windows will open to allow the air to cool the exposed concrete soffit. When the offices have been sufficiently cooled the windows will close.

mid-season – March & September
- Air enters buildings via wind scoop and at a low level (see 1 and 2).
- Solar gain assists stack driven natural ventilation, by warming air between the offices and the outer skin. This creates a negative pressure, with the office areas drawing in more air from outside via 1 and 2.

summer

offices – summer day
- During periods of high external temperature (ie. above 24°C) the building will have a tendency to overheat.
- To maintain adequate comfort conditions the mechanical ventilation system will be utilised to provide force, cooled mechanical ventilation to all office areas. Air will be supplied from the air-handling units.
- Cooled will result from a combination of air cooling and radiant cooling from the underside of the exposed concrete soffit, thus requiring a smaller amount of ventilation.

offices – summer night
- By night the mechanical ventilation system will operate and drive cooled air through the offices. The slabs will accordingly be cooled, and the exhaust air will be extracted at high level.

summer
- During peak summer conditions, the building is mechanically ventilated.
- The air handling plant makes use of full fresh air, but will require additional comfort cooling to offset maximum heat gains.
- The air is extracted from the atrium by the wind tower.

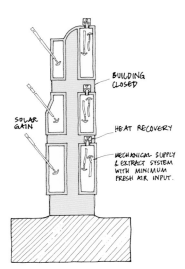

- BUILDING CLOSED
- SOLAR GAIN
- HEAT RECOVERY
- MECHANICAL SUPPLY & EXTRACT SYSTEM WITH MINIMUM FRESH AIR INPUT.

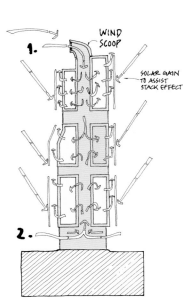

1.

- WIND SCOOP
- SOLAR GAIN TO ASSIST STACK EFFECT

2.

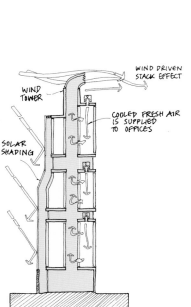

- WIND DRIVEN STACK EFFECT
- WIND TOWER
- COOLED FRESH AIR IS SUPPLIED TO OFFICES
- SOLAR SHADING

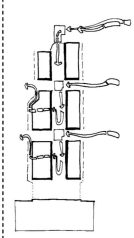

IN

OUT

- BUILDING USERS ARE MORE TOLERANT OF HIGHER TEMPERATURES IF THERE IS GREATER AIR MOVEMENT.

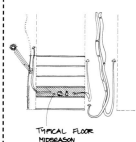

TYPICAL FLOOR MIDSEASON

winter period	mid-season period	summer period

During the day, fresh air is pre-heated in the thermal flue and mechanically supplied to each floor. At night the louvres within the thermal flue close to provide insulation, preserving heat stored during the day.

The outside air temperature suits the internal requirements and the building transforms to optimise natural ventilation. The skycourts are opened to the atria. The thermal stack effect works by the thermal flue drawing air from the atria across the floor plates. A wind scoop at the top of the atria forces cool fresh air through the building.

At night the air temperature drops. By ventilating the building overnight the structure is pre-cooled for the following day. During the very high summer temperatures, mechanically cooled air is supplied. the air is vented through the thermal flue or atria.

daytime

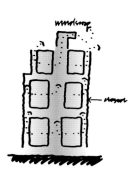

nighttime

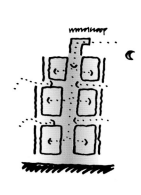

energy management

global warming

• The energy demand profile throughout the year and over the day has been moderated.

• With more consistent energy demand throughout the year and day, a combined heat, cool and power plant becomes more economically viable as the size and the capacity of the plant has been minimised and it will run a full capacity for longer durations making the payback period very favourable.

• The CHP plant will be powered by gas, however, renewable energies such as wind power, solar power and heat sink capacity of ground water will also contribute to minimise the use of fossil fuels.

winter period

• The 'peak lopping' of the winter energy demand will be achieved by the following energy strategy:-

1 minimise heat loss by:
• good insulation
• minimise surface area
• protect building envelope from the wind.

2 maximise solar gain by:
• large glazed area to the south
• maximise exposed area to the sun.

Utilising the thermal mass of the structure as 24-hour heat store and to dampen sudden temperature changes.

summer period

• The 'peak lopping' of the summer energy demand may be achieved by:

1 minimising solar gain with adequate shading devices

2 minimising heat gain or cooling loss by:
• good insulation
• protection from winds
• minimising surface area.

3 utilising the thermal mass of the structure as a 24-hour thermal regulation - storing the coolness at night for the following day and dampening climatic changes.

mid-season period

• During mid-season, there is no need for either heating or cooling and the building may be naturally ventilated.

• As building comes out of winter, the heating is switched off and the building will open up to a warmer climate, however, as the climate warms further, the internal temperature rises and cooling will be required as summer begins. However, higher temperatures are more acceptable if there is good ventilation.

• Thus, if the switching on of the cooling system for the building is to be delayed the building should enhance natural cross ventilation as much as possible – wind and solar power may be used to drive the ventilation of the tower by solar stack effect or wind suction or wind pressure.

• The ventilation of the tower is driven by both wind and sun during mid-season period. The temperature rise during the day is minimised by night time ventilation – the cool night time is used to pre-cool the structure for the following day.

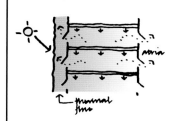

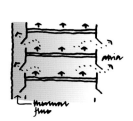

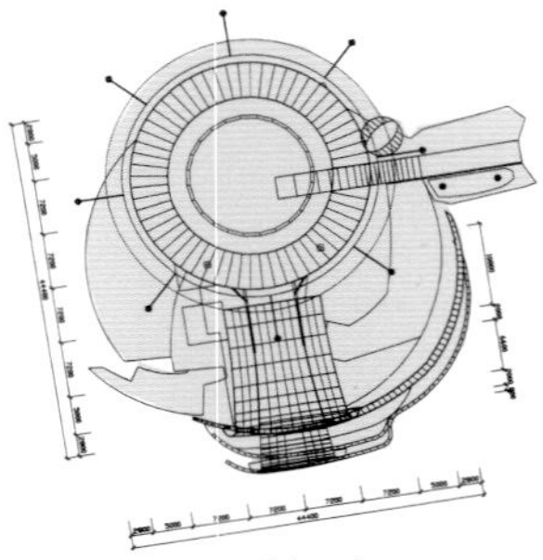

roof level

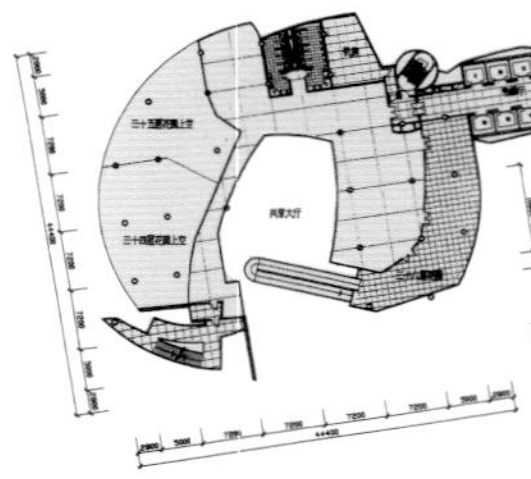

level 21

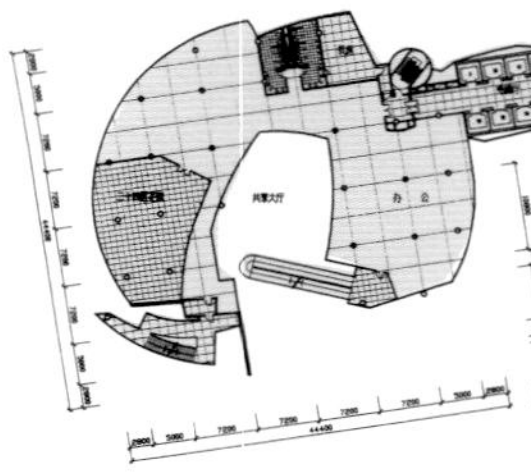

level 15

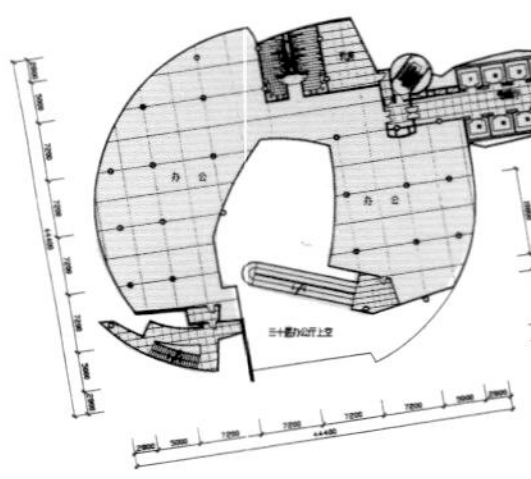

level 5

level 36

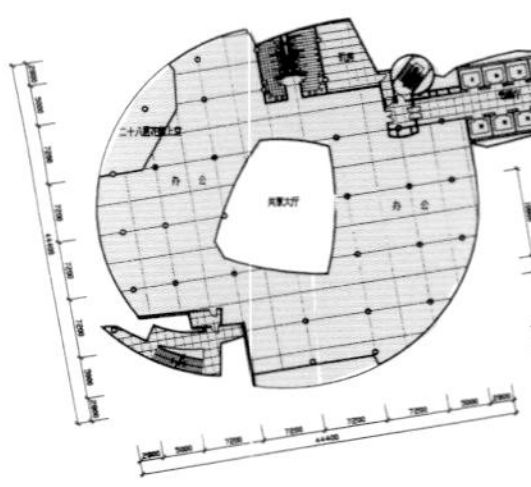

level 20

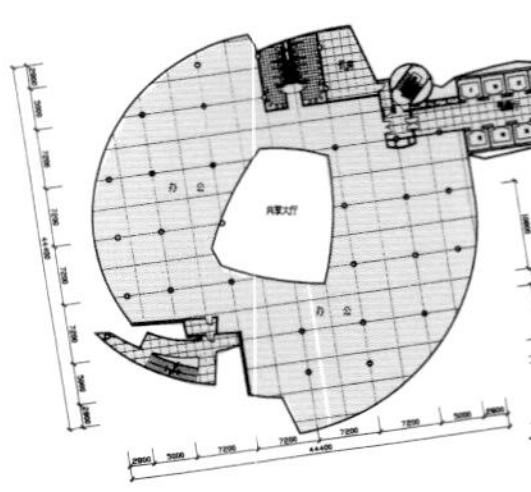

level 11

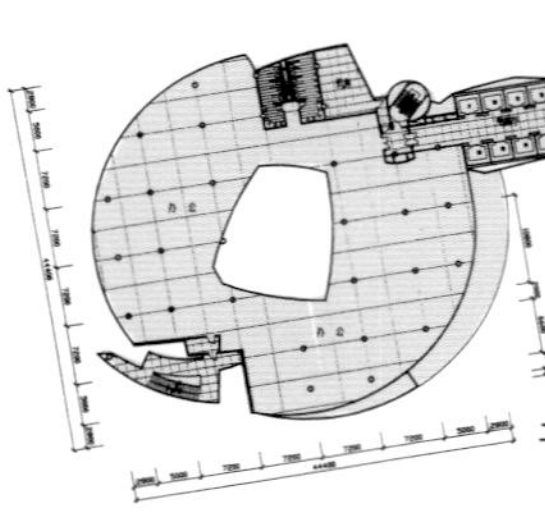

level 4

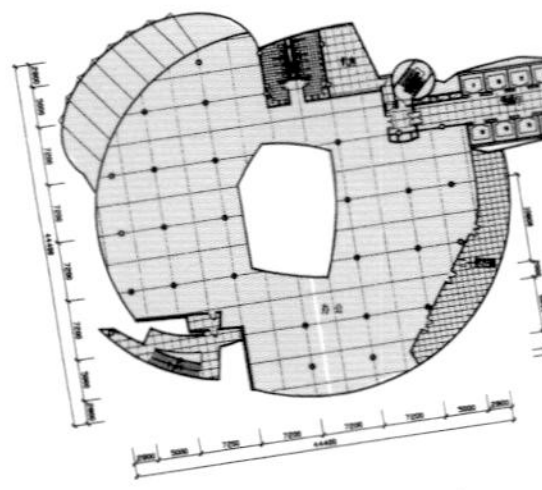

level 34

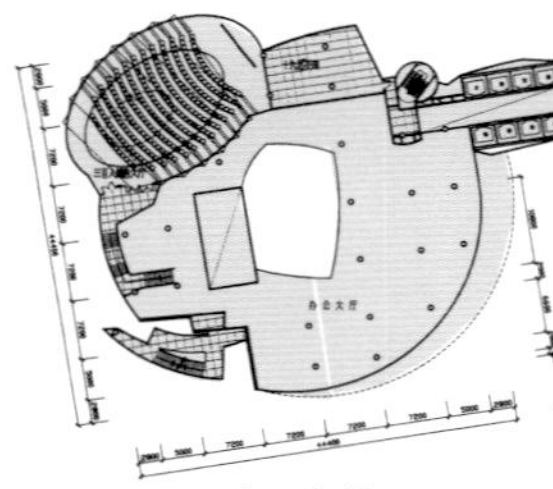

level 19

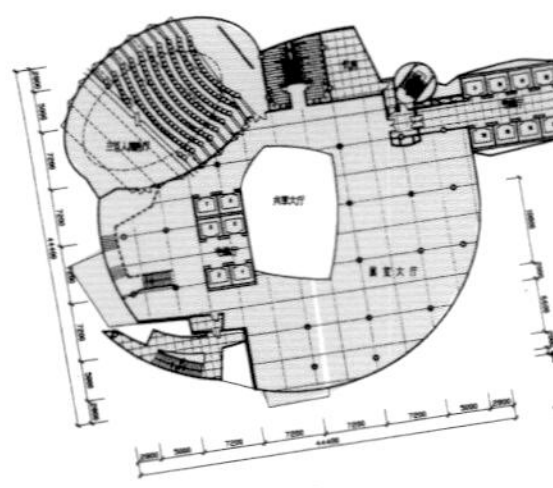

level 10

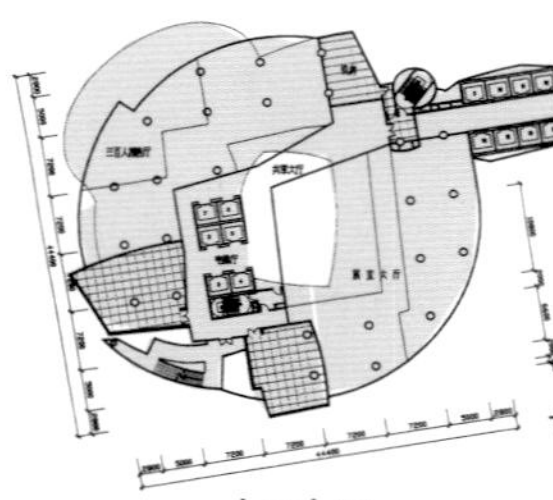

level 2

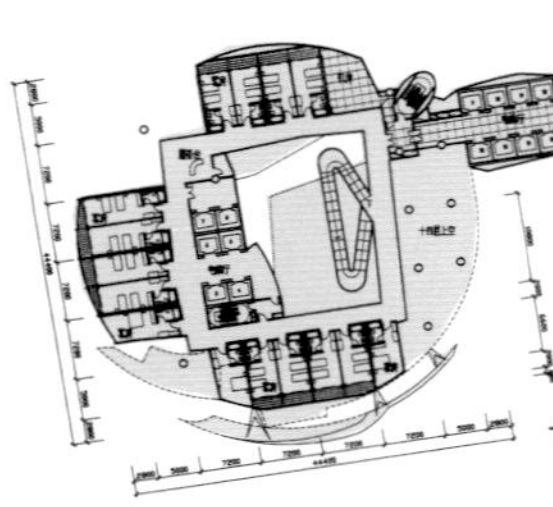

level 31

level 18

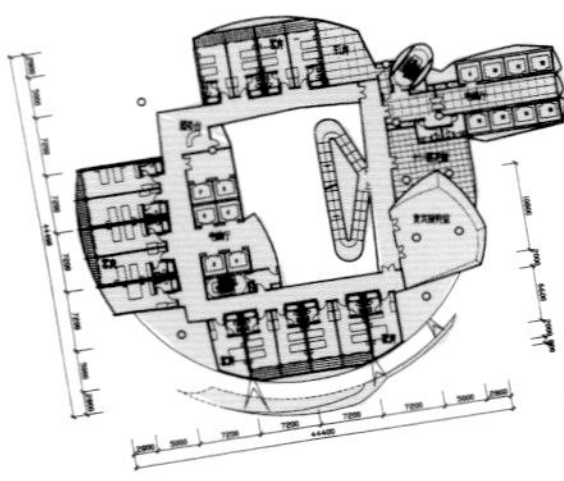

level 9

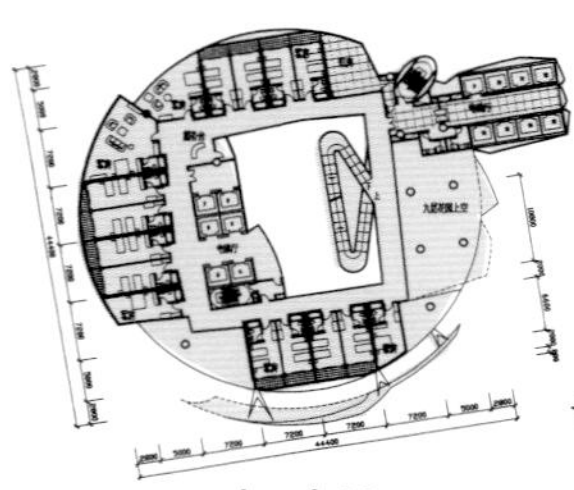

level 1

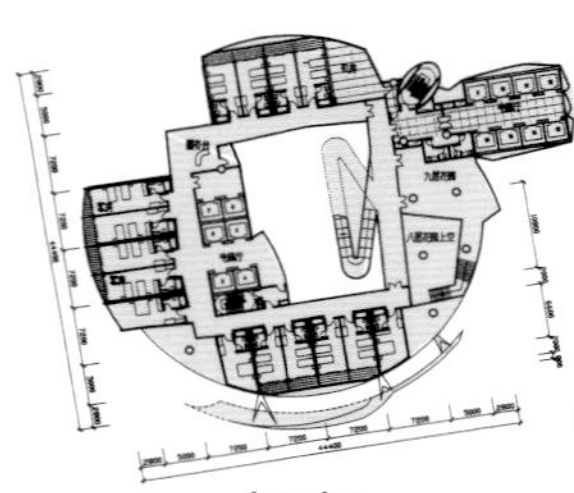

level 29

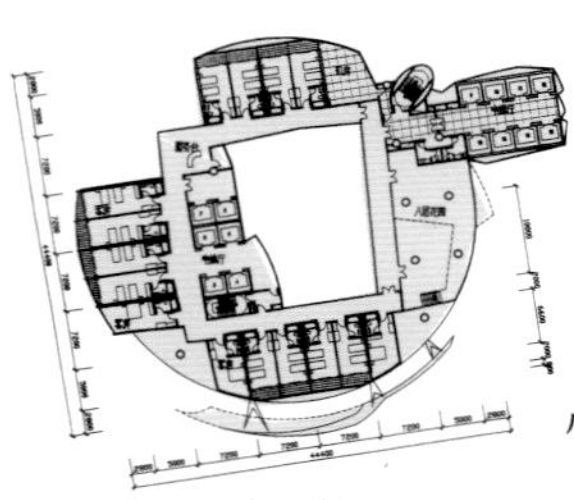

level 17

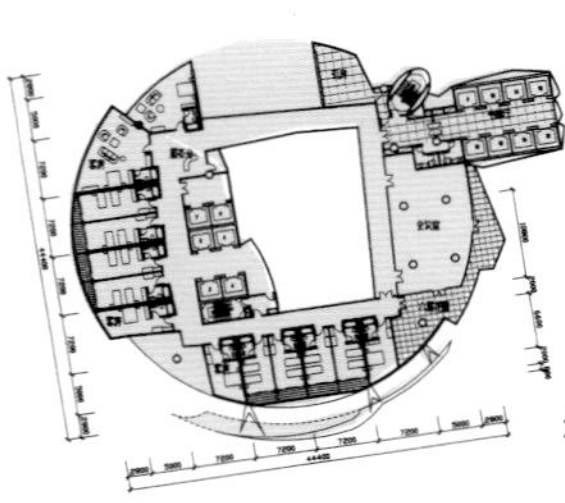

level 8

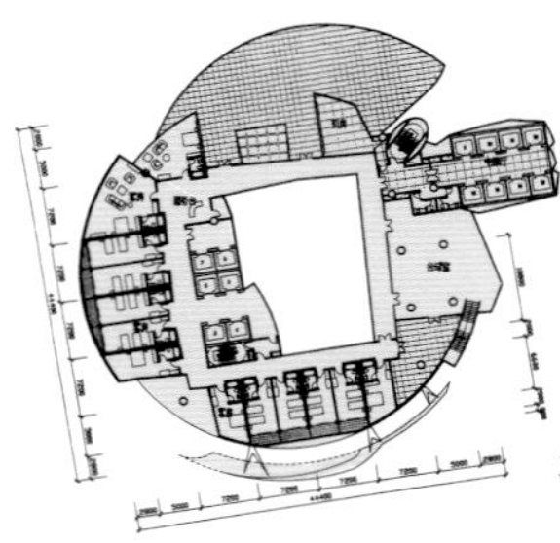

level 26

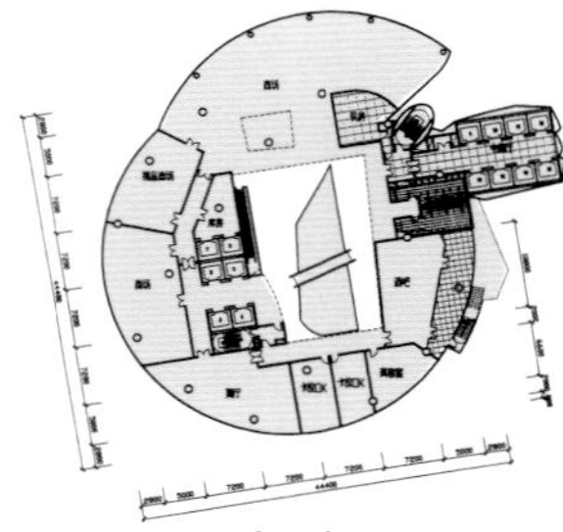

level 16

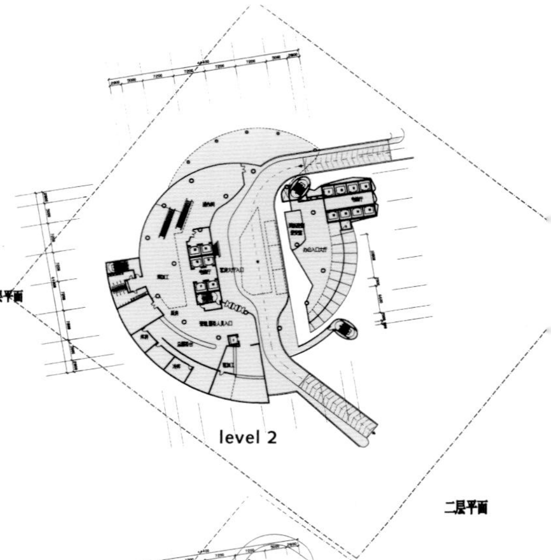

level 6

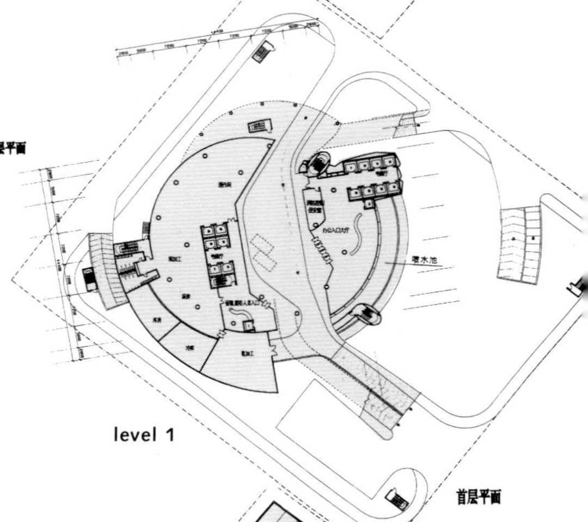

basement

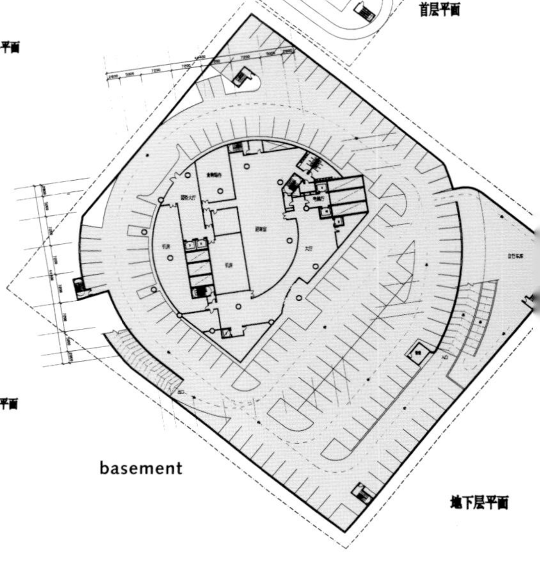

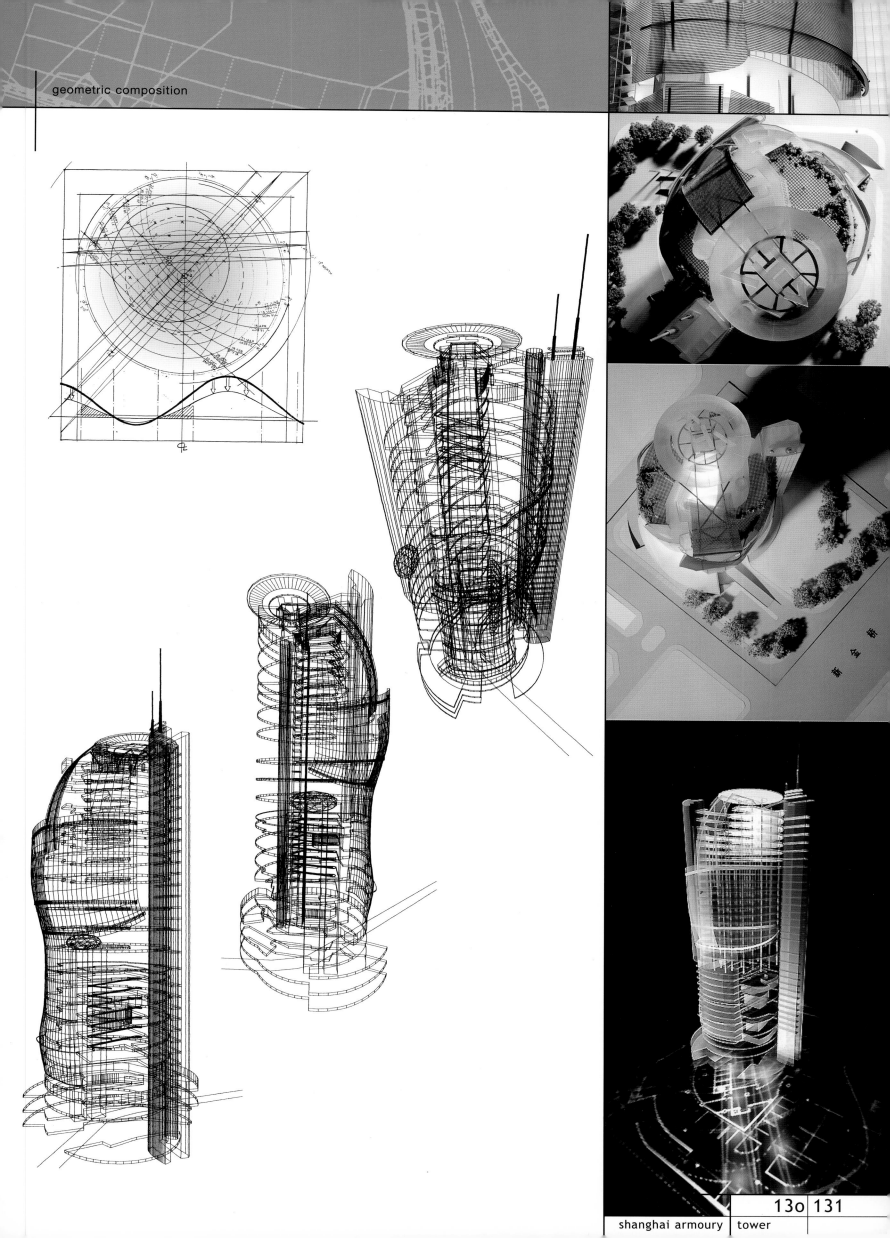

offices @ periphery

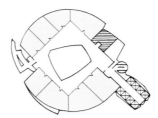

large rooms

small rooms

variation

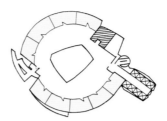

large rooms

small rooms

offices @ centre

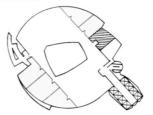

large rooms

variation

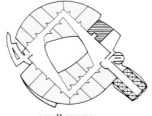

small rooms

open concept

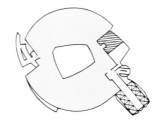

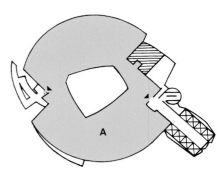

single tenant
arrangement
net leasable area = 82% typ. flr.

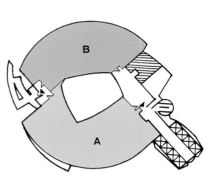

double tenant
arrangement
net leasable area = 78% typ. flr.

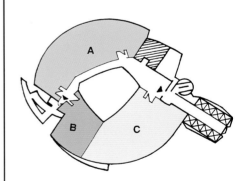

triple tenant
arrangement
net leasable area = 75% typ. flr.

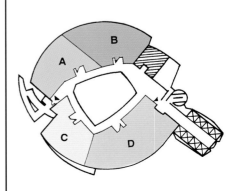

multiple tenant
arrangement
net leasable area = 74% typ. flr.

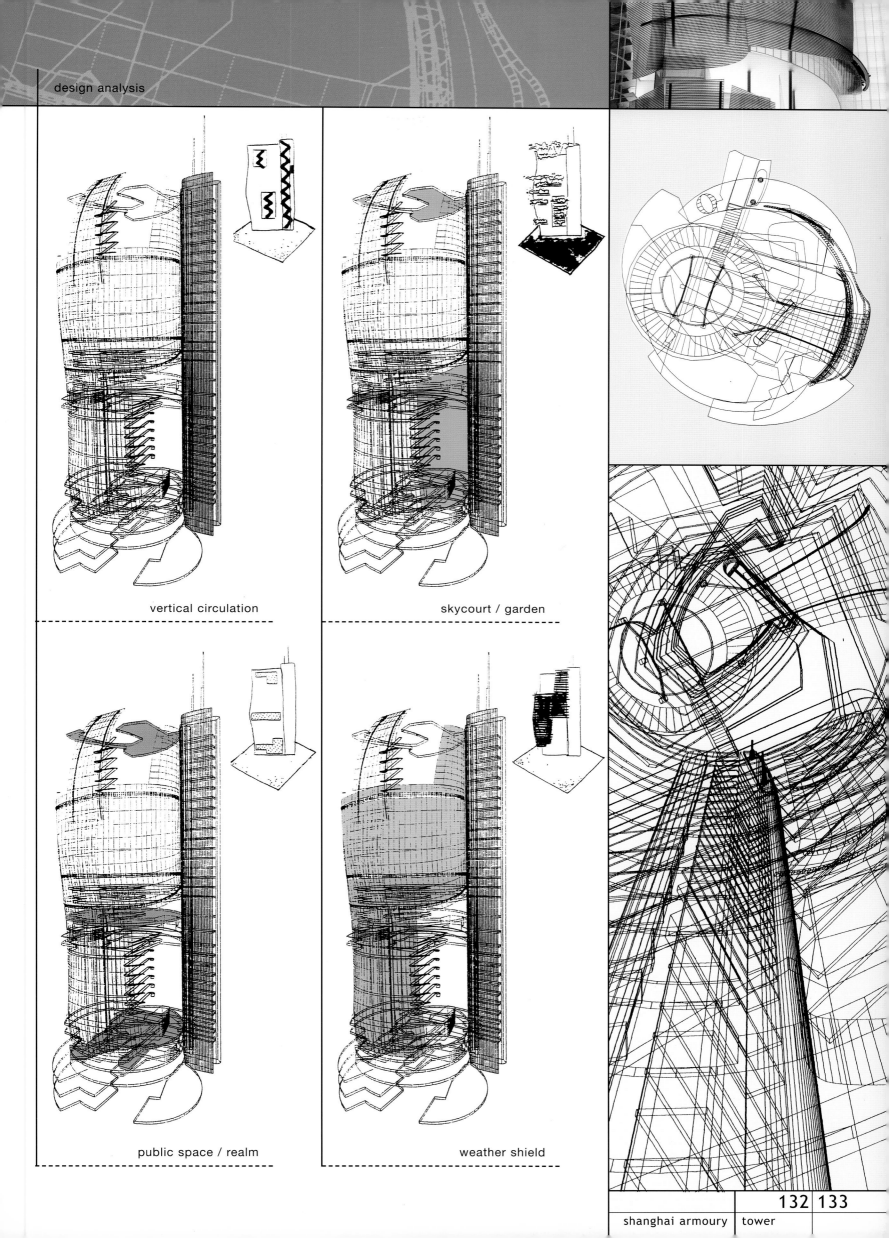

vertical circulation

skycourt / garden

public space / realm

weather shield

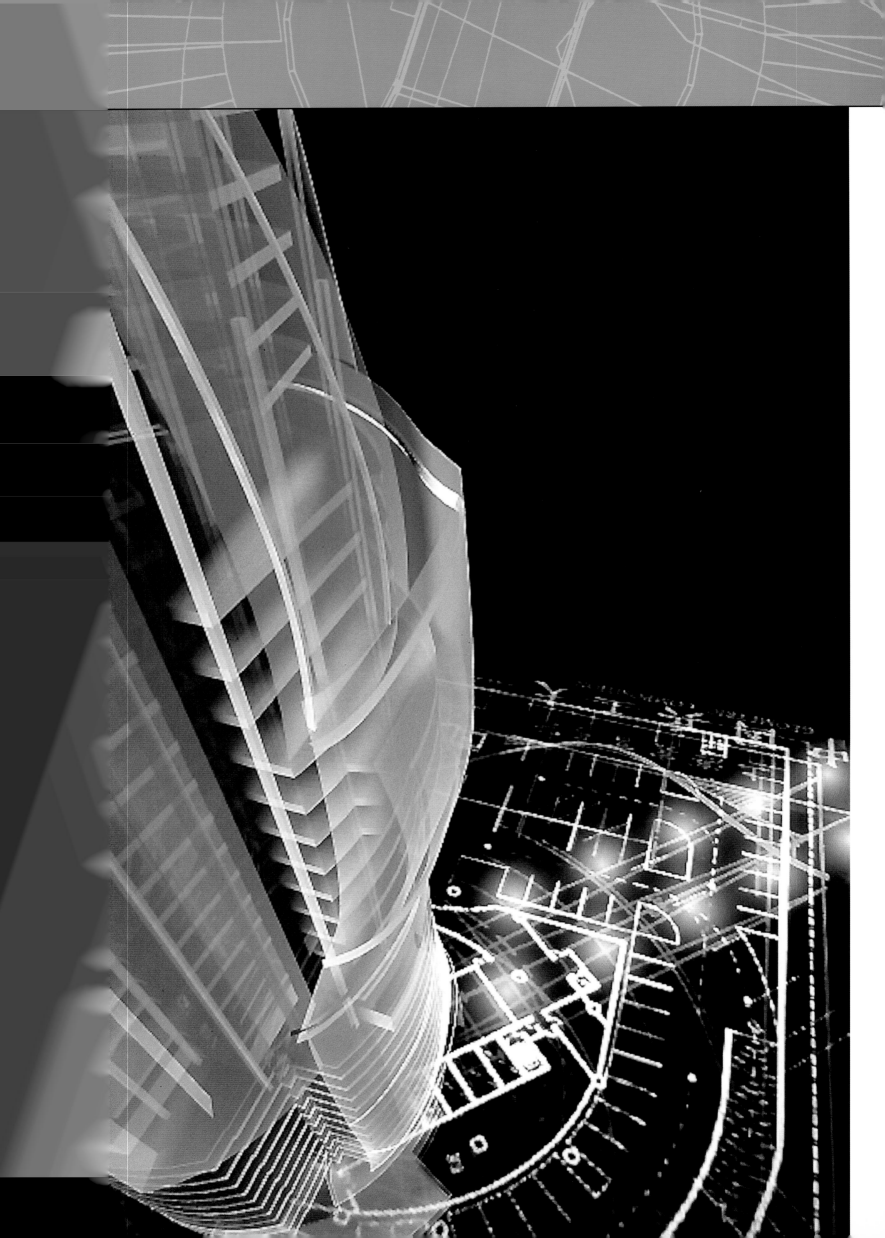

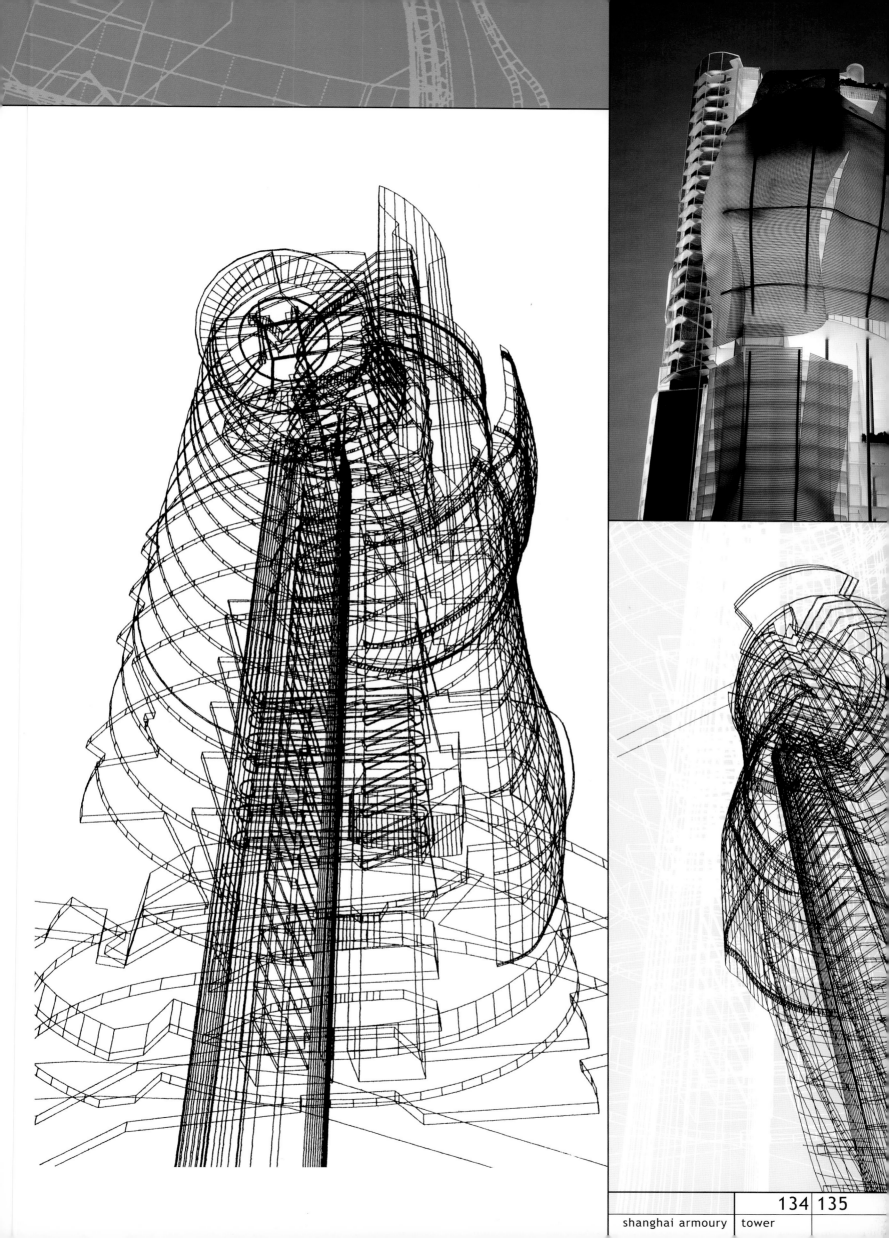

Shah Alam, Malaysia

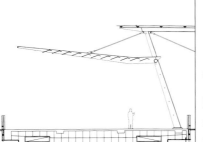

gamuda headquarters

owner Gamuda Berhad
location Kota Kemuning Business Park,
Shah Alam, Malaysia
latitude 3.2°N
nos of storeys 10 storeys
date start 1996
completion date pending
areas Total gross area 31,800 sq m
Site area 12,145 sq m
plot ratio 1:2.6

design features
• The focus of the new HQ building is the visually exciting elliptical atrium created by the two curved wings of the office tower.
• The office floors are raised 12 metres above the ground plane to allow this public atrium space to blend into the extensive ground level water and tropical garden system which continues through the business park. This central space is visible from all floors.
• A sculptural roof structure screens the atrium from the rain while allowing natural light in to promote the growth of a garden oasis within.
• The design of the building also takes advantage of the prevailing winds to naturally ventilate the atrium space and the building's skycourts to create an environment that is both pleasant and soothing.
• Sensitive attention is paid to the landscaping not only at ground level but in the building itself through the generous provision of lush green skycourts, elevated garden terraces and roof gardens.
• Sunscreens and solar filters are strategically incorporated into the design of the building to minimize the heat gain from the sun thereby reducing energy costs. The building is designed as a passive low-energy building in response to the United Nations' agenda for sustainable buildings.

Within Ken Yeang's progressive development of projects for headquarters' facilities, offices and associated executive and training spaces, certain generic forms occur. The most obvious examples must include the enduring nature of Menara Mesiniaga, and transmuted – the design for the Shanghai Armoury Tower with its central atrium. Both of these are responsive **cylindrical** compositions which are capable of development into a series of related types, depending on the emphasis.

The Gamuda Headquarters is a subtle development of this lineage. Within the encirclement of a powerful **ellipse**, arises the creation of an enormous external public space – **a garden atrium**. While the built version is some 10 storeys in height, the same essential ideas and organisation could apply to a skyscraper of 100 storeys, or more.

That is to say that the essential principles of a peripheral ring of occupied space, a naturally ventilated centre, and a light central roof structure are all elements of an archetype – a summary of a generic type within Yeang's emergent architectural enquiry.

Taken as it stands, the composition of the Gamuda Headquarters is essentially simple, geometrically pure and bioclimatic in its response. The main principles of orientation, shielding and the resultant plan composition are all inherited from the earlier models, but what is dramatically different here is the focused development of the **inner atrium** – on a grand scale – and the study of wind-flow pattern on both the elliptical atrium and the peripheral surround of accommodation, which includes landscaped skycourts, elevated garden terraces and roof gardens.

In designing the building to take advantage of prevailing winds, both the elliptical atrium and the elevated skycourts benefit from an environment where supportive air-flow sustains the occupants in a pleasant and beneficial manner. The heavy and appropriate emphasis on landscape as a major element of the project is further enhanced by the raising of the lower office floors some 12 metres above the ground plane. This sectional arrangement allows the central garden oasis of the elliptical atrium to flow into and unite with the water and tropical garden system which is prevalent throughout the business park setting.

The plan is an exemplar of major principles applied in a direct and simple parti: the major shielding service cores are situated at the hot east and west ends, whose external wall surface is minimised by the elliptical geometry. The long north and south faces are cut open by a slanting sliced bisection, which both opens the atrium, creating airflow and is crossed by breezeway bridges on both facades.

The wind tunnel test report by the consultant on the proposed Wisma Gamuda Berhad Headquarters was received and studied. There are copious amounts of data contained in that report however some are more critical than others at the current stage of design.

The shape of the building, its proximity to other nearby buildings and its orientation with respect to prevailing winds determines the local wind speeds affecting people's comfort and safety. Estimates of local wind speeds and their associated % time of occurrence for four speeds intervals were calculated from the maximum wind speed coefficients for each location measured in the wind tunnel study. In addition extreme conditions that might be expected based on 50-year return period gradient winds which approach 30m/s were calculated.

Design wind loads on cladding points in kPa from 141 measurement points on the wind tunnel model based on a gradient height height design wind speed of 35 m/s are provided in Table 3c of the wind tunnel test report. The maximum value is 0.4844 kPa for location 89.

Estimates of natural ventilation are provided for minimum wind speeds needed to achieve 6 air changes per hour and the percentage of time winds from that direction equal or exceed that minimal wind speed. More extensive estimates of natural ventilation will be provided in the final report.

It is clear from the estimates of natural ventilation due to wind and stack effect that:
- While calms can occur for up to 45% of time most occurrences are at night.
- Openings in external walls will need to be significantly larger than those currently indicated, probably similar in area to associated doorway openings.
- During the 55% of time when there is wind these winds could provide 6 air changes per hour in stairwells and lift lobbies for approximately 35% of time.
- In spaces with vertical continuity such as stairwells stack effect can provide significant ventilation.

Local wind speeds during normal wind conditions in the locations studied on the wind tunnel test model did not exceed Beaufort 4 (moderate breeze). However in the case of extreme 1 hour in 50 year storm events Beaufort numbers at a few locations reached 9 (strong gale) or blow down velocities. This suggests that provisions be made in the design to prevent pedestrians access to these locations, RO2, RO3 and EO7 during such events.

Design wind loads on cladding in kPa from 141 measurement points on the wind tunnel model based on a gradient height design wind speed of 35 m/s are provided in the wind tunnel test report. The maximum design wind pressure in these data is 0.4844 kPa for location 89.

location of pressure tapping points

----

level 3/ points 65 - 98 (ie. between 7 to 9 flr)

maximum value (on gradient height design wind-speed of 35 m/s) is 0.4844 kPa @ location 89 (level 3)

bridge 2 north (B2N)

bridge 1 east (B1E)

bridge 2 east (B2E)

skycourt east (SE 1-2)

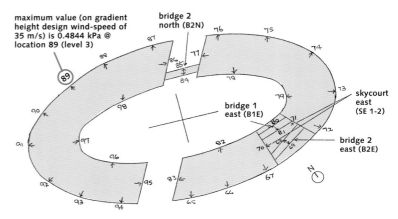

Wind and speed effects at 10m

(1m/s = 1.94 knots = 2.25mph)

beaufort scale	description	mean wind speed range (m/s)	effects at 10m
B0	calm	0 - 0.2	
B1	light air	0.3 - 1.5	No noticeable wind
B2	light breeze	1.6 - 3.3	Wind felt on face
B3	gentle breeze	3.4 - 5.4	Wind extends light flag
B4	moderate breeze	5.5 - 7.9	Raises dust and loose paper. Hair disarranged, clothing flaps
B5	fresh breeze	8.0 - 10.7	Limit of agreeable wind on land
B6	strong breeze	10.8 - 13.8	Umbrellas used with difficulty. Force of wind felt on the body. Noisy, frequent blinking.
B7	near gale	13.9 - 17.1	Inconvenience felt when walking, difficult to walk steadily. Hair blown straight.
B8	gale	17.2 - 20.7	Generally impedes progress, walking difficult to control. Difficulty balancing in gusts.
B9	strong gale	20.8 - 24.4	People blown over. Impossible to face wind; ear ache, headache, breathing difficult. Some structural damage occurs; falling roof tiles, tree branches, etc. Hazardous for pedestrians.
B10	storm	24.5 - 28.4	Seldom experienced inland. Trees uprooted; considerable structural damage occurs.

location of velocity measurements

----

plan view

bridges (north)

skycourt & bridges (west)

1 hour in 50 year storm, Beaufort 9 @ R02, R03 and E07

skycourt & bridges (east)

bridges (south)

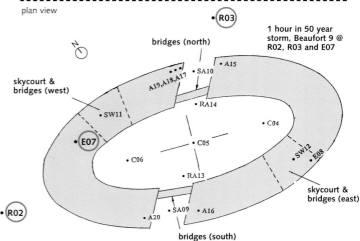

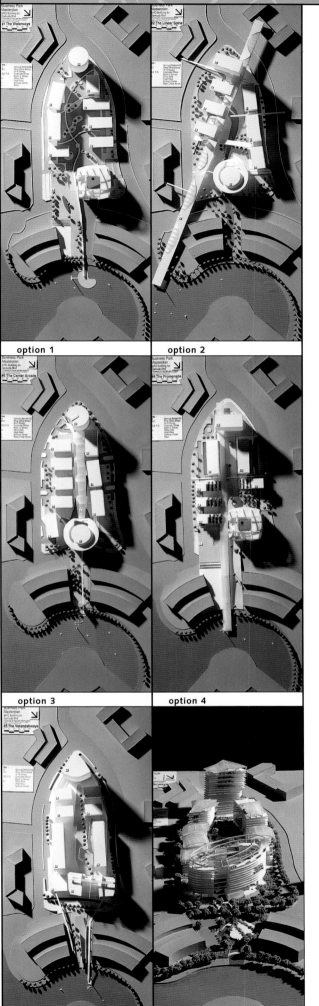

option 1

option 2

option 3

option 4

option 5

selected option

The whole of the enclosed accommodation is served by a continuous inner ring of single-loaded circulation, which encircles and views the elliptical atrium. Equally, the office space can view inwards across the circulation, or outwards from the periphery of the essentially 'thin' plan-form. This arrangement also maximises the provision of extensive natural-light and affords a first-class working environment for all occupants.

Detail studies of the sunscreen louvre banks and solar filters determine the appropriate level of solar protection and modify the daylight, while minimising heat gain and reducing energy costs.

The final major element is the over-sailing 'free' sculptural roof structure of the elliptical atrium, which is designed as a transparent umbrella rain-screen, allowing daylight to penetrate to the garden oasis beneath its sheltering presence. At the same time, the cantilevered outriggers of the roof-umbrella are intended to shield extensive roof-gardens.

What is clearly evidenced in this project is the well-rehearsed repertoire of Yeang's **passive low-energy** building agenda; all the elements are present, from the naturally ventilated lift-core lobbies to the skycourt gardens and partially open circulation. To this basic framework he has added the 'big idea' of the sheltered atrium and the elliptical geometry. The whole is gathered together into a sustainable building in response to the United Nations' agenda and towards a responsible 21st century architecture. For instance, in this case (as with all others that follow) Yeang has incorporated an **Embodied Energy Study** of the major building fabric – an aspect of his proposition that future design quality will be based upon **knowledge** – a substantiation of facts and of performance, quite as much as a spatial and aesthetic construct.

The Gamuda building, in its summary form is at once both simplistic and profound. Consistent rehearsal of principles and constant manipulation of form have enabled Yeang to reinvent the bioclimatic skyscraper in a number of notable types – the **Gamuda-type**, in itself, serves to inform a series of following developments, and in this sense, together with Menara Mesiniaga, is a benchmark project.

OTTV (Overall Thermal Transmission Value) studies of alternative configurations of service cores and orientation of the built form

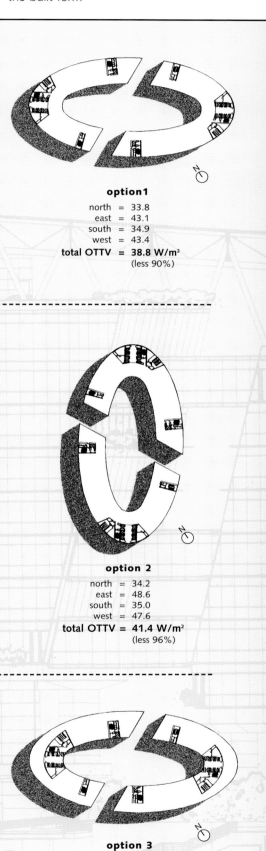

option 1

north = 33.8
east = 43.1
south = 34.9
west = 43.4
total OTTV = 38.8 W/m²
(less 90%)

option 2

north = 34.2
east = 48.6
south = 35.0
west = 47.6
total OTTV = 41.4 W/m²
(less 96%)

option 3

north = 35.3
east = 50.2
south = 36.0
west = 50.3
total OTTV = 42.9 W/m²
(100%)

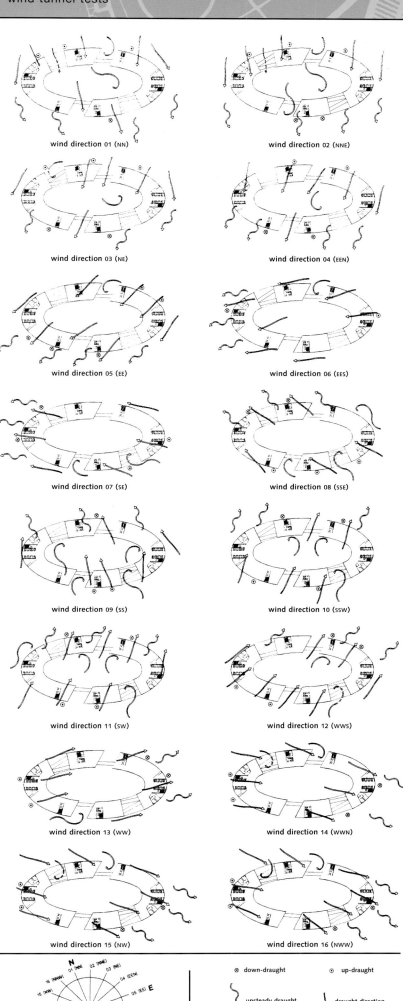

wind direction 01 (NN)

wind direction 02 (NNE)

wind direction 03 (NE)

wind direction 04 (EEN)

wind direction 05 (EE)

wind direction 06 (EES)

wind direction 07 (SE)

wind direction 08 (SSE)

wind direction 09 (SS)

wind direction 10 (SSW)

wind direction 11 (SW)

wind direction 12 (WWS)

wind direction 13 (WW)

wind direction 14 (WWN)

wind direction 15 (NW)

wind direction 16 (NWW)

wind directions (16 nos.)

notation

⊗ down-draught   ⊙ up-draught

unsteady draught   draught direction
other than up or down

circulation

internal flow

wind tunnel test

by Professor TS Lee, Professor YT Chew & Associates
Faculty of Engineering, National University of Singapore

Atmospheric boundar layer simulation
in industrial wind tunnel model with
surroundings (view from the South)

Instrumentation for pressure
measurement

Instrumentation for wind speed
measurement

Measurement for wind speed with
Omni-directional probe

Instrumentation for on-line data
acquisition

Setup of the thermal couples in the
test model

wind direction: 01 (NN)

Wind direction: 02 (NNE)

wind direction: 03 (NE)

wind direction: 04 (EEN)

wind direction: 05 (EE)

wind direction: 06 (EES)

wind direction: 07 (SE)

wind direction: 08 (SSE)

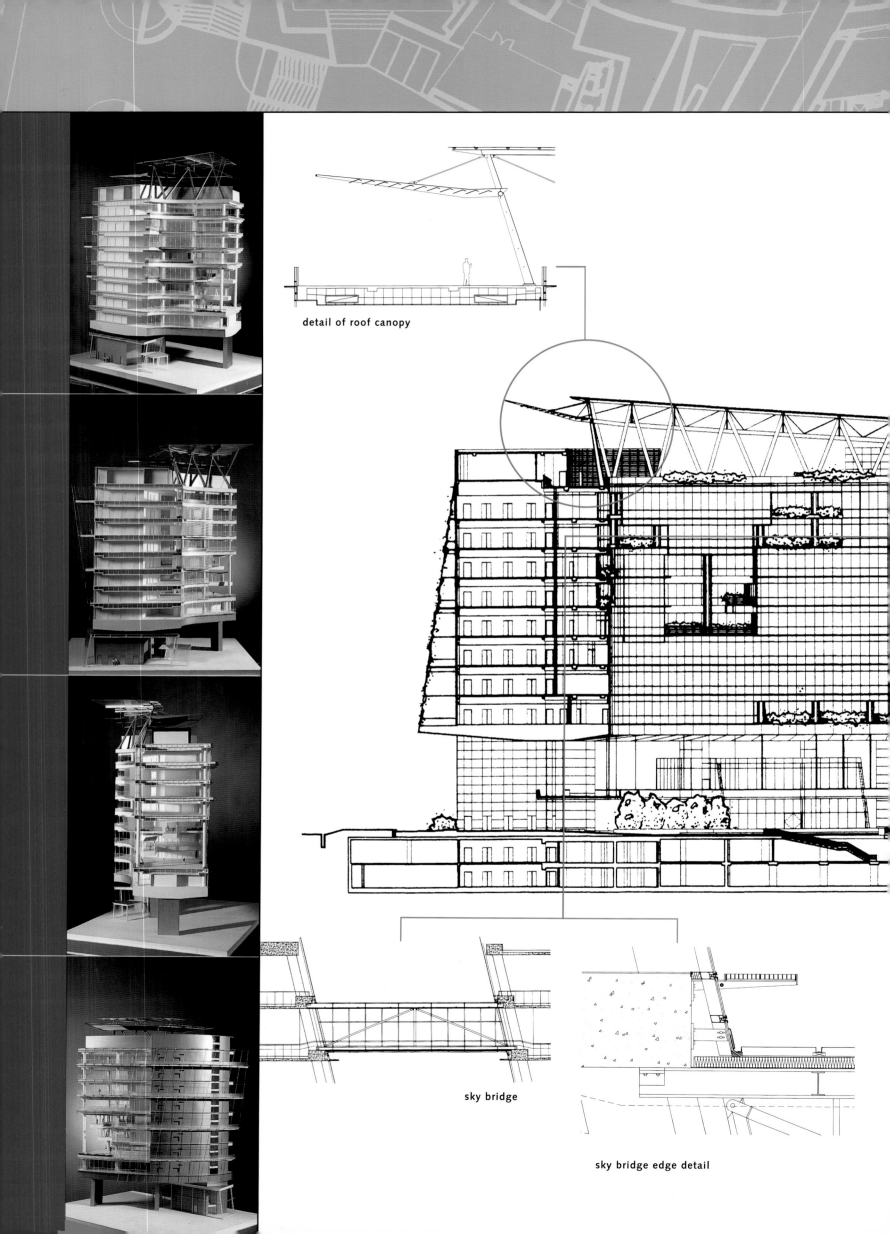

detail of roof canopy

sky bridge

sky bridge edge detail

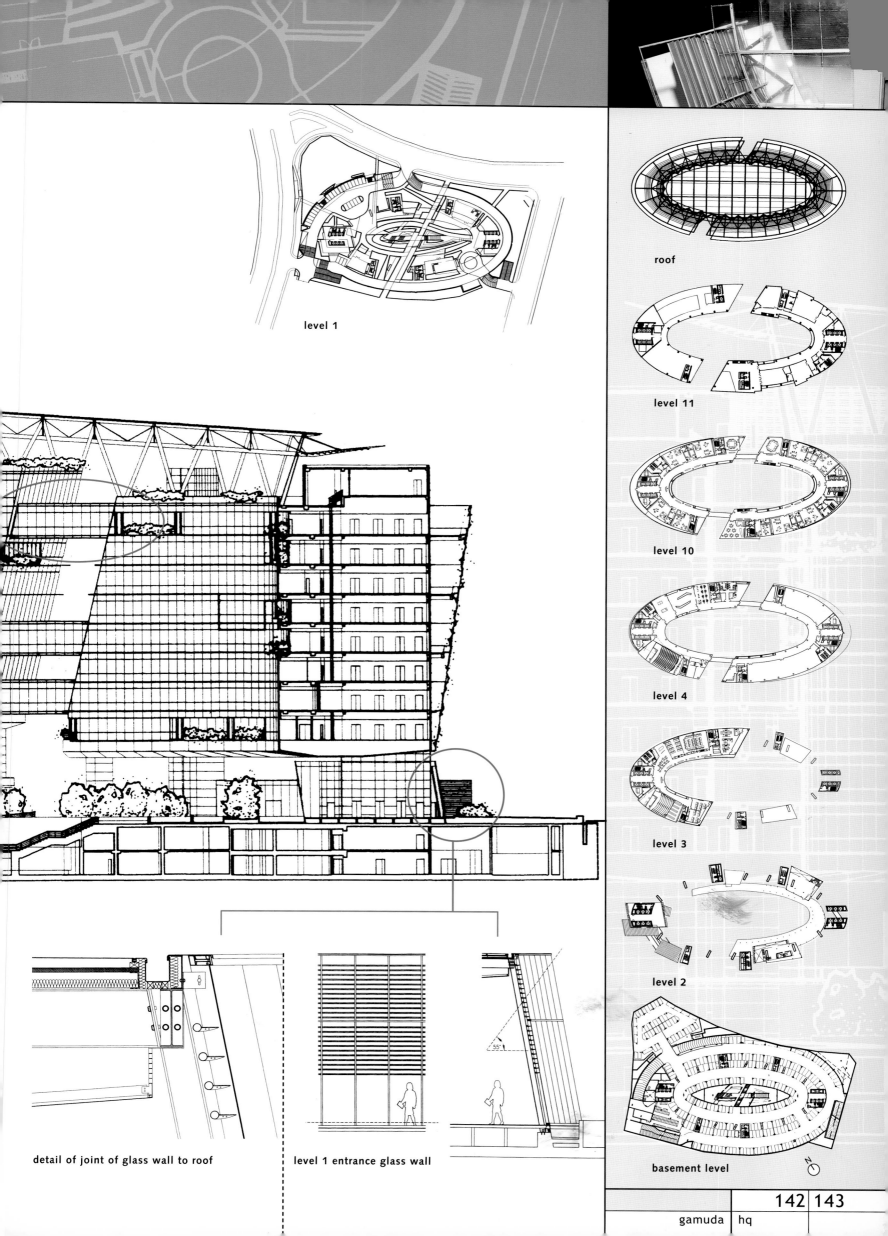

level 1

roof

level 11

level 10

level 4

level 3

level 2

basement level

detail of joint of glass wall to roof

level 1 entrance glass wall

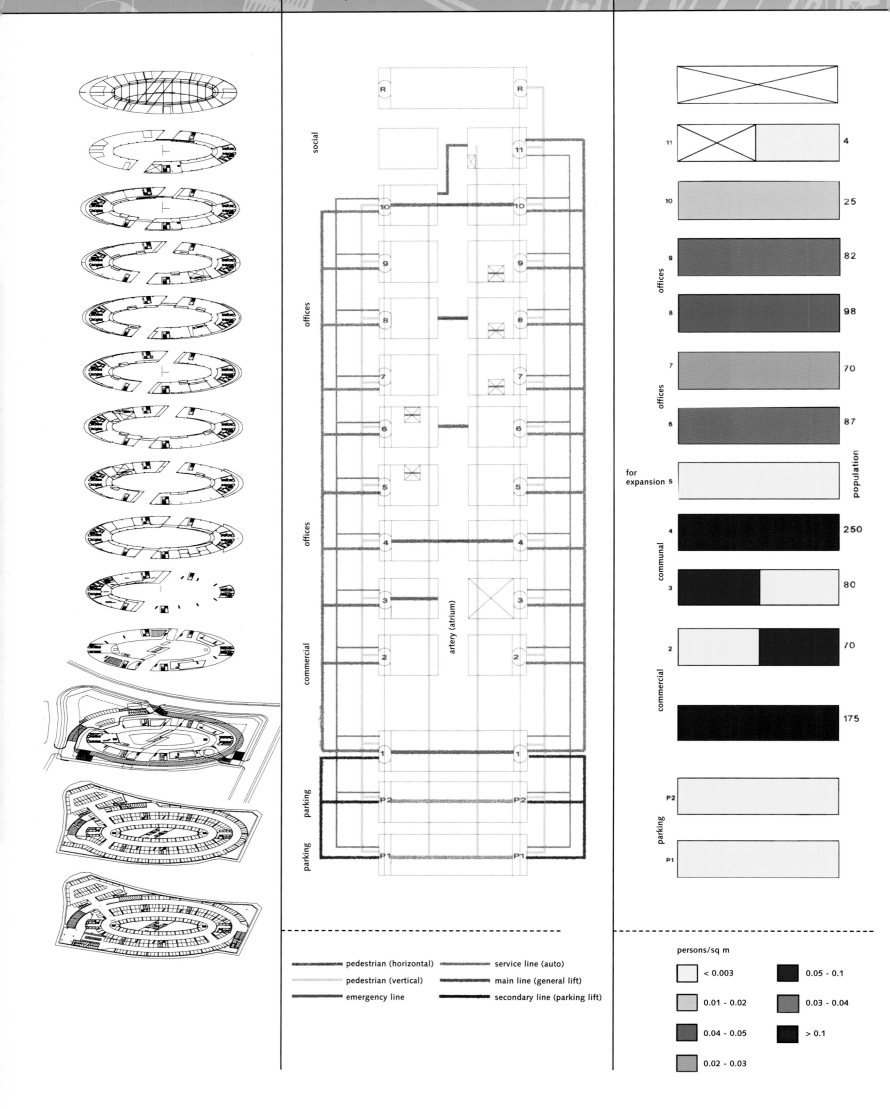

landuse mapping of the skyscraper
(© T.R.Hamzah & Yeang Sdn Bhd 2001)

'subway map'

population density

social

offices

offices

offices

commercial

artery (atrium)

parking

parking

R
11
10
9
8
7
6
5
4
3
2
1
P2
P1

population

offices
11   4
10   25
9   82
8   98

offices
7   70
6   87

for
expansion 5

communal
4   250
3   80

commercial
2   70
175

parking
P2
P1

——— pedestrian (horizontal)   ——— service line (auto)
——— pedestrian (vertical)   ——— main line (general lift)
——— emergency line   ——— secondary line (parking lift)

persons/sq m

☐ < 0.003   ■ 0.05 - 0.1

☐ 0.01 - 0.02   ■ 0.03 - 0.04

☐ 0.04 - 0.05   ■ > 0.1

☐ 0.02 - 0.03

% of Open Space

open space

11	
10	2.16
9	6.5
8	5.4
7	11.14
6	6.47
5	6.3
4	12.41
3	12.37
2	74.6
1	66
P2	
P1	

offices

artery (atrium)

communal

commercial

parking

parking

void space

open space

circulation zone

landuse map

social

offices

artery (atrium)

offices

commercial

parking

parking

Utility Lines

void space

office zone

office space

service zone

social zone

circulation zone

communal zone

business zone

climatic buffer zone

form studies

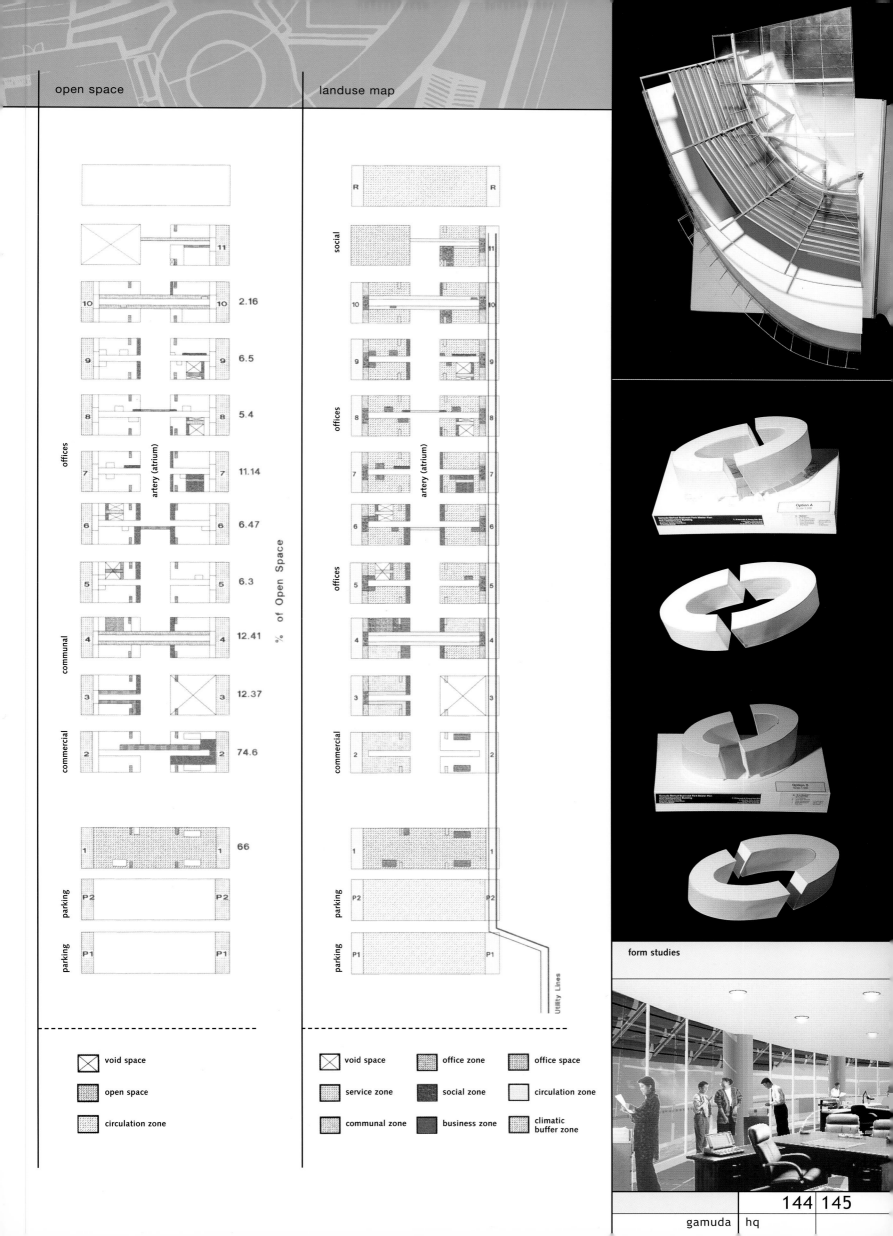

In order to assess the design for its embodied energy attributes, Davis Langdon & Everest Energy & Environmental Group were consulted. This group are internationally respected for their work on the embodied energy of construction materials an the consequential emissions of greenhouse and acid gases. They are particularly experienced in assessing designs over their full life cycle. They often contribute to the design process to help minimise the embodied energy and emissions without compromising the operational energy performance of a design.

The group use the technique of sensitivity analysis to focus on critical date and hence ensure that accurate and specific data is used for critical parameters whilst date of lower quality or less certain origin can be used for non-critical parameters. This allows accurate results to be obtained at minimum effort and cost. To facilitate their work, they have devised a range of tools:

- A database of internationally published embodied energy factors containing over 5,000 items.
- Detailed process analysis spreadsheets for the seven key materials that comprise about 70% of the embodied energy of buildings, eg. for:
  - aggregates } hence concrete
  - cement
  - brick and clay products
  - wood
  - steel
  - plaster and plasterboard
  - glass
- An elemental estimator of embodied energy & CO_2 for use at inception and the early design stage. The estimator provides both initial and life cycle results.
- Estimating tools for assessing the transport components of embodied energy for the 4, largest mass and most transport sensitive materials:
  - aggregates } hence concrete
  - cement
  - brick and clay products
  - wood

These materials contain over 99% of the mass of most buildings.

approach

The approach used to assess the life cycle embodied energy mirrors that used for estimating the cost of the buildings. Estimates can be built up at different levels of detail appropriate for the different stages of design:

- embodied energy/CO_2 benchmarks to help the client set a design target in the brief.
- an initial estimate to assist the deign team at inception and sketch design stages
- refinement of the estimate for the design as it evolves throughout the design process.

benchmarks of likely performance for Gamuda

Hence for Gamuda, which is a large prestigious air conditioned medium/high rise building specified to high standards, he would expect the following performance:

Table 1 - typical benchmarks of performance			
attributes	**units**	**range**	
		low	high
initial primary embodied energy	GJ/m² GFA	10	18
Initial embodied CO_2	kg CO_2/m² GFA	500	1000
life cycle primary embodied energy	GJ/m² GFA	8	14
life cycle embodied CO_2	kg CO_2/m² GFA	600	1300
operational delivered energy	KWhrs/m²/yr	100	200

Hence minimising the operational energy should be the first priority before considering embodied energy/CO_2.

Elemental results summary

Table 2 sums up the results from a more detailed design study. These results show that Gamuda will lie toward the middle of the range of embodied energy/CO_2 performance. The exercise was only undertaken to the shell and core design stage and hence data on fit-out and services has not been elaborated further than an initial estimate. The principle way in which the design has been made more embodied energy/CO_2 efficient is by ensuring that the floor loadings are not over specified and are structurally efficient. The extensive use of curtain walling is also beneficial due to their relatively low mass compared to alternative forms of construction.

lessons learnt

Gamuda is an inherently high quality, high cost, high specification office development. As a result, its embodied energy/CO_2 is likely to be higher than that for a more modest specification. It is also a fairly high-tech building which is engineered for structural efficiency. This allows it to be a moderate mass building which is beneficial for embodied energy/CO_2. Modest physical mass (good for embodied energy/CO_2) can be achieved without compromising thermal mass. This is because accessible thermal mass used for stabilising diurnal temperature fluctuations requires only about 75 mm thickness of concrete which is small compared to the thickness required for structural purposes.

the dream

The ultimate low embodied energy/CO_2 building might be constructed from a low (engineered) mass of mainly locally sourced natural and renewable materials (eg. wood). The design would moderate the local climate without the need for external energy sources to always provide comfort, health and productivity for the users of the building. The materials used would need a minimum of processing to make them suitable for construction and would not require toxic or noxious materials and by product wastes from production.

The constructed buildings would have a very long, flexible and adaptable life. At the end of their life, the materials would be reusable or recyclable locally with minimal processing energy. Alternatively, they may be useful as fuels for heating and electricity cogeneration without the release of toxic flue gases. at the very least, demolition material should be inert and non-toxic for simple disposal.

Clearly practical buildings must be a compromise between these aspirations and all of the other functional, aesthetic, and physical requirements of the building and our state of knowledge in being able to construct and operate them.

Table 2 - elemental study of improved design									
Gamuda HQ summary results	measured (m²)	embodied energy (GJ prim)	embodied energy (GJ del)	embodied CO_2 (kg CO_2)	life cycle embodied energy (GJ prim)	life cycle embodied energy GJ del	life cycle embodied CO_2 (kg CO_2)	primary % initial	primary % life cycle
Substructure	13527	155405	98778	16795429	155405	98778	16795429	28%	13%
structural frame	24481	226882	126659	23693701	242201	139343	24884596	41%	20%
external walling and finishes	20377	40754	20377	3056550	122262	61131	9169650	7%	10%
roof coverings etc	6414	11452	6449	1023177	23481	13352	1922352	2%	2%
internal walling	944	415	363	35896	2492	2176	215374	0.1%	0.2%
internal finishes	N/A	49587	28623	3665561	285424	162046	20052644	9%	23%
joinery finishes, etc	49157	0	0	0	0	0	0	0%	0%
services	49157	62291	46227	3868386	404632	291795	23839758	11%	33%
GJ/m²	49157	546786 11.1	327476 6.7	52138700 1061	1235897 25.1	768621 15.6	96879803 1971	100%	100%

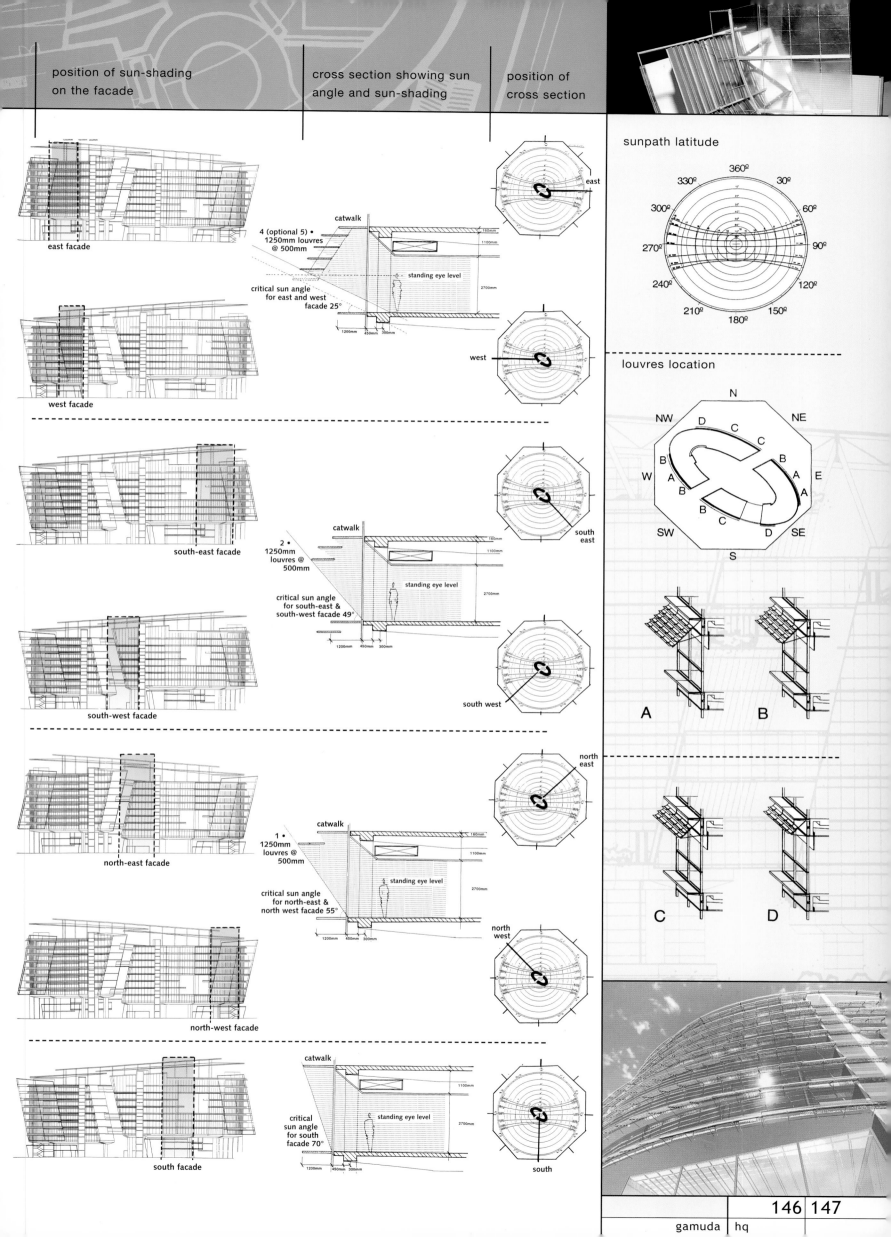

position of sun-shading on the facade

east facade

west facade

south-east facade

south-west facade

north-east facade

north-west facade

south facade

cross section showing sun angle and sun-shading

catwalk

4 (optional 5) • 1250mm louvres @ 500mm

critical sun angle for east and west facade 25°

standing eye level

160mm
1100mm
2700mm

1200mm 450mm 300mm

catwalk

2 • 1250mm louvres @ 500mm

critical sun angle for south-east & south-west facade 49°

standing eye level

160mm
1100mm
2700mm

1200mm 450mm 300mm

catwalk

1 • 1250mm louvres @ 500mm

critical sun angle for north-east & north west facade 55°

standing eye level

160mm
1100mm
2700mm

1200mm 450mm 300mm

catwalk

critical sun angle for south facade 70°

standing eye level

1100mm
2700mm

1200mm 450mm 300mm

position of cross section

east

west

south east

south west

north east

north west

south

sunpath latitude

360°
330°   30°
300°   60°
270°   90°
240°   120°
210°   150°
180°

louvres location

N
NW   NE
D C
C
B   C   B
W A   A E
B   A
B
C   D
SW   SE
S

A   B

C   D

The Menara TA2 is seen as a related development for a residential and leisure assembly associated with the Menara TA1 office tower which stands on an adjacent linked site, within the Golden Triangle of Kuala Lumpur City, and in the immediate vicinity of the Petronas Towers.

Within Yeang's range of tower forms, and in a basic generic sense, Menara TA2 and the MBF Tower in Penang share a fundamental typology that sets these projects apart. Both are residential developments with the main core of elevators and staircases within the **centre of plan**, leaving the encircling periphery free to accommodate the residences. Both towers share the principle of **natural ventilation** throughout the central space, supporting the occupied areas.

The Menara TA2 remains a project, but its clear characteristics establish a definitive **bioclimatic typeform** within an urban setting. The plan is composed of two interconnected, spatially separated, reversed L-form towers. The towers comprise a loft wing with 6 metre ceiling height, and a standard wing with 3.1 metre ceiling height. The condominium units in both wings are a mixture of one and two bed-room units, and each one has unobstructed outward views across Kuala Lumpur city.

The space between the two towers rises as a vast **central atrium**, where the central elevator and stair cores rise around a cruciform of circulation that connects to encircling circulation bridges, giving level by level access to the sets of residential condominium units. The openness of this central volume and the vertical separation of the towers at the corners enables a free air-flow within the atrium inducing **natural ventilation** – this also assists the condominiums in that no unit requires mechanical ventilation. In turn the placement of common facilities at vertically strategic locations throughout the building, further introduces openness, creates a sense of community coupled with he atrium, and generates a sense of **living, vertical urbanism**.

Kuala Lumpur, Malaysia

menara TA2

owner TA Properties Sdn Bhd
location The Golden Triangle,
Kuala Lumpur, Malaysia
latitude 3.2°N
nos of storeys 42 storeys (plus 2 basements)
areas Total gross area 39,331 sq m
Total nett area 30,746 sq m
Total built up area 55,495 sq m
plot ratio 1:6.5

design intentions and features

This mixed condominium / service apartment tower is designed
to incorporate all aspects of high-end residential lifestyle
system. Located within the 'Golden Triangle' and financial
district, the tower was designed for a young corporate market.
Included within the building features were fibre optic
connection to every room, the digital business centre, indoor /
outdoor gym, railed multi-function sport park, members
'sky-club', courtyard terraces and squash courts. Units were
split between single and mezzanine apartments with double-
height living room and full-height solar-protected glazing.
• The form of the building was derived to allow maximum
views across and surrounding jungle terrain while maintaining
a naturally vented control atrium space and core. The plan was
split in two to allow cross as well as stack ventilation.
As a result, every room, toilet and kitchen in each apartment
are naturally ventilated. Inside the atrium is column free
planted corridors linking each unit to the lift lobby.

The vertical incidents of common facilities include a gymnasium,
racquet club and health spa with swimming pool, a main club house
and various skycourt garden voids, together with a high-level
business center. The roof level of the seven storey
car-parking podium is expressed as a
multipurpose park – an exercise space
and a venue for social events at the
heart of the tower assembly. Each of
these facilities together with the
separation gaps between the towers,
and the rising atrium, develops
interstitial air-flow, and equally these
separation gaps and the translucent
atrium roof provide natural light
throughout the internal void.

The sense of amenity is enhanced
by the exploitation of elevation and
prospect – both the health spa,
swimming pool and main club house
lounge, restaurant and sky-terrace
have potentially spectacular views
over the surrounding city. Equally the
diagonal corner units, and end units
of both towers have especially strong
locations and command of the
outward vistas over the city and
beyond to the landscape.

It is possible to imagine, that
particularly during the calmer
moments of the tropical evening,
with balcony terraces open to the
inner living spaces and with all the
communal facilities in full-swing, the
potential of the hedonistic lifestyle
possible in a city such as Kuala
Lumpur, could be realised in this
building.

In its sleek form and relaxed
arrangement this proposition is much
more than a 'condo' – it is a
residential mega-type of
high quality that both offers
the opportunity to celebrate
the openness the climate
suggests and collectively
forms a crucial element in
Yeang's vision of the city,
imbued with the release and
stimulation of a
vertical
urbanism, as a
new cultural
form.

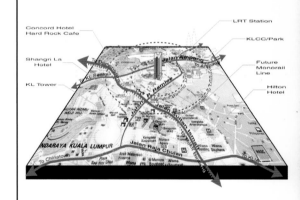

north west

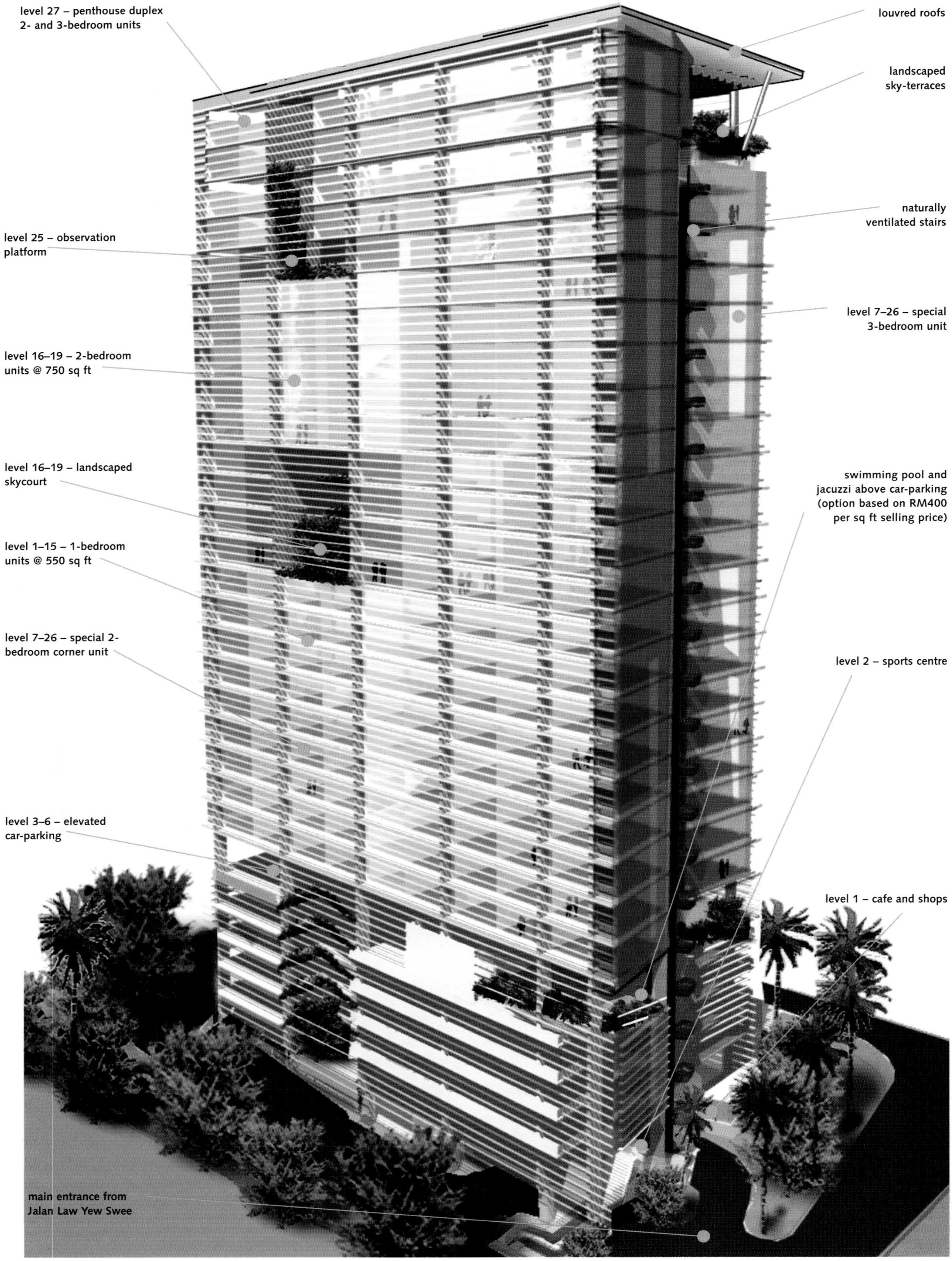

level 27 – penthouse duplex
2- and 3-bedroom units

louvred roofs

landscaped
sky-terraces

level 25 – observation
platform

naturally
ventilated stairs

level 7–26 – special
3-bedroom unit

level 16–19 – 2-bedroom
units @ 750 sq ft

level 16–19 – landscaped
skycourt

swimming pool and
jacuzzi above car-parking
(option based on RM400
per sq ft selling price)

level 1–15 – 1-bedroom
units @ 550 sq ft

level 7–26 – special 2-
bedroom corner unit

level 2 – sports centre

level 3–6 – elevated
car-parking

level 1 – cafe and shops

main entrance from
Jalan Law Yew Swee

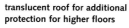

What the project demonstrates is that both the living and working environment can be united within the very heart of the city, rather than the separation of functions that creeping suburban condo-developments impose, with all the attendant problems of traffic pollution and transportation.

The united forms of TA1 and TA2 – the related condo-tower, propose a new urbanism appropriate to an emergent capital such as Kuala Lumpur, within the urban construct of the 21st century.

gap in between provides constant natural lighting throughout the internal void

translucent roof for additional protection for higher floors

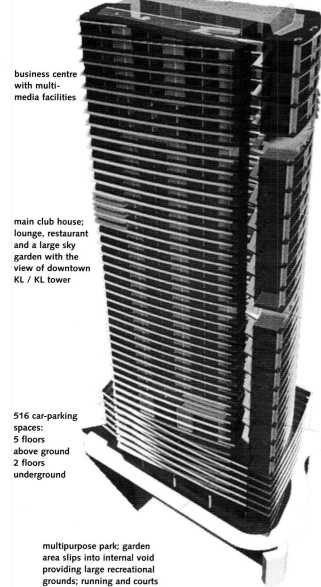

business centre with multi-media facilities

main club house; lounge, restaurant and a large sky garden with the view of downtown KL / KL tower

516 car-parking spaces: 5 floors above ground 2 floors underground

multipurpose park; garden area slips into internal void providing large recreational grounds; running and courts

health spa, changing room, mini bar, garden and a swimming pool with a view of KLCC.

gymnasium with indoor / outdoor facilities

garden void : also provides internal void ventilation

racquet club connecting directly to the park below

all Loft wing @ 6m ceiling height 100 – one-bedroom units 50 – two-bedroom units

circulation bridges connecting elevators to units and other functions on each floors

all standard wing @ 3.1 m ceiling height 100 – one-bedroom units 50 – two-bedroom units

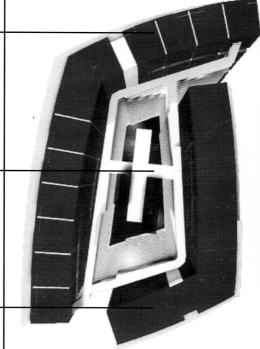

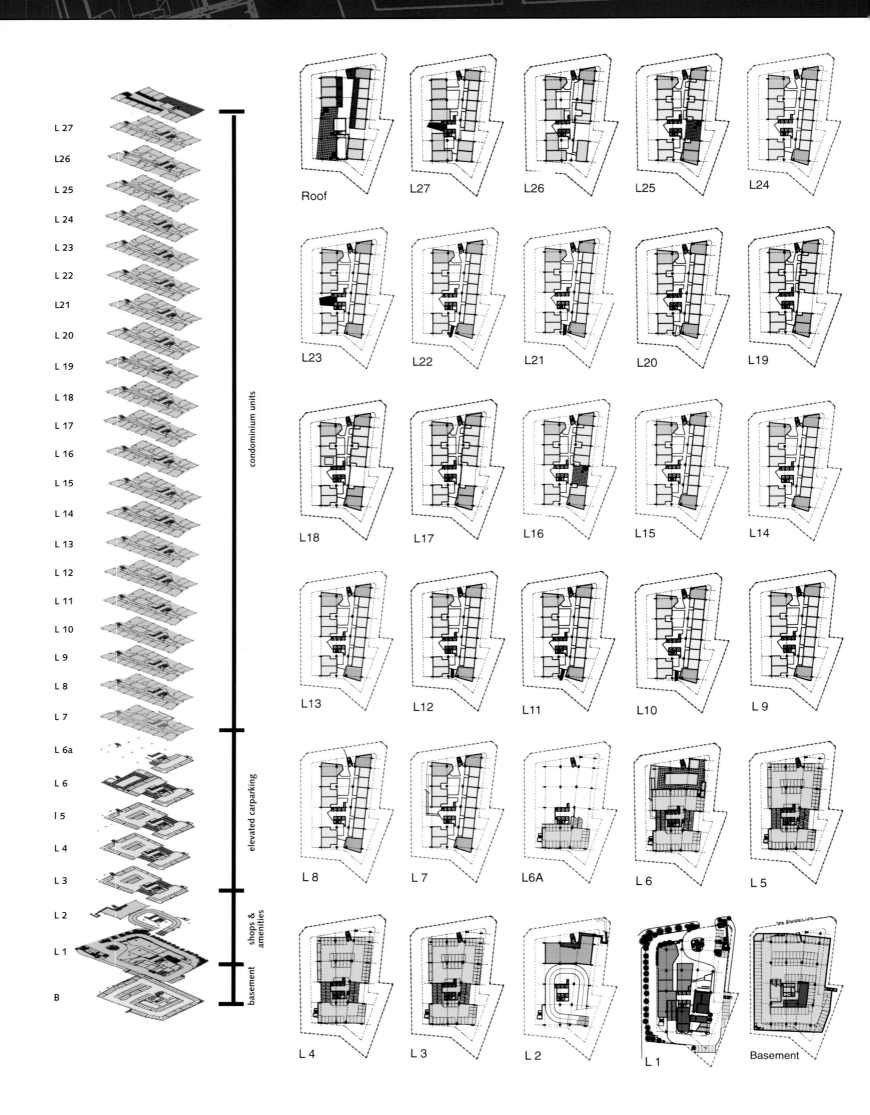

L 27
L26
L 25
L 24
L 23
L 22
L21
L 20
L 19
L 18
L 17
L 16
L 15
L 14
L 13
L 12
L 11
L 10
L 9
L 8
L 7

condominium units

L 6a
L 6
I 5
L 4
L 3

elevated carparking

L 2
L 1

shops & amenities

B

basement

Roof

L27

L26

L25

L24

L23

L22

L21

L20

L19

L18

L17

L16

L15

L14

L13

L12

L11

L10

L 9

L 8

L 7

L6A

L 6

L 5

L 4

L 3

L 2

L 1

Basement

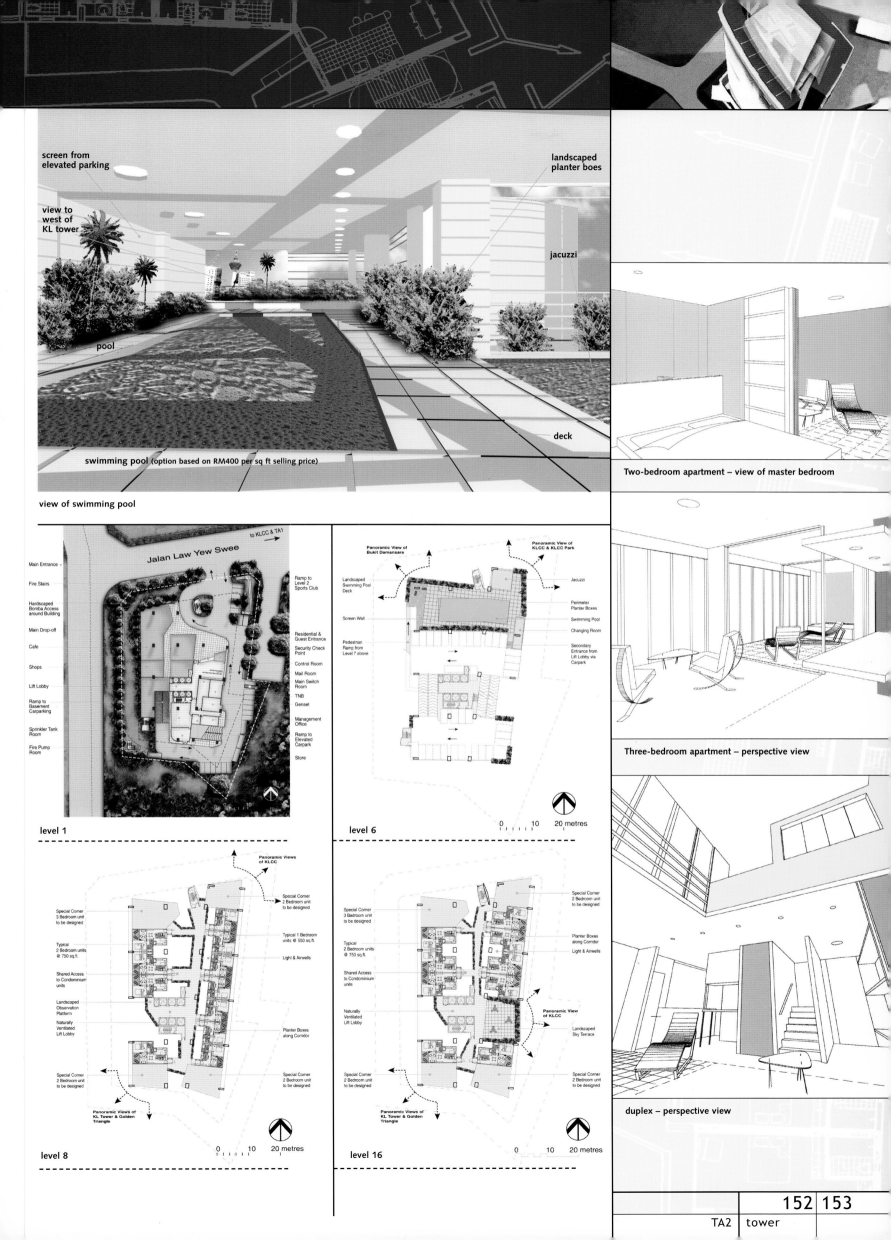

screen from
elevated parking

landscaped
planter boes

view to
west of
KL tower

jacuzzi

pool

deck

swimming pool (option based on RM400 per sq ft selling price)

view of swimming pool

Two-bedroom apartment – view of master bedroom

Three-bedroom apartment – perspective view

duplex – perspective view

level 1

Main Entrance

Fire Stairs

Hardscaped
Bomba Access
around Building

Main Drop-off

Cafe

Shops

Lift Lobby

Ramp to
Basement Carparking

Sprinkler Tank
Room

Fire Pump
Room

Jalan Law Yew Swee

to KLCC & TA1

Ramp to
Level 2
Sports Club

Residential &
Guest Entrance

Security Check
Point

Control Room

Mail Room

Main Switch
Room

TNB

Genset

Management
Office

Ramp to
Elevated
Carpark

Store

level 6

Panoramic View of
Bukit Damansara

Panoramic View of
KLCC & KLCC Park

Landscaped
Swimming Pool
Deck

Jacuzzi

Screen Wall

Perimeter
Planter Boxes

Swimming Pool

Pedestrian
Ramp from
Level 7 above

Changing Room

Secondary
Entrance from
Lift Lobby via
Carpark

0   10   20 metres

level 8

Panoramic Views
of KLCC

Special Corner
3 Bedroom unit
to be designed

Special Corner
2 Bedroom unit
to be designed

Typical
2 Bedroom units
@ 750 sq.ft.

Typical 1 Bedroom
units @ 550 sq.ft.

Shared Access
to Condominium
units

Light & Airwells

Landscaped
Observation
Platform

Naturally
Ventilated
Lift Lobby

Special Corner
2 Bedroom unit
to be designed

Planter Boxes
along Corridor

Special Corner
2 Bedroom unit
to be designed

Panoramic Views of
KL Tower & Golden
Triangle

0   10   20 metres

level 16

Special Corner
3 Bedroom unit
to be designed

Special Corner
2 Bedroom unit
to be designed

Typical
2 Bedroom units
@ 750 sq.ft.

Planter Boxes
along Corridor

Shared Access
to Condominium
units

Light & Airwells

Naturally
Ventilated
Lift Lobby

Panoramic View
of KLCC

Special Corner
2 Bedroom unit
to be designed

Landscaped
Sky Terrace

Special Corner
2 Bedroom unit
to be designed

Panoramic Views of
KL Tower & Golden
Triangle

0   10   20 metres

The Maybank project defines a point in Yeang's work overall, where **the vertical scale** of the skyscraper begins to be really significant.

In this case the vertical scale is enhanced by the insertion of **tropical terraces**, a version of the skycourt principle, which divides the building into four vertical office zones, with banking hall at the base and tropical roof garden at the summit.

Situated within the Singapore downtown of major tower-forms with a riverside plaza that terminates the Boat Quay waterside walk, the Maybank tower rises as a slender 'blade' of articulated floors, sheathed on the hot west face with a massive vertical plane of service cores, elevators and staircases. The east face is sheathed in a **sophisticated double skin**, which varies its physical condition according to time and user need. This facade is composed of three elements: an outer solar-filter layer, an operable glazed facade, and supporting structure and spaces. This facade assembly allows users to control their internal environment both with regard to air-flow and natural light. The variable nature of the transparent inner skin acts as a glass filter, changing its translucency relative to time of day and the need for solar control and ventilation. Thus the **facade engineering** takes over a major expressive role, in the life of the building and its occupancy. During the day the inner floor plates suggest a series of inner spaces, delicately visible beneath the porous outer skin, while at night the radiant inner volumes expose the variety of inner space and its levels of occupancy. This counter sensation of **opacity and porosity**, transforms the tower into an interactive shaft of light, which stands in sharp contrast to the other surrounding, monolithic tower forms. Set in its context,

the Maybank Tower will be highly visible both from within Singapore city and on the high-rise skyline. As such it is truly a landmark project.

Elements of Yeang's vertical urbanism are in evidence: these include bistro and café facilities, the extensive tropical terraces with panoramic vistas and the use of ramps within selected vertical zones as additional space integrators. The whole assembly has the intensity of movement and occupation that ensures a visibly permeable, living organism. In itself, the design is a complete transformation of the skyscraper, and clearly exemplifies Yeang's **bioclimatic architecture**.

owner Maybank Singapore Operations
location 2 Battery Road, Singapore
latitude 1.2°N
nos of storeys 54 storeys (plus 4 basements)
site area 1,132 sq m
areas Total gross area 15,678 sq m
  Total nett area 12,373 sq m
  Total construction area 17,507 sq m
plot ratio 1:13.8

design features • The site is located within the major financial district of Singapore. To the north is the Singapore River and the Boat Quay pedestrian walkway, to the south is Fullerton Square and Raffles MRT Station. The building is highly visible from within the city and will have a major impact on Singapore's skyline.

The features of the design are:
• The east and west facades are constructed in three elements: the outer solar-filter layer; the operable glazed facade; the supporting structure and spaces. This configuration enables the buildings' users to control their internal environment at a personal and local level.
• During the day the facade and various floor plate engender a sense of spatial texture beneath the porous outer-skin. The inner skin is a transparent glass filter changing it's translucency according to the time of the day and the individual need for solar control and natural ventilation.
• At night the facade appears as a thin gossamer skin over a series of colonised spaces. The floor plates and their respective volumes radiate from behind the facade exposing the variety of spaces from within the building. The tower is no longer a impermeable vertical stacking of bored concrete trays but allows social interaction, increased user activity and enhanced productivity.
• The service core to the west side acts as solar buffer to the hot west sun. The curved east facade is fully glazed allowing natural daylight onto the office floor plates and gives unobstructed views across the Singapore River and the Marina Bay.
• The building gradually changes its opacity and porosity not only during the day and the night but also according to ones approach and passage through the building. On Fullerton Square the tower opens on the long axis exposing physical access to the Boat Quay and visual glimpses through the towers voids to the sky beyond.
• A small north facing plaza connects the river front with the building base and the entrance lobby. This provides a termination to the Boat Quay waterside walk and is the threshold between the river and the building. The plaza is a covered outside area servicing the Maybank's Banking Hall and own offices with an upmarket lunch-time bistro. The public plaza opens up and expands the physical and visual links between Marina Bay and the Boat Quay.
• The tower is designed to have seven vertical zones separated into open public and office spaces. The raised entrance plaza connects all three open public spaces – the banking zone is reached with a series of ramps; the mid-height interchange level and cafe is accessible from the express lift which continues to the Tropical Roof Garden. In between the Banking and Tropical Roof Garden are four zones of office space.
• Each zone is connected to the main lift core. Within each lift zone are additional space integrators linking the floors with ramps. These enable movement within a zone to be very efficient and conducive to multiple tenancy situations. The various zones are inter-linked to their immediate neighbours via smaller shuttle lifts. Spaces between the vertical zones are equivalent to tropical terraces. Each terrace has a panoramic view across the water and skyscape of Singapore.

south elevation

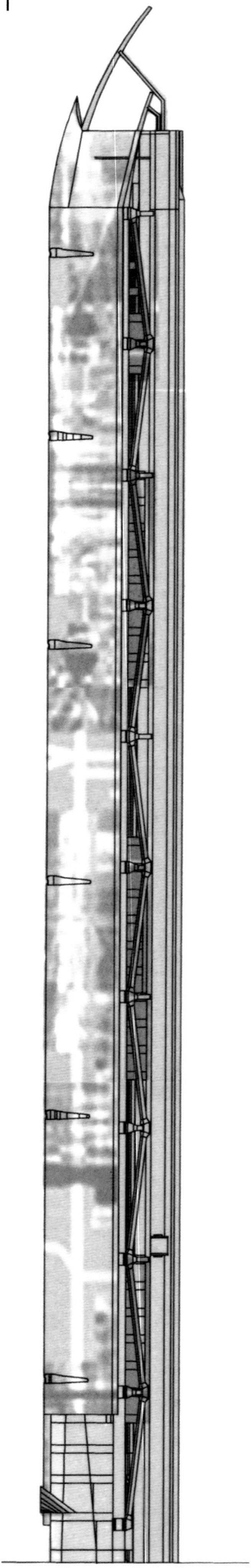

east elevation

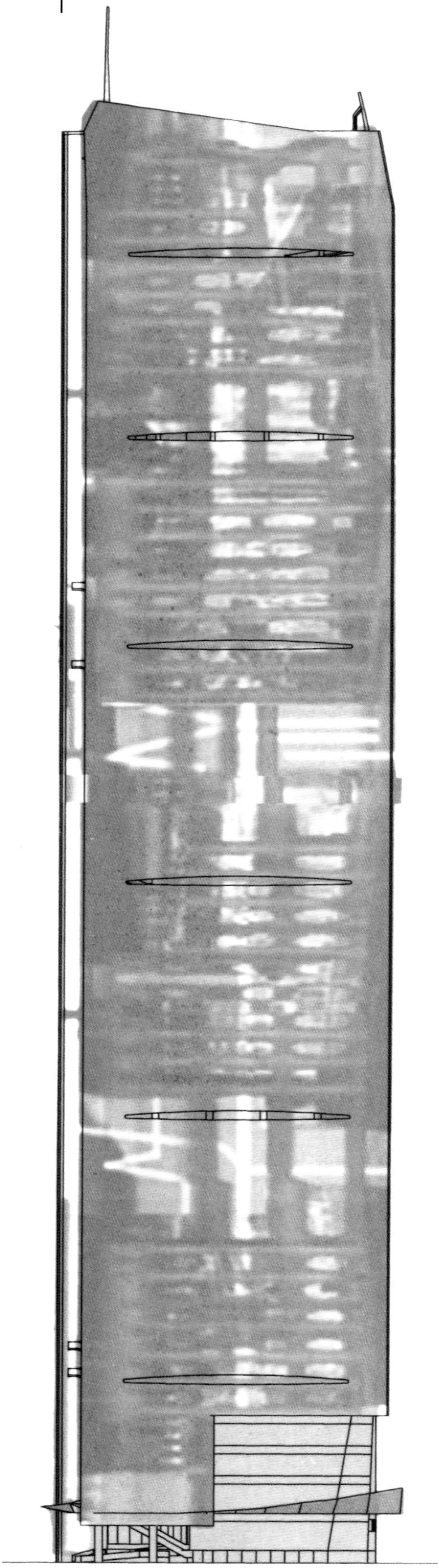

north elevation

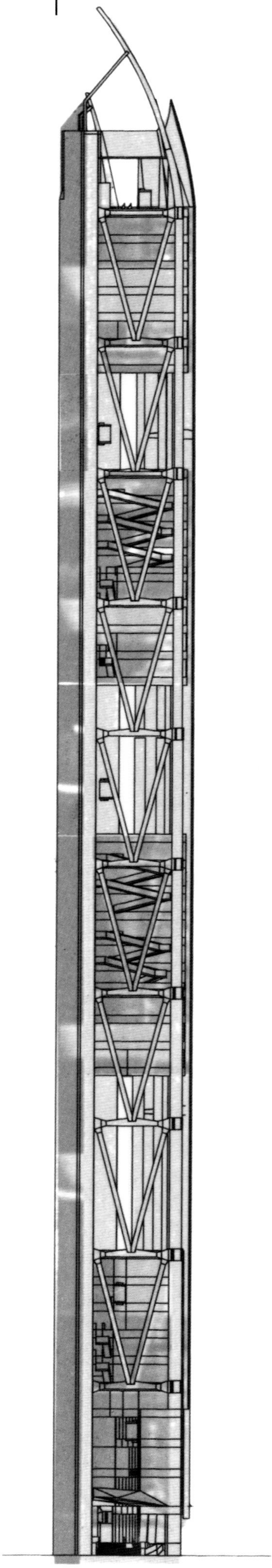

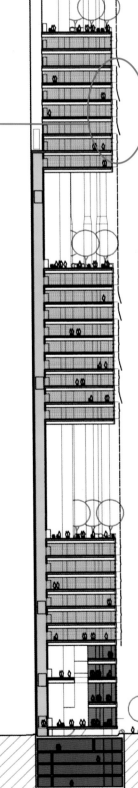

At first sight, the project has clear precedent in Yeang's work. The overall 'thin' form with its contrasting facades recalls the UMNO Tower, while the V-braced structure of the north and south ends has a root in Central Plaza. Equally the use of the double-skin facade finds its origin in the Shanghai Armoury Tower, and the vertical clusters of offices and skycourt separators recall Hitechniaga.

While it is reassuring to find this rehearsal of typological elements within successive projects, it is an affirmative satisfaction to find the continuous research and application of developed systems – in this case the double-skin façade – which Yeang brings to each progressive design. His formative method of research, design and development continues to be the central discipline that maintains the quality and inventive nature of his architectural production.

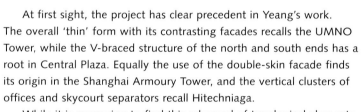

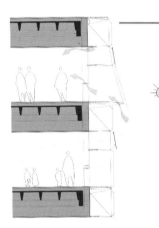

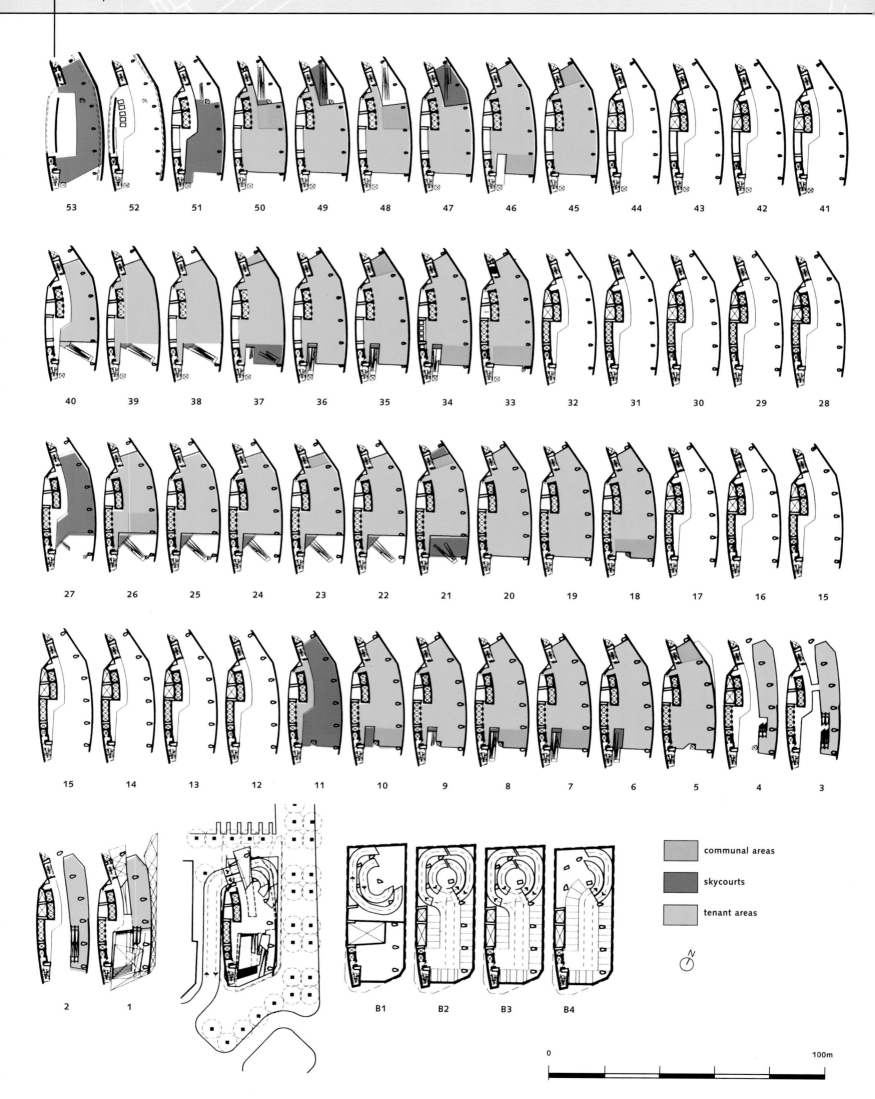

floor plans

53 52 51 50 49 48 47 46 45 44 43 42 41

40 39 38 37 36 35 34 33 32 31 30 29 28

27 26 25 24 23 22 21 20 19 18 17 16 15

15 14 13 12 11 10 9 8 7 6 5 4 3

2 1 B1 B2 B3 B4

communal areas

skycourts

tenant areas

N

0 100m

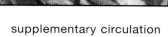

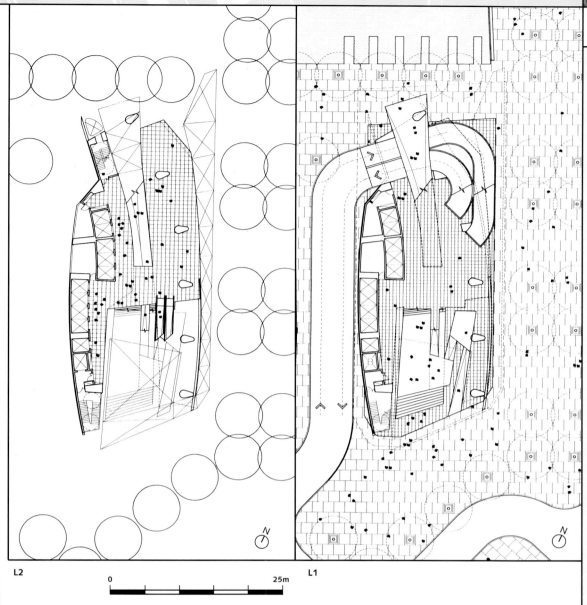

L2

0   25m   L1

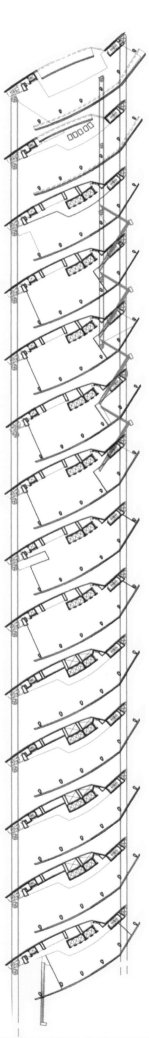

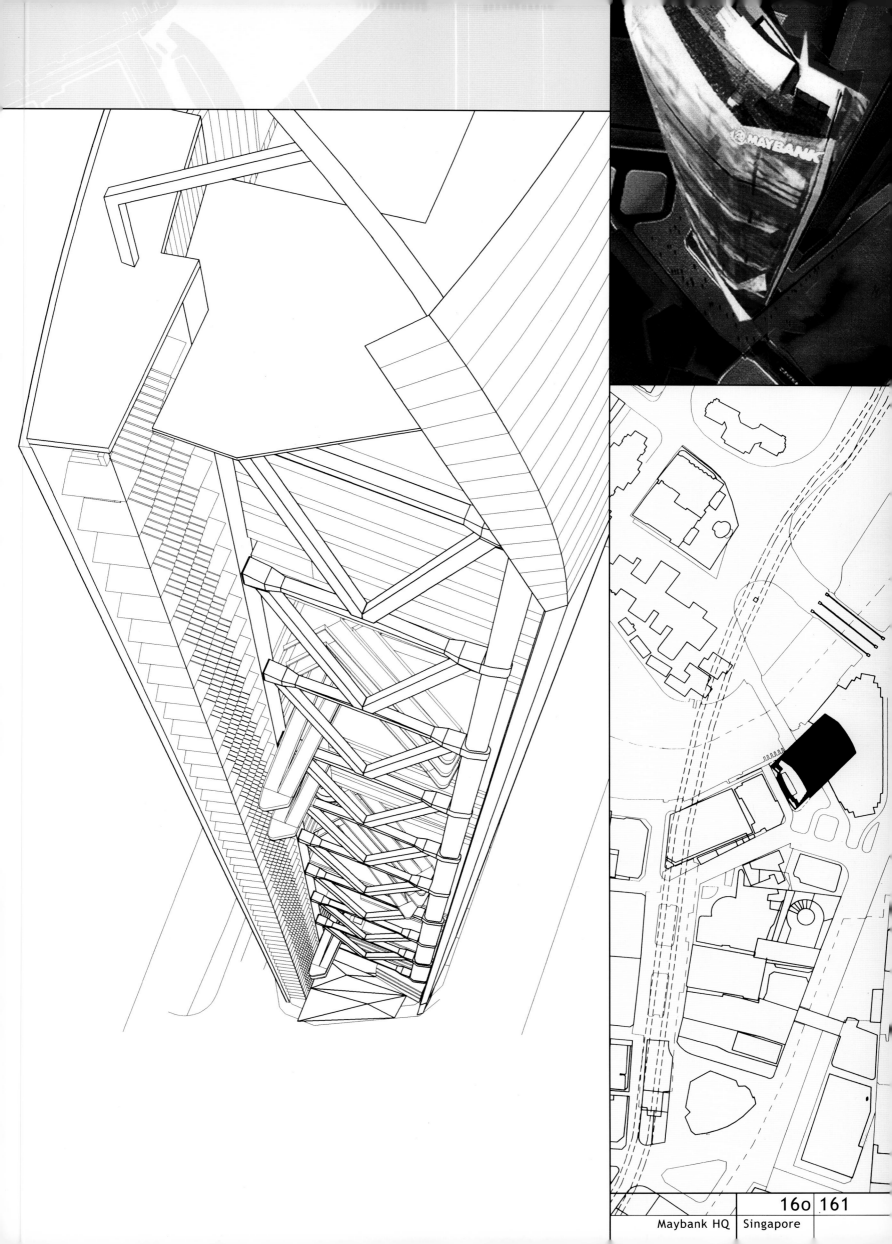

Maybank HQ | Singapore

Kuala Lumpur, Malaysia

owner Waterfront House Sdn Bhd
location Jalan Pinang, adjacent to the Petronas Twin Towers, Kuala Lumpur, Malaysia
latitude 3.2°N
nos of storeys 28 storeys
(approx. 143 m height)
date start June 2000 (design)
completion date –
areas (tower 1) total gross area 32,436 sq m
total nett area 22,973 sq m
skycourts, terraces &
garden balconies 3,300 sq m
carparking 16,330 sq m
site area 3,817 sq m
plot ratio 1:8.5

design features • The tower, predominantly a speculative high quality office, has been seen by the client and architect as an object that should enhance the special nature of its surroundings in the heart of Kuala Lumpur's most prestigious city center development. The 26-storey building is intended to also house the client's headquarters in the upper tiers and present a fresh and innovative corporative image.
The building is formed by three distinct sections:
• The plinth is made up of four floors providing commercial banking and cafe facilities.
• The column forms the majority of the open plan office space.
• The capital of four floors creates the headquarters including a roo top garden breaking downwards through three floors with two eastern pavilions providing dramatic views all round.
The ideas behind the tower and its form:
• The client's push to enhance rather than maximise the site has allowed the creation of a green 'skirt'. With extensive landscaping banking up and over the vehicular access pedestrians filling the KLCC Plaza and its neighbouring park are given priority over city's ever present cars. Entering the main lobby or pedestrian plaza through the planting and greenery without crossing driveways is designed to extending the park concept and welcoming occupants and visitors into the building.
• The plinth, column and capital are similarly separated by organic areas. In keeping with the garden tower principles a lower double and upper triple height skycourt in combination with terraces at every level provide 'lungs' for the building and its surroundings. These reduce its impact on the city centre while providing public, semi-public and private spaces for the users.
• Shading has been carefully analysed to maximise the service core's thermal damping effect by placing the buildings back bone to the mid-day sun, while rapping the sun-path with a flowing rib cage of louvres. The aim has been to reduce solar gains, while scooping in light and natural ventilation passively before investigating active systems.
• The horizontal shades are broken adjacent to each stair core by two vertical wing walls projecting from the facade and cutting back into the terrace alcoves linked to the service core corridor and lift lobbies. These are used to maximise natural air flow and gain from the building height and increased wind impact inherent in tower structures.
• The structure formed by the service core and reinforced concrete columns gives expansive clear span floors for instant flexibility and long term adaptability. Raised floors and deep ceiling plenums combined with generous risers are designed to avoid the problems of obsolescence with the rapid advancement in IT requirements.

The project, essentially a high quality office tower, is both related in its form and response to two major sets of criteria, as well as to the general agenda of the Yeang green skyscraper typology. The first response is to the important urban location of Kuala Lumpur's most prestigious city centre development, including the Petronas Twin Towers. The building form addresses collectively KLCC, KLCC Park and the Mandarin Oriental Hotel, and offers extensive vistas. Much of the site area at ground level has been formed into a major garden and includes both a grand entrance plaza and a pedestrian plaza with café and entertainment area. The intention is to extend the adjacent park concept and to give priority to occupants and visitors to the building.

The second response is both functional/programmatic and at the same time formally symbolic, resulting in a vertical **tripartite composition**, of **plinth column and capital**. The **plinth** of four major floors includes a commercial banking hall and café facilities, grand entrance lobby and atrium, and together with a fifth level skycourt, function rooms, restaurant and club provides five levels inter-connected by a rising grand ramp. The **column** of open plan office space then forms the major element of the vertical mass. This assembly is concluded by a **capital** of four floors, which provides the headquarters for the client, with a rooftop garden that cascades through three floors, together with two eastern pavilions with panoramic vistas.

The bank logo appropriately signals its presence, mounted outboard of this crowning cluster of accommodation, with executive penthouse and pool.

The formal and symbolic idea is framed in Yeang's description:

"... the three tiered building allows the tailoring of technology and environmental aspects for each zone while projecting the Feng Shui philosophical image of a healthy man with his feet firmly on the ground, full well-fed body and wise head held high. Standing with its strong back to the sun, which carries the solar ribs up and over the roof top garden to create a shaded 'hat' ..." [1]

What Yeang is referring to here is both the ecological form of the architecture and the implications of the distinctive imagery the building is intended to create as an innovative, inhabited landmark within the city.

[1] Ken Yeang: 'Waterfront House', Project Notes 2000

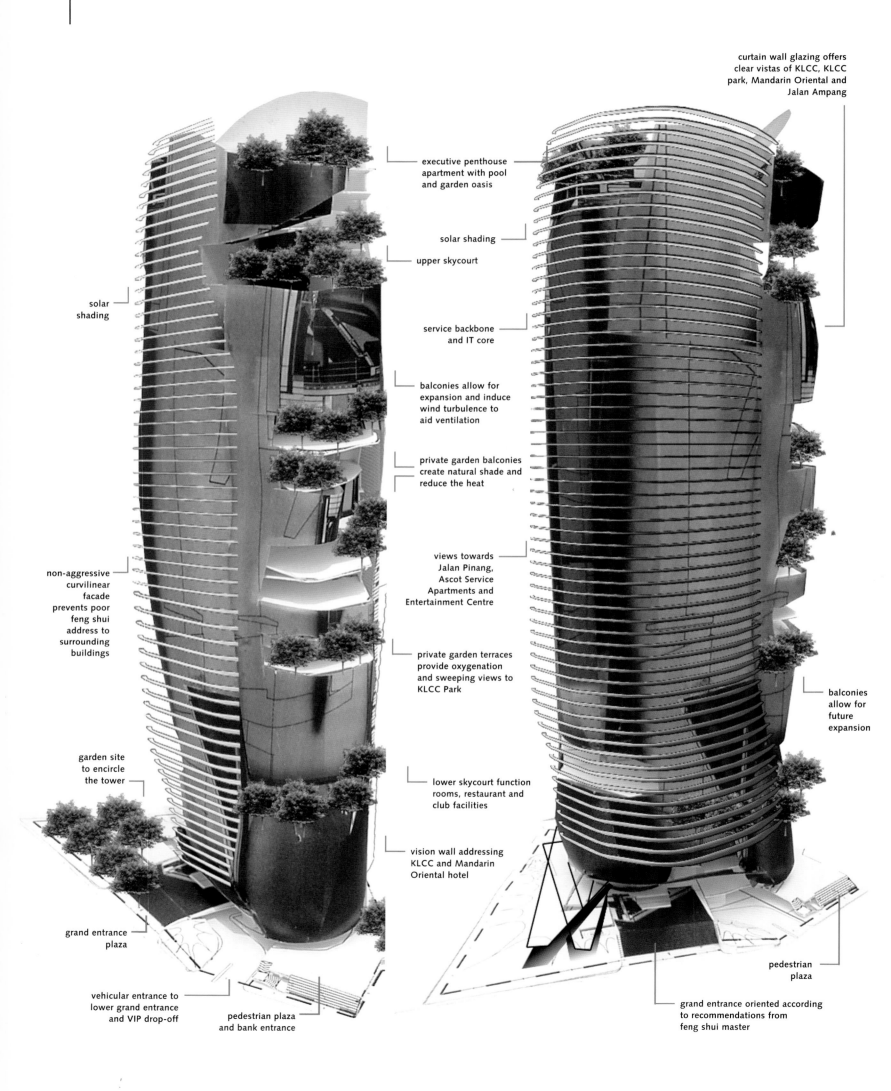

curtain wall glazing offers clear vistas of KLCC, KLCC park, Mandarin Oriental and Jalan Ampang

executive penthouse apartment with pool and garden oasis

solar shading

upper skycourt

solar shading

service backbone and IT core

balconies allow for expansion and induce wind turbulence to aid ventilation

private garden balconies create natural shade and reduce the heat

non-aggressive curvilinear facade prevents poor feng shui address to surrounding buildings

views towards Jalan Pinang, Ascot Service Apartments and Entertainment Centre

balconies allow for future expansion

garden site to encircle the tower

private garden terraces provide oxygenation and sweeping views to KLCC Park

lower skycourt function rooms, restaurant and club facilities

grand entrance plaza

vision wall addressing KLCC and Mandarin Oriental hotel

pedestrian plaza

vehicular entrance to lower grand entrance and VIP drop-off

pedestrian plaza and bank entrance

grand entrance oriented according to recommendations from feng shui master

The **skycourts and terraces** form a major expressive element in the vertical composition and its landscape:

> "... the plinth, column and capital are...separated by organic areas ... in keeping with the garden tower principles a lower double and upper triple height skycourt in combination with terraces at every level provide 'lungs' for the building and its surroundings. These reduce its impact on the city centre while providing public, semi-public and private spaces for the users." [2]

The balconies also allow for expansion of floor-plate area and induce wind turbulence to aid ventilation. At the same time, garden balconies and terraces create natural shade and oxygenation, and assist heat reduction, while providing vistas to the city and adjacent park.

The shading of the whole building form has several important elements which influence both the plan-form and the external envelope. This includes maximising

> "... the service core's thermal damping effect by placing the building's backbone to the mid-day sun, while wrapping the sun path with a flowing ribcage of louvres (applied to the tower). The aim has been to reduce solar gains, while scooping in light and natural ventilation passively before investigating active systems." [3]

The project also includes two projecting **vertical wing walls**, which break the horizontal shades adjacent to each stair core, and cut back into terrace alcoves linked to the service core corridor and lift lobbies. The wing-walls maximise **natural air flow** induced by the tower's height and increased wind impact. These elemental devices of building configuration, vertical landscaping, shading and ventilation are all aspects of Yeang's sustainable, green architecture and are joined here by many other design features which are graphically catalogued, in vertical series, as part of the project documentation that communicates clearly to the client, the benefits of Yeang's overall methodology.

Important amongst these features are the structure

> "... formed by the service core and reinforced concrete columns [which] gives expansive clear span floors for instant flexibility and long term adaptability ... raised floors and deep ceiling plenums combined with generous risers are designed to avoid the problems of obsolescence with the rapid advancement in IT requirements." [4]

In another sense, this design is carefully considered in its overall **address of context**. At the lower levels, the form incorporates a double sided **vision wall** which acknowledges both KLCC and the Mandarin Oriental Hotel, and in so doing arises as a major curvilinear determinant of the tower and its base. Balancing this element, the 'non-aggressive' curved facade of the tower is intended to prevent poor Feng Shui address to surrounding buildings. Similarly, the grand entrance plaza is oriented according to recommendations from a Fung Shui Master.

- The three-tiered building allows the tailoring of technology and passive environmental aspects for each zone while projecting the Feng Shui philosophical image of a healthy person with his feet firmly on the ground, full-well feed body and wise head held high. Standing with its strong back to the sun, which carries the solar ribs up and over the roof top garden to create a shaded 'hat'. The building similarly projects the architect's philosophical intention to develop the health of its occupants and visitors while offering a modern urban element which recognises its responsibility to its surroundings.

[2] Ken Yeang 'Waterfront House', op cit.
[3] Ibid.
[4] Ibid.

ground floor (level 1)

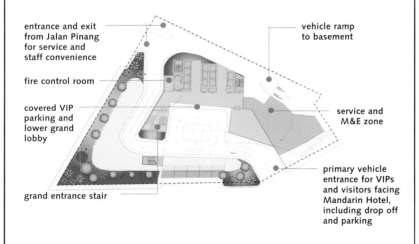

entrance and exit from Jalan Pinang for service and staff convenience

fire control room

covered VIP parking and lower grand lobby

grand entrance stair

vehicle ramp to basement

service and M&E zone

primary vehicle entrance for VIPs and visitors facing Mandarin Hotel, including drop off and parking

typical lower zone

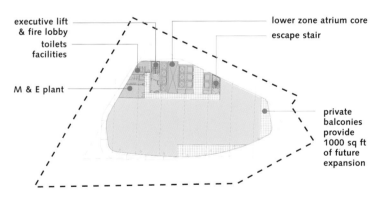

executive lift & fire lobby

toilets facilities

M & E plant

lower zone atrium core

escape stair

private balconies provide 1000 sq ft of future expansion

level 2

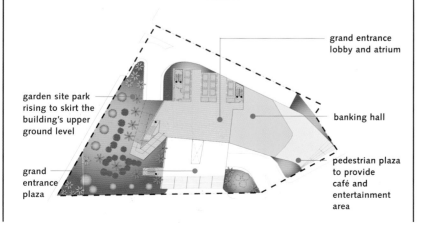

garden site park rising to skirt the building's upper ground level

grand entrance plaza

grand entrance lobby and atrium

banking hall

pedestrian plaza to provide café and entertainment area

typical upper zone

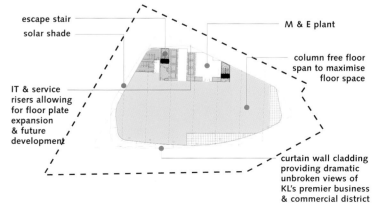

escape stair

solar shade

IT & service risers allowing for floor plate expansion & future development

M & E plant

column free floor span to maximise floor space

curtain wall cladding providing dramatic unbroken views of KL's premier business & commercial district

Seen overall, what Yeang is increasingly disposed to deliver in his ever expanding range of projects centred on the comprehensive basis of the green skyscraper, is a balanced unity of technology, functionalism and tradition. In the case of Waterfront House, his expectations of a vertical urbanism are most in evidence in the rising levels of spectacular skycourts and private gardens, while greater emphasis of public use is focused in the building's plinth and its appropriate facilities and spaces.

Within the teeming context of Kuala Lumpur city, the project registers as a fresh and radically different office-building typology and provides exactly the innovative corporate image requested by the client at the outset.

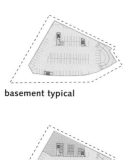
basement typical

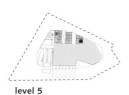
level 5

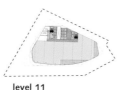
level 11

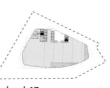
level 17

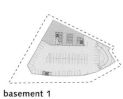
basement 1

level 6

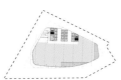
level 12 (transfer floor)

level 18

level 1

level 7

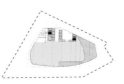
level 13

level 19

level 2

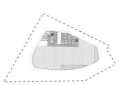
level 8

level 14

level 20

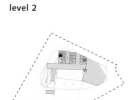
level 3

level 9

level 15

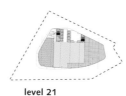
level 21

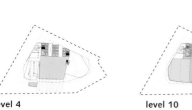
level 4

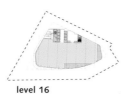
level 10

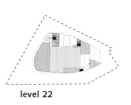
level 16

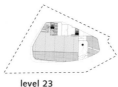
level 22

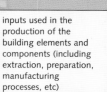
level 23

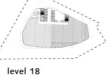

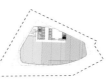

management of energy and materials in the life cycle of a designed system

ecological interactions in the recovery of the designed systems	input used in site rehabilitation, recolonisation by species, site recovery
	input used in recovery processes
	input used in preparation for recycling, reuse, reconstruction, and/or disposal and safe discharge into the environment
	input used in removal demolition
ecological interactions in the operation and consumption of the designed systems	input used in operation of built system, maintenance, ecosystem protection measures, system modifications, etc
ecological interactions in the provision of the physical substance and form of the designed systems of the designed systems	input used in construction and site modification
	input used in distribution, storage, transport to site
	inputs used in the production of the building elements and components (including extraction, preparation, manufacturing processes, etc)

inputs in the recovery phase

inputs in the operation phase

inputs in the construction phase

inputs in the production phase

wind

In one sense, the UMNO Tower belongs to the family of 'thin' plan types exemplified by Central Plaza and Menara TA1, both in Kuala Lumpur.

And, while all three demonstrate certain principles and witness Yeang's great skill in delivering a commercial product in a harsh market place, with added values beyond the client's expectation, the UMNO Tower stands apart. The reason for this lies in the realm of applied **natural ventilation**, its dynamic effect upon the building form, and the factor of aesthetic development this innovation has brought to Yeang's pursuit of an ecological architecture, situated within the skyscraper.

The composition of the UMNO Tower takes the familiar format of a base, with banking hall auditorium and car-parking levels, together with 14 floors of office space above.

The plan-form makes the best of a restricted narrow corner site with one massive shield-wall of elevators, services and of end-to-end staircases facing east/south east, defending the space from solar gain. The opposite west/north west facade is glazed and shielded with solar-orientated linear solar shades. For Yeang these design moves are natural and common place within his work. However, what makes the design exceptional is the formation of the two extreme ends of the plan.

In these key locations, relative to the wind-rose and prevailing winds, Yeang has introduced soaring vertical wall-fins that he describes as **'wind wing-walls'** that direct wind to special balcony zones and act as pockets with 'air locks' for natural ventilation via opening, full-height sliding doors.

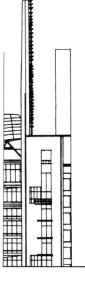

Essentially these devices introduce **natural ventilation** by the creation of pressure at the inlet, induced by the **wing-walls,** which effectively 'catch' the wind from a range of directions. The position of the wing-walls and air-locks within the plan-form are based on Yeang's own assessment, assisted by data from the wind patterns of the locality. The overall experimental nature of this system has been subsequently verified by CFD analysis with positive results.

The key reason for this experiment lies in the economics of the original project. Because of the low rental rates perceived to be applicable in Penang, the original project was designed for tenants to install their own air-conditioning units. Yeang therefore proposed the use of **natural ventilation** not simply as a source of fresh air supply, but as a true modifier of comfort conditions internally. Consequently, Yeang was able to claim that the UMNO Tower is probably the first high-rise office building that uses **wind** as natural ventilation relative to internal comfort conditions, as a general overall principle.

The fact that central air-conditioning was subsequently installed, now means that the natural ventilation design provides a back-up system to the building, in the event of power-failure. This factor, together with the natural ventilation and lighting of the service cores and stairs and the protective measures in orientation of the building's mass, collectively results in a genuinely low-energy design proposition.

Aside from the simple and brilliant technical resolution of a plan-form generated by pure principles from studies of **wind and sun path**, all of which feed Yeang's following projects, he has also extended the **expressive** dimension of these forces in the overall architectural composition.

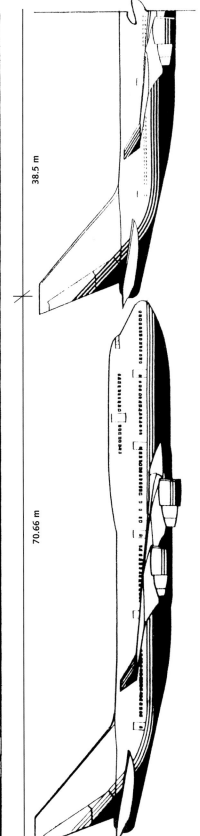

38.5 m

70.66 m

menara umno

owner South East Asia Development Corporation Berhad
location Jalan Macalister, Penang, Malaysia
latitude 5.2°N
nos of storeys 21 storeys
date start 1995
completion date 1998 (March)
areas Total gross area (incl. carpark) 10,900 sq m
Total net area 8,192 sq m
nos of carpark bays 94 bays
site area 1,920 sq m
plot ratio 1:5.5

design features • The proposed tower on this site is 21 storeys and contains spaces for banking hall at the ground floor and at level 1 and an auditorium for meetings and assemblies at level 6. The auditorium is also accessible by a separate external staircase. Above this are 14 floors of office space.

The building's design features are as follows:
• All office floors (although designed to be air-conditioned) can be naturally ventilated.
• The building has wind wing-walls to direct wind to special balconies zone that serve as pockets with 'air-locks' (having adjustable doors and panels to control the percentage of openable windows) for natural ventilation. This building is probably the first high-rise office that uses wind as natural ventilation for creating comfort conditions inside the building. Other claims of 'natural ventilation' in high-rise towers use natural ventilation simply as a source of fresh air supply to the interior and not for internal comfort.
• The building was originally designed for tenants to install their own split-unit air-conditioning as it was perceived that the poor rental rates did not justify the installation of a central system. However a central air-conditioning system was subsequently installed.
• All the lift lobbies, staircases and toilets have natural sunlight and ventilation making the building safe to use (ie. naturally lit stairs and lobbies in the event of power failure or other emergencies) and also low energy to operate.

energy consumption
• The cooling load of the building is 6,000,773 BTU (500 RT).
• The air-conditioning consumption is 126 kWhr/sq m/annum.
• The total energy consumption of the building is 244 kWhr/sq m/annum.
• The energy consumption, if naturally ventilated (ie. without air-conditioning) 118 kWhr/sq m/annum.

(Source: Ranhill Bersekutu Sdn Bhd)

One of the ways in which natural ventilation can improve occupant comfort as a form of passive low-energy cooling of building, is through a direct physiological effect on the occupants. For example, by opening the windows, we let the wind in and in doing so, we provide a higher indoor air speed, which make the occupants inside feel cooler. This approach is generally called comfort ventilation.

Introducing the outdoor air with a given speed into a building may provide a cooling effect even when the cooling temperature is actually elevated. This is particularly true when the humidity is high and the higher wind speed entering the space increases the rate of sweat evaporation from the skin of the occupants, thus minimising the discomfort that they feel when their skin is wet.

Such comfort ventilation may be desirable from the physiological viewpoint, even when the outdoor temperature is higher than the indoor temperature, because the upper temperature limit of comfort is shifted upwards with a higher air speed. Therefore even if the indoor temperature is actually elevated by ventilation with the warmer outdoor air, the effect of the comfort of the occupants (up to a given temperature limit) might be beneficial.

The important factor is the airspeed over the body of the occupants. This air speed can be further increased by the greater opening of the windows and also by the use of such devices as ceiling fans in closed buildings.

Contrary to popular belief that the incident impact of wind on the external wall gives better ventilation, it is in fact the oblique wind with angles of 30° to 60° away from the normal. That can provide better ventilation conditions in rooms. When the wind is oblique to the building, a pressure gradient is created along the windward walls. This pressure gradient can be further increased by adding a single wing-wall (a vertical projection one side of the wind).

The wing-wall is simply a short wall placed perpendicular to an opening in the building (ie. the orifice leading to the insides of the building), that is used in combination with the orifice as a device like a pocket to collect and direct the greater range of prevailing winds (where these come from a range of incidences) into the insides of the building. The device can be used to enhance the internal conditions of comfort (eg. internal air changes, temperature, humidity, etc). The design of this device depends on local wind conditions, the plan depth and built form, and would need to be tested by wind-tunnel tests or by CFD (Computational Fluid Dynamics) simulations to ascertain effectiveness, size of openings, control components, wing-wall size and shape, wing-wall orientation and location in relation to the built form, etc.

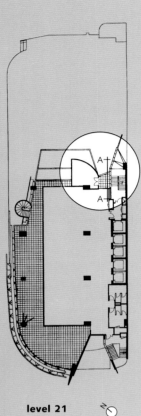

level 21

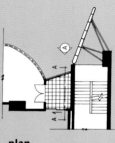

plan

elevation A

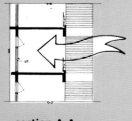

section A-A

figure 1 > shows the conditions without the wing-wall. Wind 'A' from a perpendicular angle of incidence hits the wall and the orifice. The flow that enters the orifice is 'a', which is generally smaller in dimension than the orifice's opening dimension 'x'.

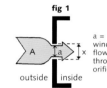

fig 1

$a =$ wind flow through orifice

outside | inside

figure 2 > shows the situation when wind comes from an incline incidence to the wall and the orifice. The wind 'B' hits the building's external wall, generating flow 'b' into the interior. Assuming that wind speeds 'A' and 'B' are the same, then flow 'b' is smaller than 'a', since wind 'B' comes from an inclined angle of incidence.

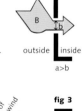

fig 2

outside | inside

$a > b$

figure 3 > shows the situation with the addition of a perpendicular wing-wall. The wall is located on that side of the orifice that should enable it to collect the greater range of prevailing winds. Which side of the orifice for the wing-wall to be located depends upon an assessment by the designer of the wind-data of that locality. In this instance, this is assumed to be primarily within 45° incidence from direction 'A' and 'B'. The flow through the orifice is 'c' which is equal to or greater than flow 'a' or 'b' due to the wing-wall.

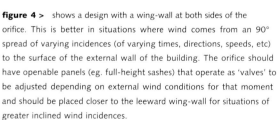

fig 3

range of prevailing wind

outside | inside

wing-wall $c \geq b > a$

figure 4 > shows a design with a wing-wall at both sides of the orifice. This is better in situations where wind comes from an 90° spread of varying incidences (of varying times, directions, speeds, etc) to the surface of the external wall of the building. The orifice should have openable panels (eg. full-height sashes) that operate as 'valves' to be adjusted depending on external wind conditions for that moment and should be placed closer to the leeward wing-wall for situations of greater inclined wind incidences.

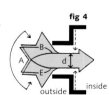

fig 4

outside | inside

The perpendicular wing-wall configuration is more effective at stagnating the approaching air-flow which results in flow more perpendicular to the opening and with less contraction. In addition, the wing-wall devices should also have compatible adjustable horizontal 'spoilers' at each floor level to minimise vertical flow over the face of the building and to further control the incoming winds in the event of conditions of very high wind speeds.

figure 5 > shows a single wing-wall option which is more efficient for winds coming from inclined incidences than **figure 4**.

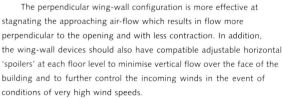

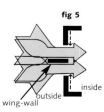

fig 5

inside

outside

wing-wall

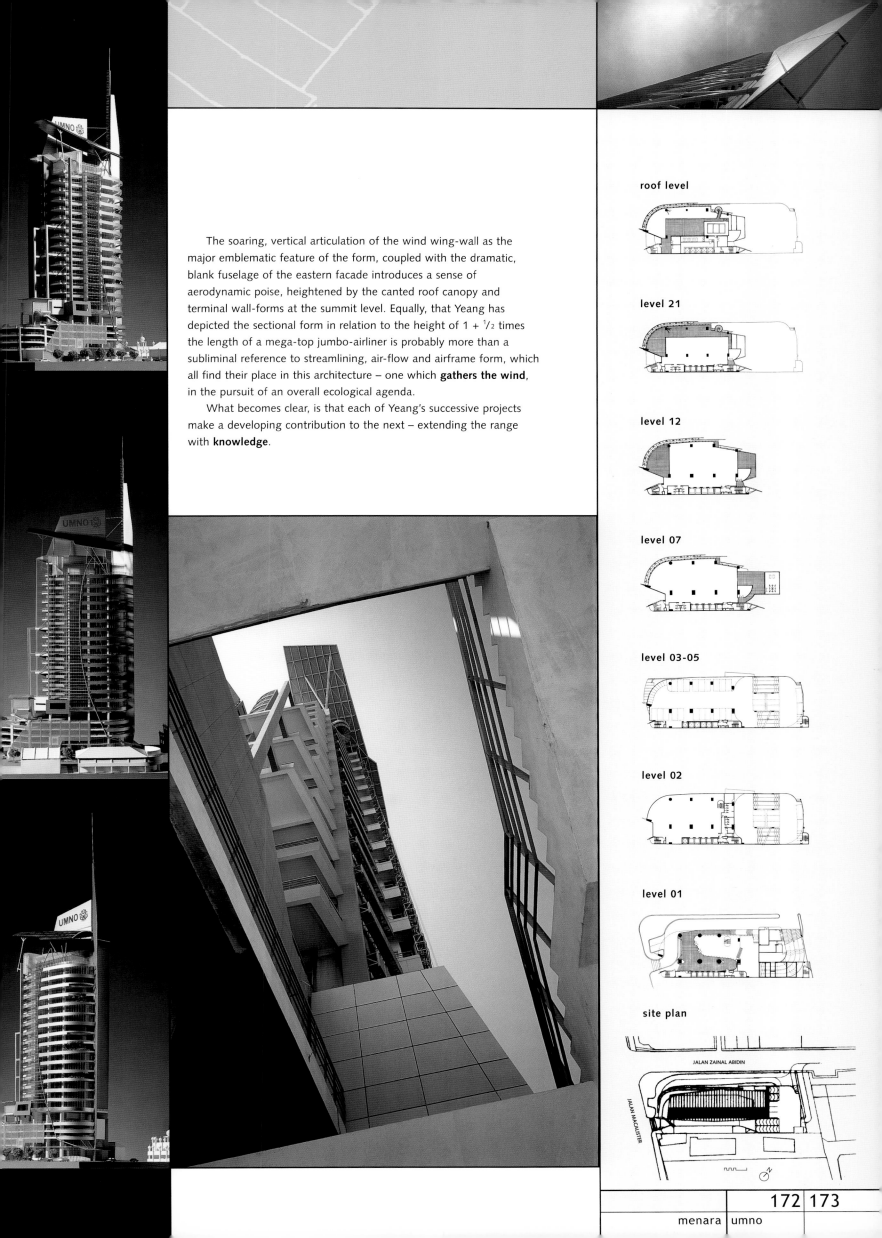

The soaring, vertical articulation of the wind wing-wall as the major emblematic feature of the form, coupled with the dramatic, blank fuselage of the eastern facade introduces a sense of aerodynamic poise, heightened by the canted roof canopy and terminal wall-forms at the summit level. Equally, that Yeang has depicted the sectional form in relation to the height of $1 + \frac{1}{2}$ times the length of a mega-top jumbo-airliner is probably more than a subliminal reference to streamlining, air-flow and airframe form, which all find their place in this architecture – one which **gathers the wind**, in the pursuit of an overall ecological agenda.

What becomes clear, is that each of Yeang's successive projects make a developing contribution to the next – extending the range with **knowledge**.

roof level

level 21

level 12

level 07

level 03-05

level 02

level 01

site plan

APRIL 1996

16 JUNE 1997

AUGUST 1997

10 SEPTEMBER 1996

11 AUGUST 1997

SEPTEMBER 1997

5 NOVEMBER 1996

AUGUST 1997

SEPTEMBER 1997

19 NOVEMBER 1996

24 NOVEMBER 1996

AUGUST 1997

OCTOBER 1997

17 DECEMBER 1996

AUGUST 1997

15 JANUARY 1997

NOVEMBER 1997

AUGUST 1997

25 MARCH 1997

NOVEMBER 1997

AUGUST 1997

DECEMBER 1997

14 APRIL 1997

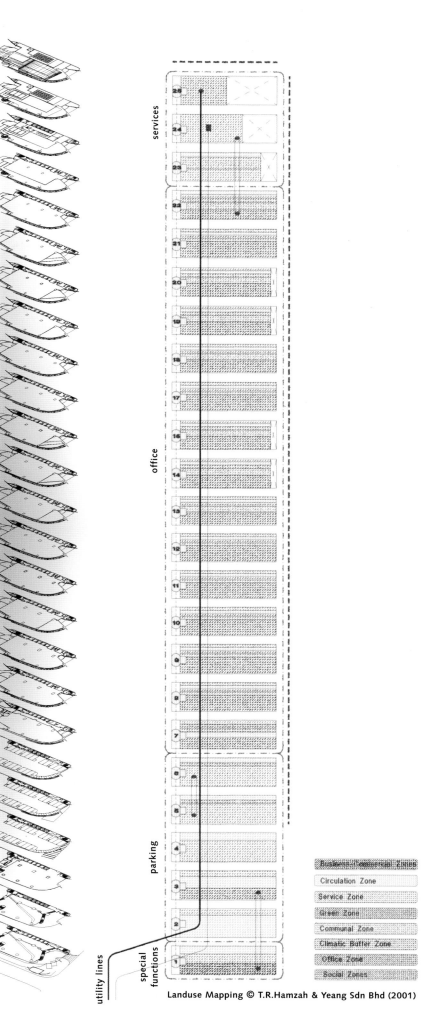

services

office

parking

special functions

utility lines

28
24
23
22
21
20
19
18
17
16
15
14
13
12
11
10
9
8
7
6
5
4
3
2
1

Business / Commercial Zones
Circulation Zone
Service Zone
Green Zone
Communal Zone
Climatic Buffer Zone
Office Zone
Social Zones

Landuse Mapping © T.R.Hamzah & Yeang Sdn Bhd (2001)

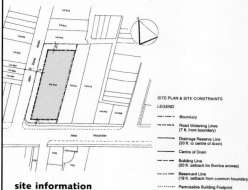

feasibility notes presented
to client at inception of project

introduction
These notes contain feasibility study for the
proposed commercial development on the
mentioned parcels of land.

SITE PLAN & SITE CONSTRAINTS
LEGEND

Boundary
Road Widening Lines
(7 ft. from boundary)
Drainage Reserve Line
(20 ft. to centre of drain)
Centre of Drain
Building Line
(20 ft. setback for Bomba access)
Basement Line
(19 ft. setback from common boundary)
Permissible Building Footprint

site information
site location: lot 912
total site area: 21,290 sf (1,977.84 sq m)
site constraints and building footprint
- site area: 21,290 sf
- site area after road widening, building lines and
  drainage reserve setback: 14,357 sf (approx.)
- site area after basement line or full basement
  area: 13,543 sf (approx)
- permissible building footprint: 14,357 sf (approx.)
(NB The above information was obtained from MPPP
on 16 April 1993)
Gross built-up area
- plot ratio: 1:5
- gross built-up area: 106,450 sf

these feasibility notes are based on the following assumptions:
- assume setback line from all boundary lines.
- total land are: **21,290 sf**
- take proposed development to have a plot ratio of 1:5
  (approved by MPPP)
- therefore, gross floor area (GFA) excluding carpark:106,450 sf
- assume 75% efficiency, nett area: 79,837.5 sf
- assume building carpark requirements: for every 400 sf area,
  one car bay to be provided.

proposed building area
- proposed GFA (excluding carpark): 106,500 sf
- assume typical floor @ 8,200 sf - 106,500 sf ÷ 8,200
- no of floors: 13 storeys
- assume building footprint per block: 78 x 110 = 8,200 sf
- total gross area (excluding carpark): **106,450 sf**
- assume 75% nett efficiency, total nett area: 79,837 sf

carpark calculations
- assume for every 400 sq ft nett, 1 car bay to be provided
- therefore, nos of car bays required: 79,837 ÷ 400 = 200 bays
- assume 30% reduction for Bumiputra status: 140 bays
- total nos of bays to be provided: 140 bays
- assume 1 car bay: 350 sq ft
- total carpark area: 140 x 350 - 49,000 sf

proposed built form
the proposed built form shall consist of:
- 4 floors of basement parking: 49,000 sf (140 bays)
- 13 floors of office block
- gross floor plate area: 8,200 sf
- nett floor plate area: 6,150 sf

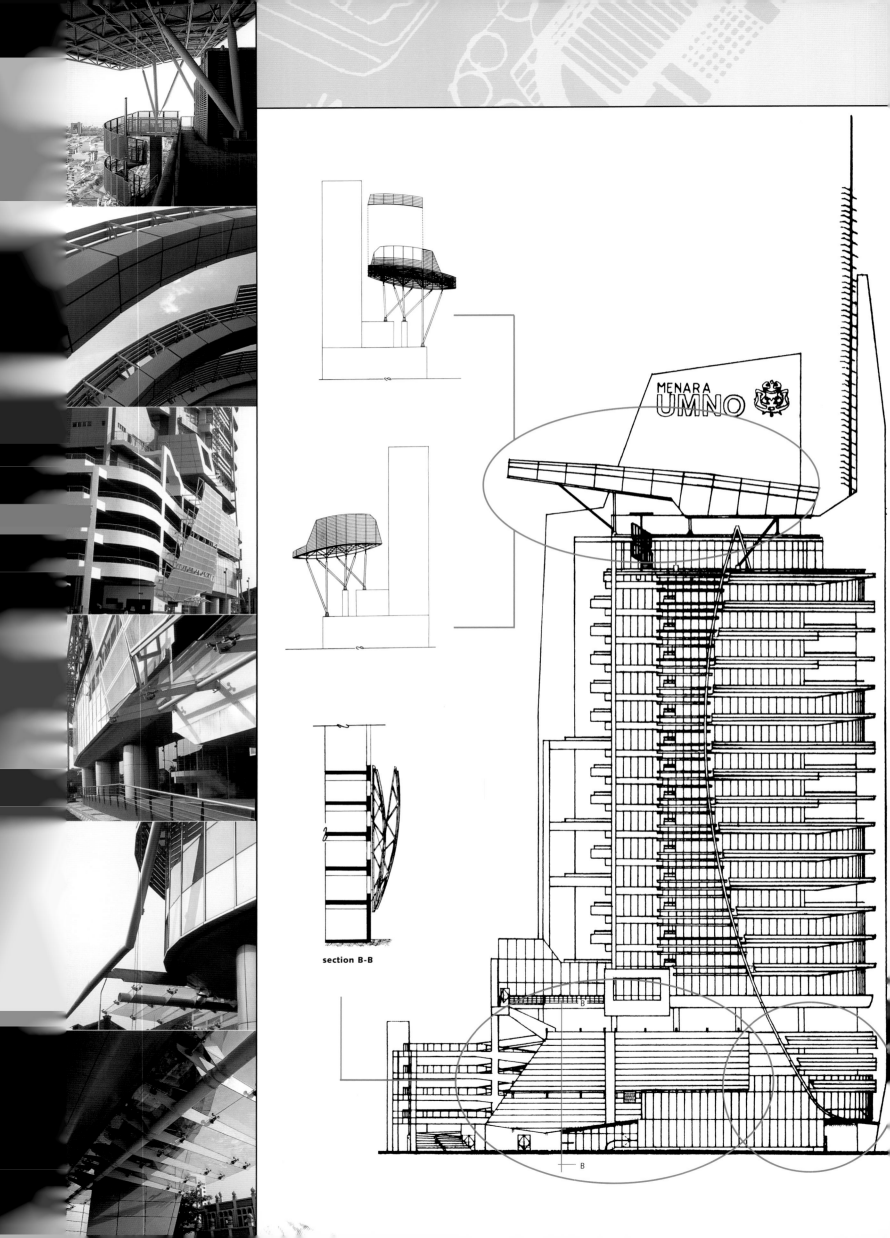

MENARA UMNO

section B-B

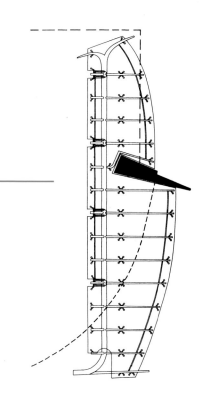

section C-C

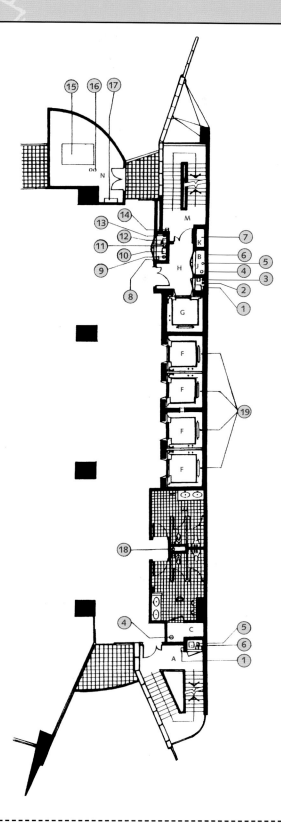

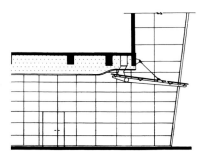

service core detail
legend

1. telecommunication Box
2. telecommunication Riser
3. audio-visual/PA system riser
4. main water riser
5. hose-reel rIser
6. hose-reel
7. pressurisation duct
8. electricity junction box (consumer risers)
9. electricity rIser conduit (main)
10. electricity junction box (main)
11. electricity conduit riser (M&E)
12. electricity junction box (M&E)
13. fire-fighting communication conduit
14. fireman's telephones
15. air handling unit
16. M&E Risers up/return
17. air handling unit control panel
18. sanitary rIser
19. pressurised shaft

A. staircase
B. hose-reel room
C. storage
D. male toilet
E. female toilet
F. lift
G. fireman's lift
H. smoke lobby
I. telephone room
J. hose-reel room
K. pressurisation duct
L. electrical room
M. staircase 2
N. air-conditioning room

structural & substructural engineering

by Dr Gerry Wong

Tahir Wong Sdn Bhd (Civil / Structural Engineer)

Four test boreholes were conducted, to a depth of about 64 m for the sub-structure design. Generally, these indicate the site to be underlain by successive layers of very soft to soft clay, followed by medium stiff to very stiff silt and silty sand. Ground water table is between 2.7 m to 3.5 m below ground level.

Column loadings vary from 3,200 tonnes to 1,800 tonnes for the widely-spaced columns. For the more closely spaced columns, the loading is about 740 tonnes.

In the selection of foundation for the structure, shallow foundation like pad footing and raft was considered to be obviously not suitable in view of poor soil (N-value of 3) to a depth of 9 m below ground level. Bored piling was not adopted in consideration of high water table with silty sand and low N-values at the upper layers. The requirements of long length of steel casings associated with boring in such soil to prevent collapse of bore holes would not merit value engineering decision.

For such soil condition and medium range column loadings, it was considered appropriate to adopt driven reinforced concrete piles. Further reasons to justify the use of driven r.c. piles are that they are economical (compared to steel piles) and could be installed relatively quickly. Piles used are as follows:

size 400 mm x 400 mm, with welded joint
grade of concrete G45
driven length average 55 m
working load 185 tonnes
maximum no of piles/column 8

Essentially, these are skin friction piles which mobilise the good soil resistance properties at depth of 30 to 55 m.

The idealised structure consists of moment resisting frames coupled to a shear wall. Horizontal and vertical r.c. members are rigidly connected together in a planar grid form which resists lateral wind loads primarily through the flexural stiffness of the members. This type of structural system is efficient to enhance the sway serviceability performance of the building. The structural analysis was carried out using the computer software STAAD-III, with the appropriate gravity loads and wind loads, derived from a basic wind speed of 35.8m/s (80mph).

The maximum computed horizontal deflection of 98mm, is well within the deflection limit of H/500 (85m/500 = 170mm).

The building was designed for conventional r.c. beam and slab construction which is economical for such medium height range. The quantity of concrete (G30) and steel reinforcement (Fy = 460 Mpa) used for the superstructure are as follows: **Concrete** 5,696 m^3
Steel 1,195 tonnes

To achieve an early hand over of the lift r.c. wall for lift installation, the contractor adopted the 'Jump Form'™ construction with a construction cycle time of 8 days for 3.9 m height of wall. With this method, the contractor completed the r.c. wall construction 3 months ahead of the other areas which was constructed using normal steel and timber framework. The entire project, including piling works, was completed in 22 months.

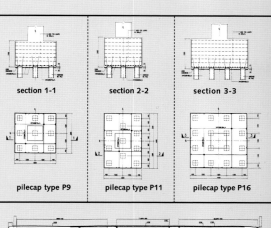

section 1-1   **section 2-2**   **section 3-3**

pilecap type P9   **pilecap type P11**   **pilecap type P16**

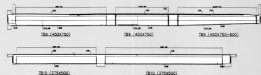

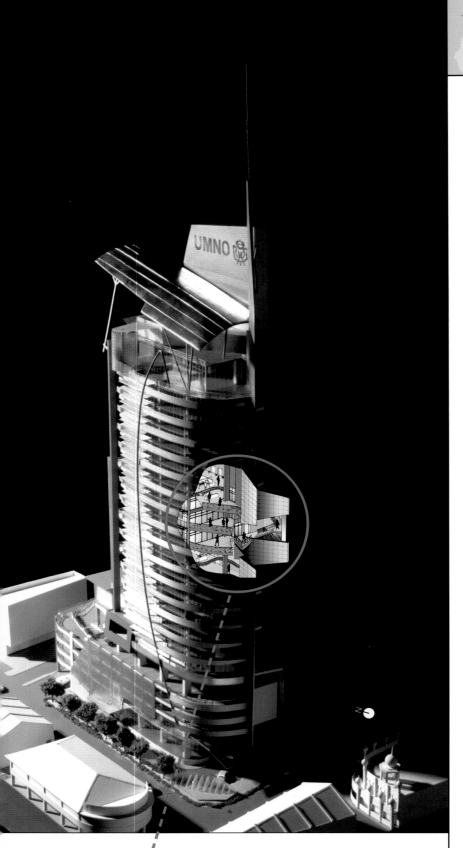

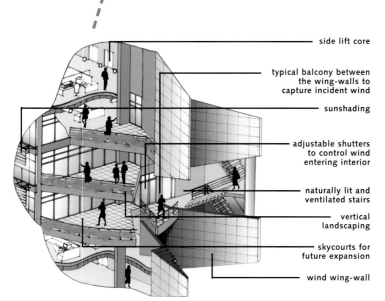

side lift core

typical balcony between
the wing-walls to
capture incident wind

sunshading

adjustable shutters
to control wind
entering interior

naturally lit and
ventilated stairs

vertical
landscaping

skycourts for
future expansion

wind wing-wall

The wing walls are orientated to 'catch' the prevailing wind and the windows and balcony doors are adjustable to control the wind-induced ventilation. The building is situated on an open site with no interference from other high-rise buildings. **Figure 1** shows the building on its site together with the wind rose for Penang.

Described here is the analysis of the building in relation to its potential for natural ventilation. It first discusses the analysis of the wind impact in relation to the building form. Computational fluid dynamics (CFD) airflow modeling was used to predict the wind pressures on the building, in particular at the location of the openings. From this, surface pressures at openings were obtained, which could then be used for the prediction of ventilation rate, internal air movement and temperature distribution. These predictions were obtained for 'stack' (that is, for calm conditions with no wind) and for a range of window opening conditions with wind forces.

Ventilation and comfort

Ventilation is needed for occupants breathing and to exhaust odours. It can also be used to exhaust heat gains, although generally, this requires higher levels of ventilation. For example, for a typical density of office occupation, 1-2 ac/h of fresh air ventilation may be needed to supply the ventilation needs. However, the order of 5 ac/h, or more, may be required to exhaust typical office heat gains, such that the internal air temperature is within about 1°C of external air temperature. The air movement associated with ventilation can provide comfort cooling for people especially in the hot humid conditions of Malaysia, where air movement across the skin can increase evaporative heat loss. Indeed, traditional Malaysian building design promotes high levels of natural ventilation and air movement, by using large openings in the external facade in order to encourage wind-driven cross ventilation. This, together with solar shading provides an environmentally selective design that can produce internal comfort conditions for much of the time. However, modern buildings in noisy polluted city locations tend to be designed such that they totally reject the climate and rely on air-conditioning and artificial lighting. But air-conditioning carries with it high energy and operating costs, and there is a growing concern over the quality of indoor environments in air-conditioned buildings, and the health of the occupants in relation to complaints of 'sick building syndrome' and poor indoor air quality. In Europe, there is an increasing interest in buildings that combine the benefits of natural and mechanical ventilation in some hybrid form, with mechanical ventilation only operating in spaces or at times when it is needed. The design provides the potential for using this hybrid approach to environmental design.

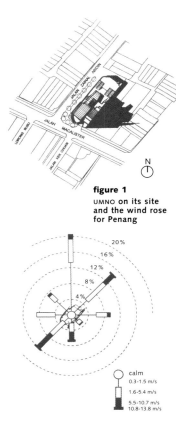

figure 1
UMNO on its site
and the wind rose
for Penang

UMNO form, orientation and location of openings

The form of the building with its wing-walls and balconies has been designed to direct the wind pressure to the main ventilation openings. Each floor of office space is open plan with most work places having access to an openable window /door and natural light. The main openings are in the form of windows and balcony doors, and are located on the south-west and north-east elevations. These allow for cross-ventilation driven by the prevailing wind conditions. Other windows are located along the north-west facade for user controlled ventilation. **Figure 2** shows a typical office floor plan with the main openings identified.

Wind Analysis

The wind speed will increase in height according to a power law relation as shown in **figure 3**. In order to assess the potential for natural ventilation, the wind pressure over the building's external surfaces needed to be estimated at the opening locations. This would normally be carried out using a physical scale model in a wind tunnel. However, this was not an option in this design and therefore a mathematical wind tunnel analysis was carried out using the CFD airflow model DFS-AIR.

A model of the building was constructed mathematically in the computer and used to obtain an estimate of the surface pressures at each opening. The wind rose for the site, shown in **figure 1**, indicates that a typical wind condition for the site would be a speed of 2.5 m/s (at a height of 10 m from ground level) and a south-west prevailing wind direction. The power law relationship in **figure 3** was then used in the airflow model to calculate the boundary layer wind speed at increasing heights.

The results of the simulation are shown in **figures 4** and **5**. **Figure 4** describes the wind flow around the building in the form of air pressure contours. The maximum wind impact on the windward elevation is at about 75% the height of building, which is a general rule for buildings on an open site. **Figure 5** shows the pressure distribution around the building for a typical office.

figure 2

It shows a positive pressure of about 6Pa at openings on the windward balcony and a negative pressure of about 3Pa on the downwind balconies and side openings. These surface pressures were then used in the internal air-flow simulation to predict the wind-induced ventilation rates for typical wind conditions.

Internal Airflow Analysis

The aim of the internal airflow simulations was to predict internal ventilation rate, air speeds and temperature distribution in order to assess the potential for natural ventilation and to provide advice on window opening strategies. The CFD airflow model DFS-AIR was again used, but this time to predict the internal air movement in relation to a range of operating conditions for natural ventilation. The model is able to account for the pressure boundary conditions at the openings, based on the wind pressure simulation data described above, as well as simulating internal heat gains and heat transfer at internal surfaces, for example heat gains through the windows.

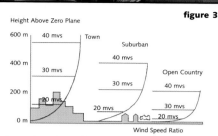
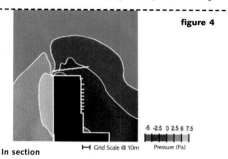

The simulations were carried out for a typical external air temperature of 30°C. Internal heat gains, due to people, lights and small power, were assumed to be 35W/m². Simulations were carried out in two stages.

Case		A (1.8)	B (1.8)	C (4.2)	D (5.1)	X (2.0)	
1	Stack	open	Open	Open	open	open	Table 1
2	Wind	open	Open	Open	closed	closed	Schedule of simulations
3	Wind	open	Open	Open	open	closed	for stack and wind
4	Wind	open	Open	Closed	open	open	(areas of opening in
5	Wind	closed	Closed	Open	open	closed	brackets (m2)

figure 3

Power law relation for varying wind speed with height.

Stage 1

The simulations were carried out:

- for a calm day with no wind and ventilation driven by the stack forces generated due to internal external temperature differences;
- for average wind conditions (2.5 m/s; south-westerly) and a range of window opening configurations.

Case		m³/s	ac/h	Average internal air temperature (°C)	Average internal air speed (m/s)	
1	Stack	0.45	1.0	31.5	0.1	Table 2
2	Wind	10.8	24.0	31.0	0.47	Summary of results
2 repeat	Wind	5.6	12.6	31.2	0.35	
3	Wind	15.2	33.8	30.9	0.57	
4	Wind	2.9	6.3	31.4	0.34	
5	Wind	12.6	28.0	30.5	0.3	

figure 4

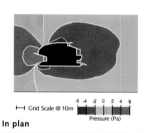

In section

The situations modeled are shown in **table 1**. **Table 2** summarises the main results from the simulations. For windows and doors fully open on the up-wind and down-wind facades, ventilation rates were very high for the wind condition considered. Case 4 has only small openings (at X) and this has a more controllable ventilation rate of about 6.3ac/h. Case 2 was repeated with a smaller area of window opening on the upwind doors, C (1.5 m² instead of the fully open area of 4.2 m²). This again reduced the ventilation rate considerably.

The results for the stack only condition, Case 1, are shown in **figure 6**. **Figure 6** presents the internal temperature distribution and the air speed vectors at 1.2m height.

Figure 7 presents the internal temperature distribution and air speed vectors respectively for Case 2 (repeat).

figure 5

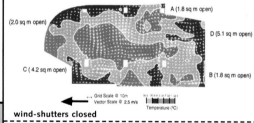

In plan

Stage 2

Following these tests, further tests were performed for low (-1m/s at 10m height) and high (-5m/s at 10m height) wind speeds, in order to derive some guidance on window opening for the prevailing wind directions. Results from stages 1 and 2 are presented in **table 3** and an approximate set of curves extrapolating from this data are presented in **figure 8**.

Wind Direction → X   C   A,B,D   Location of windows on building

figure 6

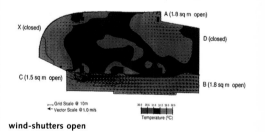

wind-shutters closed

Table 3 NOTES

- For stack effect only (i.e. calm conditions) the ventilation rate with all windows open is about 1 ac/h.
- At low wind speeds (1-1.5m/s) the ventilation rate is about 4ac/h.
- At medium wind speeds (2.5m/s) the ventilation rate increases significantly and upwind windows need to be closed down to 50% (or less), or completely closed and side windows open, to give ventilation rates between 6 and 12 ac/h.
- At high wind speeds (5m/s) the upwind windows need to be closed to 20% or less. Closing down wind windows is of secondary importance (closing them to 50% only reduces the ventilation rate from 11.9 to 10.8 ac/h.).

	Upwind	Side	Downwind	Ac/H	
Stack	C (100%)	X (100%)	A, B, D (100%)	1.0	Table 3
Low Wind	C (50%)	0	A, B (100%)	2.1	Wind user table
	C (100%)	0	A, B (100%)	4.1	
Medium Wind	C (100%)	0	A, B (100%)	24.0	
	C (50%)	0	A, B (100%)	12.6	
	C (100%)	0	A, B, D (100%)	33.8	
	0	X (100%)	A, B, D (100%)	6.3	
	C (100%)	0	D (100%)	28.0	
High Wind	C (20%)	0	A, B (100%)	11.9	
	C (20%)	0	A, B (50%)	10.8	

figure 7

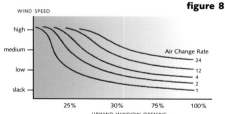

wind-shutters open

Discussion and conclusions

The wind condition was successfully simulated to provide external pressure values at the opening door and window locations. The building's shape appears to respond well to the prevailing wind directions, with the combination of wing-walls and balconies providing relative high/low pressure areas at ventilation openings on the upwind and downwind elevations. For wind directions other than the prevailing winds, the pressure gradient across the building may be less, however the openings along X should provide sufficient control.

For the stack only situation the ventilation rate is not very high, at about 1ac/h. The internal external air temperature difference is greatest (1.5°C higher) for the stack only case. This relatively small temperature difference, together with the relatively low ceiling height with respect to the stack effect, does not provide a strong stack force. The internal air speed is low and would not provide a significant comfort cooling effect.

For the window opening situations, where there are large openings upwind and downwind, the ventilation rates are very high (up to about 30 ac/h). Obviously, this is too high for comfort as the corresponding internal air speeds are between 0.4 and 0.5 m/s, which could give rise to mechanical problems, such as papers moving. Closing down the openings on the upwind side appears to be the best solution for controlling ventilation. For example, Cases 3 and 2 (repeat) provide controlled ventilation without excessive internal air speeds.

The pattern of internal air movement for wind-driven ventilation appears to be localised in relation to the inlet openings. There are strong paths of air-flow originating from the inflow openings, which appear to mainly coincide with internal circulation routes, but there may be much lower air movement in the main occupied zone. There may be the need to consider some form of device that would diffuse the incoming air 'jet', such that the ventilation air is more evenly distributed and to avoid any 'short-circuiting' between supply and exhaust openings. This might be in the form of a 'spoiler' or 'deflector' located near to the openings.

The ventilation strategy should be to ensure that windows and doors can be opened wide, for low wind and calm conditions, but that they can have adjustable openings to allow them to be operated under average and high wind conditions (refer to curves in **table 3**). During medium to high wind situations it appears to be advisable to close down on the windward direction openings to a minimum. It appears that the openings on the down-wind facades have only a secondary effect on ventilation rates although they may have a larger influence on patterns of internal air movement.

A table and graph of window opening guidance has been extrapolated from the simulation data.

figure 8

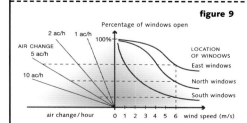

Window opening related to wind speed (zero, low, medium and high), air change rate, for the prevailing wind direction.

figure 9

Example of occupant's guide to natural ventilation
(1 graph for each wind direction eg. north-west and vertical zone)

daylight simulations

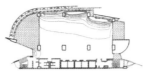

level 9
10.00am

level 9
3.00pm

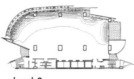

level 8
10.30am

level 8
3.30pm

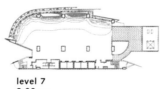

level 7
9.00am

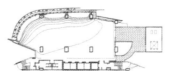

level 7
4.00pm

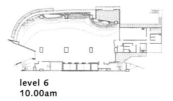

level 6
10.00am

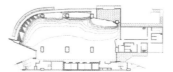

level 6
4.00pm

The effects of direct/global solar radiation is significantly intense in this type of climate and the presence of glazed facades of the western 'front' of the menara pose problem in terms of controlling this effect.

The problem is however, concentrated on the curvature of the facade (where it most directly faces west) and hence this 'component' is where the shading system has to be most effective.

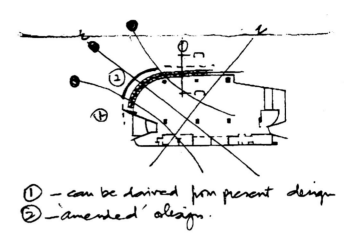

① – can be derived from present design
② – 'amended' design.

Climate data on solar radiation also shows that it is about 4:00pm to 5:00pm that direct/diffuse radiation (and also temperature) start to significantly 'drop' (Vertical cut-off angles for this time shows about 18-20 deg).

What is recommended is a shading system with two main components:
1 one whose dimensions/cross section can be derived from the present one
2 a 'separate' component dealing with the high intensity incident of the curvature.

To deal with the intensity of direct radiation (**2**) should either be:
1 a vertical shading system that cantilever about 2 or 1.75 x the 'length' of the existing frame of present shading system possibly made with perforated metal to admit usable amounts of daylight

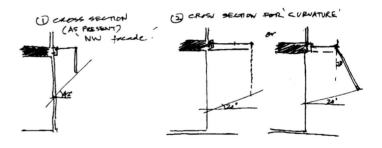

or

2 a 'tilted' system, with the present 'cantilever' with an approx 18–20 deg tilt from vertical can be made by present construction materials/components. (**2**) might serve better in satisfying the requirement of provision of view for occupants.

An additional feature which has resulted in improved 'daylighting efficacy' is the integration of a lightshelf system into the design.

Research in temperature summer season has shown that besides reflecting light into internal space, the lightshelf provides more uniformity for illuminance values at the worst illuminated point in a room compared with other (vertical/horizontal/tilted) shading system.

To control the effects of heat gain, it is recommended that the upper glazed portion above the light shelf be made of glazing material that is 'lower' in shading coefficient values. What would be ideal is also the use of glazing, in this portion of the glazed wall with high efficacy (low-shading coefficient and high transmittance) such as tinted or reflective Low-E glass.

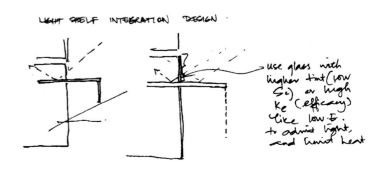

LIGHT SHELF INTEGRATION DESIGN

use glass with higher tint (low Sc) or high Ke (efficacy) like low-E. to admit light and limit heat

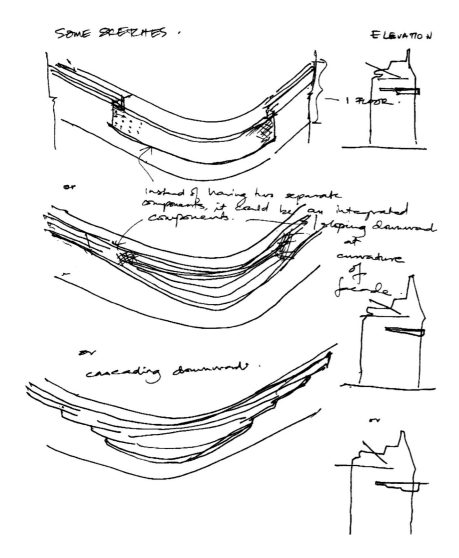

SOME SKETCHES.

ELEVATION

1 FLOOR.

or

instead of having two separate components, it could be an integrated components. — sloping downward at curvature of facade.

or cascading downward.

sketches for improvements to west facade sunshading

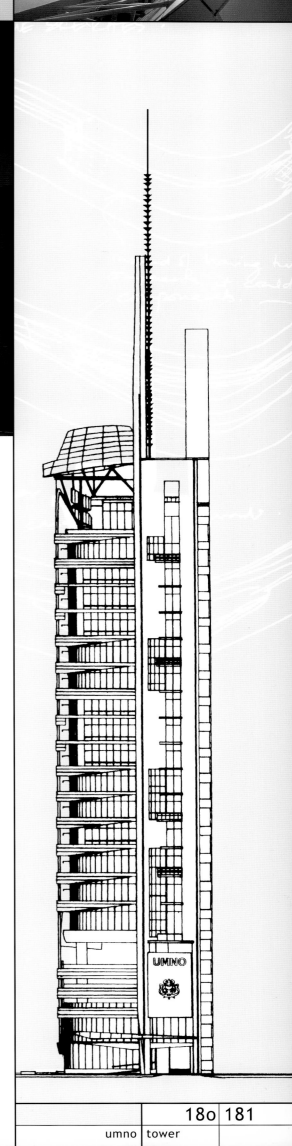

UMNO

public and private marina   waterfront residential blocks   pedestrian boulevard   floating mosque

Dubai, United Arab Emirates

dubai towers

owner Dubai Municipality, United Arab Emirates
location Dubai, United Arab Emirates
latitude 25.1°N
nos of storeys up to 18 storeys (over 27 blocks)
date start 1998 (design)
completion date -
areas Total built-up area 863,550 sq m gross
Site area 124,688 sq m
plot ratio 1:4.5

design features • The project is located in a prominent
waterfront site between five famous sectors in central Dubai;
Clock Tower, City-center, Dubai International Golf Club,
Alkhor Park and AlMaktoum Bridge.
The site enjoys panoramic views across the river to Alkhor and
Alkhor Park to the south and Alkhor Park and the Golf Club
to the south-east.
The site has an area of over 1.3 million sq ft with a permissible
Floor Area Ratio (FAR) of 1:5, which gives the development
great flexibility in design and use, and high potential economic
returns. However, there is a building height restriction of 13
storeys or 55 m which places a constraint on the site's building
massing.
The site is located in a heavy traffic zone area at the crossing
of AlMaktoum interchange expansion with Baniyas main road.
Due to its proximity the intersection, the site has limited
vehicular access points off the main road. The road frontage is
also limited as the south-western boundary is taken up by the
water front.
The brief calls for a mixed-use complex with housing, offices,
touristic and commercial uses, as well as landscape areas.

masterplanning • The project's masterplan overall
objective is to address the street frontage and the river
frontage. Water is brought into this site to enable access by
boat and to contribute to lowering the ambient temperature
of the development (see below).
site massing • The massing proposal for this scheme addresses
the existing site density and height restriction as follows:
• All car-parking spaces are located in the basement in order
to free up the ground level for landscaping and recreational
use. By placing the cars in the basement, the building height
can also be reduced.
• Water is brought into the site to create internal views and to
increase the waterfront recreational space (eg. marina, waterfront promenade, etc).
• The buildings fronting the water is elevated at ground level,
freeing up extra space for recreational use.
• Increase in building height to 70 m. Informal discussions
held with the Dept. of Civil Aviation suggests that there may be
a relaxation in building height restrictions from 55 m to 70 m.
hotel • The hotel is located at the most visible position from
the main road at the northern corner on the site.
The hotel is served by a high-class vehicle drop-off with
convenient car-parking located underneath.
The hotel suites has views both to the waterfront to the west
and the city centre to the north. Its 'horse-shoe' shape frames
the swimming pool deck while directing the views towards the
creek beyond.
The hotel serves the business demand generated by the
proposed office buildings as well as tourists to this location.
The nearby tourist attractions such as the City Centre shopping
mall, Dubai Creek Golf Club and Creekside Park would
be further enhanced by the proposed new waterfront
development and shopping mall.
serviced apartments • The serviced apartments are
connected to the hotel for central servicing and shared use
of club facilities. The apartments have direct views towards
the waterfront and new marina bay.
The hotel and serviced apartments are located on the
northern segment of the site separated by the new marina
bay to differentiate it from the rest of the development.
This allows for better security of its premises.
apartments • The apartments are located at the waterfront
edge and command the best views in the development.
The apartments benefit from a close relationship to the office
towers and retail shopping mall.
Each apartment block has a separate car drop-off to the
main lobby and are directly accessible from the basement
car-parking underneath.

double-glazed west facade   skycourts   vegetation on mounted landscape

Al Maktoum bridge

hotel tower

waterfront apartments

office blocks facing Beniyas Rd

mounted landscape

public/private marina

floating mosque

waterfront apartments

building elements – overall concept

----

site plan

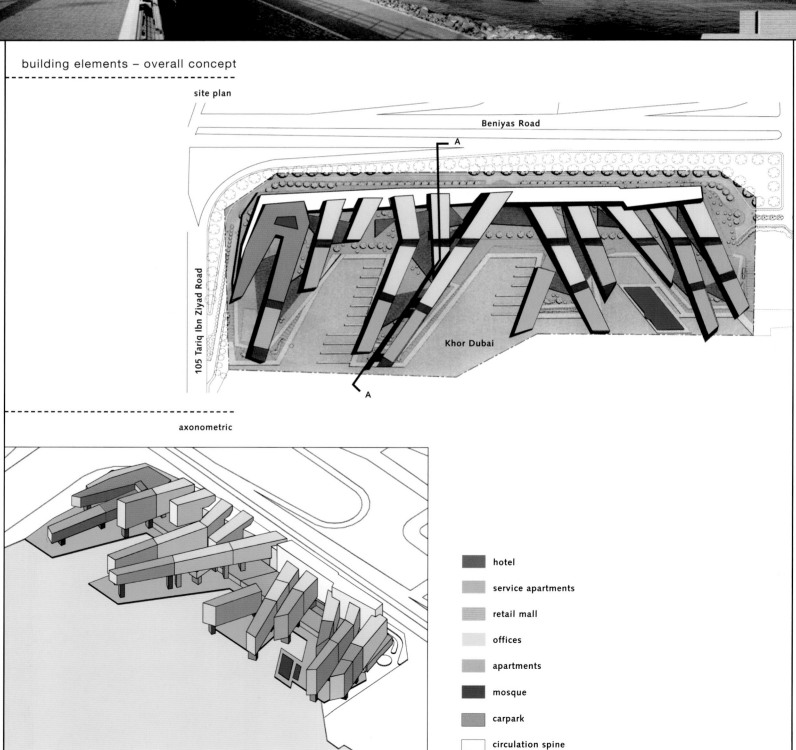

Beniyas Road

A

105 Tariq Ibn Ziyad Road

Khor Dubai

A

----

axonometric

- hotel
- service apartments
- retail mall
- offices
- apartments
- mosque
- carpark
- circulation spine

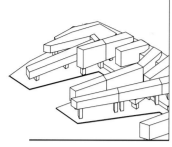

The Dubai Towers project is essentially very different from Yeang's definitive skyscraper typology, in both its form and location.

Set in a distinctive **waterfront** position, in central Dubai, the site and buildings enjoy panoramic vistas across the river to parkland. The permissible building height is restricted to 70 metres maximum, and road access is limited to the linear highway frontage of Baniyas Road.

Yeang's overall design strategy is essentially that of a huge partially buried plinth which houses car-parking and retail shopping mall with a landscaped roof which descends gently to a new waterfront promenade and marina, and which brings water into the site-enhancing views and recreational space. Over this massive landscaped base Yeang has located a series of canted **linear-towers**, whose ends are lifted above the lower landscape, and are set at approximate right-angles to the waterfront. The towers are separated but linked, for ease of circulation. The overall result of this arrangement is a 'sliced' form which is entirely driven by considerations of **wind** and **natural ventilation** and the maximising of the vistas and prospect.

Yeang's summary of the **bioclimatic response** contained in the formal arrangement makes two significant points: first, that channeled air movement between the linear towers increases air movement and cooling effect, and next that complementary shading between the linear towers lowers radiant air temperature. Coupled with these overall principles Yeang has utilised a traditional concept of the **'wind tower'**, to ventilate basement car-park levels through to the podium roof. Thus, in overall terms the whole intensive layered form can be seen as a direct conceptual model, which is **harnessing wind** and hence ventilation, and providing shade over new landscape of planting and water. Yeang's policy is developed in more detail:

> **"… the proximity of the creek water mass with the city water mass behind the development can give reversal of wind directions during the daily cycle. During the afternoon when the land mass is warmer the cooler sea breeze moves in from the water towards the land. In the early morning when the land and building masses have been cooled with night radiation to the sky, the dense cool air moves towards the water mass."** [1]

The design is inextricably evolved from this statement, and then enhanced in detail throughout the programme of mixed-uses.

Of all the bioclimatic elements, beyond the wind and ventilation strategy, the **landscaping** is the most significant, re-introducing organic mass and lowering ambient micro-climate temperatures. The project includes both ground and vertical landscaping, and including water coverage represents 90% of the entire site area. This is largely due to the massive landscaped ground plane extending from the promenade upwards, over the whole podium. Landscaped skycourts are also incorporated into the higher levels of the buildings.

offices • The Offices are located on the east side of the development to take advantage of the road frontage. It is essential that these offices are very visible from the surrounding streets.
The office blocks sit above the retail podium.
Each office block has a separate car drop-off on the lower ground (promenade) level and are directly accessible from the basement carparking underneath.

retail • The retail shopping centre directly faces Baniyas Road and has its main entrances off the street level.
The roof of the shopping centre is landscaped with shopping pavilions. They command panoramic views over the marina and creek.
The car-parking is located underneath the mall and are directly accessible via escalators and lifts.

mosque • The mosque is located on an 'island' site directly at the waterfront. The mosque faces west towards Mecca.

car-parking • The car-parking for this development is located on the lower ground and basement levels due to space limitations and height restrictions. Very little ground level parking is provided and where this is provided it is with dropping VIPs, women and families in mind.
The top level of the car-parking (lower ground floor) is the drop-off level for the offices. This level is semi-submerged and receives natural light and ventilation. It is served by a wide and spacious 'boulevard' road which has views of the water.

section concept • Pedestrian and vehicular traffic are separated through a device of vertical segregation of people above and vehicles below.
In this way, the linkage between building elements is optimised and conflicts with external traffic conditions and circulation are avoided.

bioclimatic aspects

landscaping • Landscaping and planting to lower ambient micro-climate temperatures as well as to re-introduce organic mass back into the essentially urban and mostly inorganic location.
Ground and vertical landscaping is used extensively around the development. This is achieved by extending the landscaping from the waterfront promenade level up to the retail podium roof in one continuous plane, below the elevated the building blocks. Landscaped skycourts are introduced in the upper floors of the buildings.
Earth excavated from the new marinas are used to create landscaped mounds between the elevated buildings and the basement carparking roof, reducing costly export of earth from the site. The earth acts as thermal insulation for rooftops.

wind and natural ventilation • The orientation of the building blocks at right angles to the water front encourage free movement of air between the building blocks assisting the natural cooling of the buildings. The porosity of the building facades assists in channeling air through the site while vertical gaps act as thermal flues moving air vertically and in doing so cools the building fabric.
In traditional buildings this movement of air has been utilised in the use of 'Towers of Wind' to ventilate occupied accommodation. This principle is used in the development to ventilate the carpark floors. Large light and ventilation wells from the podium roof into the basements function as wind towers, drawing fresh air into the basement and extracting used air out.

shading • Shading of both primary and external spaces is an essential and important part of the design. The need is there to protect the treated internal environment from direct solar radiation and in doing so reduce the energy demand of the building's environmental systems and at the same time improve the overall comfort of the spaces.
Sunshade structures emanate as external louvered screen attachments to the facade of the buildings. The space between the external screen and the windows are cooled by wind movement (see external wall section).

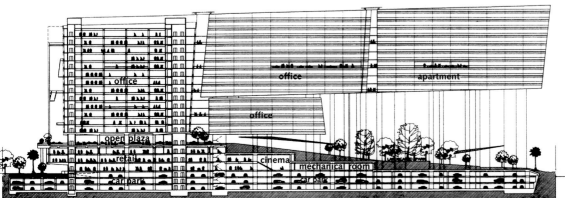

[1] Ken Yeang: 'Dubai Tower', Project Notes 1998

section A-A

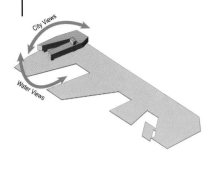

hotel

The hotel is located at the most visible position from the main road at the northern corner on the site. The hotel is served by a high-class vehicle drop-off with convenient car-parking located underneath.

The hotel suites has views both to the waterfront to the west and the city centre to the north. Its 'horse-shoe' shape frames the swimming pool deck while directing the views towards the creek beyond.

The hotel serves the business demand generated by the proposed office buildings as well as tourists to this location. The nearby tourist attractions such as the City Centre shopping mall, Dubai Creek Golf Club and Creekside Park would be further enhanced by the proposed new waterfront development and shopping mall.

service apartments

The serviced apartments are connected to the hotel for central servicing and shared use of club facilities. The apartments have direct views towards the waterfront and new marina bay.

The hotel and serviced apartments are located on the northern segment of the site separated by the new marina bay to differentiate it from the rest of the development. This allows for better security of its premises.

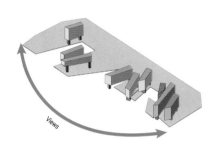

apartments

The apartments are located at the waterfront edge and command the best views in the development. The apartments benefit from a close relationship to the office towers and retail shopping mall.

Each apartment block has a separate car drop-off to the main lobby and are directly accessible from the basement car-parking underneath.

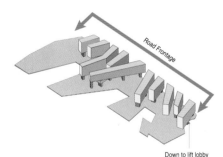

offices

The offices are located on the east side of the development to take advantage of the road frontage. It is essential that these offices are very visible from the surrounding streets.

The office blocks sit above the retail podium. Each office block has a separate car drop-off on the lower ground (promenade) level and are directly accessible from the basement car-parking underneath.

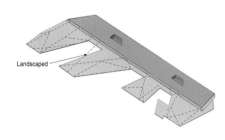

retail

The retail shopping centre directly faces Baniyas Road and has its main entrances off the street level.

The roof of the shopping centre is landscaped with shopping pavilions. They command panoramic views over the marina and creek.

car-parking

The car-parking for this development is located on the lower ground and basement levels due to space limitations and height restrictions. Very little ground level parking is provided and where this is provided it is with dropping VIPs, women and families in mind. The top level of the carparking (lower ground floor) is the drop off level for the offices. This level is semi submerged and receives natural light and ventilation. It is served by a wide and spacious 'boulevard' road which has views of the water.

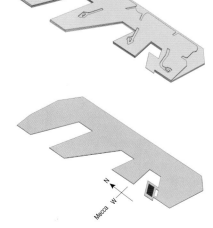

mosque

The mosque is located on an 'island' site directly at the waterfront. The mosque faces west towards Mecca.

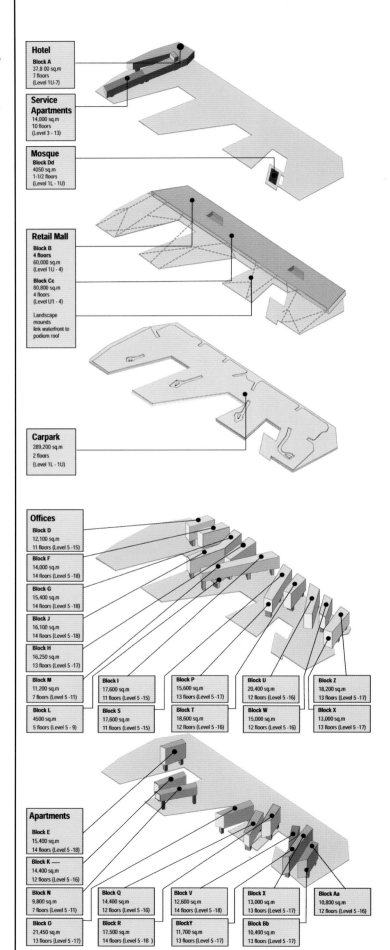

Hotel
Block A
37,800 sq.m
7 floors
(Level 1U-7)

Service Apartments
14,000 sq.m
10 floors
(Level 3 - 13)

Mosque
Block Dd
4050 sq.m
1-1/2 floors
(Level 1L - 1U)

Retail Mall
Block B
4 floors
60,000 sq.m
(Level 1U - 4)

Block Cc
80,800 sq.m
4 floors
(Level U1 - 4)

Landscape mounds link waterfront to podium roof

Carpark
289,200 sq.m
2 floors
(Level 1L - 1U)

Offices
Block D
12,100 sq.m
11 floors (Level 5 -15)

Block F
14,000 sq.m
14 floors (Level 5 -18)

Block G
15,400 sq.m
14 floors (Level 5 -18)

Block J
16,100 sq.m
14 floors (Level 5 -18)

Block H
16,250 sq.m
13 floors (Level 5 -17)

Block M
11,200 sq.m
7 floors (Level 5 -11)

Block I
17,600 sq.m
11 floors (Level 5 -15)

Block P
15,600 sq.m
13 floors (Level 5 -17)

Block U
20,400 sq.m
12 floors (Level 5 -16)

Block Z
18,200 sq.m
13 floors (Level 5 -17)

Block L
4500 sq.m
5 floors (Level 5 - 9)

Block S
17,600 sq.m
11 floors (Level 5 -15)

Block T
18,600 sq.m
12 floors (Level 5 -16)

Block W
15,000 sq.m
12 floors (Level 5 -16)

Block X
13,000 sq.m
13 floors (Level 5 -17)

Apartments
Block E
15,400 sq.m
14 floors (Level 5 -18)

Block K
14,400 sq.m
12 floors (Level 5 -16)

Block N
9,800 sq.m
7 floors (Level 5 -11)

Block Q
14,400 sq.m
12 floors (Level 5 -16)

Block V
12,600 sq.m
14 floors (Level 5 -18)

Block X
13,000 sq.m
13 floors (Level 5 -17)

Block Aa
10,800 sq.m
12 floors (Level 5 -16)

Block O
21,450 sq.m
13 floors (Level 5 -17)

Block R
17,500 sq.m
14 floors (Level 5 -18)

Block Y
11,700 sq.m
13 floors (Level 5 -17)

Block Bb
10,400 sq.m
13 floors (Level 5 -17)

As well as the natural **sun-shading** created by the separated linear-towers, sun-shade structures in the form of louvered screen attachments are extensively applied to the linear facades. On the level of **programme and urban design** the project is intensively mixed-use, with extensive Shopping Mall including departmental store, supermarket, food court and speciality shops distributed over the basement parking levels. The linear-towers incorporate both Apartments and Offices, together with a stretched 'horse-shoe' form Hotel.

The Hotel is a major 400 bedroom and suite configuration surrounding a courtyard with swimming pool and outdoor cafes. The wings of rooms all command a variety of outward views, and the corridors include skycourts for natural light. The accommodation includes roof top garden terraces which also have spectacular **vistas** over both waterfront and park. As with Yeang's skyscrapers, such as the Singapore EDITT Tower, the consideration of **outward prospect** and **view** is always a major priority.

The eleven Apartment buildings, in linear-towers are 'thin' forms which encourages **cross ventilation** through the apartments. The terminal ends of these buildings are cantilevered over the water and include facilities such as gymnasia, coffee-houses and function rooms, together with special penthouses on upper levels. Again outward views are a concern, throughout. The offices have a similar linear-tower form, located above the retail podium. The elongated plan with minimal columns allows both flexibility of sub-division and provides maximum **natural lighting** to the interiors.

Many other aspects of the project such as structure, access and circulation have been carefully innovated and integrated into the overall concept and layout. The project also includes a Mosque, which is sited on a waterfront 'island', in a tranquil location facing west, towards Mecca.

But, what remains as singularly important to this project is not its formal arrangement alone, rather it is the manner in which the **bioclimatic-response** has driven that arrangement into a natural climate-controlled result.

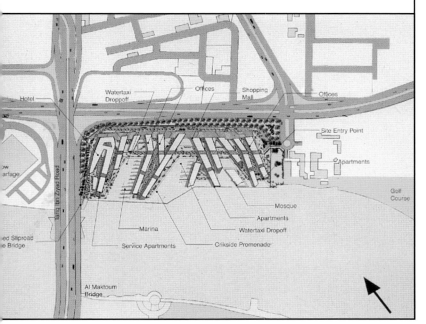

phasing

phase 1A

A • hotel (300 rooms)
B • retail mall (phase 1)
C • service apartments

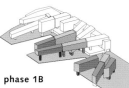

phase 1B

D • offices
E • apartments (80)
F • offices
G • offices
H • offices
I • offices

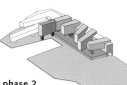

phase 2

J • offices
K • apartments (75)
L • offices
M • offices
N • apartments (50)
O • apartments (110)
P • offices
Q • apartments (75)
R • apartments (90)

phase 3

S • offices
T • offices
U • offices
V • apartments (65)
W • apartments (80)
X • offices
Y • apartments (60)
Z • offices
Aa • offices
Bb • apartments (55)
Cc • retail mall
Dc • mosque

building aspects
hotel concept • The hotel is a in the five-star luxury category with 400 large bedrooms and suites. It is laid out in a 'horse shoe' configuration with its center courtyard housing the swimming pool and outdoor cafes. Each wing has a centre corridor dividing rooms with views to the courtyard and the city centre/creek. The corridors are punctuated by common lounge areas and skycourts which provide natural light and relieves monotony. The tips of each wing is reserved for suites with direct views across the creek.
The hotel is connected to the retail mall on levels 2 and 3. On level 4, the the hotel has direct access to the podium roof garden which terraces down to the marina and waterfront promenade. The rooftop garden terraces offers spectacular views over waterfront and the creekside park beyond. Central services such as the main kitchen, laundry, and service access are located at the center of the 'horse-shoe' configuration on the lower floors of the hotel. The hotel is served by a high-class vehicle drop-off facing Baniyas Road. Underground parking is provided in the basement floors directly below.
apartment concept • There are 10 apartment blocks and one serviced apartment block in this development. These are located on the side of the development facing the creek. Nearly all apartments in this development overlook of the waterfront. This is achieved by bringing water into the site for the new marina bays, which increases the waterfront considerably.
The apartments blocks are linear in nature. This encourage cross ventilation through the apartments. The units are accessed from single loaded corridors overlooking landscaped courtyards (between two blocks of apartments). Duplex unit layout provides for greater variety of space and more access to facade with views by requiring only one access corridor every two floors.
The ends of the apartment blocks cantilevers over the waterfront edge. They house common facilities such as the gymnasium, coffee house and function rooms on the lower floors and special penthouse units on the upper floors. These spaces are given special elevational treatment to appear as beacons at night.
To maintain a relatively column-free space on the waterfront promenade level, the internal apartment columns are supported by a vierendeel trusses at the base of the apartment blocks, on level 5. All plumbing services from the apartments are diverted to service cores on this level.
retail concept • The retail shopping mall is designed to take advantage of its waterfront location and to cater to the development population mix of residents, tourists, marina users and office workers.
The shopping mall will be anchored by a departmental store and will contain a supermarket, an international food court, speciality boating shops by the marina, outdoor and indoor cafes/restaurants, souvenir shops, fashion boutiques and other speciality shops.
The site for the mall was determined to be the optimum location within the development because of the opportunity for visual exposure on three sides and good vehicular access. The mall is positioned between Baniyas Road and the waterfront area to act as a visual and noise buffer.

retail strategy • The shopping mall has several porte cochere off the main access road running parallel to Baniyas Road, facilitating auto drop-off for shoppers. The mall has a striking facade with a porous external skin, revealing in portions circulation ramps, skycourts and the interiors of the shopping mall. The facade suggests a hive of activities within the mall, and draws visual interest and curiosity into the mall from the main road.
The mall is linked to the surrounding apartments, offices and hotel component of the development via a network of landscaped pedestrian routes. These circulation networks contribute to excellent access and exposure for retailers from shoppers living or working within the complex.
Cars are brought into the shopping mall carpark on the Lower ground floor and basement 1 via wide car ramps on each end of the shopping complex, and one at the center. Once on the carpark level, shoppers drive along a lush landscaped 'boulevard' with views to the waterfront to their designated carparking areas. The entries to vertical circulation escalators leading to the shopping level is marked by large light wells. These light wells also function as wind towers, drawing fresh air from the podium roof level and extracting air from the basement.

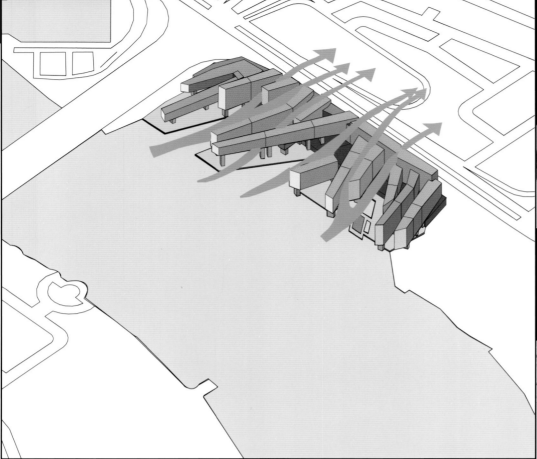

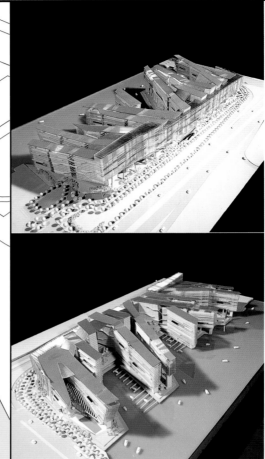

wind and natural ventilation

The proximity to the Creek water mass with the 'city' water mass behind the development can give reversal of wind directions during the daily cycle. During the afternoon when the land mass is warmer the cooler sea breezes move in from the water towards the land. In the early morning when the land and building masses have been cooled with night radiation to the sky the dense cool air moves towards the water mass. The orientation of the building blocks at right angles to the water front encourage free movement of air between the building blocks assisting the natural cooling of the buildings.

The porosity of the building facades assists in channeling air through the site while vertical gaps act as thermal flues moving air vertically and in doing so cools the building fabric.

In traditional buildings this movement of air has been utilised in the use of 'Towers of Wind' to ventilate occupied accommodation. This principle is used in the development to ventilate the carpark floors. Large light and ventilation wells from the podium roof into the basements function as wind towers, drawing fresh air into the basement and extracting used air out.

landscaping

Ecologically and bioclimatically, we should use landscaping and planting to lower ambient micro-climate temperatures as well as to re-introduce organic mass back into the essentially urban and mostly inorganic location.

Ground and vertical landscaping is used extensively around the development. The proposed scheme boasts 90% landscaping (including water coverage) of the entire site area. This is achieved by extending the landscaping from the waterfront promenade level up to the retail podium roof in one continuous plane, below the elevated the building blocks. Landscaped skycourts are introduced in the upper floors of the buildings.

The earth excavated from the new marina bays are used to create landscaped mounds between the elevated buildings and the basement car-parking roof, reducing costly export of earth from the site.

The earth acts as thermal insulation for rooftops.

sun-shading

Shading of both primary and external spaces is an essential and important part of the design. The need is there to protect the treated internal environment from direct solar radiation and in doing so reduce the energy demand of the building's environmental systems and at the same time improve the overall comfort of the spaces.

The sun-shade structures will emanate as external louvered screen attachments to the facade of the buildings. The space between the external screen are cooled by wind movement through its porous floors.

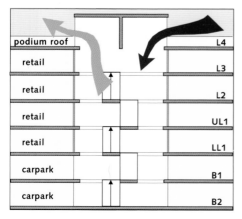

wind tower

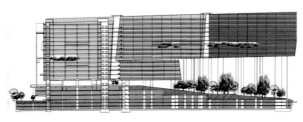

section

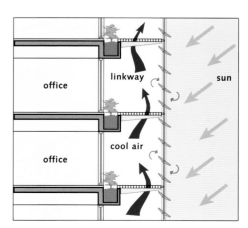

external wall section

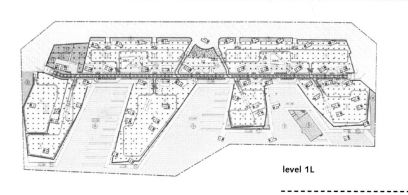

level 1L

BENIYAS ROAD

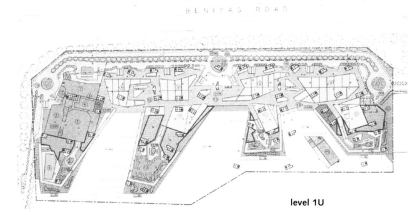

level 1U

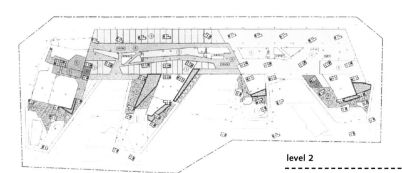

level 2

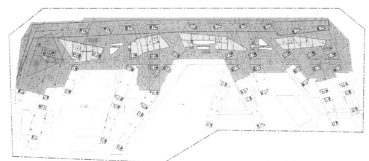

level 4

level 15

The internal circulation within the shopping mall is organised in a loop configuration along the longitudinal axis of the mall. A three-level departmental store, supermarket and food court is located at one end of the loop while speciality shops line the circulation loop.

The roof of the mall is an open landscaped plaza with retail pavilions reserved for restaurant and cafes with outdoor seating overlooking the marina.

office strategy • The offices are located above the retail podium. The offices have their entrance and car drop-off lobbies on the lower ground floor of the podium.

The lift cores are located on either ends of the office building giving uninterrupted office space for its tenants. The rectangular floor plan with minimal columns allows maximum flexibility for the interior partitioning of the floors. The elongated plan provides for maximum natural lighting into the interior spaces.

High-level links between office buildings enable one to access the next block without having to return to the ground floor lobby. This also facilitates amalgamation of office spaces between blocks for office expansion.

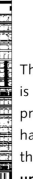

The Makkah project is amongst the largest proposals that Yeang has made, and where the emphasis shifts to **urban design** and the relationship of the whole assembly of buildings to the existing city and topography.

The linear site is framed within a major network of roads and urban highways on the periphery, with a main access road (and service road for deliveries beneath) forming a linear traffic circulation spine, with the buildings distributed alongside, on the crest of a hill above. The whole assembly is within walking and viewing distance of the al-Haram, the focus of world pilgrimage to Mecca.

Yeang's central response is to create a

"... unique, calming green park environment for the pilgrims ... careful planning and resource management can turn the Jabal Omar site into a green area, shading the external spaces and creating a pleasant environment in which to carry out pilgrimage ... a shaded place from which to view al-Haram." [1]

The whole design then springs from this conceptual basis – a series of V-form towers on and over a spinal concourse with car-parking and retail development sunk below a massive **landscaped roof.** The irrigation water supply is sourced from the recycled 'grey water' of the whole development, and planting and vegetation are selected on an indigenous basis, that require minimal amounts of water, and that can withstand the harsh climate. The major levels of horizontal planting are joined with groves of palms on the lower rock slopes, uniting to create a **'sea of green'** between the Jabal Omar site and the al-Haram.

[1] Ken Yeang: 'Jabal Omar Towers', Project Notes 2000

jabal omar towers

Yeang's concept is therefore one of a **'garden oasis'**, on a major scale, enhancing the land-form, with the accommodation towers rising above and gathering all the principal **vistas** of al-Haram and the Ka'bah.

Underpinning the overall idea, Yeang proposes that, given the densities required on the site, **high-rise** buildings are inevitable. By adopting this solution the major area of the land form can be transformed into **green landscape.**

The major range of nine **towers**, includes seven apartment towers of 35 storeys, and two hotel towers of 50 storeys, together with a retail concourse of four storeys and a further four hotels of 15 storeys. The detailed design of the first phase is centred on a landmark **50-storey hotel**, and a **35-storey residential tower** with all associated plazas, circulation and facilities.

Yeang's concept description reveals both his functional and symbolic intentions

> **"... the towers are raised above a concourse which collects the circulation and channels the population down two chutes to the praying plaza. The towers are configured to fulfill in particular the provision of a clear view to al-Haram from each apartment or hotel room, and from the concourse edge. The shapes of the towers are reminiscent of an opened Koran as a constant reminder of the pilgrimage."** [2]

The design concept is expanded in a series of studies which include Yeang's **Ecological Approach, Built Form and Sight Lines,** the collector **Promenade and Chutes, Travel Time** analysis, **Prayer Zones and Prayer Areas**. The overall concept is further studied in section, relating the height of the towers to a 450 m general height limit of the surrounding rim of mountains, with two signature towers rising above this level. Yeang envisages the idea of a **Future Rim** of mountains and towers as a model which could be extended from the Jabal Omar site into the surrounding hills, so that in this sense the project design is related to a regional vision, beyond the central city.

The **towers** and their detailed design emphasise Yeang's ecological design principles, considerations of room alignment and vista, pedestrian travel and the location of prayer areas, in particular. The Towers are generally oriented east-west with solid perimeter walls and circulation on the western and southern faces, depending upon configuration and type. A major feature of this high-rise is a roof-level **wind-scoop** which draws air into an **evaporative cooling-tower**, in the centre of the hotel plan, for example. Yeang's descriptive notes and sections define this principal element:

> **"... a cooling tower through the centre of the high rise is integral to the design of the development ... this tower brings warm air into the top of the tower where a fine mist spray cools and humidifies the air. This cooled, moist air drops down the towers, cooling the corridors and providing a fresh air supply to all rooms and apartments. The cool air exits the tower at the level of the roof garden, cooling the garden and prayer areas."** [3]

[2] Ibid.
[3] Ibid.

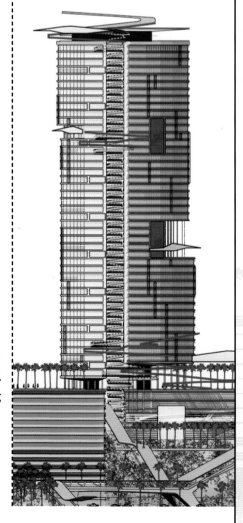

owner Makkah Construction and Development Company
location Mecca, Saudi Arabia
latitude 21.27°N
nos of storeys 7 apartment towers at 35 storeys
2 hotel towers at 50 storeys
retail concourse at 4 storeys
4 hotel blocks at 15 storeys
date start 2000 (design)
areas gross area 878,880 sq m
total nett area 565,650 sq m
prayer terraces and landscaped gardens 94,000 sq m
carpark 309,000 sq m
site area 232,000 sq m
plot ratio 1:3.8

design features • generic urban design strategy
The Haram is surrounded by five mountains that form an existing 'rim' to the Al-Haram area. Our urban design strategy is to build the inevitable high-rises fixed by a height-limit that will create a new 'protective rim' around al-Haram. This will avoid a rampant disorganised skyline around the holy area. A new benchmark building height is thus derived from the average height of the five mountains at 450 m as the new height limit for future development of the sites surrounding al-Haram. Only one or two exceptional towers at preselected locations may exceed this height limit to give some diversity to the skyline resembling the minarets of the traditional mosque.

masterplan • The proposed development at Jabal Omar uses the mountain crest to define the site into two parts, one facing al-Haram and the other sloping away from al-Haram. The parts of the development facing al-Haram contains the concourse and pedestrian links to al-Haram. Hotel and apartment towers are situated over the mountain crest, limited by our new 'rim' height for maximum views. The western side of the development is for car-parking and vehicular access.

accessibility to Al-Haram • A central promenade (ie. the concourse) at level 2 acts as a 'collector' to collect pilgrims from all the towers, who are directed to the two 'chutes' to al-Haram. A combination of elevators, escalators, travelators and pedestrian routes is used for reducing the travel time. Travel time analyses have been studied to verify the time needed to reach the Haram from the rooms of each tower.

views of Al-Haram • Tower built forms with single-loaded rooms or apartments are shaped for maximum facade area with views towards al-Haram, using a number of tower typologies (ie. the A, V, H, M and composite shapes).

green park • A green park environment is created for pilgrims, by landscaping of the carparking block roofs and the concourse roof. These are connected via landscaped bridges. The water supply for greening of the development comes from the recycled 'grey' water of the development. The concept seeks to create a balanced 'ecosystem' on the site of both organic and inorganic aspects of the ecological environment. At its simplistic level of sustainable design, the landscaping over the roofs literally provides a 'green' scheme. By covering the car-parks with earth and greenery, the carparks can be excluded from the plot ratio calculation, thereby increasing the Developer's permitted commercial area.

evaporative cooling shafts • As a passive low-energy air-conditioning design, 'evaporative cooling shafts' are located within the towers to provide cool air to the circulation spaces and to supplement the air-conditioning of the rooms and to the green gardens below.

alternative prayer zones • Alternative prayer zones are also provided. The hotel towers have ramps within the central atrium that connects to prayer rooms located at every five floors. A prayer terrace on the roof of the concourse offers an alternative prayer zone: a public, open area shaded by buildings and palms planted around it with a view to al-Haram.

The cooling tower also contains a **pedestrian ramp,** which both connects rooms to praying halls and continues into the lower retail areas delivering cooled air from above. In addition, planting and water ponds are placed on the tower roof to cool the intake air and reduce the amount of air-borne dust. The **roof gardens** also form major prayer areas, with views to al-Haram on the eastern tips and edges of the plan.

Coupled with the major **evaporative cooing tower** feature are Yeang's principles of the green skyscraper, which he relates to the whole project.

The tower design incorporates a range of spaces for the **offering of prayers,** varying between the private room to prayer halls and terraces through to the al-Haram plaza praying area. Pedestrian travel in the service of prayer, is fundamental to the project and Yeang has studied this in great detail. Central to this key function is the inclusion of a **promenade** at concourse level:

> **"... the prime function of this Promenade is to serve as a collector for the Jabal Omar population as they are called to prayer five times a day. All of the population will be brought to this level, through the lift cores of the towers above or the escalators that link the four levels of the concourse... the population is divided into four streams, to be discharged at the plaza below by chutes consisting of escalators and travelators."** [4]

Having established these major pedestrian movement systems, which bridge the Ibrahim Al-Khalil Road, to deliver pilgrims in safety to the precinct of al-Haram, Yeang has also provided an analysis of pedestrian **travel time**. This study proves the success of the development and

> **"... the speed at which the population can access the praying areas for their daily devotion."** [5]

As with all Yeang's projects vertical landscaping is incorporated at intervals, particularly in relation to prayer rooms in this instance.

The **overall plan-forms** of both hotel and apartment towers are organic in nature, and have something of the quality of Hans Scharoun, at first sight. Looked at in detail, the design of each room and linear cluster is dominated by the provision of **outward vistas** to al-Haram, which are provided by faceted glazed walls to the leading edge of each unit.

Seen as a whole, the Jabal Omar project exemplifies the **comprehensiveness** of Yeang's design method which covers the whole range of considerations from the making of a new city area to the careful design of the individual room. In turn his ecological approach, the regeneration of landscape and the organisation of movement are gathered together to form an **urban sanctuary,** which exists to serve **pilgrimage** and the purpose of the pilgrims' offering of prayers.

4 Ibid.
5 Ibid.

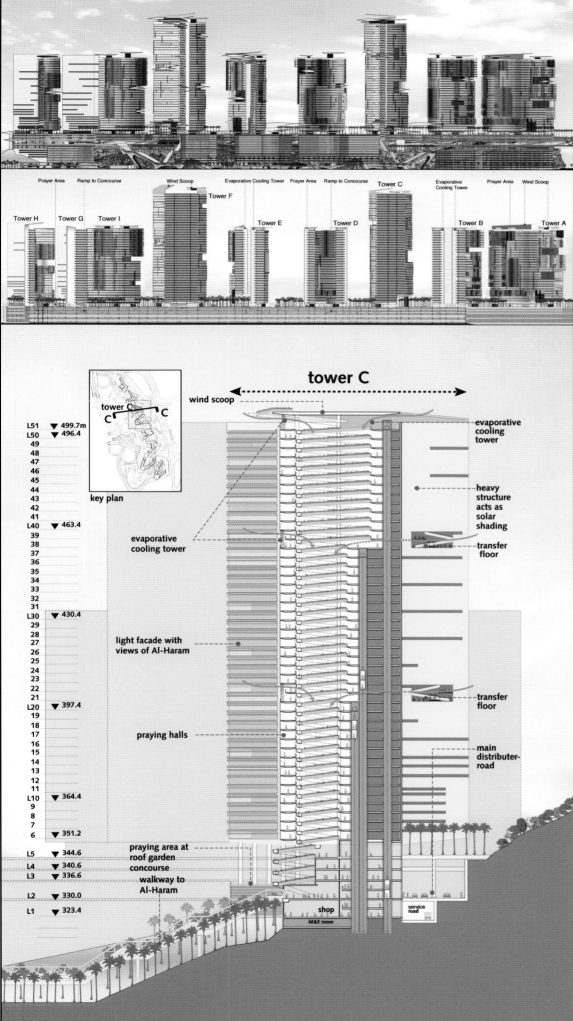

elevation and section (elevation views)

Prayer Area | Ramp to Concourse | Wind Scoop | Evaporative Cooling Tower | Prayer Area | Ramp to Concourse | Evaporative Cooling Tower | Prayer Area | Wind Scoop

Tower H | Tower G | Tower I | Tower F | Tower E | Tower D | Tower C | Tower B | Tower A

tower C

wind scoop

tower C

key plan

L51	▼ 499.7m
L50	▼ 496.4
49	
48	
47	
46	
45	
44	
43	
42	
41	
L40	▼ 463.4
39	
38	
37	
36	
35	
34	
33	
32	
31	
L30	▼ 430.4
29	
28	
27	
26	
25	
24	
23	
22	
21	
L20	▼ 397.4
19	
18	
17	
16	
15	
14	
13	
12	
11	
L10	▼ 364.4
9	
8	
7	
6	▼ 351.2
L5	▼ 344.6
L4	▼ 340.6
L3	▼ 336.6
L2	▼ 330.0
L1	▼ 323.4

evaporative cooling tower

light facade with views of Al-Haram

praying halls

praying area at roof garden concourse

walkway to Al-Haram

shop
M&E room

service road

evaporative cooling tower

heavy structure acts as solar shading

transfer floor

transfer floor

main distributer road

site cross section

the design concept

The Jabal Omar site forms one of five hills that surround the holy site of al-Haram. As such, it is the outer rim from which views of the praying area can be seen. The scheme seeks to make use of the elevation of this outer rim, developing a viewing and praying concourse along the crest of the hills.

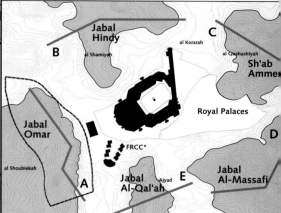

surrounding mountains as the 'Rim' for Al-Haram

The roof of this concourse contains praying areas within a landscaped garden. These praying areas form an extension to the praying platform below, whilst still allowing for the development of the lower slopes. The concourse at Level 2 also serves as the main drop-off level for those arriving by vehicles.

Below the concourse at Level 1 is a service road to meet all deliveries, refuse disposal and service requirements.

The concourse consists of four levels of commercial activity, which face the Haram. It encloses the reception areas for the towers above and acts as a collect on point for the population of Jabal Omar and the adjacent areas, from which people will be taken to their prayers along two major chutes extending into al-Haram.

There are two factors that would suggest that the development of the surrounding hills of the Haram would create a harsh, desert-like concrete jungle. The climate of Makkah is hot and dry, with little vegetation. Due to the large numbers of pilgrims, especially during haj times, the densities required to accommodate the resident, commercial and temporary populations are extremely high. However careful planning and the sensitive creation of an indigenous ecosystem can encourage vegetation to grow, providing a greened and ecologically friendly environment in which to house the pilgrims.

If taken throughout the enclosing hills the greening of the rim will create an oasis, containing and emphasising the prominence of the Ka'bah.

This design concept can be taken throughout the five hills of Makkah creating an enclosure to the holy site that allows for accommodation and commercial activity within its boundaries.

The above are the key features that make this scheme environmentally responsive and unique.

the built form

The development consists of a series of towers above a concourse at the crest of the hill. With the densities required on The site, high-rise buildings are inevitable. By going high-rise, the rest of the land can be returned to vegetation.

The towers are raised above a concourse which collects the circular on and channels the population down two chutes to the praying plaza.

The towers are configured to fulfill in particular the provision of a clear view to al-Haram from each apartment or hotel room and from the concourse edge. The shapes of the towers are reminiscent of an opened Koran as a constant reminder of the pilgrimage.

The concourse is served by a main distributor road with a service road (for deliveries) running beneath it.

As the al-Haram is the primary focus of the pilgrimage, creating towers that exploit the viewing cones which exist naturally within the site, ensures a high return on the lettable areas.

The towers are lifted above the roof garden of the concourse, allowing for free public access and movement through the site and ensuring privacy and security within the towers.

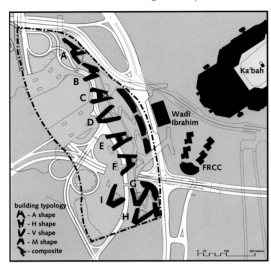

site cross sections

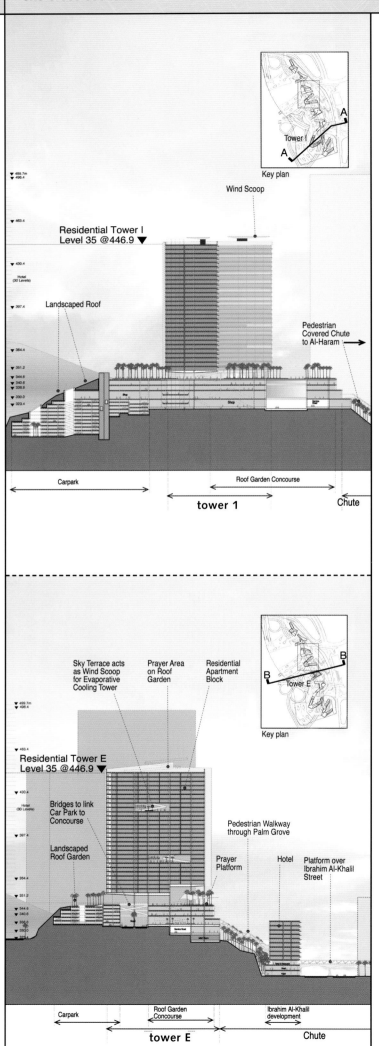

sight-lines from tower to al-Haram

The Ka'bah is the central experience of the pilgrimage to Makkah. The visual links of the development to the Haram are ensured in a series of towers that afford a view to the praying areas from each apartment.

The pilgrim is assured of a view of al-Haram from the rooms so that prayers can be offered and so a constant link to the holy site is not broken.

A hierarchy of views exists in Makkah, with the Ka'bah as the prime focus. During the haj season, when the praying area is covered with pilgrims, the secondary visual zone extends to the edges of this plaza.

The landscaped roof garden affords a view to al-Haram so that outdoor prayer areas form along its edge.

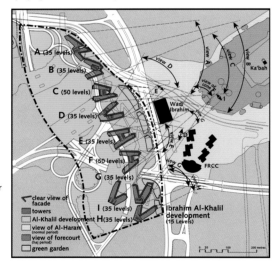

the Promenade as a 'collector' to chutes to al-Haram

The main level of the concourse has a generous 'promenade' that connects the site from the adjacent sites to the north and south. The promenade has views of al-Haram and the praying platform that surrounds it continuously referring the people within the concourse to the focus of their pilgrimage.

The prime function of this promenade is to serve as a collector for the Jabal Omar population as they are called to prayer five times a day. All of the population will be brought to this level through the lift cores of the towers above or the escalators that link the four levels of the concourse.

The population is divided into four streams, to be discharged at the plaza below by chutes consisting of escalators and travellators.

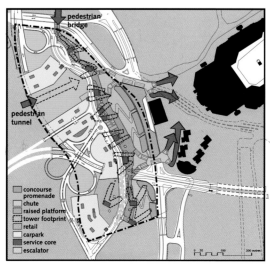

Of utmost importance to the success of the development is the speed at which the population can access the praying areas for their daily devotion.

There are a number of areas in which prayers can be offered and the time h takes to reach each place from the furthest point of the site has been calculated to ensure efficiency, with the best~case scenario and worst~case scenario expressed in minutes.

Accessibility will be by walking (either on the flat or down a ramp), elevators (within the towers or the concourse), escalators (in the concourse and down the major chutes) and travellators.

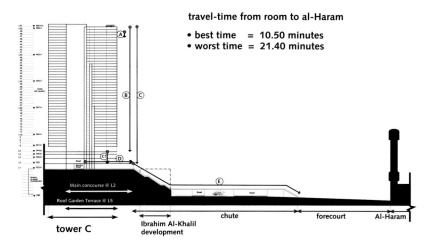

route	travel mode	from	to	Distance (m) Vertical	Horizontal	Time (min)
A	walking & ramp	typical room @ upper most floor	prayer area in tower	10	80	3
B	elevator	typical room @ upper most floor	roof of concource @ level 5	152	35	3
C	elevator	typical room @ upper most floor	concourse @ level 2	166	35	3.50
C1	elevator	level 4	level 2	11	21	1
D	walking	elevator core @ level 2	chute	/	54	1
E	elevator & travellator	chute	Al- Haram area	45	142	6

travel-time from room to al-Haram

• best time = 10.50 minutes
• worst time = 21.40 minutes

Main concourse @ L2
Roof Garden Terrace @ L5

chute | forecourt | Al-Haram

tower C

Ibrahim Al-Khalil development

cooling tower system

section A-A

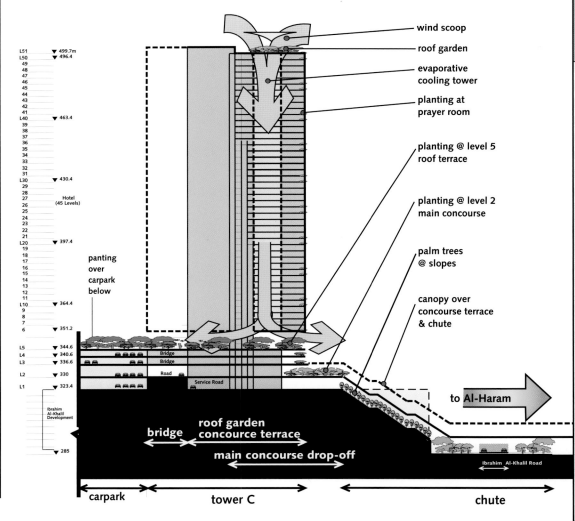

- wind scoop
- roof garden
- evaporative cooling tower
- planting at prayer room
- planting @ level 5 roof terrace
- planting @ level 2 main concourse
- palm trees @ slopes
- canopy over concourse terrace & chute

L51 ▼ 499.7m
L50 ▼ 496.4
L40 ▼ 463.4
L30 ▼ 430.4
Hotel (45 Levels)
L20 ▼ 397.4
panting over carpark below
L10 ▼ 364.4
▼ 351.2
L5 ▼ 344.6
L4 ▼ 340.6 Bridge
L3 ▼ 336.6 Bridge
L2 ▼ 330 Road
Service Road
L1 ▼ 323.4
Ibrahim Al-Khalil Development
▼ 285

to Al-Haram

bridge | roof garden concource terrace

main concourse drop-off

Ibrahim Al-Khalil Road

carpark | tower C | chute

---

the 'green park'

site area = 23 ha   **green area = 15 ha**

The central design concept is to create a unique calming green park environment for the pilgrims. Careful planning and resource management can turn the Jabal Omar site into a green area, shading the external spaces and creating a pleasant environment in which to carry out pilgrimage.

The car-parking and concourse development are sunk beneath a green, landscaped roof, visually reducing the impact of the large scale of the development while creating a green landscaped park for recreation outdoor commercial activities and a shaded place from which to view al-Haram.

The water supply for the greening of the site comes from the recycled 'grey' water of the development. The water from the ablutions, baths and basins will be filtered, stored and reused to create a greened environment year-round.

Planting and vegetation are selected which are indigenous to the locality and which require minimal amounts of water for irrigation. The plants are all chosen to withstand the harsh climate while serving to soften it. The lower slopes of the development where bare rock is exposed will be planted with palms so that there is a sea of green to be seen between the Jabal Omar development and the al-Haram.

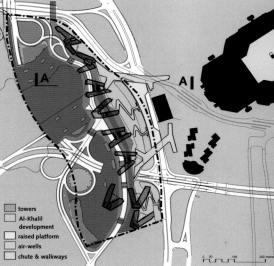

- towers
- Al-Khalil development
- raised platform
- air-wells
- chute & walkways

• **ecological approach**

A cooling tower through the centre of the high rise is integral to the design of the development. This tower brings warm air into the top of the tower where a fine mist spray cools and humidifies the air.

This cooled, moist air drops down the tower, cooling the corridors and providing a fresh air supply to all rooms and apartments. The cool air exits the tower at the level of the roof garden, cooling the garden and prayer areas.

The ramp that extends through the cooling tower continues into the retail area on level 4, bringing in the cooled air from above.

Planting and water ponds are placed on the tower roof to cool the intake air and to reduce the amount of air-borne dust. The roof garden on top of the concourse is cooled by these series of towers along its length.

The concerns that this project have addressed are:
• low energy inputs
• low energy outputs
• recycling of outputs
• recycling of energy
• extending the planting into the building

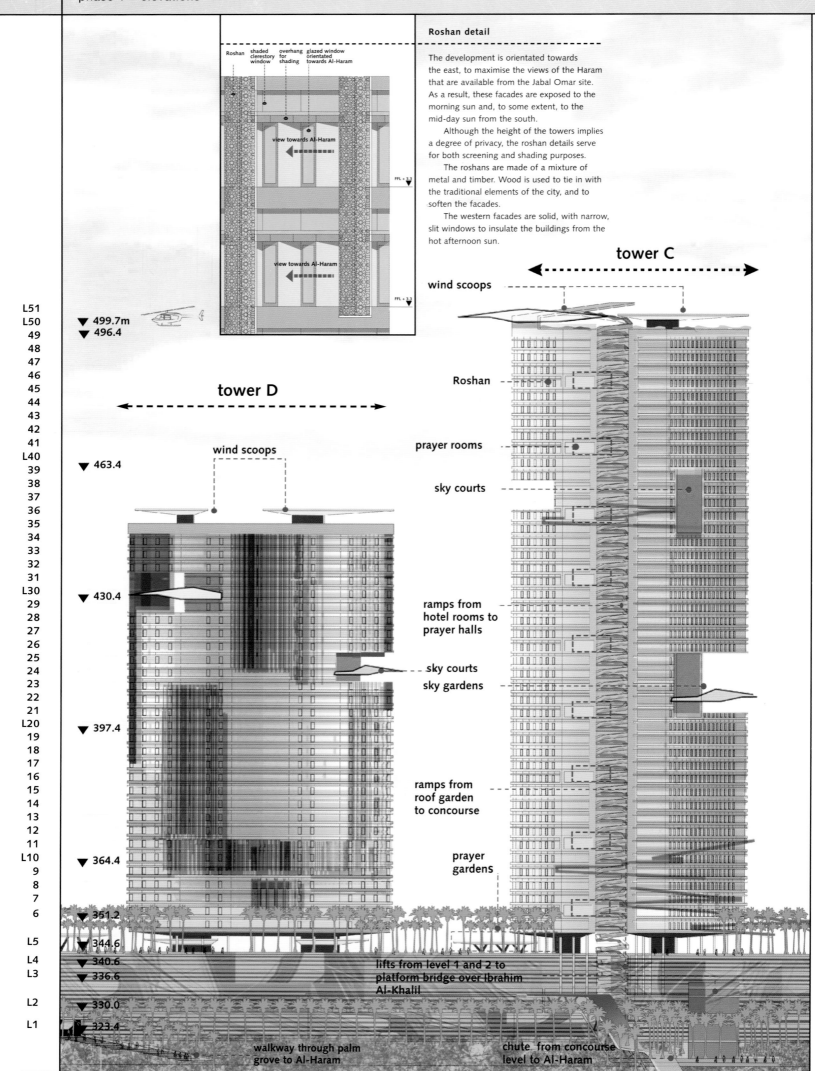

Roshan detail

Roshan | shaded clerestory window | overhang for shading | glazed window orientated towards Al-Haram

view towards Al-Haram

view towards Al-Haram

FFL + 3.3

FFL + 3.3

The development is orientated towards the east, to maximise the views of the Haram that are available from the Jabal Omar site. As a result, these facades are exposed to the morning sun and, to some extent, to the mid-day sun from the south.

Although the height of the towers implies a degree of privacy, the roshan details serve for both screening and shading purposes.

The roshans are made of a mixture of metal and timber. Wood is used to tie in with the traditional elements of the city, and to soften the facades.

The western facades are solid, with narrow, slit windows to insulate the buildings from the hot afternoon sun.

tower C

wind scoops

Roshan

prayer rooms

sky courts

ramps from hotel rooms to prayer halls

sky courts

sky gardens

ramps from roof garden to concourse

prayer gardens

tower D

wind scoops

L51
L50   ▼ 499.7m
49   ▼ 496.4
48
47
46
45
44
43
42
41
L40
39   ▼ 463.4
38
37
36
35
34
33
32
31
L30
29   ▼ 430.4
28
27
26
25
24
23
22
21
L20
19   ▼ 397.4
18
17
16
15
14
13
12
11
L10
9   ▼ 364.4
8
7
6   ▼ 351.2
L5   ▼ 344.6
L4   ▼ 340.6
L3   ▼ 336.6
L2   ▼ 330.0
L1   ▼ 323.4

lifts from level 1 and 2 to platform bridge over Ibrahim Al-Khalil

walkway through palm grove to Al-Haram

chute from concourse level to Al-Haram

scale 1:400   0 15   125   250m

The Ka'bah is the focus of all the pilgrim's prayers (6) and the area immediately around it is of prime importance with concentric circles of decreasing importance radiating out from it.

The most remote place would be to take one's prayers within the private apartments and hotel rooms (1) Within the towers themselves there are further dedicated prayer areas (2). Each hotel has a prayer area every fifth floor for people to congregate.

The second zone is the plaza around the al-Haram (5). This plaza is connected the base of Jabal Omar by a platform that bridges over the Inner Ring Road, forming a secondary, elevated plaza from which prayers can be offered (4). The chutes that lead from the concourse bring the population of Jabal Omar down to the level of the raised platform. The concourse roof garden at Level 5 (3) offers the fourth praying zone: a public, open area shaded by the buildings and palms planted around it with a view to Al-Haram.

This prayer zone is accessed from the towers concourse and car-parks via elevators and escalators.

landscape concept

proposed landscaping zones and major plant groupings
zone A: front slope landscaping
The slopes ranging in elevation from 295 m to 325 m forms a major open space facade facing the holy mosque. Here, a single specie palms is proposed to dominate the slope with planting distance about 6m apart. The planing holes could be edged in rocks with ground covers planted on top of the planter holes.
palm: Phoenix dactylifera
ground cover and low shrubs: Lantana camara, Bougainvillaea, Duranta repens.

zone B1: rooftop planter and connecting walkways
The planting on this zone will serve as ornamental as well as functional – shade palms, ornamental Rowenng shrubs and sweet smelling night blossoms to fragrant the spaces between the building masses. The planting of this level will be in a series of raised planters with differing heights for palms as well as for shrubs. Also present at this level are other hardscape landscaping elements such as walkways, paving for prayer areas ablution points water fountains, stepped decks and seating areas.
palms: Phoenix canarierisis, Phoenix theophrastii, Washingtonia robusta
shrubs: Nenum oleander, Plumeria culfolia, Tecoma stans, Hibiscus nisa-sinensis, Caesalpinia pulchenma, Bougainvilla spp, Jasmmimum var, Agave americana, Agave attenuata, Yucca elephantipe, Yucca filamentosa
Groundcovers: Gomphrena globosa, Impatiens balsamina, Vinca rosea, Amartanthus caudatus Cosmos spp, Rhoeo discolor, Zebrina penadula, Lantana montevidensis

zone B2: rooftop planter and connecting walkways
Cascading planters facing the holy mosque will be planted with colorful Bougainvillaea to give Zone B2 rooftop planter and connecting walkways a hanging garden effect. The planting on this zone is similar to Zone B1 except that this zone is more functional than ornamental with more shade shrubs and trees forming the bulk of the bio-massing instead of the flowering varieties of B1.

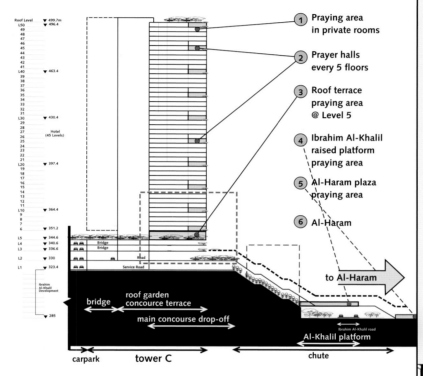

1. Praying area in private rooms
2. Prayer halls every 5 floors
3. Roof terrace praying area @ Level 5
4. Ibrahim Al-Khalil raised platform praying area
5. Al-Haram plaza praying area
6. Al-Haram

to Al-Haram

bridge | roof garden concource terrace
main concourse drop-off
Al-Khalil platform

carpark | tower C | chute

the Promenade as a 'collector' to chutes to al-Haram

Access from the hotel rooms to the public prayer areas is by either the ramps through the central atrium or by the elevators that deposit people either at the hotel prayer rooms, the roof garden prayer areas or at the main concourse. The concourse is connected to the parking blocks by bridges.

Movement between the roof garden and the main concourse is through escalators.

The main thoroughfare from the concourse to Al-Haram is via the chutes by escalators and travellators. Throughout the scheme there are elevators to service the disabled population.

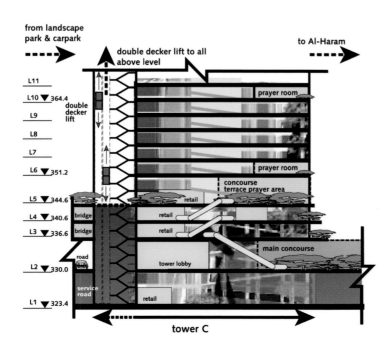

from landscape park & carpark
to Al-Haram
double decker lift to all above level

L11
L10 ▼ 364.4
double decker lift
L9
L8
L7
L6 ▼ 351.2
prayer room
prayer room
L5 ▼ 344.6
concourse terrace prayer area
retail
L4 ▼ 340.6 bridge
retail
L3 ▼ 336.6 bridge
retail
road
main concourse
L2 ▼ 330.0
tower lobby
service road
L1 ▼ 323.4
retail

tower C

Recycled water source from "grey water" at base of towers

Recycled water pumped to storage tank

Water tanks; related to phasing development & irrigation land coverage

Major watering points.

Minor watering points through a series of perforated PVC pipes buried within the planter beds. Supply through dripping methods with timer.

vertical urban design

The MAX Tower project has significance in Yeang's work, not just because it stands in the realm of his **'green skyscraper'** series, but that it also marks his entry into a range of European commissions, that have subsequently advanced into the UK itself. This advance not only brings his architecture into a new and receptive marketplace, but it also presents the context of a completely different **climatic condition**, from that of his major range of projects in the Far East.

The tower and its site stand very close to Norman Foster's landmark Commerzbank in Frankfurt, which is highly appropriate as both designs are part of a new tradition of environmentally conscious architecture.

Within the context of Yeang's work, the MAX Tower plan is markedly different, for in this case the service cores are inboard, and form two sides of a **square atrium**, which rises through the whole-form as part of its environmental strategy, and brings natural light to both offices and circulation, depending on the internal arrangement. The peripheral office space, encircling the core of services and atrium, is a regular band of 15 metres in width, which facilitates a whole array of optional internal space arrangements and a high degree of natural day-lighting. Variable office groupings can also be inter-linked by a system of ramps, which cross the atrium void, at intervals. The office plan-form is therefore an efficient, rational overall arrangement incorporating great flexibility, and variety of occupant orientation and outward views over the city.

frankfurt max tower

owner Deutsche Grundbesitz Management Gmbh
location Grosze Gallusstrasze, Frankfurt, am Main
latitude 52.3 °N
nos of storeys 50 storeys
date start July 1999 (Design)
completion date –
areas 90,000 sq m

design features
- Incorporating vertical planting into the facade from the site to balance the inorganic aspects of the city environment (with more organic mass).
- Transformation of the site into a green park to link to the city's green belt.
- Continuous planting up the tower as an ecological system from street level spiralling up the facade to create a continuous and stable ecosystem
- Earth mounds and recessed courtyards at the point where the tower meets the ground to blend the building with the ground.
- Puncturing of the park with skylight openings to bring natural light and vegetation to the basement car-park.
- All-year round public plaza within a greenhouse environment, controlled by openable windows and walls.
- Tower has planted skycourts, balconies, viewing decks, and movable internal greening inside the office spaces.
- Tower has movable shutters (within the skycourts) for control of the internal office environment to cater for seasonal changes.

The building in general is technologically sophisticated, and includes a variety of systems and details, such as a double-skin facade and the use of photovoltaics, contributing to its energy-efficient content.

However, the aspect of the design which is at once most evident, and has the greatest impact on the architecture, is the **greening** of both the site and overall building form and its interiors. This is particularly evident in the section and on the facades, where an extensive system of fully landscaped skycourts are linked vertically by a spiralling range of planted inserts. While this is common place in Yeang's work as a whole, it becomes a remarkable event in the context of the high-rise in an European city. As such, it openly exhibits the qualities of the 'green skyscraper', and the very different nature of the environment offered to its occupants.

Yeang's approach to this transformation begins at ground level, which is designed as a green park with the continuous vertical planting on the tower running from street level to the summit. In establishing a stable ecosystem, it is Yeang's stated intention

"... to balance the inorganic aspects of the city environment ... with more organic mass". [1]

Coupled with this, earth mounds and recessed courtyards are included at the base of the building to assist integration with the ground form, and natural light and planting penetrate into the basement car-park through skylights punctured into the park. Within the extensive facilities of the spreading, linear street-level podium Yeang has formed a public plaza, with a glass enclosure that provides a **'greenhouse environment'** – controlled by openable windows and walls. This space – a form of winter garden – provides an all year facility, and appropriate to the variable seasonal climate.

As well as the general overall provision of planted skycourts, balconies and viewing decks, in this case Yeang has also provided a form of **localised skycourt**, serving clusters of office space, with movable internal planting. These skycourts have **adjustable shutters**, which provide control for the associated office space, depending on the seasonal conditions, and the comfort conditions required by the occupants. This device, which is illustrated in a series of plans demonstrating the variables is particular to this project and again, extends the principle of the **winter garden** idea, an urban tradition in German cities such as Frankfurt and Berlin.

Yeang's proposition for the **green skyscraper** in the European context both contains the landscaping within its internal space and offers this literal greening to the city on its exterior. The tower architecture is transformed to a vehicle of organic inhabitation – an **ecological symbol**.

[1] Ken Yeang: 'Max Tower', Project Notes, 1999

1 • Dachflaechenregenwasser
2 • Gruenbewaesserung Außen
3 • Wasserbecken
4 • Zisterne
5 • Grundwasserspiegel 95m ue.NN
6 • Sprinkler
7 • WC-Spuelung
8 • Gruenbewaesserung Innen
9 • Kaeltemaschine f r Kuehl oder Heizbetrieb
10 • Waermetauscher
11 • Rueckkuehlwerk mit Regenwassernutzung
12 • PV Module 90 sq m Leistung 12kW (Peak)

Indoor plants for improving indoor air quality (IAQ)

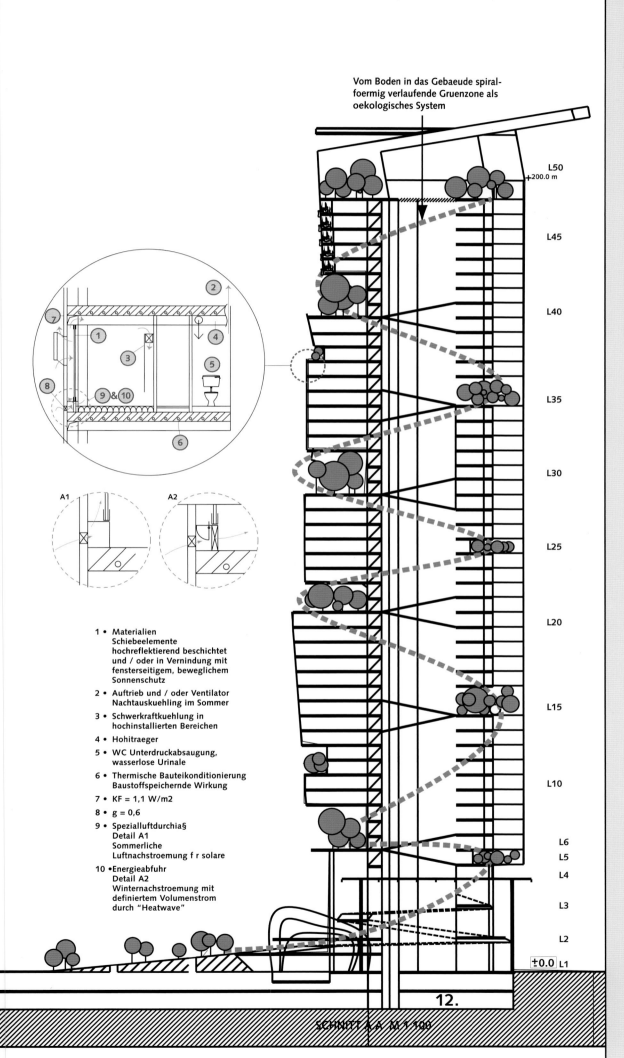

Vom Boden in das Gebaeude spiral-
foermig verlaufende Gruenzone als
oekologisches System

L50
+200.0 m

L45

L40

L35

L30

L25

L20

L15

L10

L6
L5
L4

L3

L2

±0.0 L1

SCHNITT A-A M 1:100

A1   A2

1 • Materialien
   Schiebeelemente
   hochreflektierend beschichtet
   und / oder in Vernindung mit
   fensterseitigem, beweglichem
   Sonnenschutz

2 • Auftrieb und / oder Ventilator
   Nachtauskuehling im Sommer

3 • Schwerkraftkuehlung in
   hochinstallierten Bereichen

4 • Hohitraeger

5 • WC Unterdruckabsaugung,
   wasserlose Urinale

6 • Thermische Bauteikonditionierung
   Baustoffspeichernde Wirkung

7 • KF = 1,1 W/m2

8 • g = 0,6

9 • Spezialluftdurchia§
   Detail A1
   Sommerliche
   Luftnachstroemung f r solare

10 •Energieabfuhr
   Detail A2
   Winternachstroemung mit
   definiertem Volumenstrom
   durch "Heatwave"

12.

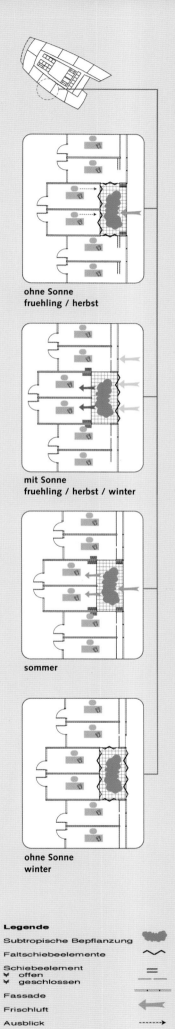

ohne Sonne
fruehling / herbst

mit Sonne
fruehling / herbst / winter

sommer

ohne Sonne
winter

Legende

Subtropische Bepflanzung

Faltschiebeelemente

Schiebeelement
   offen
   geschlossen

Fassade

Frischluft

Ausblick

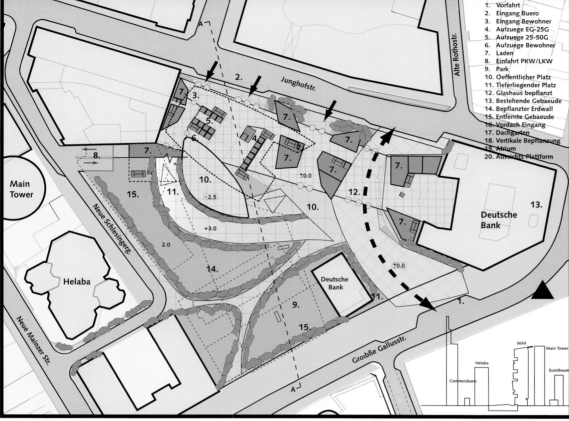

±0.0

Legend:
1. Vorfahrt
2. Eingang Buero
3. Eingang Bewohner
4. Aufzuege EG-25G
5. Aufzuege 25-50G
6. Aufzuege Bewohner
7. Laden
8. Einfahrt PKW/LKW
9. Park
10. Oeffentlicher Platz
11. Tieferliegender Platz
12. Glashaus bepflanzt
13. Bestehende Gebaeude
14. Bepflanzter Erdwall
15. Entfernte Gebaeude
16. Vordach Eingang
17. Dachgarten
18. Vertikale Bepflanzung
19. Atrium
20. Aussichts Plattform

Main Tower
Helaba
Deutsche Bank
Deutsche Bank

Neue Schlesingerstr.
Neue Mainzer Str.
Junghofstr.
Alte Rothofstr.
Groboße Gallusstr.

MAX Main Tower Helaba Eurotheum Commerzbank

Ein Gleichgewicht zwischen Stadtstruktur und Gruenbereichen
• Ein Park zum Verweilen, regenerieren und ein Ort für Veranstaltungen
• spiralenfoermige Gruenbereiche an der Fassade und im Gebaeude
• Gruenbereiche im Glashaus Erdgeschoß für ganzjaehrige Nutzung
• offene begrunte Innenbereiche als Verbindung zwischen dem Sockelgeschoß und Max

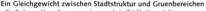

D	J	F	M	A	M	J	J	A	S	O	N

20°
10°
0°

Weihnachtsmarkt | Kunst-und Skulpturgarten zur ART Frankfurt | Open-Air Konzerte | Lesungen zur Frankfurter Buechermesse

MAX Veranstaltungen

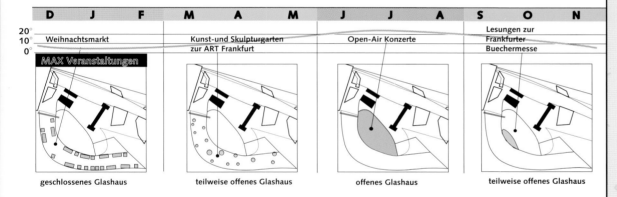

geschlossenes Glashaus | teilweise offenes Glashaus | offenes Glashaus | teilweise offenes Glashaus

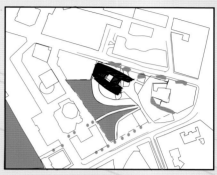

Bepflanzung

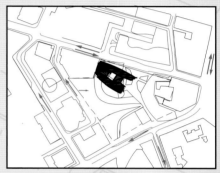

Verkehr

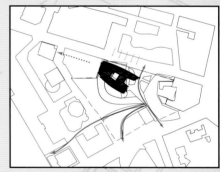

Fußgaenger

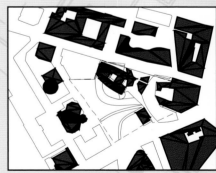

Massenstudie

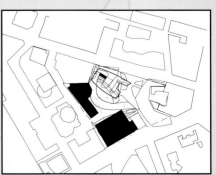

Alternative: Gebaeude nicht abgerissen

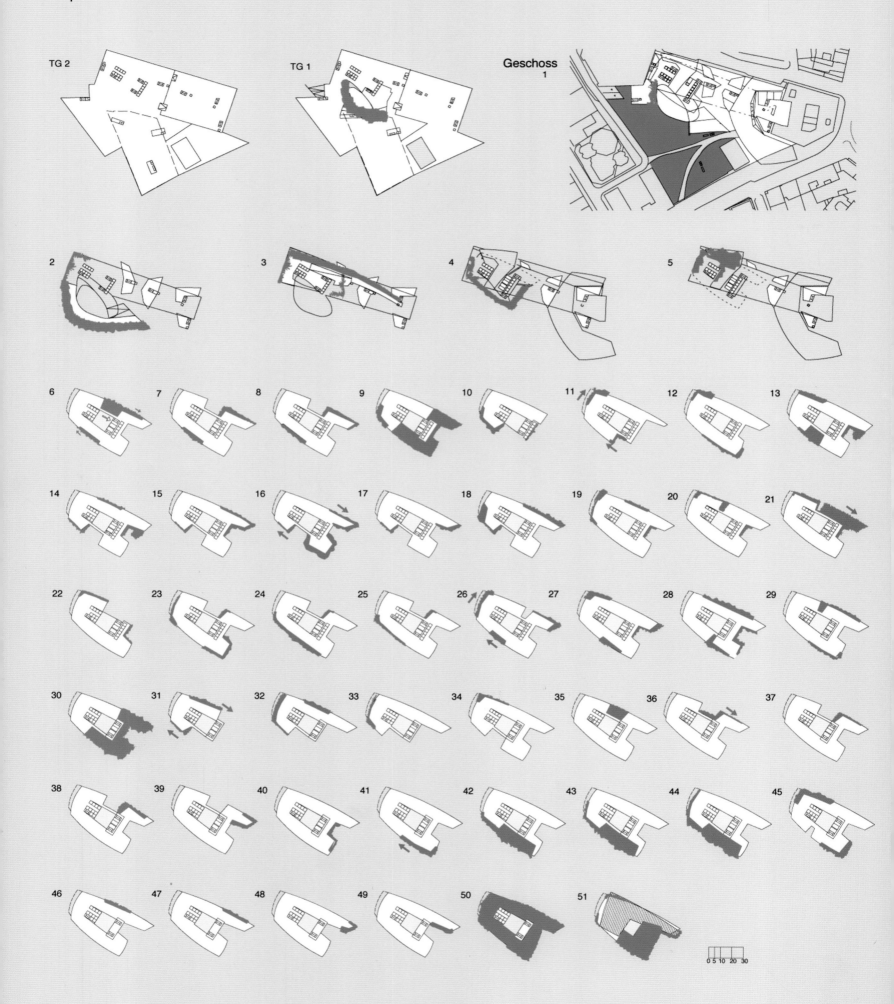

TG 2

TG 1

Geschoss 1

2
3
4
5

6 7 8 9 10 11 12 13

14 15 16 17 18 19 20 21

22 23 24 25 26 27 28 29

30 31 32 33 34 35 36 37

38 39 40 41 42 43 44 45

46 47 48 49 50 51

0 5 10 20 30

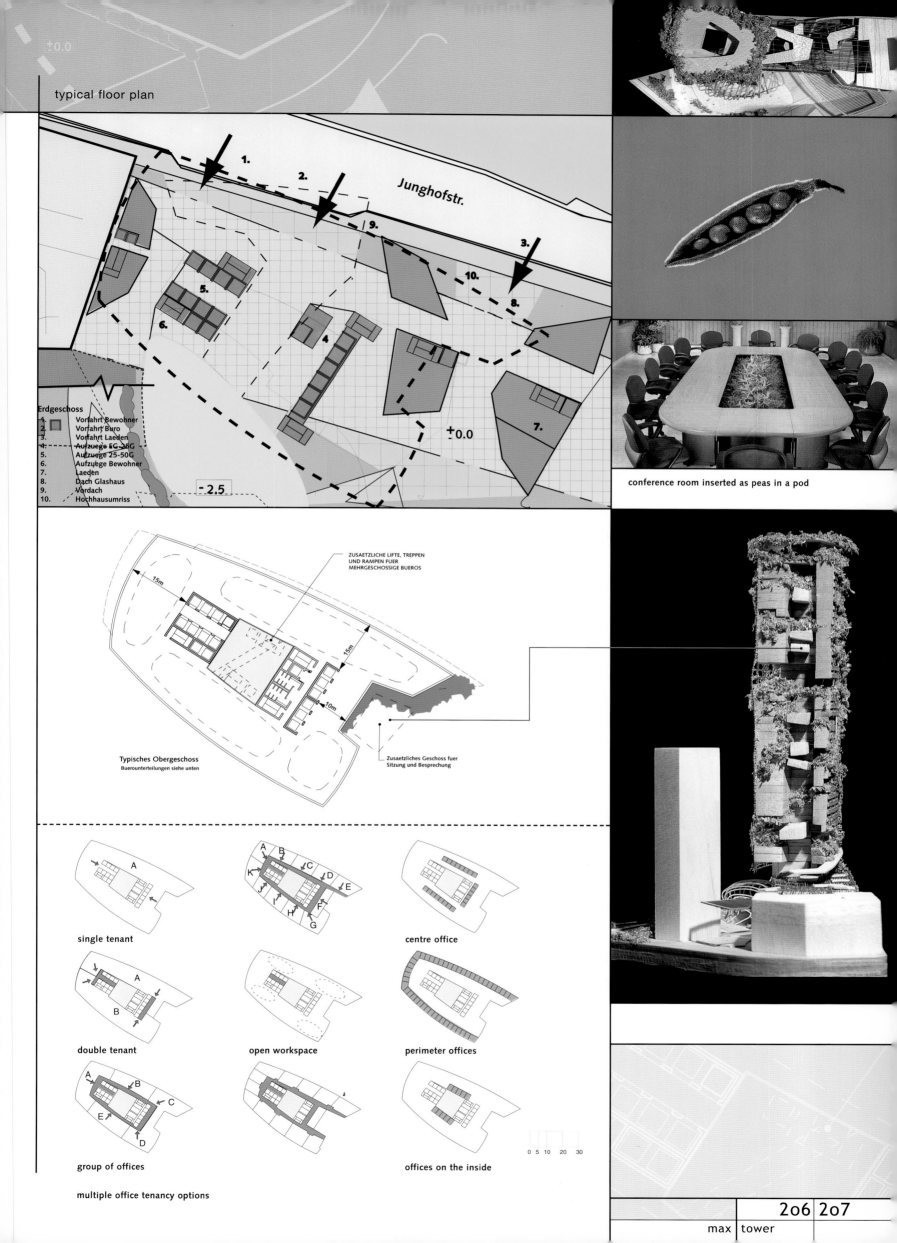

Junghofstr.

Erdgeschoss
1. Vorfahrt Bewohner
2. Vorfahrt Büro
3. Vorfahrt Laeden
4. Aufzuege EG-25G
5. Aufzuege 25-50G
6. Aufzuege Bewohner
7. Laeden
8. Dach Glashaus
9. Vordach
10. Hochhausumriss

±0.0

−2.5

ZUSAETZLICHE LIFTE, TREPPEN
UND RAMPEN FUER
MEHRGESCHOSSIGE BUEROS

15m

15m

10m

Typisches Obergeschoss
Buerounterteilungen siehe unten

Zusaetzliches Geschoss fuer
Sitzung und Besprechung

conference room inserted as peas in a pod

single tenant

centre office

double tenant

open workspace

perimeter offices

group of offices

offices on the inside

multiple office tenancy options

0 5 10 20 30

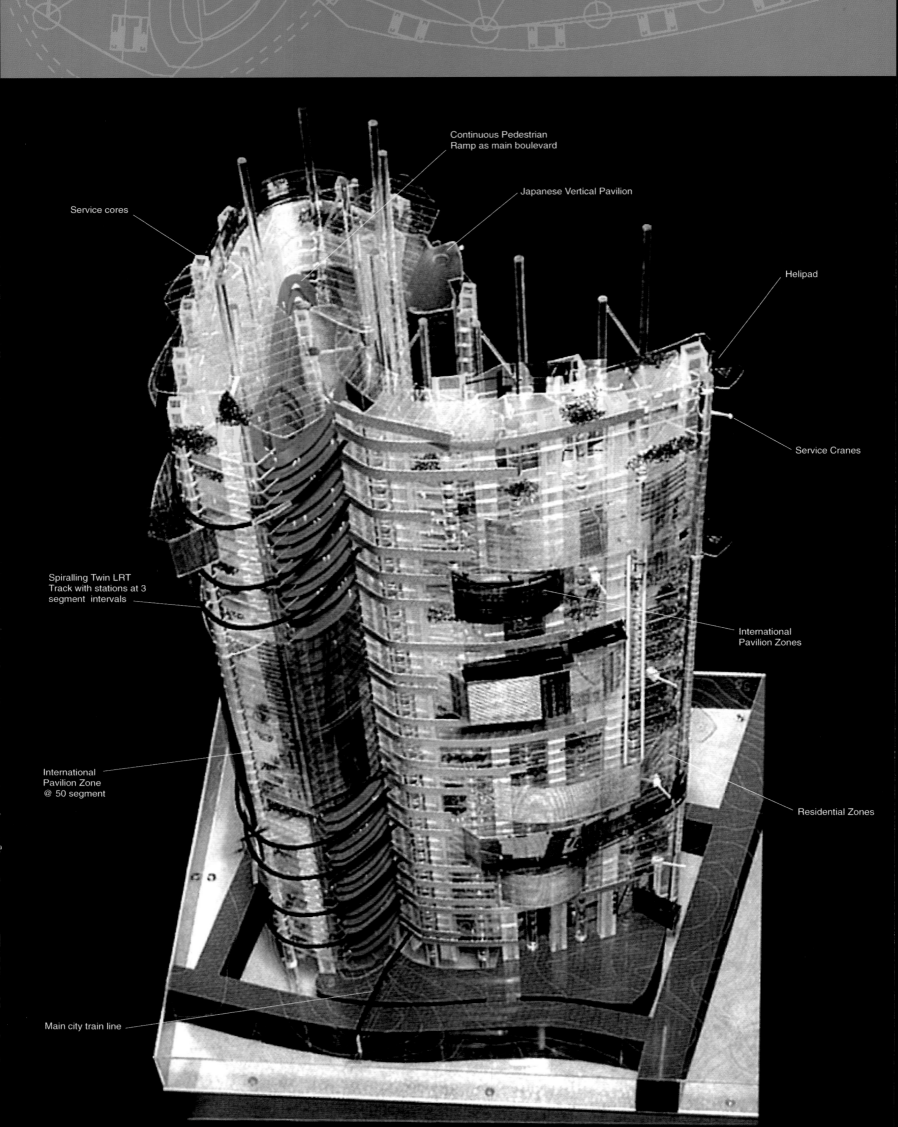

Service cores

Continuous Pedestrian Ramp as main boulevard

Japanese Vertical Pavilion

Helipad

Service Cranes

Spiralling Twin LRT Track with stations at 3 segment intervals

International Pavilion Zones

International Pavilion Zone @ 50 segment

Residential Zones

Main city train line

Nagoya, Japan

owner 2005 Committee
location Nagoya, Aichi Prefecture, Japan
latitude 35.1°N
nos of storeys 50 floor segments
date start 1998 (design)
completion date –
areas Total gross area 223 ha
Total nett area 156 ha
Site area 150 ha

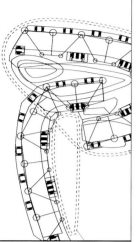

At the very centre of Yeang's proposals for the Nagoya 2005 World Exposition, lies a clear commitment to the preservation of the ecosystem of the locality.

Instead of adopting a conventional **horizontal** layout for the Expo, which would spread over most of the 150 hectares of site area, Yeang has proposed a **vertical alternative**, with a building footprint of just 2 hectares occupied by a 50-storey Hypertower of 12 metres per storey, rising to 600 metres in height. This solution effectively creates 'artificial land' in the sky, as each platform of the mega-structure can be occupied by the various Pavilions, that form the World Exposition.

The overall proposal is thus framed in two fundamental ideas: that of a **vertical mega-structural system** interlaced with a series of concepts, and a set of optional **vertical circulation** systems. This proposition is generated entirely, by a direct response to the theme set out by the Expo 2005 Committee for the Exposition to: "... **express the need to reconsider the natural world through the adoption of an innovative attitude to urban planning, infrastructure, building design and information, proposing new standards for quality of life in an ecologically friendly environment.**" [1]

Yeang's competition proposals, which were submitted under the Sponsors main headline of: "... **Beyond Development: Rediscovering Nature's Wisdom**", were underscored by a clear statement of undisputable advantage : "... **in going vertical, the proposal will preserve more than two-thirds of the existing ecosytem of the locality ... (and) will therefore avoid extensive land clearance and disruption to the site's existing mature ecology.**" [2]

The design proposals are based on a distribution of landuse within the 50 segments, with a system of 'horizontal' and vertical zoning of uses.

design features

The Nagoya Expo 2005 Tower is the alternative proposal as the vertical option to the conventional horizontal layouts used in the previous Expos elsewhere in the world. This proposal is currently being considered by the Expo 2005 Committee.The Expo 2005 Committee had earlier declared that the exhibition theme has to "express the need to reconsider the natural world through the adoption of an innovative attitude to urban planning, infrastructure, building design and information, proposing new standards for quality of life in an ecologically friendly environment". The site is near Seto City in Nagoya in Japan and is a 150 hectare site with a pristine matured ecosystem (following a period of secondary ecological succession). It is contended here that to build the new Expo facilities on this site with an expected 25 million visitors trampling over this ecosytem will appear contrary to the declared intentions of the Expo Committee. It will likely generate an uproar from environmentalists worldwide. The vertical solution proposed here addresses the issue of the ecological sensitivity of the site by creating 'artificial land' in the sky. In going vertical, the proposal will preserve more than two-thirds of the existing ecosystem of the locality. The fundamental benefit of the vertical solution is that it will have a smaller building-footprint at the ground-plane (ie. @ 2 Ha compared to that of the horizontal version @ 150 Ha). This vertical Expo will therefore avoid extensive land clearance and disruption to the site's existing mature ecology. The tower design will in effect be a working prototype of the "1000 m Hypertower project" mooted and researched by the Japan's Ministry of Construction. The tower will be 600 metres high and will have 50 segments of platforms @ 12 m height that will enable the various pavilions to be built (up to three storeys) within each segment. The tower's distribution of landuse within the 50 segments will be on the basis of a system of 'horizontal' as well as 'vertical' zoning of uses. Horizontal zoning enables pavilions and facilities to be located within one or more of the 50 segments of 12 m height. Vertical zoning provides for certain pavilions and facilities to be accessible at all floors (eg. the International Pavilion, the Japan Pavilion, the Administration/ Security/Services Facilities, etc). The key circulation system is by means of a spiralling monorail with its twin tracks placed on the periphery of the tower with 'stations' at six segment intervals (ie. 2 minutes travelling time between stations). This connects to the LRT system at the ground-plane. In addition to these, there will be supplementary systems of elevators, escalators and inclined travelators. However as with most Expos, there will be a main promenade for use by pedestrians from which all pavilions will be accessible. This promenade in the tower will be in the form of a large gentle ramp that traverses from the ground-plane all the way up to the top of the tower. Such a new urban development constitutes an opportunity to test the concept of the vertical organisation and integration of local resources, environmental demands and the specific needs of an international exhibition. The building's operational and environmental systems will address the challenges of the new century giving respect to nature in a technological response, using clean and efficient energy technologies and recycling systems. The intention of the Expo 2005 Tower will demonstrate a new policy toward preservation of the natural environment and the freeing of existing urban landscape for vegetation. It will likely be an example for future urban expansion spaces (eg. the proposed relocation of the Japan Government facilities outside Tokyo).

[1] Ken Yeang: 'The Nagoya Expo 2005 Tower', Project Notes
[2] Ibid.

(1)

(2)

(3)

Japan, covering 378,000 square kilometers over the four main islands (Hokkaido, Honshu, Shikoku and Kyushu), lies mostly in the temperate zone and has a humid monsoon climate. Extending over 25° of latitude, there is considerable variation of temperature with Hokkaido in the north registering a winter mean of –3°C and Okinawa in the south experiencing a summer mean of 28°C.

With a population of 125 million, Japan also has one of the world's highest densities at 335 persons per square kilometer (USA at 28 persons per square kilometer) with a rapidly diminishing resource of arable and habitable land.

One of the simplest way to accommodate high densities and yet preserve nature and to avoid building over valuable arable land (eg. rice fields) is to go upwards. This is a critical issue which needs to be addressed not only in Japan but worldwide. The Expo 2005 becomes an ideal platform for this debate and re-assessment of existing attitudes and ideas regarding intensive buildings. The proposal here offers the 'vertical' solution to these issues.

infrastructure of Seto City, Aichi Prefecture

Aichi Prefecture is home to the city of Nagoya, one of the three largest metropolitan areas in Japan. Its central location gives it convenient access nationwide. Nagoya is the important mid-point along the shinkansen line running from Tokyo and Osaka. The Meishin Expressway connects Nagoya to Osaka while the Chuo and Tomei Expressways links it to Tokyo. The ports of Nagoya and Toyohashi serve the region with a proposed new international airport in Chubu further enhancing and ensuring the future growth of this area.

Traveling Time to Major Cities

	Bullet Train	Car
Tokyo	96 minutes	4.0 hours
Kyoto	36 minutes	2.0 hours
Osaka	52 minutes	2.5 hours

The vertical expo enables a vertical continuation of the horizontal train railway system with a new spiraling SRT that will traverse around the facade of the vertical expo tower.

Satoyama woodlands

Seto which is 20 km south-east of Nagoya has a 1,300-year history as a ceramics center. During this time, the land was mined for the native clay and trees logged to fire up the kilns. This exploitation of the local natural resources resulted in a ravaging cycle of deforestation and reforestation which peaked in the 1940s and lasted until recently.

With a heightened awareness of forest conservation, switching to other sources of fuel and an ambitious reforestation program, the area is now rehabilitated into a viable mixed-growth matured forest habitat. The site is a maintained ecosystem referred to as the satoyama woodlands. The illustration here shows the results of successful ecological succession in which re-vegetation and reforestation has taken place over a formerly devastated site.

flora and fauna of Aichi Prefecture

The Satoyama Woodlands together with the Kaisho Forest on the outskirts of Nagoya are the habitat for a diverse collection of valuable plants, birds and insects. Over 800 species of plants live in these forests.

A recent research surveyed 61 species of butterflies, 41 species of dragonflies, 300 species of moths, 121 species of birds, 15 species of amphibians and reptiles, many of which are rare and endangered. For example, the magnolia stellata (star magnolia) found here, grows in less than 100 areas around Japan. The goshawk (Accipiter gentilis) also lives and breeds in this area. This species is particularly rare in Japan as its natural habitat continues to disappear. Another species at risk is the gifucho butterfly (Luehdorfia japonica) which is endemic to Japan.

This proposal for Expo 2005 aims to proactively address the preservation of these indigenous species. A horizontal expo layout over this site will without doubt eliminate many of these valuable species.

the viable alternative to the 'horizontal' expo

The modern expositions of the last two decades generally comprised of low-rise purpose-built or proto-typical pavilions laid out over a large site and is usually connected by a vast transport network of rail, road and sometimes marine craft systems. The impact of a horizontal built-form on the site is evident. It will result in widespread destruction of this matured ecosystem.

In pursuing an alternative layout and specifically to minimize the impact of the built form on the existing woodlands and the indigenous wildlife, the traditional expo masterplan is re-interpreted and re-organized in a 'vertical' configuration. The comparison of the built footprint on the locality is illustrated below. Clearly the 'vertical' solution is much preferred over the 'horizontal' one as it will have a smaller footprint on the ecologically mature site.

Satoyama woodlands

The comparison of the coverage of the built form between the horizontal and vertical planning concept is as follows:

A horizontal Expo 2005 Development
- total area of site = 540 ha 100.0%
- proposed area of development = 75 ha 14.0%
- area reserved for natural environment = 455 ha 86.0%

B vertical Expo 2005 Prototype Tower
- total area of site = 540 ha 100.0%
- proposed area of development = 75 ha 14.0%
- proposed footprint @ 25 segment levels = 75 ÷ 25 = 3 ha 0.5%
- area reserved for natural environment = 537 ha 99.5%
- increase in area for natural environment = 147 ha 18.0%

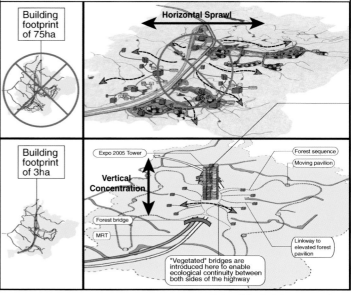

Building footprint of 75ha

Horizontal Sprawl

Building footprint of 3ha

Expo 2005 Tower

Forest sequence

Moving pavilion

Vertical Concentration

Forest bridge

MRT

Linkway to elevated forest pavilion

"Vegetated" bridges are introduced here to enable ecological continuity between both sides of the highway

reduced footprint on ecosystems

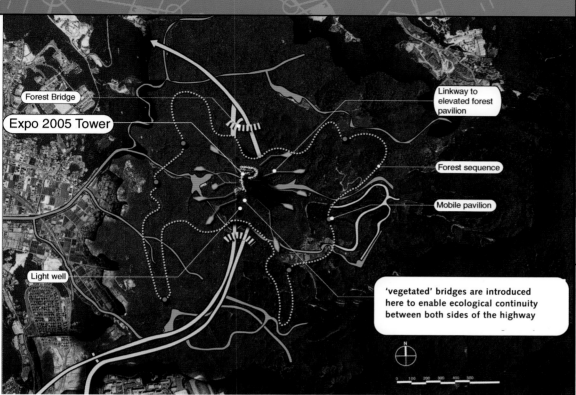

Forest Bridge

Expo 2005 Tower

Linkway to
elevated forest
pavilion

Forest sequence

Mobile pavilion

Light well

'vegetated' bridges are introduced
here to enable ecological continuity
between both sides of the highway

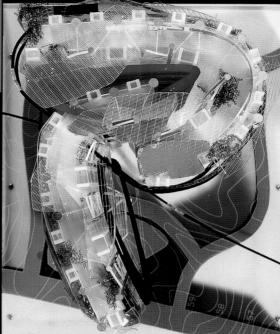

Essentially this allows horizontally zoned pavilions to be located in one or more of the vertical 12 m spaces, or for vertically zoned pavilions to occupy a multiple of levels – such as the International Pavilion or the Japan Pavilion.

The major plan arrangement – an interlocking U- and L-formation – is configured to incorporate a multiple set of systems. Most important amongst these is a **spiralling monorail** with twin tracks set on the tower's periphery, and with stations at frequent intervals, the whole connected to the LRT at the ground plane. This basic system is supported by elevators, escalators and inclined travelators. A further pedestrian promenade is included, between pavilions, by a large gentle ramp that continues from the ground plane to the summit of the tower.

In certain respects there is a similarity to Yeang's earlier proposals for the Tokyo Nara Tower, for instance in the Nagoya Tower's **vertical landscaping** strategy, and in the nature of its triangular **mega-structure** and horizontal cross-bracing. However, in this case, the especially different elements are the structural floors which form foundation plates for construction in each vertical zone. Equally, Yeang has given specific instances of how the **zoning** might be applied: in the horizontal case, office administration, light industry, residential units and urban infrastructure are proposed; in the vertical case exposition pavilions, hotels and commercial units are applied volumes.

To this mix is added a host of facilities including an arts and crafts village, convention hall and theatres. The main U-form of the curved plan is orientated to acquire views and natural light, with vistas that include Mount Fuji itself, and the Nagoya bay Ise Shrine.

As with all Yeang's projects there is a major emphasis on this as an ecological architecture: **"... the building's operational and environmental systems will address the challenges of the new century giving respect to nature in a technological response, using clean and efficient energy technologies and recycling systems."**[3] The project, he proposes, can also be seen as a model for future urban expansion, such as the relocation of the Japan Government facilities outside Tokyo.

This project, in its deliberate and sensitive response to the local ecosystem is at one stage beyond all Yeang's previous proposals. It is not just a proposal for a Hypertower, but a signal initiative which addresses the nature of a whole region. Its deserves to be built.

The Expo 2005 Tower is the alternative proposal as the 'vertical' option to the conventional horizontal layouts used in previous international expositions. This supports the goals for Expo 2005 in addressing concerns of the environment and the world's burgeoning population.

In addition, the 'vertical' solution here, is in line with the Expo's aims to develop a new mutually respecting relationship of nature with mankind and technologies related to the protection of the environment well as the preservation of the Satoyama Woodlands.

The proposal for the 'vertical' expo is ecologically further enhanced as it sits on the proposed platform links over the proposed expressways (which will bisect the woodlands) as forested bridges between the adjacent woodlands. These connectors (interspaced with generous lightwells) may re-establish ground level migration routes and encourages specie migration between each micro-habitat. This engenders a more stable ecosystem and enhances the ecological diversity of the immediate site and the surrounding Satoyama Woodlands.

[3] Ibid.

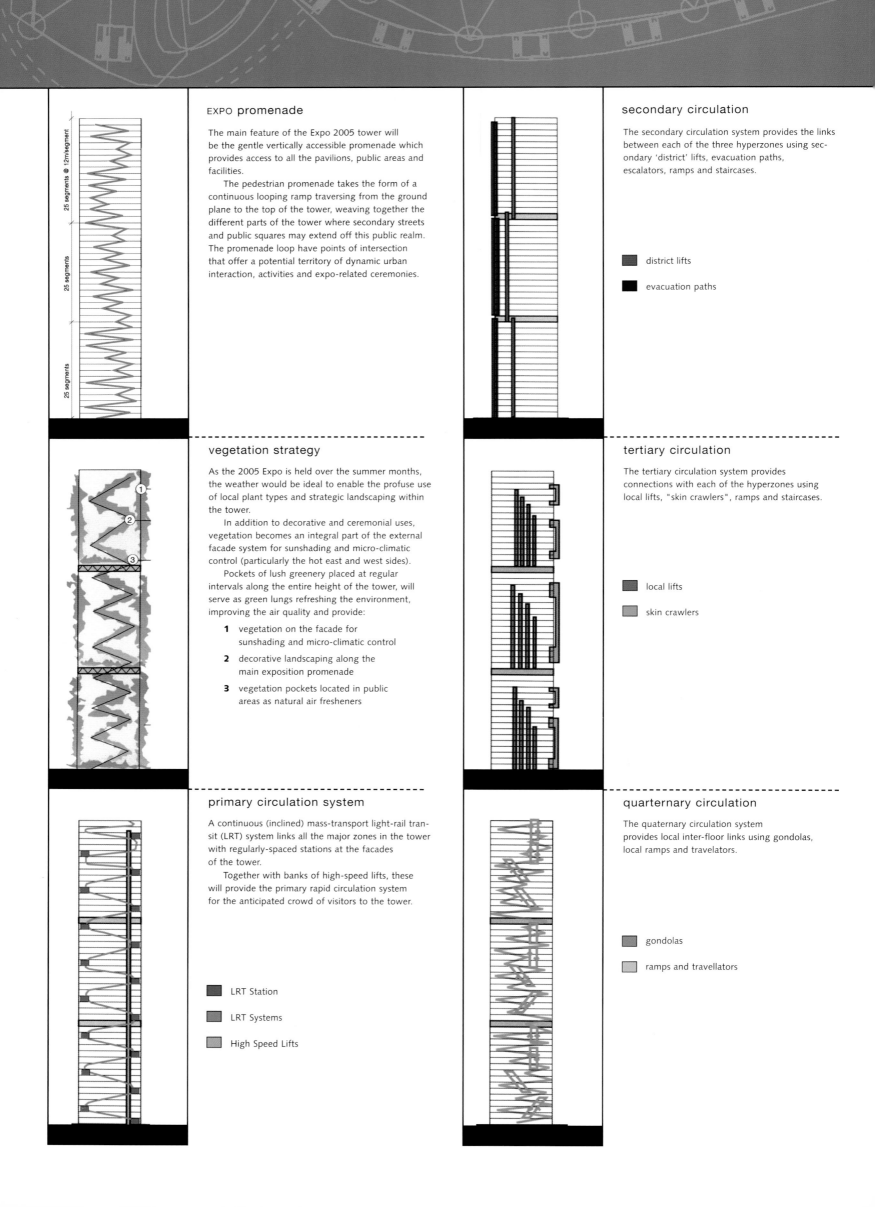

EXPO promenade

The main feature of the Expo 2005 tower will
be the gentle vertically accessible promenade which
provides access to all the pavilions, public areas and
facilities.

The pedestrian promenade takes the form of a
continuous looping ramp traversing from the ground
plane to the top of the tower, weaving together the
different parts of the tower where secondary streets
and public squares may extend off this public realm.
The promenade loop have points of intersection
that offer a potential territory of dynamic urban
interaction, activities and expo-related ceremonies.

secondary circulation

The secondary circulation system provides the links
between each of the three hyperzones using secondary 'district' lifts, evacuation paths,
escalators, ramps and staircases.

- ⬛ district lifts
- ⬛ evacuation paths

vegetation strategy

As the 2005 Expo is held over the summer months,
the weather would be ideal to enable the profuse use
of local plant types and strategic landscaping within
the tower.

In addition to decorative and ceremonial uses,
vegetation becomes an integral part of the external
facade system for sunshading and micro-climatic
control (particularly the hot east and west sides).

Pockets of lush greenery placed at regular
intervals along the entire height of the tower, will
serve as green lungs refreshing the environment,
improving the air quality and provide:

1 vegetation on the facade for
sunshading and micro-climatic control

2 decorative landscaping along the
main exposition promenade

3 vegetation pockets located in public
areas as natural air fresheners

tertiary circulation

The tertiary circulation system provides
connections with each of the hyperzones using
local lifts, "skin crawlers", ramps and staircases.

- ⬛ local lifts
- ⬛ skin crawlers

primary circulation system

A continuous (inclined) mass-transport light-rail transit (LRT) system links all the major zones in the tower
with regularly-spaced stations at the facades
of the tower.

Together with banks of high-speed lifts, these
will provide the primary rapid circulation system
for the anticipated crowd of visitors to the tower.

- ⬛ LRT Station
- ⬛ LRT Systems
- ⬛ High Speed Lifts

quaternary circulation

The quaternary circulation system
provides local inter-floor links using gondolas,
local ramps and travelators.

- ⬛ gondolas
- ⬛ ramps and travellators

The key circulation system is by means of a spiraling monorail (Skyscraper Rapid Transit – SRT) with its twin tracks placed on the periphery of the tower with 'stations' at three segment intervals (ie. two minutes traveling time between stations) This connects to the LRT system at ground plane.

In addition, the vertical prototype Expo 2005 Tower will have a three-dimensional transportation system that is structured vertically and horizontally for high speed mass transportation as well as for personal transportation. Circulation within the tower is structured in a multi-tiered hierarchical system.

primary circulation

function: links all major programmatic zones in hypertower with the entrance links the hypertower with its environs

features: continuous SRT system with fully automated monorail twin tracks integrated SRT stations @ every three segments (36 m) high-speed lifts that connects the entrance to major pavilions

secondary circulation

function: circulation between hyperzones (15 segments separated by refuge zones)

features: district lifts that connects refuge zones evacuation routes within each hyperzone that terminates in the refuge zones

tertiary circulation

function: circulation within each hyperzone

features: local lifts that serve every segment skin crawlers that links @ every 3–5 segments

quarternary circulation

function: inter-segment circulation

features: continuous gondola system that runs between three segments continuous ramp and travellator system that runs through every segment

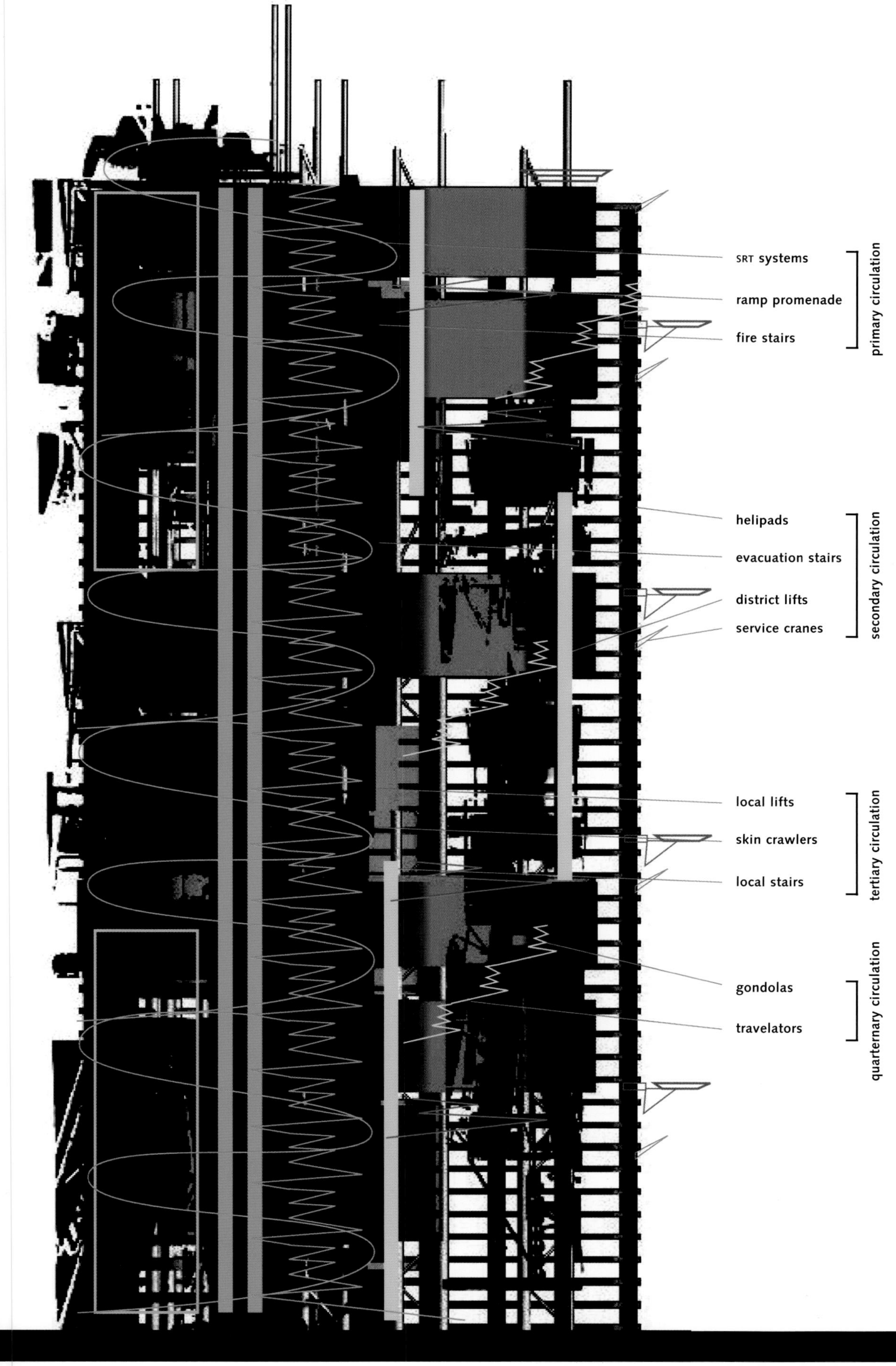

---

primary circulation
- SRT systems
- ramp promenade
- fire stairs

secondary circulation
- helipads
- evacuation stairs
- district lifts
- service cranes

tertiary circulation
- local lifts
- skin crawlers
- local stairs

quarternary circulation
- gondolas
- travelators

zoning concept

The tower will be 300 meters high and will have 25 segments of platforms @ 12m height that will enable the various pavilions to be built (up to three storeys) within each segment. The tower's distribution of land use within the 25 segments will be on a "horizontal" and "vertical" zoning basis.

"Horizontal" zoning applies to individual pavilions (eg. country, corporations, NGO's) and facilities which are located within one or more of the 25 segments of 12m height. "Vertical" zoning provides for certain pavilions and facilities to be accessible from all floors (eg. The Expo Theme Pavilion, the Japan Pavilion, Special Forest Pavilions, services and security)

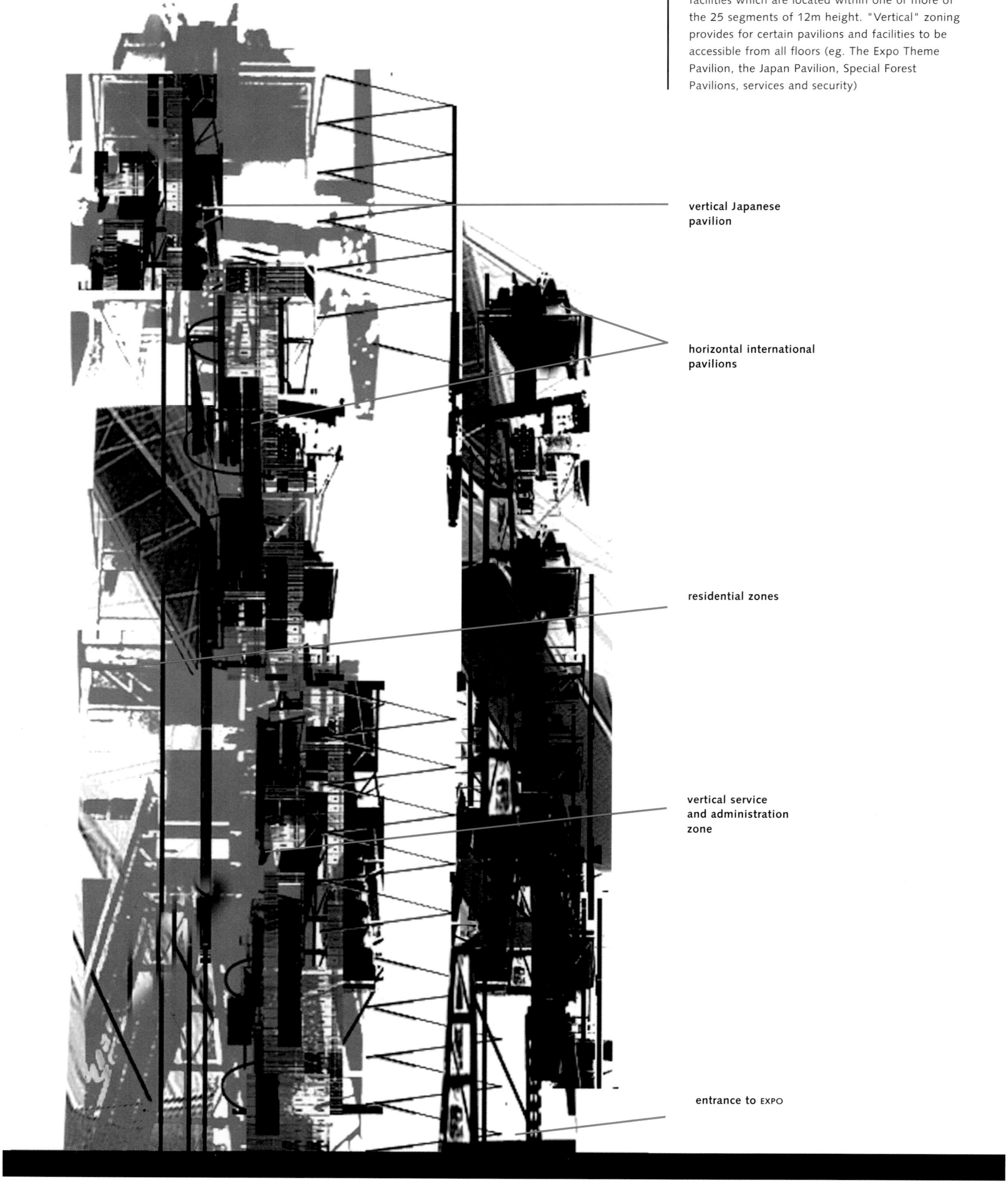

vertical Japanese
pavilion

horizontal international
pavilions

residential zones

vertical service
and administration
zone

entrance to EXPO

horizontal and vertical zoning

In contrast to the conventional stratifications of floor uses, the Expo 2005 tower has both horizontal zoning of uses as well as vertical zoning. Some uses are linked vertically and are on all floors.

zone		areas (in sq m)	%
1 EXPO **2005 pavilions**		200 000	9%
• international zone (exposition pavilions)			
• local government zone Japanese pavilion			
• theme pavilion			
• arts and crafts village (theme zone)			
2 hotels and commercial		188 000	8.4%
• convention hall			
• theater			
• event theater			
• guest house (residential units)			
3 office and administration		462 000	20.7%
• international organisation zone			
• administration (offices), security, medical			
• gate facilities			
4 light industry		19 500	0.9%
5 residential buildings		1215 000	54.5%
• dwellings	12 000		
• resident population	25 000		
• working population	15 000		
6 urban infrastructure		146 000	6.5%
• public circulation areas and plazas			
• service road			
• pedestrian road			
• bus terminals			
• main approach from railway			
• main approach from bus			
• arterial road			
• moving walk			
total built area :		2230 500	100%

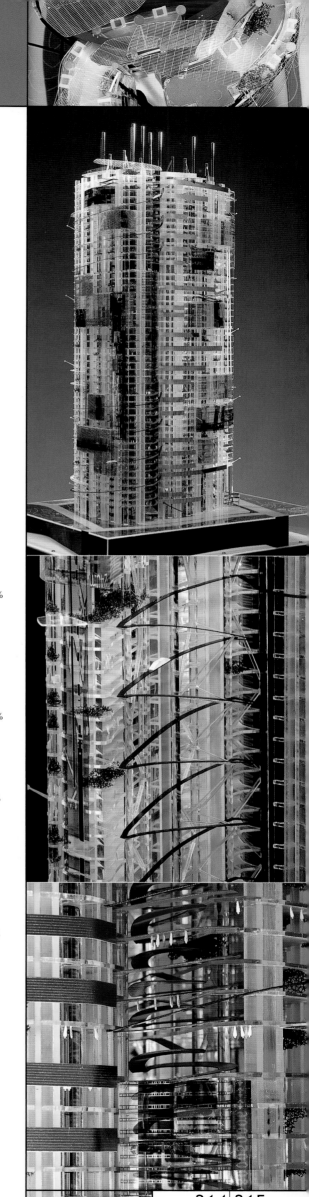

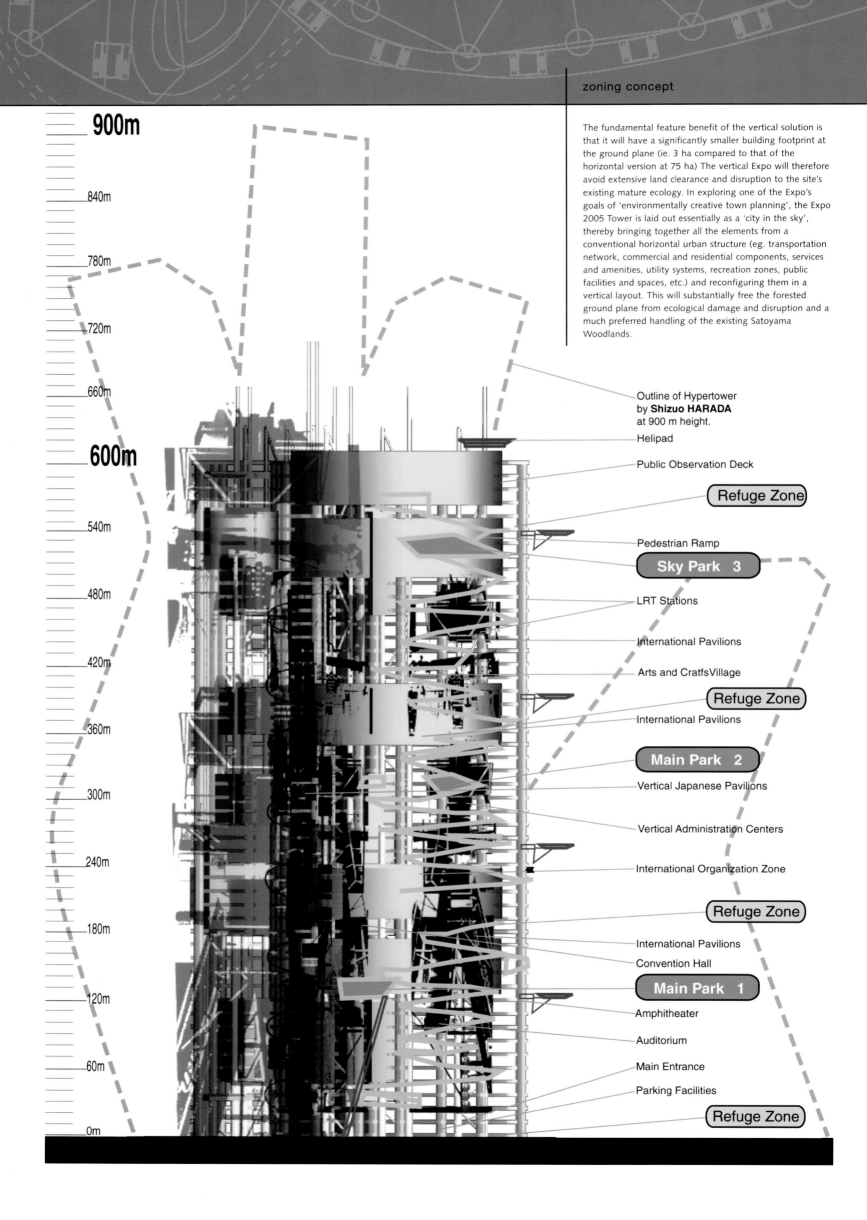

The fundamental feature benefit of the vertical solution is that it will have a significantly smaller building footprint at the ground plane (ie. 3 ha compared to that of the horizontal version at 75 ha) The vertical Expo will therefore avoid extensive land clearance and disruption to the site's existing mature ecology. In exploring one of the Expo's goals of 'environmentally creative town planning', the Expo 2005 Tower is laid out essentially as a 'city in the sky', thereby bringing together all the elements from a conventional horizontal urban structure (eg. transportation network, commercial and residential components, services and amenities, utility systems, recreation zones, public facilities and spaces, etc.) and reconfiguring them in a vertical layout. This will substantially free the forested ground plane from ecological damage and disruption and a much preferred handling of the existing Satoyama Woodlands.

900m

840m

780m

720m

660m

600m

540m

480m

420m

360m

300m

240m

180m

120m

60m

0m

Outline of Hypertower
by **Shizuo HARADA**
at 900 m height.

Helipad

Public Observation Deck

Refuge Zone

Pedestrian Ramp

Sky Park 3

LRT Stations

International Pavilions

Arts and CratfsVillage

Refuge Zone

International Pavilions

Main Park 2

Vertical Japanese Pavilions

Vertical Administration Centers

International Organization Zone

Refuge Zone

International Pavilions

Convention Hall

Main Park 1

Amphitheater

Auditorium

Main Entrance

Parking Facilities

Refuge Zone

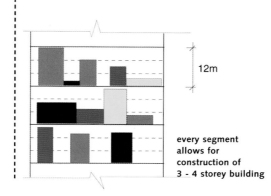

The floor plate is maintained at a maximum depth of 30 m to ensure natural light penetration into the internal display spaces. The curvilinear form also maximizes the external surface area for optimum exposure to natural light and fresh air exchanges. In addition, the generous external surfaces permits spectacular panoramic views of the surrounding Satoyama Woodlands and the adjacent environs.

The design in effect provides 'artificial land' within three-storey segments to enable users to construct three- to four-storey sub-buildings within the mega-structure.

The project therefore has a 'long-life' and 'loose-fit' ecological justification.

12m

every segment allows for construction of 3 - 4 storey building

site information

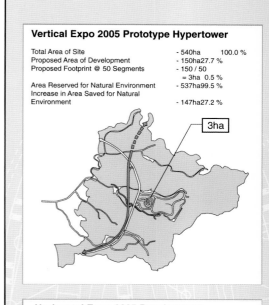

Vertical Expo 2005 Prototype Hypertower

Total Area of Site	- 540ha	100.0 %
Proposed Area of Development	- 150ha	27.7 %
Proposed Footprint @ 50 Segments	- 150 / 50	
	= 3ha	0.5 %
Area Reserved for Natural Environment	- 537ha	99.5 %
Increase in Area Saved for Natural Environment	- 147ha	27.2 %

3ha

Horizontal Expo 2005 Development

Total Area of Site	- 540ha	100.0 %
Proposed Area of Development	- 150ha	27.7 %
Area Reserved for Natural Environment	- 390ha	72.3 %

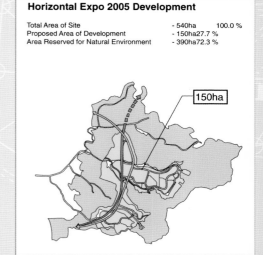

150ha

the existing pristine ecosystem

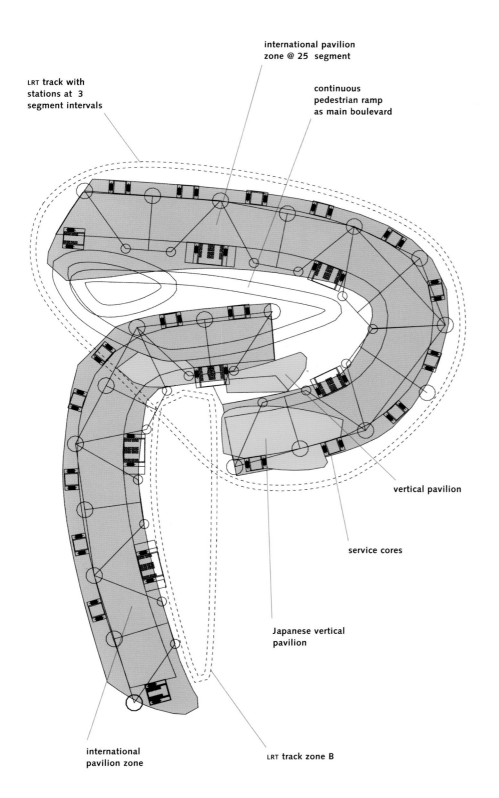

LRT track with stations at 3 segment intervals

international pavilion zone @ 25 segment

continuous pedestrian ramp as main boulevard

vertical pavilion

service cores

Japanese vertical pavilion

international pavilion zone

LRT track zone B

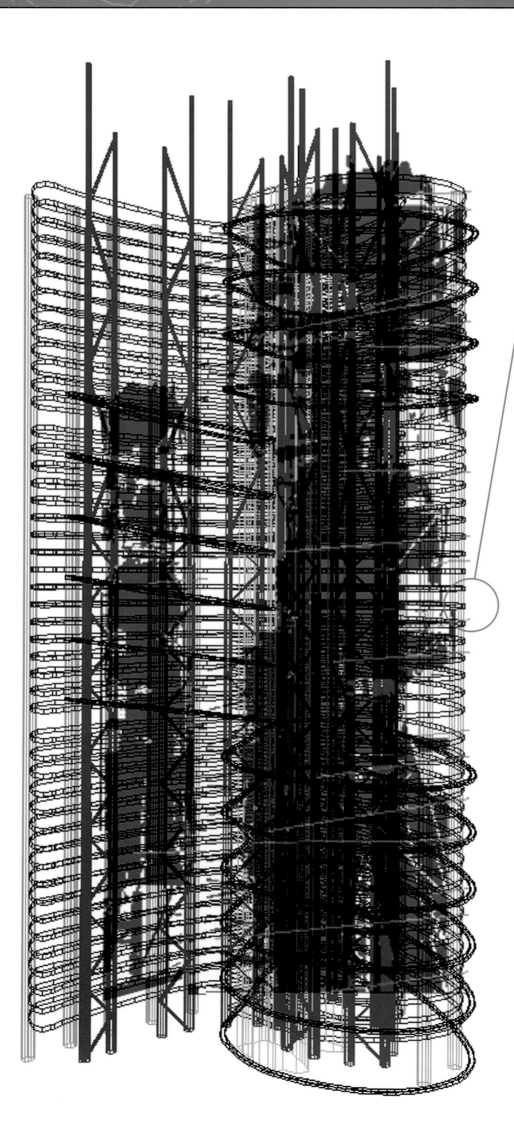

Each 12 m floor to ceiling segment height (refer to illustration below) will allow up to a three-storey pavilion construction with an independent quaternary circulation system. This space will them be converted into 'real-estate-in-the-sky' after the Expo 2005.

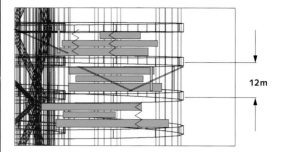

The space allocation is comparable to the land use apportionment of Expo '98 in Lisbon. The expected population density is estimated as follows:

- estimated visitor population
  = 12 million/6 months
  = 2 million/month
  = 64,500 visitors/day

- estimated staff population
  = 20% of visitor population
  = 12,900 staff

- estimated population in tower
  = about 77,400 per day during Expo

site information

In the Expo 2005 Tower, this takes the form of a fully automated continuous SRT (Skyscraper Rapid Transit) system that weaves together the different programmatic zones into a looping public zone where secondary streets and public squares may extend off this public realm. This SRT system consists of a pair of monorail twin tracks (one for ascension, the other for descending) which makes a full turn every three segments ie. 36 m. SRT stations are placed at every three segments, providing access to major pavilions and sites.

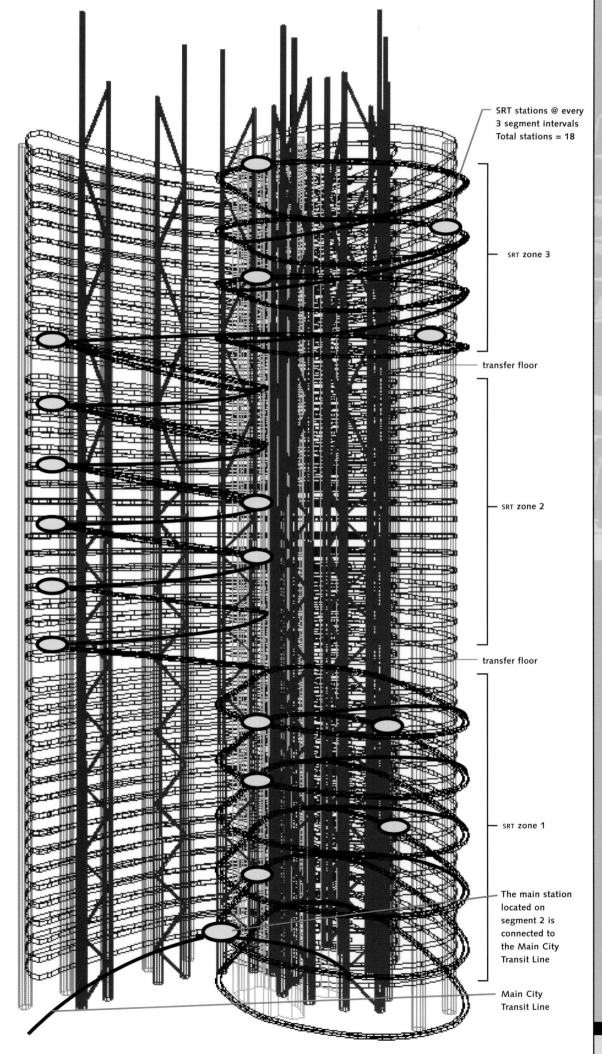

SRT stations @ every 3 segment intervals
Total stations = 18

SRT zone 3

transfer floor

SRT zone 2

transfer floor

SRT zone 1

The main station located on segment 2 is connected to the Main City Transit Line

Main City Transit Line

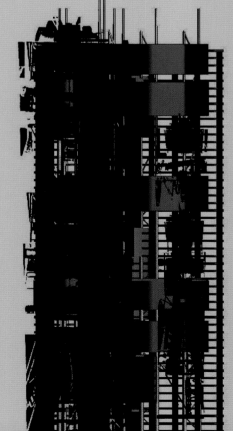

These projects, which are both centred on residential accommodation and mixed-use, and are both the subject of competitions, mark Yeang's entry into the UK scene, with proposals for two major locations in the city.

While the development briefs and sites vary in detail, both are essentially configured as a range of peripheral towers with a centralised facility, such as market square or transport interchange and plaza within the site. Both projects are associated with railways tracks, which are in boundary or centralised positions. Logically, as both projects are located in London, either north or south of the River Thames and have similar programmes with the emphasis on **residential use**, Yeang has applied similar concepts, criteria and methodology to each scheme. These factors of the designs exhibit the characteristics of Yeang's **'green skyscraper'** and **vertical urbanism propositions**.

Yeang's approach is based on three major issues and their incorporated resolution. These include **Social Sustainability, Environmental Sustainability**, and **Passive Low Energy Responses**, and expanded in detail these form the overall framework and content of the projects. Yeang's controlling concept of the **'City-in-the-Sky'**, recurring in almost all of his high-rise work, envisages the skyscraper **"... seen as a microcosm of the city, containing within itself the inherent elements of a city block ... parks, shops, entertainment centres, community facilities, social housing"** ... [1] and other residential accommodation types.

Yeang then outlines the benefits of this **intensified vertical urban** condition, which includes local employment resulting from mixed use, a balanced mixture of residents depending on income and accommodation requirements, yet with common facilities, such as parks and shopping streets provided on a shared basis. The arrangement then allows for basic amenities such as local stores, postal boxes, chemist and so on, to be provided within the building. Further, and characteristically, Yeang emphasises the creation of a healthy landscaped environment, with

"... spatial progressions of public open spaces (parks in the sky) to semi private (entrance courts) to private open spaces (balconies)." [2]

In the case of both projects Yeang's agenda for **Environmental Sustainability** is identical, and is drawn directly from his **'Green Skyscraper'** treatise, and his **open general systems framework.** [3]

This includes the interconnected set of external and internal interdependencies, together with the external-to-internal exchanges of energy and matter and vice versa, the designed systems output of energy and materials. To this Yeang then adds the considerations of **Passive Low Energy Responses**, both by Building Configuration and Orientation, and by Landscaping and Vegetation. Thus both designs, although varied in detail, are based on Yeang's full agenda for an **ecological architecture**, in this case related to the **temperate climate** of London.

From this shared conceptual basis, the two projects can be reviewed independently, within a closely **related typology**.

[1] Ken Yeang: 'Bishopsgate Towers, and Elephant and Castle Eco-Towers', Project Notes 2000
[2] Ibid.
[3] Ken Yeang: **'The Green Skyscraper,'** op cit.

Bishopsgate Goodsyard, London

bishopsgate towers

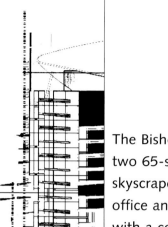

The Bishopsgate Towers include two 65-storey residential skyscrapers, and a 50-storey office and hotel associated with a convention centre.

The residential towers are sited on the southern edge of a new Market Square, which includes a linear shopping complex with retail outlets cafes/restaurants, arts and crafts centre and studio workshops, forming a new cultural hub for the neighbourhood.

The residential towers share a common **plan-form**, which has a radial configuration with the apartments forming a 'fan' arrangement on the northern and southern faces. The peripheral accommodation encloses an **internal atrium**, which rises through the building surrounded by a continuous **landscaped ramp**. This primary pedestrian circulation forms the principal element of the towers, which are essentially radial-spiral forms. The **landscaping** of the atrium is augmented by planted facades and terraces, which collectively contribute to the rehabilitation of the site, which Yeang defines as a devastated ecosystem.

The mixed-use facilities extend over several levels from the base, and occur again at vertical intervals such as level 23, which Yeang describes as a High Street, with shops, cafe and pub. Taken together, the range of mixed uses proposed is extensive, and Yeang has assembled this into a **horizontal and vertical zoning** diagram, which controls the occupation of the multi-layered and multi-level zoned masterplan of the entire building, conceived as a vertical land use pattern. This includes car-parking, vertical services, landscape, retail, housing and circulation. The housing itself includes both social/subsidised and private apartment accommodation, which provides each unit with a planted terrace/garden throughout a range of various plan-types.

As thoroughly conceived **'green skyscrapers'**, these towers exhibit all the major systems of Yeang's **ecological design** method, similar in principle to the EDITT tower, but modified to a temperate climate with sustainable objectives applied to a high-density scheme. Outstanding amongst these design studies are Yeang's **passive low energy responses**. Characteristically, the overall form is governed by the sunpath of the site, and the conditions of the summer and winter windrose.

Essentially each tower is configured as two blocks with a weather-protected landscaped core. The buildings are orientated **"... to maximise solar gain into the interior spaces in winter and mid-seasons, and to maximise solar shading in the summer months".** [4]

[4] Ken Yeang: 'Bishopsgate Towers', Project Notes, 1999

owner The Architecture Foundation (in association with) Peabody Trust British Steel (sponsor)
location Bishopsgate Goodsyard, London Boroughs of Hackney & Tower Hamlets, London E1
latitude 51.3°N
nos of storeys tower 1 & 2 – 65 storeys
tower 3 – 50 storeys
date start 1999 (design)
completion date –
areas (3 towers) total gross area 157,000 sq m
total net area 117,000 sq m
total area of plantation & circulation 110,000 sq m
site area approx. 3.4 hectares (8.4 acres)
plot ratio 1:5

design features • The brief calls for the design of 'mixed-use, mixed-income, sustainable high density settlement'. The design here addresses these issues as follows:

social sustainability

a. concept – 'city-in-the-sky'.
The design takes the model of a general geographical area of a city, with its inherent systems, zoning and social infrastructure and 'verticalises' it into skyscraper buildings. The skyscraper here is seen as a microcosm of the city, containing within itself the inherent elements of a city block, ie. parks, shops, entertainment centers, community facilities, social housing, medium-cost and high-cost housing, etc. The 'city-in-the sky' concept provides for:
• opportunities for local employment through mixture of use, both on ground and upper levels
• a healthy mix of residents within the same building. Through 'vertical zoning', resident types are grouped according to income (determined by their housing affordability) and accommodation preferences (single units, family units, luxury apartments, etc), yet common facilities (eg. parks, shopping streets, etc) are shared.
• close proximity to basic amenities, such as the local grocery store, postal boxes, chemist, etc. These are all located within the same building.
• a healthy landscaped environment, with spatial progressions of public open spaces (parks in the sky) to semi-private (front yard) to private open spaces (backyard).

b. density
A population density 750 persons/hectare is achieved in this proposal by building high-rise. This would not be possible with low- or mid-rise buildings.

c. users
Mixture of residents from different ages, incomes, occupations and family structures are accommodated by the provision of a variety of accommodation types: Social housing, subsidised housing (two- and three-bedroom types), singles apartments, two-room apartments, three-room apartments and penthouses.

d. uses
The development will incorporate housing, retail, community facilities, commercial and light industry both on the ground level and up the tower. The location of housing in close proximity to employment, retail, leisure and community facilities will reduce reliance on public transport.

e. open space requirements / outdoor space
The design seeks to re-create conditions on the ground up-in-the-sky, with features such as a front and back gardens for every unit, shared secondary and tertiary landscaped open spaces within groups of housing. The open spaces are connected via a central landscaped ramp, which spirals up the building.

f. relationship to immediate context
Urban connectivity is a key concept in the design proposal. The proposal here includes high-level bridging over the surrounding streets and earth mounding over existing train viaduct. This reduces the site's physical isolation from the surrounding created by the existing railway track and roads, and allows free multi-directional connections across the site for pedestrians and cyclists.

rain collection pan — M&E / ROOF

photovoltaic panels — 58

pub — 54

multi-layered environmental moderator — 52, 51, 50

creche — 46

restaurant — 45

photovoltaic panels — 43, 42, 41

pub

60, 59, 57, 56, 55, 53, 49, 48, 47, 44

sandwich shop

intermediate garden 'squares'

private front and back gardens

intermediate garden 'squares'

public parks (commons) in the sky

secondary programmed places in the sky

launderette
pub

mini market
IT knowledge centre

bank

35, 34, 33, 32, 31

secondary circulation systems

intermediate garden 'squares'
retail, general

William Hill — 27

28, 26, 25, 24

pub

electronics shop — 23

library / bookshop

22

hardware store

cafe on the ramp — 21

intermediate garden 'squares'

20, 19, 18, 17

sandwich shop

creche — 16

15

oxfarm

launderette — 14

pub — 13

retail, general

12

urban agriculture — 11

academia

10

restaurant

9

research laboratory — 8, 7

pub

6

bird sanctuary — 5

4

continuous landscaped ramp up the tower

3 (PARK)
2 (PARK)
1 (GROUND)

B1
B2
B3

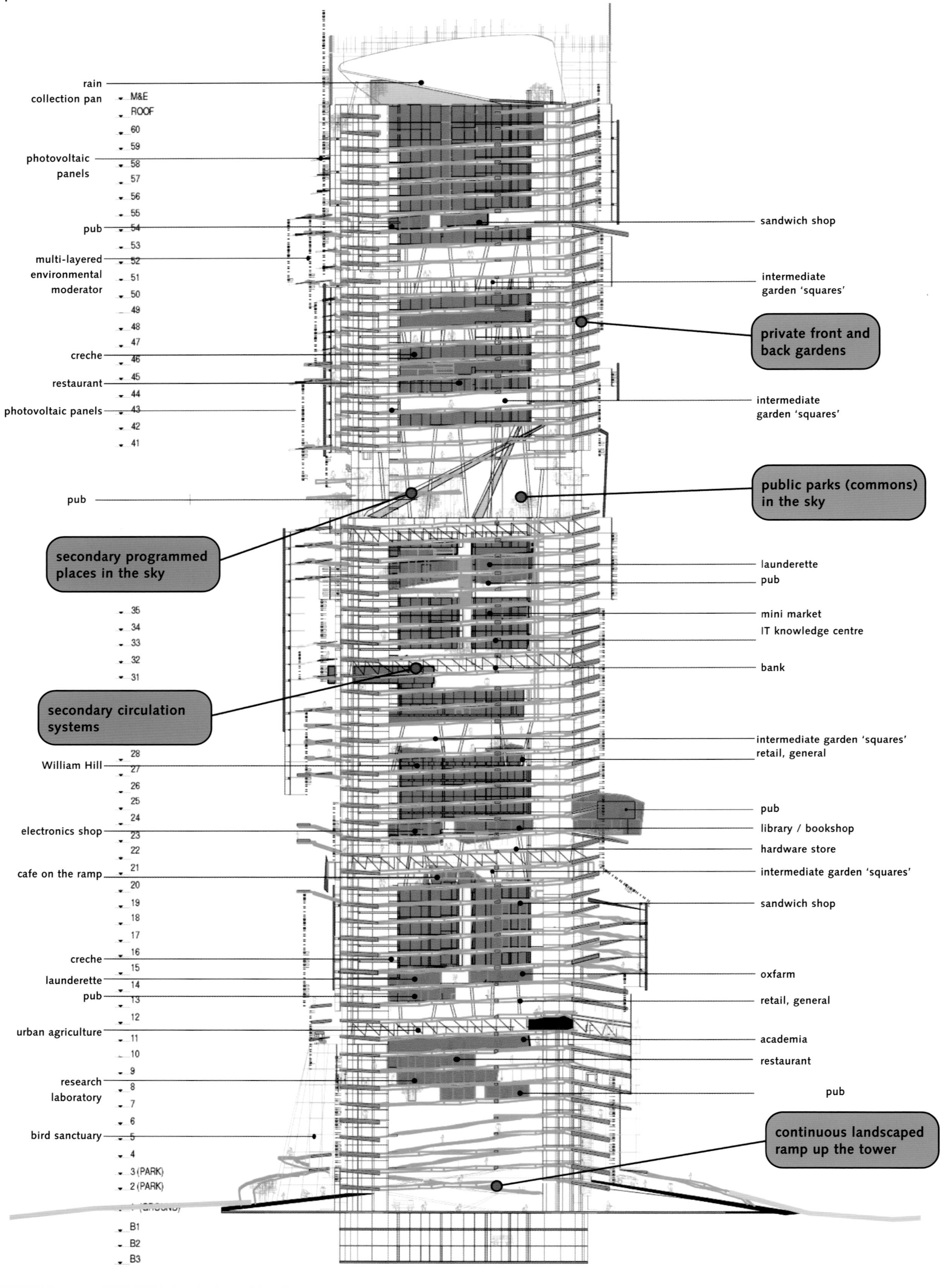

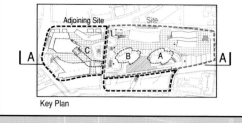

Key Plan

Adjoining Site | Site

The following map labels appear on the masterplan:

Workshops
Light Industry
Community Centre
Studio / Works

Shoreditch High St.
Retain Perimeter Wall
Escalator down to Underground Train Station
Ramp Up to Park Level
Ramp Up to Park Level
Bethnal Green Road
Existing Brickarches
Sclater Street
Ramp Up to Park Level
Gallery
Retail
Retail
Retail
Art / Craft Centre
Ramp Up to Park Level
Convention Centre
Main Drop-Off
Market Square
Community Centre
Pedestrian Entry
Studios
Workshops
Light Industry
Convention Entry
Office Drop-Off
Studio / Workshop Light Industry
Retail
Office Entry
B
A
Brick Lane
Hotel Drop-Off
Hotel Lobby
C
Office Lobby
Earth Mound
Ramp Up to Park Level
Wheler Street
Commercial Street
Existing Rail Line
Park
Park
Quaker Street
Earth Mounding over Rail Track
Up to Tower Drop-Off
Tower C (Office / Hotel)
Tower B (Residential)
Tower A (Residential)
0 20 40 100 metres
Level 60
Level 48
Secondary Programs In The Sky
Individual Private Gardens
160 m
Continuous Landscaping
Public Parks In The Sky
Secondary Circulation System
200 m
C
B
A

Legend
- Offices & Hotel
- Retails & Workshops
- Plaza
- Vegetation
- Service Core
- Park & Pavement
- Road

In this case, the lift cores are positioned on the north-east and west facades, providing a **buffer** of solar protection in summer. Conversely, during the winter months, low-angle sun can penetrate to the landscaped circulation atrium, and south-east facing residential units receive maximum solar gain. Beyond these basic principles, Yeang has applied special attention to the **facade design**, and the relationship of this, in particular, to the residential accommodation.

Essentially the facade is designed to allow maximum light into the interior spaces, while excluding cold winds by the use of a **multi-layered external wall**, which controls both the individual garden terraces and living units. This detailing includes both mesh-screen wind-breaker elements that reduce the inflow of strong winds, together with adjustable, insulated shutter doors that retain internal heat at night. This arrangement is then supported by both large double-glazed windows and internal shutters. Finally, there is the contribution of the landscaping and planting, of private gardens and communal sky-parks, that both acts as a wind buffer, and in summer as protection against solar radiation.

Seen as a whole, the detail design of the residential unit types – such as the three-dedroom duplex, which incorporates ramps between levels – all contain a great variety of articulated spaces and innovative installations, and are flexibly suited to all occupier categories.

While Yeang has typically expanded many other overall design considerations, such as the ventilation variants incorporating the central atrium, the use of south-facing photovoltaic panels as a rain-screen or the rainwater catchment scallops – all part of his **green agenda**, it is the additional detailed design of the **residential** elements that particularly marks this project. In turn the careful consideration of **occupation and lifestyle** contributes a further level of content to Yeang's **ecological architecture**.

g. ratio of affordable housing to market-rate housing

The proposal adheres to the design brief recommendations for the following minimum provisions for social and subsidised housing mix.

- 20% social housing
- 15% subsidised housing
- 65% market-rate housing

environmental sustainability

The approach to environmental sustainability here is a holistic approach, ie. it takes into account the entirety of the systems and functions of the ambient environment.

It is contended that ecological design must consider the following aspects of a building:
- its external interdependencies, consisting of the designed system's relations to its external environment and ecosystems
- its internal interdependencies, being the designed system's internal relations, activities and operations
- its external-to-internal exchanges of energy and matter – being the designed system's inputs of energy and material
- its internal-to-external exchanges of energy and matter – being the designed system's output of energy and materials

[See pages 64-65 of Yeang, K. (1999), *The Green Skyscraper*, Prestel (Munich, Germany)].

a. external dependencies :the site's ecosystem

In consideration of the external ecosystem and environmental interdependencies of our designed system, we start by looking at the site's ecosystem and its properties. It is evident that this site is a totally urbanized and 'zero culture' site. The site is essentially a devastated ecosystem with little of its original top soil, flora and fauna remaining.

The design strategy then is to increase biodiversity and organic mass by revegetating the site in order to rehabilitate the site's ecosystem. This is addressed by our provision of a park over the land and the adoption of a system of continuous planting up the towers (as 'vertical landscaping').

b. internal dependencies: building's operational systems

Internal interdependencies relate to building's environmental operational systems.

There are four levels of provisions for internal environmental operational systems:
- passive mode (ie. low-energy design without the use of any electro-mechanical systems)
- mixed mode (ie. partially electro-mechanically assisted systems that optimise other ambient energies of the locality)
- full mode (ie. active systems, with low energy and low environmental impacts)
- productive mode (ie. systems that generate on-site energy, eg. photovoltaic systems).

Our design strategy must be to maximise the usage of passive-mode systems (because of its lowest level of energy consumption), with the remaining energy needs to be met by mixed-mode systems, then full-mode systems and productive mode systems (where affordable).

ecological strategies

Ecological design starts with looking at the site's ecosystem and its properties. Any design that do not take these aspects of the site into consideration is essentially not an ecological approach.

A useful start is to look at the site in relation to an 'hierarchy of ecosystems' (see right).

From this hierarchy, it is evident that this site is an urban 'zero culture' site and is essentially a devastated ecosystem with little of its original top soil, flora and fauna remaining. The design approach is to rehabilitate this with organic mass to enable ecological succession to take place and to balance the existent inorganicness of this urban site.

The unique design feature of this scheme is in the well-planted facades and vegetated terraces, which have green areas that approximate the gross useable-areas (ie. GFA @ 42,820 sq m) of the rest of the building.

The vegetation areas are designed to be continuous and to ramp upwards from the ground plane to the uppermost floor in a linked landscaped ramp. The design's planted areas constitute 40,700 sq m which is @ ratio 1:1 of gross useable area to gross vegetated area.

hierarchy of ecosystems

ecosystem hierarchy	site data requirements	design strategy
ecologically mature	complete ecosystem analysis and mapping	• preserve • conserve • develop only on no-impact areas
ecologically immature	complete ecosystem analysis and mapping	• preserve • conserve • develop only on least-impact areas
ecologically simplified	complete ecosystem analysis and mapping	• preserve • conserve • increase biodiversity • develop only on low-impact areas
mixed artificial	partial ecosystem analysis and mapping	• increase biodiversity • develop on low-impact areas
mono culture	partial ecosystem analysis and mapping	• increase biodiversity • develop in areas of non-productive potential • rehabilitate ecosystem
zero culture	mapping of remaining ecosystem components (eg. hydrology, remaining trees, etc.)	• increase biodiversity and organic mass • rehabilitate ecosystem

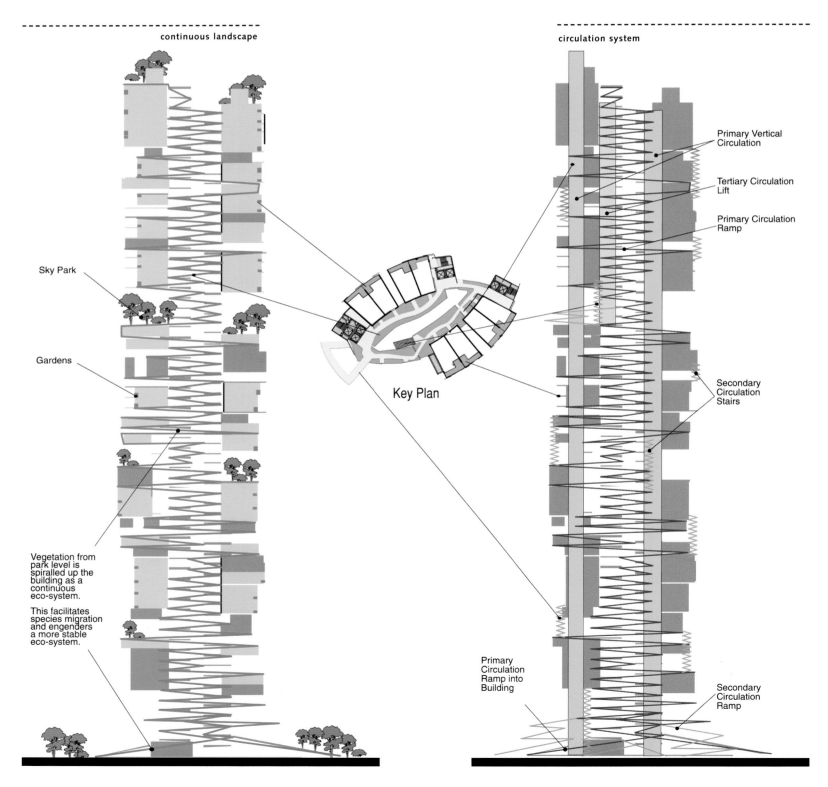

continuous landscape

Sky Park

Gardens

Vegetation from park level is spiralled up the building as a continuous eco-system.

This facilitates species migration and engenders a more stable eco-system.

Key Plan

circulation system

Primary Vertical Circulation

Tertiary Circulation Lift

Primary Circulation Ramp

Secondary Circulation Stairs

Primary Circulation Ramp into Building

Secondary Circulation Ramp

installation of
wind generators on the roof
(option)

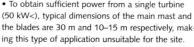

N

March / September

December

S

- -

photovoltaics system

Photovoltaics Panel

Array Meter
Array Energy

SMA 5 kW
Inverter

Inverter

Demand
Switch

REC Meters
Energy Import
Energy Export

Load Demand
Office Energy
Power Current

To The Utility
Connection

Distribution Board

Rain water
catchment
Scallops

South Facing
Photovotaic
Panels as
Rain Screen

Structural Transfer
Level as Water
Collectors

• site (ie. the roof) is termed as 'ideal' for this type of application located in city surroundings. Optimal orientation is 220° due north, as the majority of the prevailing winds come from this direction.

• The most widely used wind turbine types (ie. most economically feasible) is the upwind, three-blade horizontal axis type whether the rotor spins in front of the tower about a line parallel to the horizon. The vertical axis primarily lift type turbines, as the Darrious model shown on the sketches are not so efficient in energy production and their use can be justified as an architectural element of the integrated design for this building.

• To obtain sufficient power from a single turbine (50 kW<), typical dimensions of the main mast and the blades are 30 m and 10–15 m respectively, making this type of application unsuitable for the site.

• Small wind turbines (6–10kW) have dimensions of up to 4.5 m (blades), making them more suitable for the Bishopsgate towers. In addition, most applications use tail vanes to point the rotor into the wind.

• For obtaining approximately a 1% of the total annual building.

• Load (70MWh), the following two combinations may be chosen: 7 x 6kW units at 10,000 Mwh/unit or 5 x 10kW units at 15,000 Mwh/unit.

• Strong, rigid supports required to protect installations from strong gusts of wind.

• Noise can present a potential problem, as it can be in the range of 35–45 dB.

• Cost estimate : £75,000, assuming £1,700/kW.

• The payback period of the wind generator is approximately 23 years.

photovoltaics

- -

Photovoltaics can be used to achieve greater energy self-sufficiency.
An assessment of the environmental options for the two 50-storey mixed use residential towers are as follows:

Annual building energy use

type	area	energy (kWh/m2)	annual energy consumption(MWh)
housing	22990	200	4580
retail	8660	250	2165
			6745

Figures based on "Good Practise" energy use in the building from its owners.

installation of PV cells in SE facade
• Optimal positioning of PV cells : South oriented, tilted at an angle of 30°.

• For this project: Either cover the whole SW facade of the inclining ramp (ash shown on sketch diagrams) or cover the whole SE vertical face of the building envelope, tilted at a 30° angle, as shown on the diagram provide (panel strips placed on low level of each storey for the whole facade).

• Taking the second case, as the one covering a larger area, total area covered:
31 m x 0.5 m x (50-storeys) = 775 m²

• Potential power output, assuming PV cell efficiency of 13% : 100 kWp (kW peak).

• Potential energy generation from an 100 kWp source, assuming no shading from surrounding buildings, optimal orientation and optimal angle of tile: 70 Mwh. After allowance for surrounding buildings and actual positioning of panels (SE instead of S) : 50 Mwh.

• This represents 0.7% of the total building load.

• Cost estimate: £500,000, assuming the cost of panels as £5,000/kWp of installed power.

• The payback period of the PV installation is far in excess of the life expectancy of the units, making their installation an uneconomic solution.

• However, this is provided as a demonstration of the productive mode option for this building

c. external-to-internal exchanges of energy and matter (the inputs of energy and materials to the buildings)
This includes the embodied energy and ecological impact of the use of energy and materials in the building, which reflects the impact of production of the material or component (both globally and locally) at the source of manufacture, as well as the chain of activities leading up to its delivery to the construction site and it's eventual recycling (at the end of its useful life).

The initial design strategy is to select materials based on their potential for reuse and recycling, in order to reduce the impact on the natural environment and to positively renew, restore and enhance the natural environment. Priority is given to materials that have been previously used (ie. 'waste' from an earlier structure) or that have been recycled. This immediately lowers the overall embodied energy figures in the building's mass.

d. internal-to-external exchanges of energy and matter (systems output) (management of outputs into the environment)
This includes consideration of waste production and disposal in the life cycle of the building.

A central objective of our design method is to limit the quantity of materials and energy expelled by the building into the environment. In the selection of materials, we should avoid use of materials which pollutes the environment.

Other aspects considered are the reuse and recycling of building parts and building materials at the end of the building's useful life, and the management of consumer wastes during the use of the building (eg. through the use of a waste separator for waste recycling, etc.)

water collection and recycling system

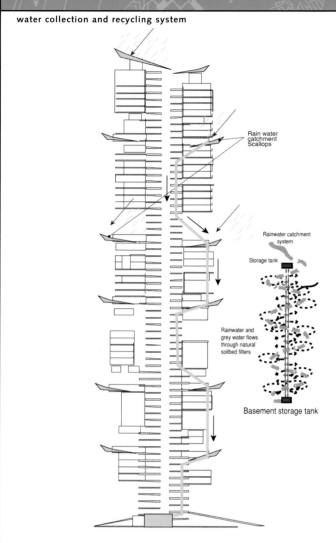

Rain water catchment Scallops

Rainwater catchment system

Storage tank

Rainwater and grey water flows through natural soilbed filters

Basement storage tank

- -

rainwater purification system

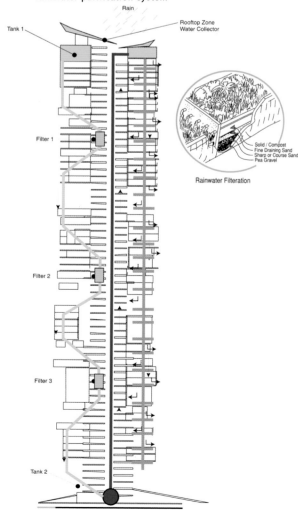

Rain

Tank 1

Rooftop Zone Water Collector

Filter 1

Rainwater Filteration

Solid / Compost
Fine Draining Sand
Sharp or Course Sand
Pea Gravel

Filter 2

Filter 3

Tank 2

key areas summary (tower A)

- housing total net area = 22,990 sq m
- shops and others total net area = 8,660 sq m
- housing units breakdown
- social housing = 41 units
- subsidised housing = 28 units
- Market rate apartments = 109 units
- Total = 178 units

building population

a housing population:
Population @ 2 rooms (average) per unit x
2 persons per room x 178 units = 712 persons

b retail / commercial population
- nett retail/commercial area = 8,660 sq m
- population @ 1 person per 10sq.m net area = 866 persons

c total population (per tower) = 712 + 866 = 1,578 persons

water recycling

Water self-sufficiency (by rainwater collection) in the tower is at 2.9%.

(Note: Recycling of grey-water will further increase the water self-sufficiency)

- Building population = 1,578 persons
- Water consumption = 60 litres/day / person
- Total requirements = 60 x 1,578 persons
  = 94,680 litres/day
  = 94.68 m³ per day x 365 day
  = 34,558 m³ per annum
- Total rainfall catchment area = 1,200 sq m.(roof) + 500 sq m
  (scallops) = 1,700 sq m
- London average rainfall/annum = 0.593 m
- Total rainwater collection = 1,008 m³ per annum
- Water self-sufficiency from rain
  water collection = 1,008 ÷ 34,558 x 100% = 2.9%

water purification

Rainwater-collection system comprises of 'roof-catchment-pan' and layers of 'scallops' located at the building's facade to catch rain-water running off its sides. Water flows through gravity-fed water-purification system, using soil-bed filters.

The filtered water accumulates in a basement storage tank, and is pumped to the upper-level storage-tank for reuse (eg. for plant-irrigation and toilet-flushing). Mains water is only here for potable needs.

raw (underground) water

Another, topical, addition to the rainwater / greywater system could be the addition of a raw water. With London's deep aquifer water level rising at an alarming rate it would be a responsible move to use some of this water for toilet flushing, etc. Investigations would of course be necessary to establish that a borehole could provide sufficient yield.

notes:

The nature of the building generally suits greywater reclamation quite well, although peoples acceptance of using greywater may prove a barrier.

Greywater can only be stored for a short time (it actually turns septic faster than blackwater). The storage would therefore be based upon a 24–48-hour turnover, although rainwater could be stored separately for longer periods allowing for the volume that would be necessary in order to maximise the water captured from infrequent rainfall.

- It is estimated that the demand for greywater would be in the region of 31,000 litres per day for each of the two towers. A separate rainwater collection tank in the region of 3x3x2 m or equivalent capacity would be recommended in conjunction with the separate greywater storage of approximately 4x4x2 m and treated storage of 2x2x2 m.

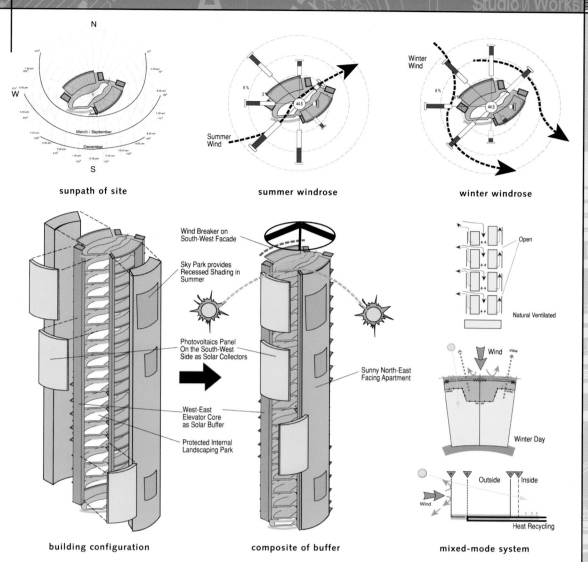

sunpath of site   summer windrose   winter windrose

building configuration   composite of buffer   mixed-mode system

Wind Breaker on South-West Facade

Sky Park provides Recessed Shading in Summer

Photovoltaics Panel On the South-West Side as Solar Collectors

West-East Elevator Core as Solar Buffer

Protected Internal Landscaping Park

Sunny North-East Facing Apartment

Open

Natural Ventilated

Winter Day

Heat Recycling

passive low-energy responses

The design here starts by optimising all the passive mode opportunities (ie. optimising the use of ambient energies of the locality) in relation to the temperate climate. The passive methods used are as follows:

a. by building configuration
The building is configured as two blocks with a weather protected central landscaped core.

b. by building orientation
The building has been orientated to maximise solar gain into the interior spaces in winter and mid-seasons, and to maximise solar shading in the summer months.
• lift cores are located at the north-east and west facades of the building to provide solar protection in summer
• during the winter months when the sun is low, central landscaped circulation area and south-east units receive maximum solar gain.

c. by facade design
The facade is designed to allow maximum light into the interior spaces while keeping out cold winds, by means of a multi-layered external wall with:
• wind breaker mesh screen to reduce inflow of strong winds
• insulated shutter doors to retain building heat at night
• large double-glazed windows
• internal shutters.

d. by landscaping and vegetation
Vegetation and landscaping within the private gardens and sky-parks building act as wind buffer while giving users a more humane environment.
In summer, vertical landscaping acts to obstructs, absorb and reflects a high percentage of solar radiation thus reducing ambient temperatures. The damp surfaces of grass and soil will also contribute to a cooler and healthier building.

energy & materials input: mixed mode concepts

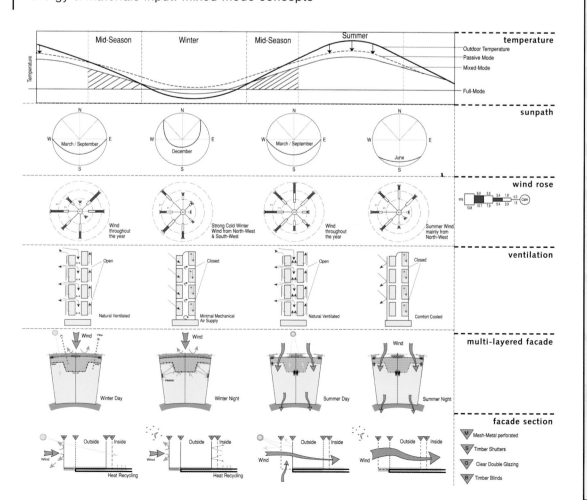

temperature
Outdoor Temperature
Passive Mode
Mixed-Mode
Full-Mode

Mid-Season   Winter   Mid-Season   Summer

sunpath

March / September   December   March / September   June

wind rose

Wind throughout the year   Strong Cold Winter Wind from North-West & South-West   Wind throughout the year   Summer Wind mainly from North-West

ventilation

Open   Closed   Open   Closed
Natural Ventilated   Minimal Mechanical Air Supply   Natural Ventilated   Comfort Cooled

multi-layered facade

Winter Day   Winter Night   Summer Day   Summer Night

facade section

Outside | Inside   Outside | Inside   Outside | Inside   Outside | Inside
Heat Recycling   Heat Recycling

M Mesh-Metal perforated
S Timber Shutters
G Clear Double Glazing
B Timber Blinds

mixed mode concepts

The basic mixed-mode strategy employed here is to encourage natural ventilation during the summer and mid-season months when the outside temperatures are conducive, and in winter, to minimise energy losses and changing over to a mechanically assisted ventilation system.

The exterior facade for the apartment units is considered from both the bioclimatic as well as an aesthetic angle for the city of London environment. The facade is multi-layered. The outermost layer is a moveable wind shield of perforated metal mesh, which can be opened to improve ventilation where required.

Next are timber folding doors which may be shut or angled to keep the terraces shielded from the sun in summer yet allow views out.

The third layer is double glazing for improved insulation properties. And lastly, all apartments are specified with adjustable timber blinds for further heat insulation.

On a windy winter day, the wind-shield is drawn but due to the low altitude of the sun, the rays penetrate the perforated mesh and on through the opened interior blinds.

On a cold winter's night, all movable layers are drawn, allowing higher heater efficiency.

On a breezy summers' day, the windshield and glass doors are opened to allow breeze into the apartment while the timber folding doors allow only desired sun to enter through the opened glass-doors, thus allowing the terrace to be enjoyed. The movable floor grating is also removed for inter-floor cooling the metal mesh acting as sun shields.

On a hot summer night, all layers are open for maximum natural-cooling and cross-ventilation.

Pedestrian
Entry

Centre

Convention
Entry

Office
Drop-Off

eler Stree

Studios

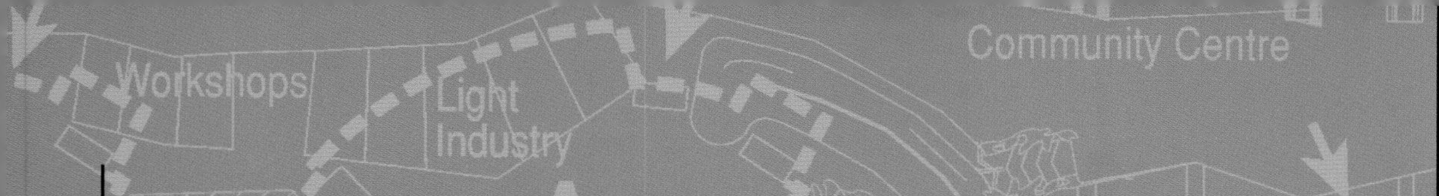

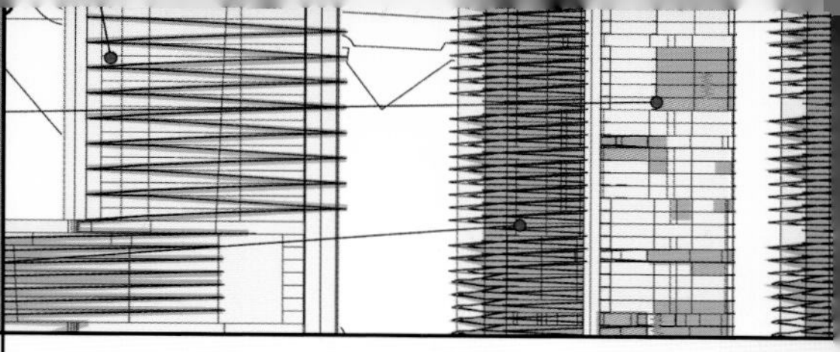

social / subsidized housing – tower A

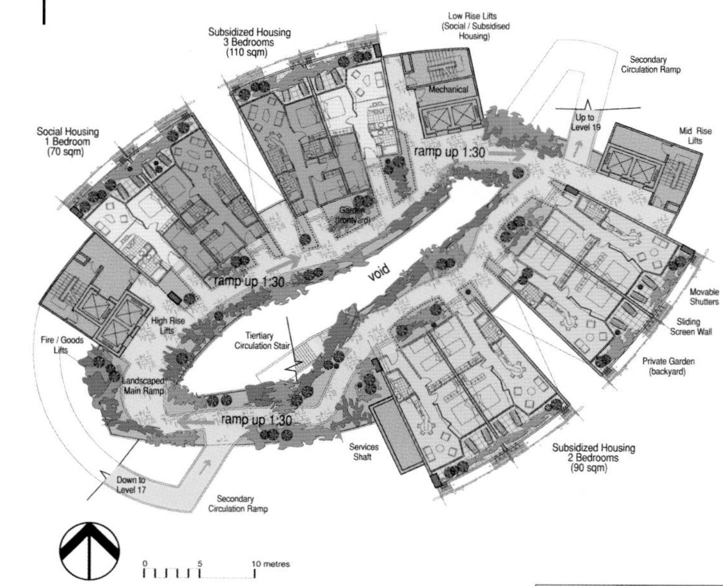

Social Housing
1 Bedroom
(70 sqm)

Subsidized Housing
3 Bedrooms
(110 sqm)

Low Rise Lifts
(Social / Subsidised
Housing)

Mechanical

ramp up 1:30

Secondary
Circulation Ramp

Up to
Level 19

Mid Rise
Lifts

ramp up 1:30

void

Movable
Shutters

Sliding
Screen Wall

High Rise
Lifts

Tertiary
Circulation Stair

Private Garden
(backyard)

Fire / Goods
Lifts

Landscaped
Main Ramp

ramp up 1:30

Services
Shaft

Subsidized Housing
2 Bedrooms
(90 sqm)

Down to
Level 17

Secondary
Circulation Ramp

0   5   10 metres

Legend
- Single Bedroom Units
- 2 Bedroom Units
- 3 Bedroom Units
- Park & Pavement
- Garden Terrace
- Walkways
- Service Core

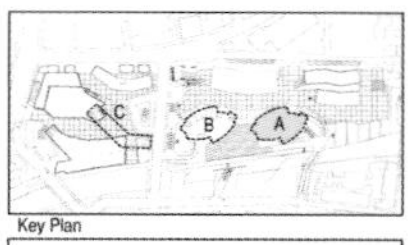

Mesh Screen
Wind Breaker

Ramp Up 1:30

Timber Shutters   Private Garden   Mesh Screen
Wind Breaker

Front
Yard

Ramp Up 1:30

Key Plan

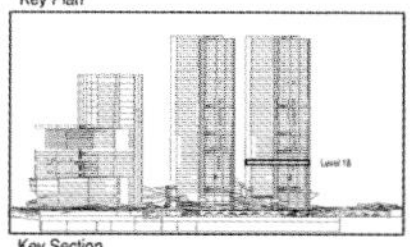

Key Section

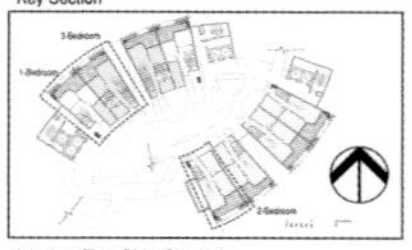

Level 18 Floor Plan (Tower A)

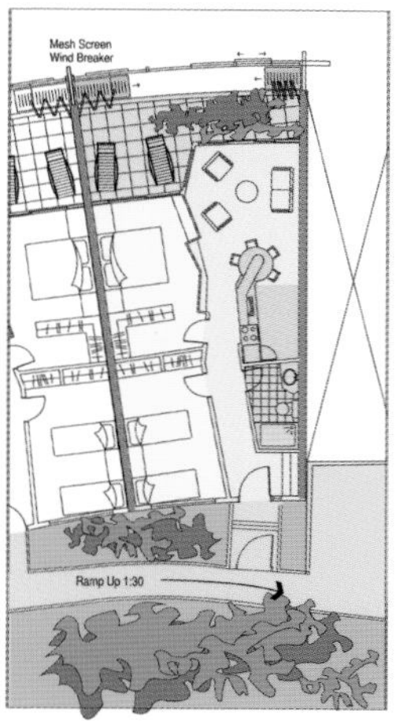

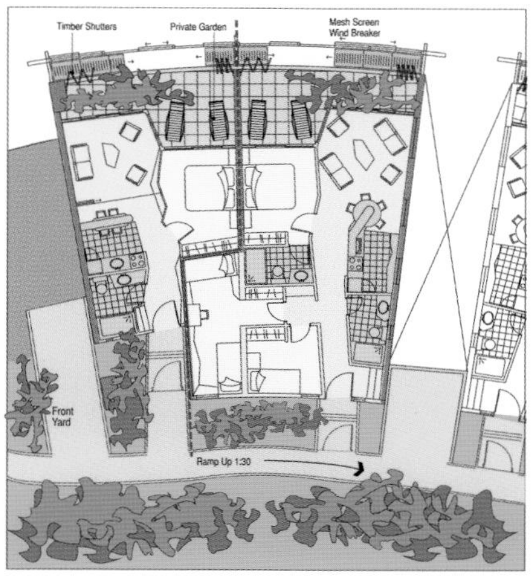

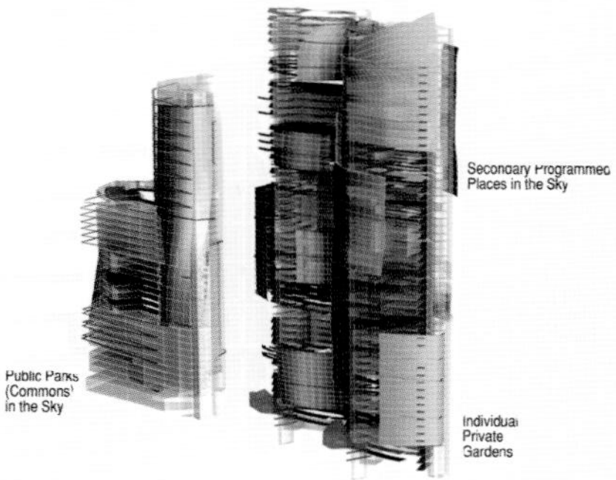

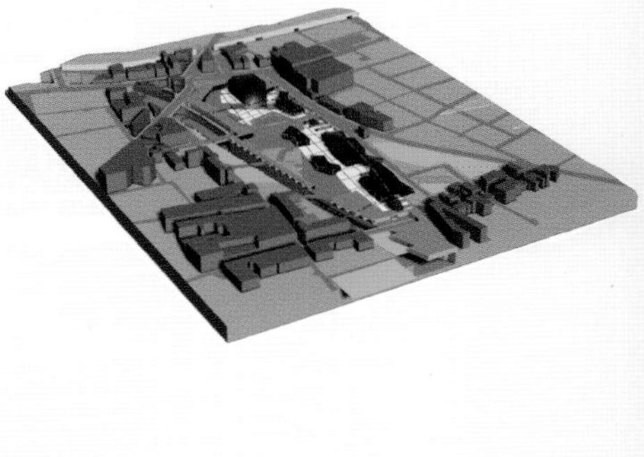

apartments - tower A

3 Bedroom Duplex
Apartment Upper Floor
(160 sqm)

Low Rise Lifts
(Social / Subsidised
Housing)

Movable Shutters

Mechanical

3 Bedroom Duplex
Apartment Lower Floor
(160 sqm)

ramp up 1:30

Mid Rise
Lifts

Sliding
Screen Wall

Lounge / Bar

Garden
(frontyard)

void

ramp up 1:30

Fire / Goods
Lifts

High Rise
Lifts

Single Bedroom
Apartment
(80sqm)

Landscaped
Main Ramp

ramp up 1:30

Private Garden
(backyard)

Secondary
Circulation Ramp

Down to
Level 40

Services
Shaft

2 Bedroom Apartment
(100 sqm)

Photovoltaic

0   5   10 metres

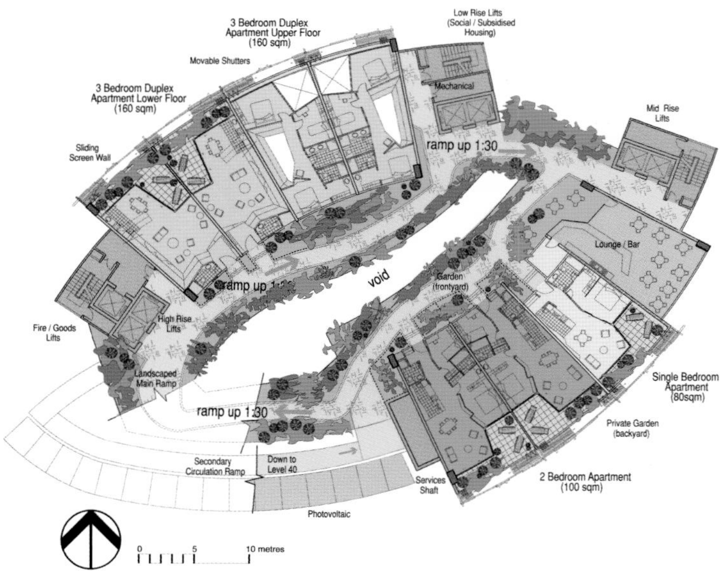

Legend
- Single Bedroom Apartments
- 2 Bedroom Apartments
- 3 Bedroom Apartments
- Lounge / Bar
- Garden Terrace
- Walkways
- Park & Pavement
- Service Core

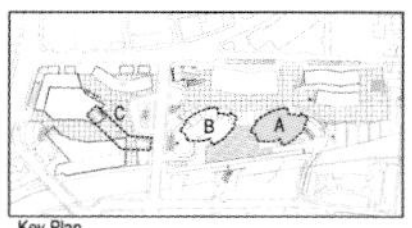

Key Plan

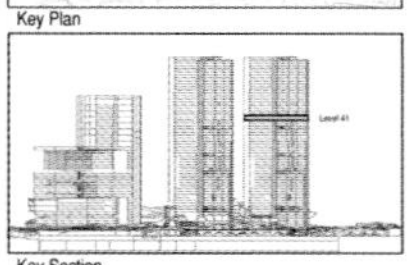

Key Section

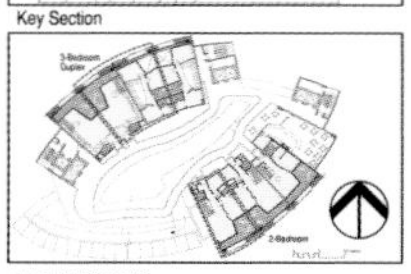

Level 41 (Tower A)

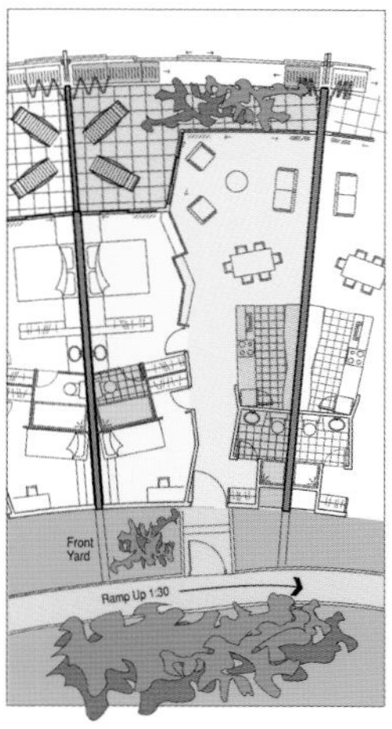

Front
Yard

Ramp Up 1:30

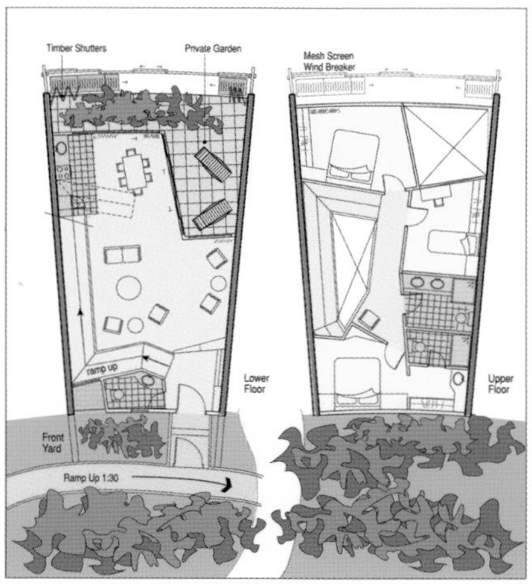

Timber Shutters   Private Garden   Mesh Screen
Wind Breaker

Front
Yard

Ramp Up 1:30

Lower
Floor

Upper
Floor

Secondary Programmed
Places in the Sky

Public Parks
(Commons) in the Sky

Individual
Private
Gardens

upper park level

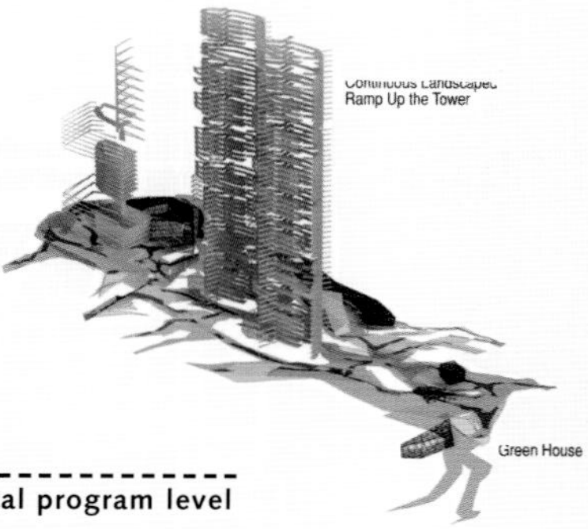

Continuous Landscaped
Ramp Up the Tower

Green House

ecological program level

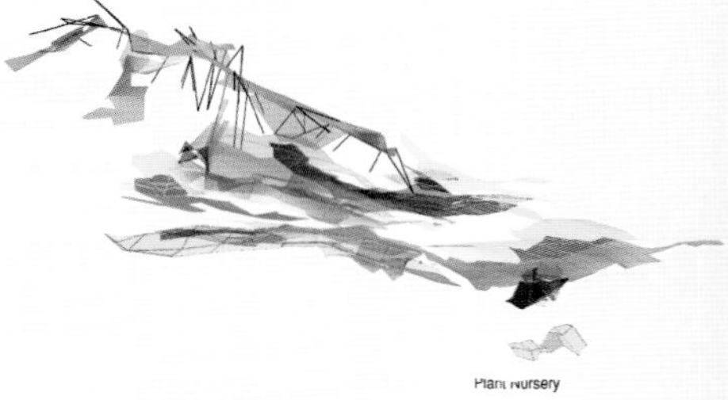

Plant Nursery

lower park level

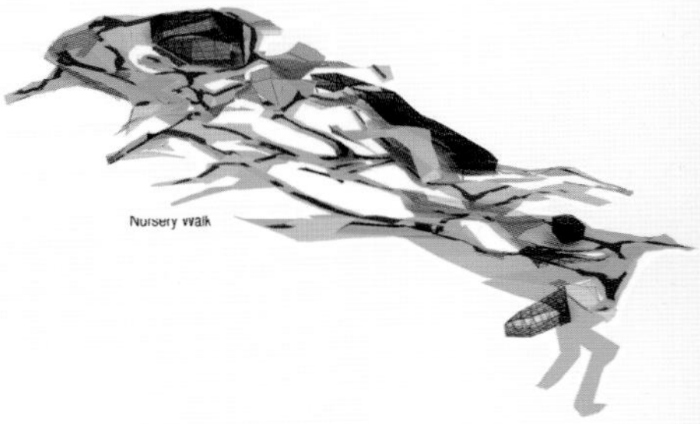

Nursery Walk

ground level

Public Program & Units Legend

1. Open Aviary / Bird Sanctuary
2. Aviary Complex Shop
3. Research Laboratory
4. Observation Deck
5. Urban Agriculture
6. Commons / Squares Gardens
7. Pub
8. Creche
9. Language School
10. Newsagents
11. Laundrette
12. Cafe
13. Sandwich Shop

14. Post Office
15. Bank
16. Bank Tellers
17. William Hills
18. Hardware Store
19. Electronics / IT
20. IT Knowledge Centre
21. Retail General
22. Library / Bookshop
23. Restaurant
24. Mini-Market
25. Charity Shop

A. Social Housing
   1-Bed
   2-Bed
B. Subsidised Housing
   2-Bed
   3-Bed
C. Apartments
   1-Bed
   2-Bed
   3-Bed
D. Penthouse

Residential
Commercial
Landscape / Park
Walkways
Service Core

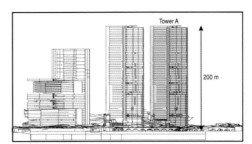

Key Section

Tower A

200 m

Level 1 +0.00
Level 2 +6.00
Level 3 +9.50
Level 4 +12.60
Level 5 +15.70
Level 6 +18.50
Level 7 +21.90

Level 11 +34.30
Level 12 +37.40
Level 13 +40.50
Level 14 +43.60
Level 15 +46.70
Level 16 +49.80
Level 17 +52.90

Level 21 +65.30
Level 22 +68.40
Level 23 +71.50
Level 24 +74.60
Level 25 +77.700
Level 26 +80.80
Level 27 +83.90

Level 31 +96.30
Level 32 +99.40
Level 33 +102.50
Level 34 +105.60
Level 35 +108.70
Level 36 +111.80
Level 37 +114.90

Level 41 +139.70
Level 42 +142.80
Level 43 +145.90
Level 44 +149.00
Level 45 +152.10
Level 46 +155.20
Level 47 +158.30

Level 51 +170.70
Level 52 +173.80
Level 53 +176.90
Level 54 +180.00
Level 55 +183.10
Level 56 +186.20
Level 57 +189.30

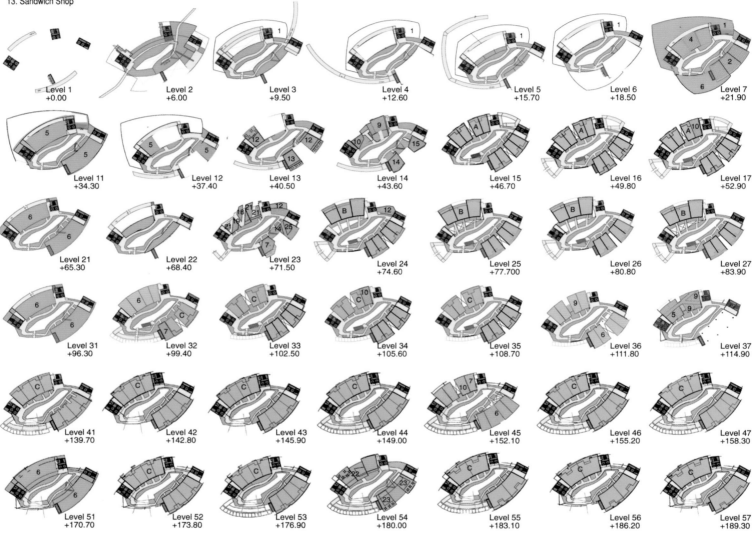

level 2 and 3

A central park is located above the street level, accessible by landscaped ramps. The park and high-level planting on the towers serve as 'green lungs' for the locality. The park also extends as 'green-fingers' into neighbouring plots through high-level bridge linkages, providing greater urban connectivity and providing safe vehicle-free pedestrian routes via bicycle lanes and footpaths.

Within the park are shops, recreational spaces, urban agriculture and plant nurseries (within glass house enclosures) and also an aviary at the base of the towers.

The park is continued up the towers via gradual spiraling landscaped ramps, making the transition from ground to tower as seamless as possible.

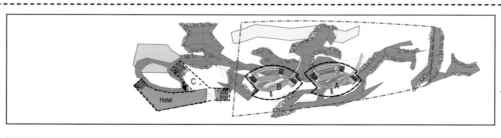

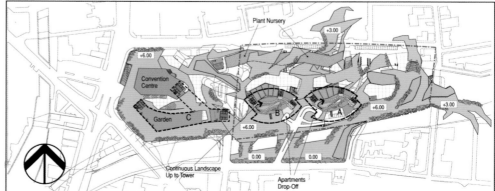

level 2 park level

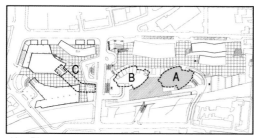

Key Plan

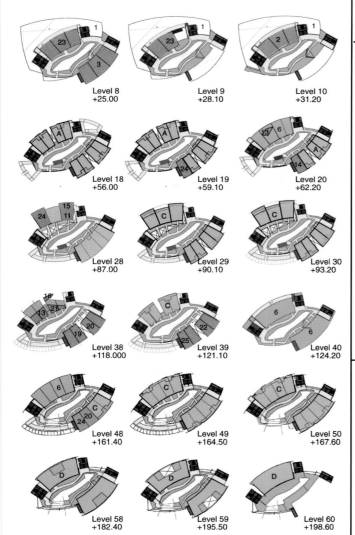

Level 8
+25.00

Level 9
+28.10

Level 10
+31.20

Level 18
+56.00

Level 19
+59.10

Level 20
+62.20

Level 28
+87.00

Level 29
+90.10

Level 30
+93.20

Level 38
+118.000

Level 39
+121.10

Level 40
+124.20

Level 48
+161.40

Level 49
+164.50

Level 50
+167.60

Level 58
+182.40

Level 59
+195.50

Level 60
+198.60

Key Plan

Key Section

Legend

 Offices & Hotel

Retail

 Park

Service Core

 Green House

Basement Car Park

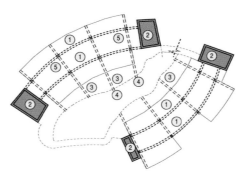

transfer structure floor

① Deep (storey height) steel trusses span between lift cores/service cores.

② R/C lift/service cores pick up load from transfer trusses and transmit loads to foundations.

③ Secondary trusses cantilever to edge or walkway zone.

④ Macaloy hanger rods support walkway slabs for 10th floors zone.

⑤ Columns pick up floor loads from 10-floor zone and transmit to transfer trusses.

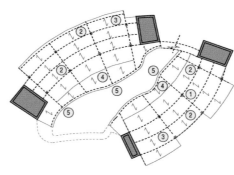

typical floor plan

① Rolled steel UB sections per as primary floor beams cantilever from columns to slab edge.

② Rolled steel UB secondary floor beams approx. 6.0m c/c.

③ Prefabricated timber floor panels span onto secondary UB's. Fire protection will be received.

④ Precast hollow core units form structural slab for walkway.

⑤ Walkway slab supported by macaloy hanger rods from transfer floor above.

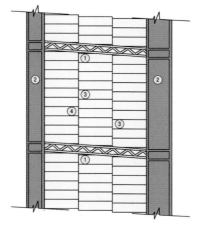

typical '10-Floor zone' & transfer levels

① Deep (storey height) steel trusses span between lift/services cores.

② R/C lift/service cores transmit loads from transfer trusses to foundations.

③ Steel columns (UC) pick up floor loads from "10-floor zone" transfer to transfer trusses.

④ Macaloy hanger rods support walkways.

structure
by Buro Happold Consulting Engineers (London)

The structural system for a building of this height is governed more by lateral (wind) loads than by vertical (gravity) loads. The concept of an internal frame with braced cores may not be the most effective solution for buildings of this height. It is often most efficient to engage perimeter structures such as the facade to provide bracing.

The proposed structural system has transfer floors at every (say) 10th level of the building, which distribute the gravity loads out to the cores. The transfer floors can occur concurrently with the utility / plant floors, so not taking up valuable public space. The cores would act as large hollow columns.

The four cores would then become the 'legs' of the building. By carrying the vertical loads out at the perimeter of the structure it is inherently more stable for lateral loads. Note that this couples the two halves of the building structurally. The cores are to be constructed from high strength reinforced concrete. 10–15 square metres cross-sectional area of concrete would be required for each core at the lower floors.

This 'megastructure' frame, made up of the four 'legs' and the transfer floors at every 10th level, would then form the multistorey building platform for hanging / supporting the various shapes of floorplate and the sloping levels. These 10-storey infill floors would be built after the main frame, and could be modifies / rebuilt at a later date without disturbing the main frame.

The 'megastructure' frame would be diagonally braced. Foundations for structures this size are difficult in London because of the large depths of clay. Piles for the building would be 40–50 metres long in order to bear on granular sands. In order to limit settlements these are likely to be as grouted. A large cluster of piles will be required under each leg, approximately twice the area of the core footprint. The capping slab will be several metres deep.

Not having a deep basement makes resisting the lateral loads more difficult in the foundations, increasing the number of piles required. Constructing these pile groups close to the existing railway lines while keeping them in operation would be very difficult. Consequently the buildings are located so that at least the 'legs' are as far away from the rail lines as possible.

specifications and ecological benefits

substructure – RC piles
structure – structural steel framing
  • enables mechanical joint connections
    (facilitates reuse and recycling at end of building's useful life)
  • speed and efficiency of construction
  • light (reduces structure load)
  • enables large spans to be achieved
RC lift cores
flooring system – fire-rated timber floor cassettes
  • low-embodied energy
  • 100% recyclable
  • easy assembly on site
external walls – plastered and painted AAC blocks
  • low-energy usage (aerated autoclaved concrete)
  • low raw material consumption
  • high insulation value (reduces cooling and heating costs)
  • light (reduces structure load)
  • no environmentally toxic byproducts
windows – recycled aluminium and glass double-glazing unit
  • high insulative value
  • recycled aluminium reduces embodied energy
  • large windows improve natural lighting
doors – timber-framed, plywood flushed doors
external floor – generally terra cotta tiles and cement screed combination
internal wall – timber stud wall with gypsum partitions board lining
  • low-embodied energy
internal floor – generally carpet
ceiling – mineral fibre ceiling (social housing)
  • high recycled material composition
  • plasterboard ceiling (others)

programmatic distribution

horizontal and vertical zoning of land use

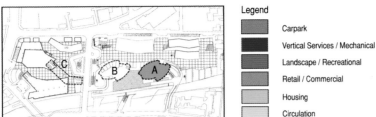

Key Plan

Legend

- Carpark
- Vertical Services / Mechanical
- Landscape / Recreational
- Retail / Commercial
- Housing
- Circulation

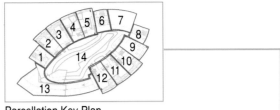

Parcellation Key Plan

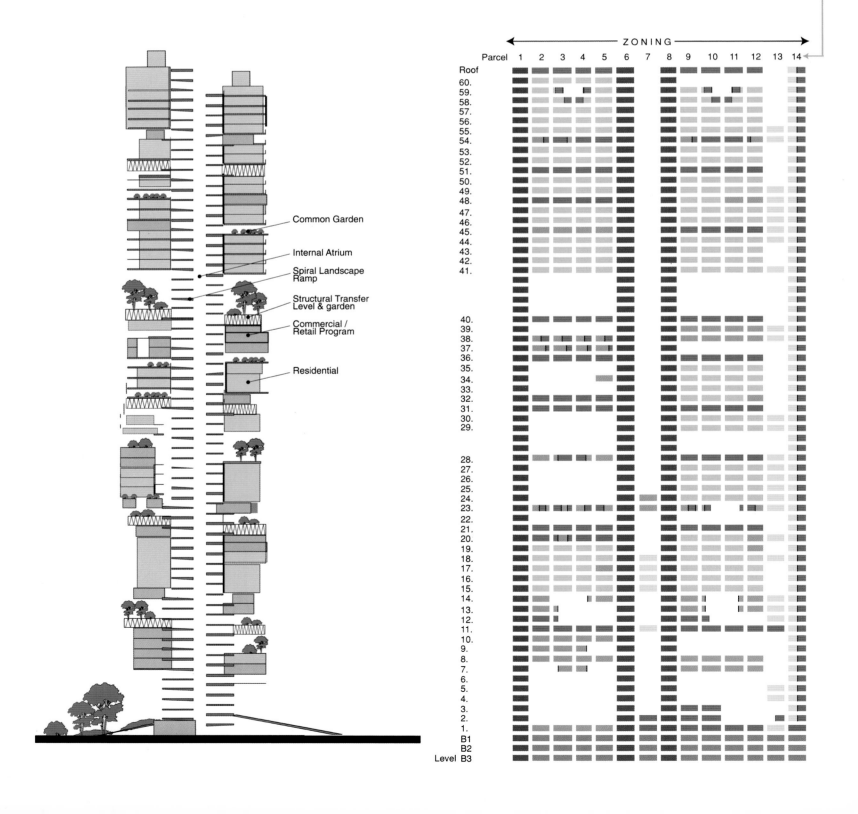

Common Garden

Internal Atrium

Spiral Landscape Ramp

Structural Transfer Level & garden

Commercial / Retail Program

Residential

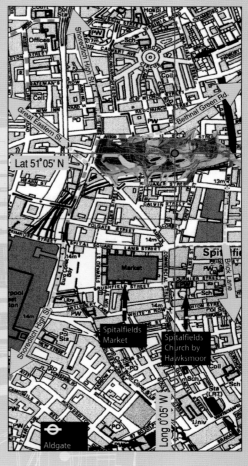

marketplace

Lat 51° 05' N

Long 0° 05' W

Aldgate

vehicular traffic and pedestrian routes

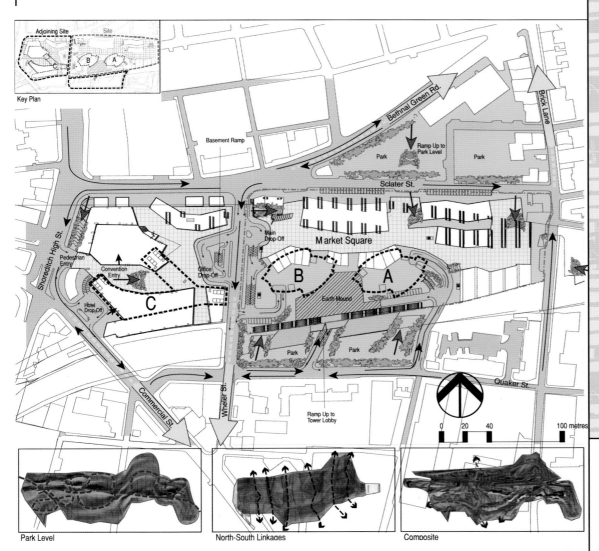

Key Plan

Adjoining Site | Site

Bethnal Green Rd.

Brick Lane

Basement Ramp

Park

Ramp Up to Park Level

Park

Sclater St.

Shoreditch High St.

Pedestrian Entry

Main Drop-Off

Market Square

Convention Entry

Office Drop-Off

B

A

Hotel Drop-Off

C

Earth Mound

Park

Park

Commercial St.

Wheler St.

Quaker St.

Ramp Up to Tower Lobby

0   20   40   100 metres

Park Level

North-South Linkages

Composite

vehicular access

The main vehicular access for the residential zone shall be via the south, from Quaker Street. A new ramped bridge is proposed across the existing railway viaduct to the residential drop-off lobby.

The main vehicular access into the adjoining commercial site is via Wheler Street.

car-parking

Public and resident carparking shall be located in basements. The lowest basement level shall approximate the level of the lower rail track. Limited roadside parking is also provided on Sclatter Street.

The location of the new East London underground railway station within the site will encourage residents and workers to make journeys to and fro from this development by public transport. Coupled with close proximity to basic amenities within the site, it is anticipated that demand for car-parking spaces in this development will be reduced.

pedestrian

The northern, western and eastern borders of the site is envisaged to be 'porous', allowing pedestrian easy flow into the retail and commercial areas within.

The design is 'pedestrian-friendly' and provides for easy and pleasant journey by foot and bicycle within and through the development.

The roof level of the existing goodsyard structure is a park, with high-level landscaped links to adjoining parcels and public parks.

Legend

Plaza

Vegetation

Park & Pavement

Road

Landscape Ramp Up to Park Level

Traffic Direction

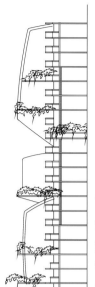

Elephant and Castle, London

The massive regeneration project for the Elephant and Castle, includes three Eco-Towers by Yeang on the east, and a central transportation – railway interchange, with a further project by Foster and Partners to the west, surrounding a major plaza. The overall project also incorporates social housing, which is financed by revenue from the towers, intended for private ownership. As well as a huge shopping and leisure facility, and other communal provisions, the development envisages three major parks.

Yeang's three buildings, known as the **Garden Towers**, represent his first competition success in London that may form a built proposition. In most major respects these towers, which vary in height between 12 and 35 storeys, repeat much of the concept of the Bishopsgate Towers, as a precedent. That is to say, that building configuration, orientation, façade design and landscaping policy directly reflect the earlier model. However, in this instance the lifts and staircores are brought together into a more compact arrangement, but again within a centralised, landscaped, access-galleried atrium. The typical floor-plan, for instance of Eco-Tower 1, is again a two-sided arrangement, which offers a variety of unit-orientation and outward views. To the overall form, in addition to the **skycourts and apartment** balconies, Yeang has added generous **'sky-pod'** volumes for communal facilities and the summit incorporates a major **winter garden**, which outwardly signals the building's ecological presence.

Key Plan

B ——— B

winter garden

apartment balcony

skycourt

transfer floor with public areas

elevated railway

ground

retail

retail

basement parking

owner Southwark Land Regeneration Plc
location Elephant and Castle, London – building on the west side of the railway line
latitude 51.3 °N
nos of storeys tower 1 – 35 storeys
tower 2 & 3 – 12 storeys
date start 2000 (design)
completion date –
areas (tower 1) total gross area 276,304 sq ft
total net area 232,095 sq ft
total area of plantation & circulation 44,209 sq ft
areas (tower 2&3) total gross area 95,765 sq ft
total nett area 79,485 sq ft
total area of plantation & circulation 16,280 sq ft
site area 170 acres

development brief • The Elephant and Castle development encompasses a vision to transform over 180 acres in South Central London into a scheme that will provide:
• over 1 million sq ft shopping and leisure
• 3,500 new homes for sale
• over 1,100 new social homes
• new public transport interchange
• 500,000 sq ft of offices
• one hotel
• 800,000 sq ft key worker accommodation
• new community facilities
• three major parks (one of 15 acres)

design features • The Elephant and Castle regeneration project was jointly designed by a number of consultants. A new railway interchange divides the site into two. The west side of the railway track was designed by Foster & Partners and the residential apartments on the east side of the railway track by T.R. Hamzah & Yeang, HTA Architects and Benoy Limited. Benoy Limited designed the retail spaces while T.R. Hamzah & Yeang designed the towers with HTA Architects. The brief calls for the design of three Eco-Towers for residential use, above a retail and commercial area. Our design addresses these issues as follows:

social sustainability
a. concept – 'city-in-the-sky'
The design takes the model of a general geographical area of a city, with its inherent systems, zoning and social infrastructure and inverts it into skyscraper buildings. The skyscraper and its retail and commercial base is seen as a microcosm of the city, containing within itself the inherent elements of a city block, ie. parks, shops, entertainment centers, community facilities and housing etc. The 'City-in-the Sky' concept provides for:
• opportunities for local employment through mixture of use, both on ground and upper levels
• healthy mix of residents within the same building. Through 'vertical zoning', resident types are grouped according to accommodation preferences (single units, family units, luxury apartments), yet common facilities (eg. parks, shopping streets, etc.) are shared
• close proximity to basic amenities, such as the local grocery store, postal boxes, chemist, etc. These are all located within the ground development and/or within the tower.
• a healthy landscaped environment, with spatial progressions of public open spaces (parks in the sky) to semi-private (entrance courts) to private open spaces (balconies).

b. orientation
The towers make the most of a southerly aspect to catch the winter sun. The views of the city to the north are also maximised. The internal void and walkways capture the sun, creating a series of light wells to brighten the service areas in the apartments. The wings of the building allow cool breezes in the summer to enter the central atrium while shielding it from the winter wind.

c. users
Mixture of residents from different ages, incomes, occupations and family structures are accommodated by the provision of a variety of accommodation types: studio apartments, two-room apartments and penthouses.

elephant and castle eco-towers

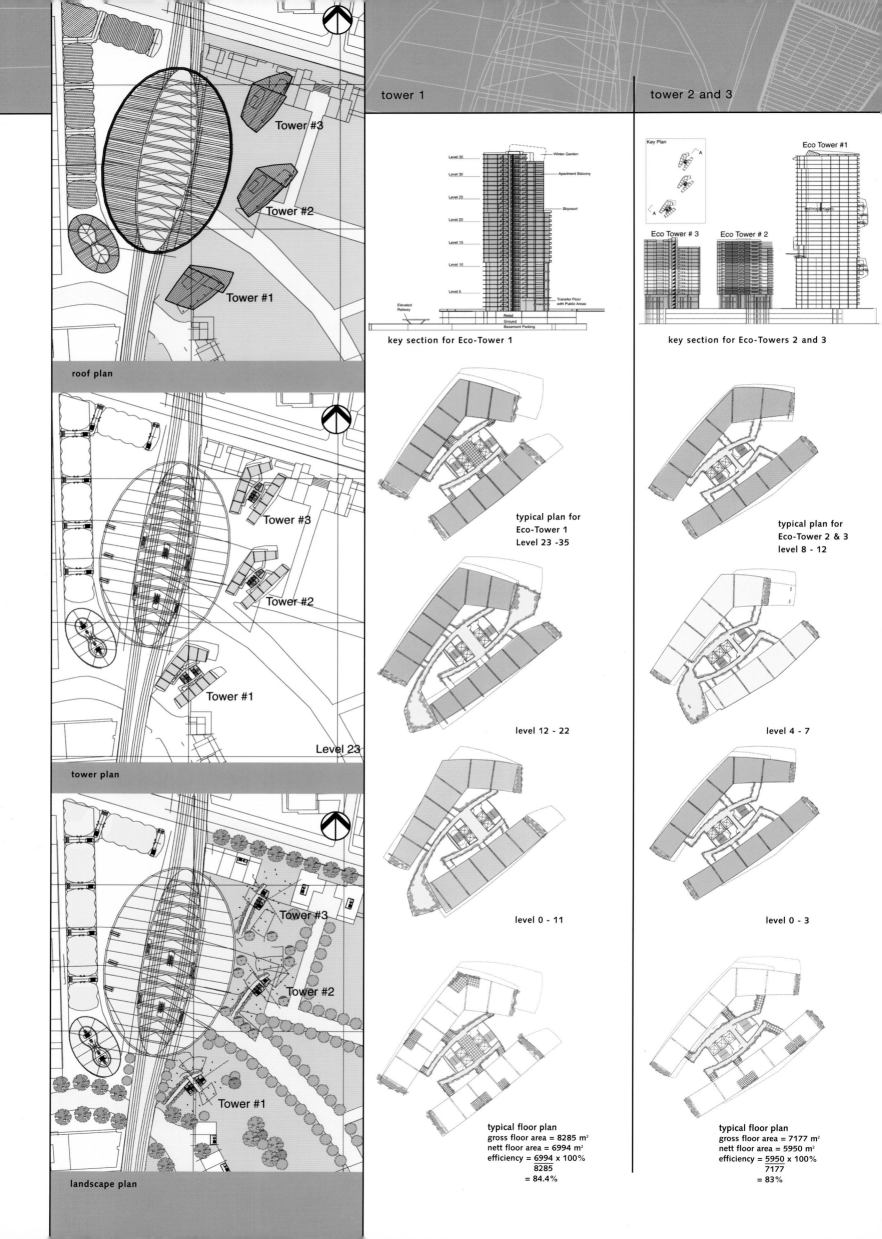

roof plan

tower plan

Level 23

landscape plan

tower 1

key section for Eco-Tower 1

typical plan for
Eco-Tower 1
Level 23 -35

level 12 - 22

level 0 - 11

typical floor plan
gross floor area = 8285 m²
nett floor area = 6994 m²
efficiency = 6994 x 100%
8285
= 84.4%

tower 2 and 3

key section for Eco-Towers 2 and 3

typical plan for
Eco-Tower 2 & 3
level 8 - 12

level 4 - 7

level 0 - 3

typical floor plan
gross floor area = 7177 m²
nett floor area = 5950 m²
efficiency = 5950 x 100%
7177
= 83%

The singular difference here, contrasted with the Bishopsgate project, is the design of regular floor levels instead of the spiralling ramped solution. Similarly, the apartment floor plans have been rationalised into a rectilinear format, with **winter-gardens** or balconies, similar to the Bishopsgate principle.

What is in evidence here, is the accomplished virtuosity of Yeang's form-giving process, and the essential simplicity that results from this discipline. The Eco-Towers are a genuine reflection of Yeang's evolving **ecological architecture**, which incorporates and develops its own aesthetic - largely that of an **elevated landscape**, and a visible social-openness. Providing that the buildings are **built** with a matching standard of constructional quality and materiality, the Eco-Towers are set to achieve landmark status, within London's regeneration.

Eco-Tower 1

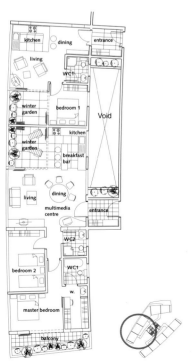

Eco-Tower 2 & 3

d. uses
The development will incorporate housing, retail, leisure, communal facilities and commerce on the retail levels and up the tower. The location of housing in close proximity to employment, retail, leisure and community facilities will reduce reliance on public transport.

e. open space requirements / outdoor space
The design seeks to re-create conditions on the ground up-in-the-sky, with features such as an entrance lobby, light wells and balconies for every unit and shared secondary and tertiary landscaped open spaces and sky pods within groups of housing in the form of sky courts and communal pods. The rooftop of the retail is designed as a roof garden.

f. relationship to immediate context
Urban connectivity is a key concept in the design proposal. The proposal here includes a high level bridge over the proposed railway station and direct connections onto the garden terrace and into the retail zones.

environmental sustainability
The approach to environmental sustainability here is a holistic approach, ie. it takes into account the entirety of the systems and functions of the ambient environment.
It is contended that ecological design must consider the following aspects of a building:
• its external interdependencies, consisting of the designed system's relations to its external environment and ecosystems
• its internal interdependencies, being the designed system's internal relations, activities and operations,
• its external-to-internal exchanges of energy and matter – being the designed system's inputs of energy and material
• its internal-to-external exchanges of energy and matter – being the designed system's output of energy and materials.
[see pages 64–65 of Yeang, K. (1999), *The Green Skyscraper*, Prestel (Munich, Germany)].

a. external dependencies: the site's ecosystem
In consideration of the external ecosystem and environmental interdependencies of our designed system, we start by looking at the site's ecosystem and its properties. It is evident that this site is a totally urbanized and 'zero culture' site. The site is essentially a devastated ecosystem with little of its original topsoil, flora and fauna remaining.

The design strategy then is to increase biodiversity and organic mass by revegetating the site in order to rehabilitate the site's ecosystem. This is addressed by our provision of a park over the land and the adoption of a system of continuous planting up the towers (as 'vertical landscaping').

ecosystem hierarchy	site data requirements	design strategy
ecologically mature	complete ecosystem analysis and mapping	• preserve • conserve • develop only on non-impact areas
ecologically immature	complete ecosystem analysis and mapping	• preserve • conserve • develop only on least-impact areas
ecologically simplified	complete ecosystem analysis and mapping	• preserve • conserve • increase biodiversity • develop only on low-impact areas
mixed-artificial	partial ecosystem analysis and mapping	• increase biodiversity • develop on low-impact areas
monoculture	partial ecosystem analysis and mapping	• increase biodiversity • develop in areas of non-productive potential • rehabilitate ecosystem
zeroculture	mapping of remaining ecosystem components (eg. hydrology, remaining trees etc)	• increase biodiversity and organic mass • rehabilitate ecosystem

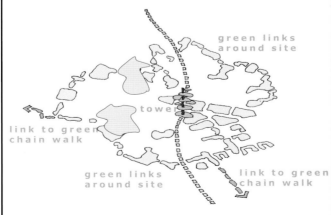

green links around site

link to green chain walk

tower

green links around site

link to green chain walk

	input used in site rehabilitation, recolonisation by species, site recovery		
ecological interactions in the recovery of the designed systems	input used in recovery processes		inputs in the recovery phase
	input used in preparation for recycling, reuse, reconstruction, and/or disposal and safe discharge into the environment		
	input used in removal demolition		
ecological interactions in the operation and consumption of the designed systems	input used in operation of built system, maintenance, ecosystem protection measures, system modifications, etc		inputs in the operation phase
	input used in construction and site modification		inputs in the construction phase
ecological interactions in the provision of the physical substance and form of the designed systems of the designed systems	input used in distribution, storage, transport to site		
	inputs used in the production of the building elements and components (including extraction, preparation, manufacturing processes, etc)		inputs in the production phase

drawings by HTA Architects

overall embodied energy and embodied CO² for various building types

building type	embodied energy delivered GJ/m²	embodied energy primary GJ/m²	embodied CO₂ kg CO₂/m²
office	5–10	10–18	500–1000
house	4.5–8	9–13	800–1200
flat	5–10	10–18	500–1000
industrial	4–7	7–12	400–70
road	1–5	2–10	130–650

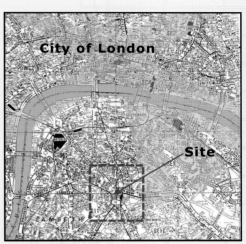

site plan

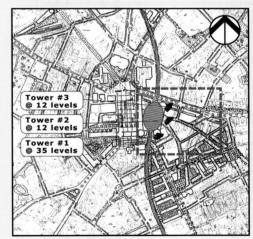

Tower #3 @ 12 levels

Tower #2 @ 12 levels

Tower #1 @ 35 levels

context plan 1: 7,500

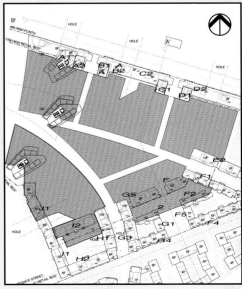

retail plan

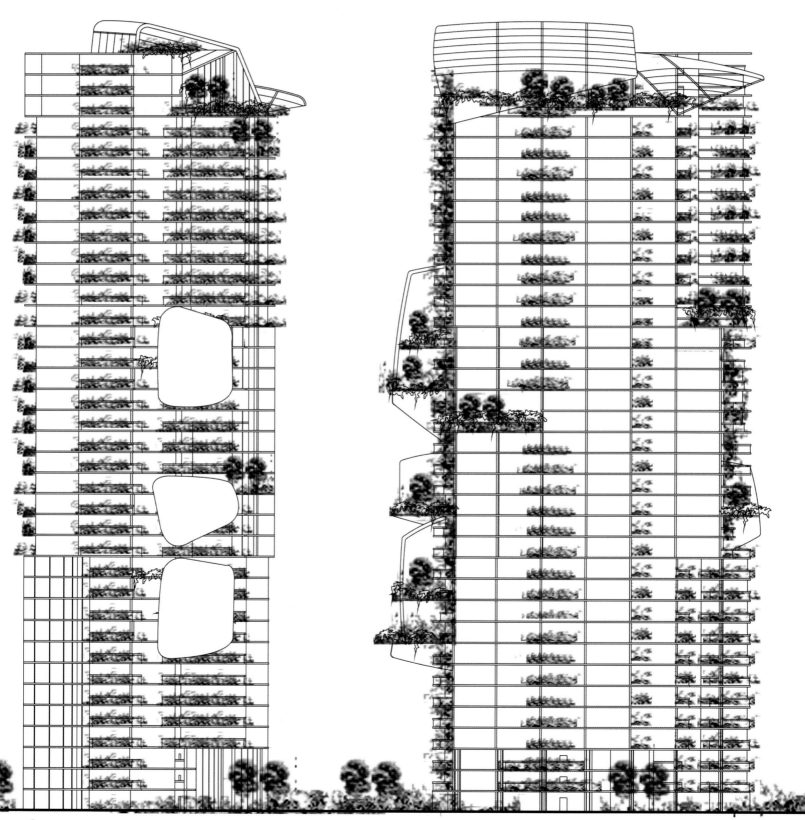

scale 1: 500

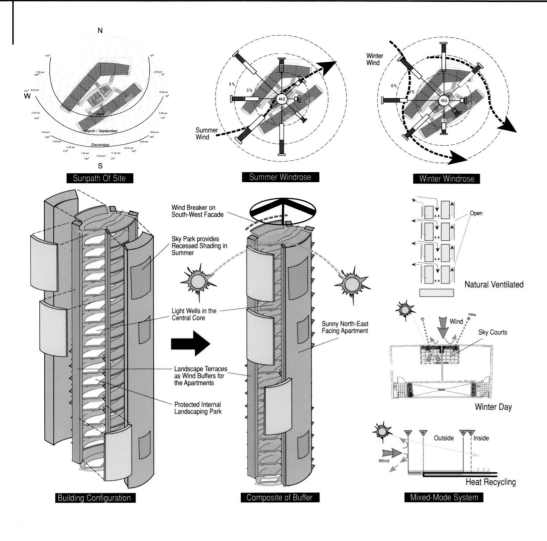

N

W — S

Sunpath Of Site

Summer Windrose

Winter Windrose

Winter Wind

Summer Wind

Wind Breaker on South-West Facade

Sky Park provides Recessed Shading in Summer

Light Wells in the Central Core

Sunny North-East Facing Apartment

Landscape Terraces as Wind Buffers for the Apartments

Protected Internal Landscaping Park

Building Configuration

Composite of Buffer

Open

Natural Ventilated

Wind — view — Sky Courts

Winter Day

Outside — Inside

Wind — Heat Recycling

Mixed-Mode System

b internal dependencies: building's operational systems

Internal interdependencies relate to building's environmental operational systems.

There are four levels of provisions for internal environmental operational systems:

- passive mode (ie. low-energy design without the use of any electro-mechanical systems)
- mixed mode (ie. partially electro-mechanically assisted systems that optimise other ambient energies of the locality)
- full mode (ie. active systems, with low energy and low environmental impacts)
- productive mode (ie. systems that generate on-site energy, eg. photovoltaic systems).

Our design strategy must be to maximise the usage of passive-mode systems (because of its lowest level of energy consumption), with the remaining energy needs to be met by mixed-mode systems, then full-mode systems and productive mode systems (where affordable).

types of modes of operational systems

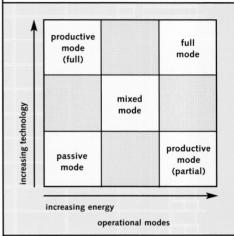

productive mode (full)		full mode
	mixed mode	
passive mode		productive mode (partial)

increasing technology

increasing energy

operational modes

comfort ranges of different modes

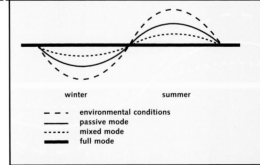

winter — summer

- – – environmental conditions
- —— passive mode
- ····· mixed mode
- ▬▬ full mode

passive low-energy responses

The design here starts by optimising all the passive mode opportunities (ie. optimising the use of ambient energies of the locality) in relation to the temperate climate. The passive methods used are as follows:

a. by building configuration

The building is configured as two blocks with a weather-protected central landscaped core.

b. by building orientation

The building has been orientated to maximise solar gain into the interior spaces in winter and mid-seasons, and to maximise solar shading in the summer months.

- during the winter months when the sun is low, the central landscaped circulation area and south-east units receive maximum solar gain
- communal skycourts and pods are positioned to catch the south sun.

c. by landscaping and vegetation

Vegetation and landscaping within the private gardens and sky-parks in the buildings act as a wind buffer while giving users a more humane environment.

In summer, vertical landscaping acts to obstruct, absorb and reflect a high percentage of solar radiation thus reducing ambient temperatures. The damp surfaces of grass and soil will also contribute to a cooler and healthier building.

mixed mode concept

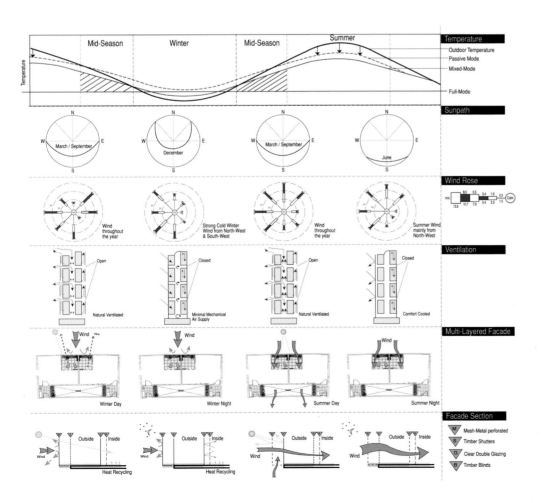

Mid-Season — Winter — Mid-Season — Summer

Temperature
Outdoor Temperature
Passive Mode
Mixed-Mode
Full-Mode

Sunpath

N — March / September — E
N — December — E
N — March / September — E
N — June — E

Wind Rose

Wind throughout the year

Strong Cold Winter Wind from North-West & South-West

Wind throughout the year

Summer Wind mainly from North-West

Ventilation

Open — Closed — Open — Closed

Natural Ventilated — Minimal Mechanical Air Supply — Natural Ventilated — Comfort Cooled

Multi-Layered Facade

Wind — Wind — Wind — Wind

Winter Day — Winter Night — Summer Day — Summer Night

Facade Section

Outside — Inside

Wind — Heat Recycling

M Mesh-Metal perforated
S Timber Shutters
G Clear Double Glazing
B Timber Blinds

project teams + collaborators

Menara Mesiniaga

Project Architect	• Too Ka Hoe
Design Architects	• Heng Jee Seng, Seow Ji Nee
Project Team	• Michael Simmonds, Don Ismail Allan, Emmy Lim, Yusoff Zainal Abidin, Yeoh Gim Seong, Yap Sait Lin, Azmin Abdullah, Ooi Poh Lye
C&S Engineers	• Reka Perunding Sdn Bhd
M&E Engineers	• Norman Disney & Young Sdn Bhd
Quantity Surveyor	• Baharuddin Ali & Low Sdn

Menara TA1

Project Architects	• Ahmad Kamil Mustapha, Seow Ji Nee, Chong Voon Wee
Design Architects	• Normala Ariffin, Paul Mathews
Project Team	• Ken Wong, Ooi Poh Lye
C&S Engineers	• Reka Perunding Sdn Bhd
M&E Engineers	• Jurutera Perunding LC Sdn Bhd
Quantity Surveyor	• Baharuddin Ali & Low Sdn

Central Plaza

Project Architects	• Yew Ai Choo, Lim Piek Boon
Design Architects	• Rachel Athis, Azahari Muhammad
Project Team	• Ng Wai Tuck, Paul Brady, Tim Mellor, Russell Harnnet
C&S Engineers	• Reka Perunding Sdn Bhd
M&E Engineers	• Jurutera Perunding LC Sdn Bhd
Quantity Surveyor	• Baharuddin Ali & Low Sdn

Casa Del Sol

Project Architects	• Andy Chong, Chong Voon Wee
Design Architects	• Heng Jee Seng, Mariani Abdullah
Project Team	• Ooi Poh Lye, Rahimah Lassim
C&S Engineers	• H P Lee & Rakan-Rakan
M&E Engineers	• Suffian Lee Perunding
Quantity Surveyor	• Kumpulan Kuantikonsult
Landscape Architect	• Malik Lip & Associates

Hitechniaga Tower

Project Architect	• Sacha Noordin
Design Architect	• Sacha Noordin
Project Team	• Ooi Poh Lye
Model Maker	• Technibuilt Sdn Bhd

MBf Tower

Project Architect	• Lawrence Lim
Design Architect	• Haslina Ali
Project Team	• Don Ismail Allan, Ooi Poh Lye
C&S Engineers	• Reka Perunding Sdn Bhd
M&E Engineers	• Jurutera Perunding LC Sdn Bhd
Quantity Surveyor	• Kuantibina Sdn Bhd

Plaza Atrium

Project Architect	• Chee Soo Teng
Design Architect	• Rahim Din
Project Team	• Mak Meng Fook
C&S Engineers	• Sentosa Reka Sdn. Bhd.
M&E Engineers	• Jurutera Perunding LC Sdn Bhd
Quantity Surveyor	• Baharuddin Ali & Low Sdn

Tokyo-Nara Tower

Design Architects	• Puvan Selvanathan, Vincent Le Feuvre
Project Team	• Syahril Nizam b. Kamaruddin, Roshan Gurung

IBM Plaza

Project Architect	• Chee Soo Teng
Design Architect	• Woon Chung Nam
Project Team	• Mak Meng Fook
C&S Engineers	• Wan Mohamed & Khoo Sdn Bhd
M&E Engineers	• Juaraconsult Sdn Bhd
Quantity Surveyor	• Juru Ukur Bahan Malaysia (KL)

Menara Boustead

Project Architect	• Chee Soo Teng, Yeoh Soon Teik
Design Architect	• Chang Sin Seng, Mun Khai Yip
Project Team	• David Fu, Rahimah Lasim
C&S Engineers	• Raja Dzulkifli Tun Uda & G Rahulan
M&E Engineers	• Khanafiah YL Jurutera Perunding Sdn Bhd
Quantity Surveyor	• Baharuddin Ali & Low Sdn

Business Advancement Technology Centre (BATC)

Project Architect	• Tim Mellor
Design Architects	• Ridzwa Fathan, Chuck Yeoh Thiam Yew, Sam Jacoby, Ravin Ponniah, James Douglas Gerwin
Model Maker	• Technibuilt Sdn Bhd

Al-Hilali Tower

Project Architect	• Seow Ji Nee
Design Architect	• Ridzwa Fathan
Project Team	• Dana Cupkova
C&S and M&E Engineers	• Battle McCarthy Consulting Engineers (London)
Quantity Surveyor	• Juru Ukur Bahan Malaysia (KL)
Model Maker	• Technibuilt Sdn Bhd

Hong Kong Bank Tower

Project Architect	• Eddie Chan
Design Architect	• Ridzwa Fathan
Project Team	• Jason Yeang, Huat Lim, Stephanie Lee, Margaret Ng
C&S Engineers	• Ranhill Bersekutu Sdn Bhd
M&E Engineers	• Norman Disney & Young Sdn Bhd
Quantity Surveyor	• Juru Ukur Bahan Malaysia (KL)
Model Maker	• Technibuilt Sdn Bhd

EDITT Tower

Project Architect	• Andy Chong
Design Architects	• Claudia Ritsch, Ridzwa Fathan
Project Team	• Azman Che Mat, Azuddin Sulaiman, See Ee Ling
Drafting	• Sze Tho Kok Cheng
C&S and M&E Engineers	• Battle McCarthy Consulting Engineers (London)
Embodied Energy Expert	• Prof Bill Lawson (University of NSW)
Model Maker	• Technibuilt Sdn Bhd

Shanghai Armoury Tower

Project Architect	• Eddie Chan
Design Architect	• Ridzwa Fathan
Project Team	• Dang Wei Dong (North Hamzah Yeang) Roshan Gurung, Yvonne Ho, Margaret Ng
C&S Engineers	• Battle McCarthy Consulting Engineers (London)
Model Maker	• Technibuilt Sdn Bhd

Gamuda Headquarters

Project Architects	• Eddie Chan, Chong Voon Wee
Design Architect	• Ann Save DeBeaurecueili
Project Team	• Matthias Schoberth, Grace Tan, Jonathan Fishlock, Paul Wiste, Rodney Ng, Louise Waters, Nik Hasliza Suriati, Ooi Poh Lye
C&S Engineers	• Ranhill Bersekutu Sdn Bhd
M&E Engineers	• Ranhill Bersekutu Sdn Bhd
Quantity Surveyor	• Juru Ukur Bahan Malaysia (KL)
Model Maker	• Technibuilt Sdn Bhd

Menara TA2

Project Architect	• Eddie Chan
Design Architect	• Ridzwa Fathan
Project Team	• Timothy Harold Wort, Alun White
C&S Engineers	• Ranhill Bersekutu Sdn Bhd
M&E Engineers	• CY Tay Perunding
Quantity Surveyor	• Juru Ukur Bahan Malaysia (KL)

Maybank HQ Singapore

Project Architect	• Ridzwa Fathan
Design Architect	• Ridzwa Fathan
Project Team	• Timothy Harold Wort, Strachan Forgan, Mark Lucas, Alun White

Waterfront House

Project Architects	• Neil Harris, Andy Chong
Design Architect	• Ridzwa Fathan
Project Team	• Renee Lee, Wong Yee Wah, Sharul Kamaruddin, Voon Quek Wah
C&S and M&E Engineers	• Ranhill Bersekutu Sdn Bhd
Feng Shui Consultant	• Jerry Too

UMNO Tower

Project Architects	• Shamsul Baharin, Mohamad Pital
Design Architects	• Tim Mellor, Ang Chee Cheong
Project Team	• Azman Che Mat, Jason Ng, Mike Jamieson, Andy Piles, Malcolm Walker, Huw Meredith Rees, Eray Bozkurt, Richard Coutts, Ooi Poh Lye, Yap Yow Kong
C&S Engineers	• Tahir Wong Sdn Bhd
M&E Engineers	• Ranhill Bersekutu Sdn Bhd
Quantity Surveyor	• Juru Ukur Bahan Malaysia (KL & Penang)
Model Maker	• Technibuilt Sdn Bhd

Dubai Towers

Project Architect	• Andy Chong
Design Architects	• Yvonne Ho, Ridzwa Fathan
Project Team	• Stephanie Lee, See Ee Ling, Azman Che Mat, Christian Kienapfel, Carene Chen, Paul Campbell, Loh Mun Chee, Margaret Ng
C&S and M&E Engineers	• Buro Happold Consulting Engineers (London)
Quantity Surveyor	• Davis Langdon & Seah
Model Maker	• Technibuilt Sdn Bhd

Jabal Omar Towers

Project Architect	• Andy Chong
Design Architects	• Ahmad Ridzwa Fathan, Portia Reynolds, Kenneth Cheong
Project Team	• Ong Eng Huat, Ng Chee Hui, Lena Ng, Peter Fajak, Loh Hock Jin, Shahrul Kamaruddin, Maulud Tawang, Wong Yee Wah, Celine Verissimo, Mah Lek, Loh Mun Chee, Margaret Ng
C&S and M&E Engineers	• Saudi Consulting Services (Riyadh)
Environmental Design Consultants	• Battle McCarthy Consulting Engineers (London), Professor Baruch Givoni
Quantity Surveyor	• Davis Langdon & Seah
Model Maker	• Technibuilt Sdn Bhd

Frankfurt 'MAX' Tower

Project Architect	• Andy Chong
Design Architects	• Ridzwa Fathan, Fred Mollring (LOG ID) Kenneth Cheong, Mona Lundborg
Project Team	• Azril Amir Jaafar, Ong Eng Huat, Stephanie Lee, Tung Swee Puan, Ho Choon Sin, Margaret Ng
Associate Architects	• Dieter Schempp, LOG ID (Tubingen)
M&E Engineers	• Planungsgruppe M + M AG (Boblingen)
C&S Engineers	• Dittrich
Model Maker	• Technibuilt Sdn Bhd

Nagoya 2005 Tower

Project Architect	• Eddie Chan
Design Architect	• Ridzwa Fathan
Hypertower Project Leader	• Kiyonori Kikutake
Megastructure Designer	• Shizuo Harada
Model Maker	• Technibuilt Sdn Bhd

Bishopsgate Towers

Project Architect	• Andy Chong
Design Architects	• Chuck Yeoh, Ridzwa Fathan, Jason Yeang
Project Team	• Ong Eng Huat, Gezin Andicen, Ooi Tee Lee, Loh Mun Chee
C&S, M&E Engineers & Urban Planners	• Buro Happold Consulting Engineers (London)
Quantity Surveyor	• Davis Langdon & Everest (London)
Model Maker	• Technibuilt Sdn Bhd

Elephant & Castle Towers

Architect	• Chong Voon Wee, Andy Chong
Design Architects	• Ridzwa Fathan, Portia Reynolds
Project Team	• Ooi Tee Lee, Loh Hock Jin, Ong Eng Huat
Associate Architects	• HTA Architects Limited
C&S & M&E Engineers	• Battle McCarthy Consulting Engineers (London)
Model Maker	• Technibuilt Sdn Bhd

index